WILEY

JOHN WILEY & SONS, INC.

THE CULINARY INSTITUTE of AMERICA

ENTERTAINING

RECIPES AND INSPIRATIONS FOR GATHERING WITH FAMILY AND FRIENDS

ABIGAIL KIRSCH

PHOTOGRAPHS BY **BEN FINK**

This book is printed on acid-free paper. ∞

Photography by Ben Fink

Cover image: Ben Fink
Cover and interior design: Vertigo Design NYC

The Culinary Institute of America

President	Dr. Tim Ryan '77
Provost	Mark Erickson '77
Associate Vice President - Branch Campuses	Susan Cussen
Director of Publishing	Nathalie Fischer
Editorial Project Manager	Mary Donovan '83
Editorial Assistant	Shelly Malgee '08

Published by John Wiley & Sons, Inc., Hoboken, New Jersey.

Published simultaneously in Canada.

For general information on our other products and services, or technical support, please contact our Customer Care Department within the United States at 800–762–2974, outside the United States at 317–572–3993 or fax 317–572–4002.

Wiley publishes in a variety of print and electronic formats and by print-on-demand. Some material included with standard print versions of this book may not be included in e-books or in print-on-demand. If this book refers to media such as a CD or DVD that is not included in the version you purchased, you may download this material at http://booksupport.wiley.com. For more information about Wiley products, visit www.wiley.com.

LIBRARY OF CONGRESS CATALOGING-IN-PUBLICATION DATA:
Kirsch, Abigail.
Entertaining: Recipes and Inspirations for Gathering with Family and Friends /
Abigail Kirsch ; photographs by Ben Fink.
p. cm.
Includes index.
ISBN 978-0-470-42132-1 (cloth); ISBN 978-1-118-32992-4 (ebk);
ISBN 978-1-118-33219-1 (ebk); ISBN 978-1-118-33269-6 (ebk)
1. Entertaining. 2. Cooking. I. Culinary Institute of America.
II. Title.
TX731.K527 2012
642'.4--dc23
2012004356

Printed in China

10 9 8 7 6 5 4 3 2 1

CONTENTS

INTRODUCTION

I was asked recently if there was a "golden era" for home entertainment. For me, the answer is the 1950s and 1960s. Some of us may still remember the dinner parties our parents hosted. As a society, we were more in tune with the manners of an era when entertaining was a more structured and formal affair. The house was polished and decorated. The table was set with china and the best silver. Flowers and candles finished the effect. The host and hostess of '50s and '60s may not have had a household staff to help with parties, but that lack was offset in two ways: Newly created convenience foods made cooking less labor-intensive, and children were often pressed into service to pass trays of hors d'oeuvre before the adults sat down to eat.

The desire to entertain at home may not really have fallen off that much, but attitudes toward entertaining have changed over the intervening years. Home entertaining today offers some great advantages: Lifestyles are generally more casual and relaxed, kitchens have a wider array of more sophisticated equipment, and markets and specialty shops offer a seemingly endless array of ethnic and exotic goods from around the world, whether you are looking for artisan chocolates for a tasting party or fenugreek for a tandoori affair.

Successful entertaining comes from confidence, and confidence comes from knowing what you like to do. If you want to boost your confidence, follow these basic guidelines:

- Have a clear idea about why you are throwing a party.
- Choose a style, whether traditional, sophisticated, "cutting edge," or casual.
- Know the capacity of your house and pick a party format that works in your house. A formal dinner party calls for a table and chairs. With a buffet, guests may eat standing or sitting in a chair (lap service).
- Assess your own cooking skills and the capacity of your kitchen. Choose a menu that you can prepare without stress (and get help with both cooking and serving if you need to).
- Give your guests advance notice and a date by which to RSVP.
- Get as much shopping and cooking done ahead of time as possible. Buy nonperishable goods far in advance. Select a few cook-and-freeze dishes.
- "Imagine" the party in the days that lead up to it and try to solve any problems that you think might crop up. You'll be able to plan for stocking adequate ice and glassware, hiring help from bartenders to servers if necessary, parking cars, and hanging coats, so that you can spend your time with your guests.

Entertaining ought to feel different from an everyday meal, but that doesn't mean that a family gathering can't be an occasion to enrich with special touches. Birthdays, anniversaries, graduations, promotions, bringing home a new baby, or even buying a new car—these are all important events that deserve to be marked with a touch or two that elevates them above run-of-the-mill. And these low-stress events boost your confidence as an entertainer.

Sometimes you have the chance to plan ahead and do it up "right" complete with handwritten invitations and RSVPs. Some entertaining occasions may occur with little or no prior notice—an impromptu potluck when neighbors or friends happen to stop by in time for lunch, or dinner or a community picnic where everyone brings their favorite dish. Maybe you are hosting a book club or a tasting party, or belong to a dinner club that meets at regular intervals. Whatever the reason for hosting a party, everyone can find an entertaining style that works for them. An intelligently stocked pantry and freezer, a repertoire of trusted recipes, a basic understanding of your capabilities and limitations, and a good plan—these are the keys to being a "natural" at entertaining. This book takes on each of these aspects of entertaining so that you can concentrate on being the kind of host you want to be: gracious, welcoming, and relaxed.

Abigail Kirsch

ENTERTAINING AT HOME CAN BE AS SIMPLE AS SERVING COFFEE AND CAKE OR AS ELABORATE AS THROWING AN AT-HOME WEDDING PARTY, COMPLETE WITH HORS D'OEUVRE, COCKTAILS, AND AN ELEGANT FOUR-COURSE DINNER. SOME GATHERINGS ARE ALL ABOUT CELEBRATING WITH FOOD: THANKSGIVING DINNER, A MOTHER'S DAY BRUNCH, OR A DINNER PARTY WITH FRIENDS. SOMETIMES, THE EVENT FOLLOWS A PRESCRIBED SEQUENCE OF EVENTS, WITH FOOD AND DRINK AS A SUPPORTING THEME. WHETHER OR NOT THE FOOD IS THE FOCUS, SERVING THOUGHTFULLY CHOSEN AND PERFECTLY PREPARED FOODS AND DRINKS IS THE HALLMARK OF A GREAT HOST OR HOSTESS. THROUGHOUT THIS BOOK, WE'VE EXAMINED THE DETAILS THAT GO INTO SELECTING, PREPARING, PRESENTING, AND SERVING FOOD AND DRINK TO YOUR GUESTS. WE BEGIN BY TAKING A LOOK AT SOME OF THE STYLES OF PARTIES YOU MIGHT UNDERTAKE AT HOME:

DIFFERENT PARTY STYLES

Cocktail Parties

Most years I attend some sort of New Year's Eve event, usually a conventional dinner out with colleagues or a casual get-together with friends from college. Now a successful twenty-something with a home of my own, I was ready to host my own New Year's Eve extravaganza this year. I wanted a formal, sophisticated feel without any of the traditional stuffiness, so I decided to build a retro lounge atmosphere on an offering of classic cocktails and glamorous décor.

A cocktail party is a great way to entertain anyone from new neighbors to close friends to business associates. Obviously the focus is on the cocktails and other drinks, but a variety of hors d'oeuvre or small-bite snacks are usually served. Cocktail parties last around two to three hours and can range from very casual to black-tie formal.

For more about cocktails and other party beverages, see chapter 9 (page 297). We've included checklists for basic bar setups, an ice-calculating chart, and other tactics for hosts planning to serve alcoholic and nonalcoholic beverages.

Dinner Parties and Brunches

We take turns choosing the book the group will focus on, and with our varied personalities, the selections have ranged from light, superficial reads to more intense, intellectual works. When my turn came around, I selected Mario Puzo's classic novel, *The Godfather*. It was a riot—just four suburban moms hashing out the nitty-gritty details of the violent gangster story. We had a great time, and since I have always loved the movie inspired by the book, I

decided to wrap up our discussion by hosting a movie night dinner in my home for the ladies and their husbands.

Dinner parties, and their close relations, brunches and luncheons, typically begin with a short reception hour, complete with drinks and hors d'oeuvre. The meal may be served at the table or guests may serve themselves from a buffet. Adding a first course makes any meal feel more refined, although it is not mandatory. A dessert course is a classic conclusion, but you may consider adding a cheese course or some after-dinner drinks. Menus for these parties can be as elaborate or basic as you wish, and the parties themselves as formal or casual and as large or intimate as you like. The type of food and the way it's served is totally up to you.

Family Celebrations

I definitely wanted to stick to tradition, so our Thanksgiving meal was anchored with family favorites and standards including turkey, mashed potatoes, dressing, and rolls and rounded out with a couple family favorites like Grandmother's Famous Savory Corn Pudding. I wanted to add a few new flavors, without stepping on anyone's toes, so I incorporated some international flavors and dishes to complement our all-American favorites.

Family parties may follow generation-spanning traditions, or they can be a spontaneous. Holiday dinners are generally the most traditional. Some hosts prefer it that way, while others may want to introduce a few of their own personal twists. Menu planning aside, these parties can be more relaxed, and it is usually fine to anticipate that the guests will lend a hand with everything from supplying missing pieces of china or chairs to handing round the hors d'oeuvre or doing the dishes.

Open Houses

Despite the busy schedules that come along with the holidays, the festive Christmastime atmosphere always gives me the itch to entertain. Last year I decided to throw a big party to celebrate the season with all our friends and family, but our small home would never accommodate a sit-down dinner for forty guests. Instead I opted to hold an open-house party, inviting guests to drop in and leave whenever they pleased during a set four-hour window. This not only solved our overcrowding issue but was also more convenient for everyone's jam-packed December calendars.

Open houses are more informal get-togethers where guests are invited to come and go as they please over the course of several hours. Generally the food is served buffet style, and you do not need to plan activities or a strict schedule like you might for other types of parties. An open house is also a great option when you need to accommodate lots of guests, because you will never be entertaining all of them at the same time.

Tasting Parties

My wife and I just returned from a trip to New York City. One of our treasured memories was attending a dinner at our favorite restaurant that included a chocolate tasting. We brought back a variety of fine chocolates and wanted to invite a group of friends to have our own tasting back home. Planning a menu that highlights the chocolate without stealing its thunder or leaving our guests too full to actually taste the chocolate was an intriguing challenge!

A tasting party is a fun way to introduce your guests to new flavors by offering a variety of something—that might be cheese, beer, coffee, chocolate, olive oil, wine, or fruit. The options are virtually limitless. No matter what item you choose, guests are offered tastes of several varieties to compare the flavor, appearance, texture, and aroma. When assembling a tray of edible items, be sure to cut the food into bite-size pieces and have descriptive, easy-to-read labels for your guests. If you are tasting beverages, whether coffee, tea, wine, or beer, serve small tastes, not full-size servings. Provide palate cleansers like plain crackers or bread and plain water.

There may be paper sheets for note taking or simply a guided discussion. Though it may seem intimidating at first, setting up a tasting sheet is a great way to get the most out of the event. Make notes about ingredient origins, aging, bottling, or curing practices. Chocolates, for example, will have varying percentages of cocoa liquor, cocoa beans may be harvested from specific regions, and the finished chocolate may have added flavors. Tasting parties are usually more casual in feel and are typically best suited for a smaller number of guests.

Backyard Parties

My husband considers himself a grilling master, so in nice weather we often invite friends to join us for dinner on our backyard patio. In addition to our many casual al fresco dinners, it has become a tradition for us to have a larger, more elaborate patio party for Fourth of July. Last year we invited four other couples to join us for drinks and dinner before heading out to see the city's fireworks display. It was a no-brainer that the meal would center on a grilled entrée, but we wanted to provide something a bit more special than the usual Fourth of July picnic staples. We decided to put a creative spin on the conventional menu of hamburgers, potato salad, and coleslaw by incorporating the fresh ingredients and Southwestern flavors that we have come to love since moving to New Mexico.

Make labels and tasting sheets for the tasting.

The best approach to any tasting party is to progress from the mildest to the most intense flavor.

Whether you know them as patio parties, backyard cookouts, barbecues, or pool parties, the main idea is dining "al fresco" with the sky above you and a fabulous meal to share. The menu, style of service, and level of formality are totally up to you. You can go the all-American route with grilled foods and salads or go as upscale or casual as you wish, from "build-your-own" dishes like pizza or tacos to an elegant four-course dinner.

Picnics And Tailgates

As soon as the weather starts warming up, my wife and I begin anticipating a summer picnic at Tanglewood. Like thousands of other concert-goers, it's our tradition to buy tickets on the lawn and arrive early to enjoy a picnic before the concert. Over the years, picnicking at Tanglewood has been elevated to something of an art; at the height of the season it's not uncommon to find epicurean spreads complete with massive canopies, elaborate tables and chairs, fine china, antique silverware, and even gold candelabras dotting the main lawn. Last June we decided to invite two other couples to join us for our annual picnic. We wanted a somewhat simpler picnic blanket experience that was elegant and sophisticated, while keeping it easy enough for us to enjoy the event from start to finish.

Picnics and tailgates are unique, because the party is taken on the road. Generally the food, drink, and other necessary accoutrements are packed up and transported to the host's chosen outdoor location. The food may be reheated or even fully cooked on site or prepared at home and then transported on ice or in hot, insulated containers. The style is typically casual, but the party may take any form, from a picnic in an open country field to a tailgate party in the rowdy parking lot of a sports stadium.

Potlucks

When we planned this get-together, I knew that I couldn't get everything done on my own, so I planned a potluck dinner, but it definitely requires a little extra time in the planning department. After determining the guest list, I devised an outline of what types of dishes would fill out the menu and then called each guest to discuss exactly which recipes they would like to contribute within those categories.

A potluck menu requires a bit of thought and advance planning. As host, you should decide what dishes you'd like to make. Typically, the host will prepare the main dish and ask guests to contribute a variety of accompaniments including simple hors d'oeuvre, salads, side dishes, and desserts. To take some of the guesswork out of the final menu, you can make suggestions that encourage a rounded selection.

WHAT'S THE THEME?

It is dark too early and cold all the time. We are all suffering from cabin fever, so I want to take a "dinner table vacation" to get us out of the cold and gloom and darkness of a February in upstate New York. It comes to me in a flash! A Spanish feast, with tapas, paella, and a fantastic torte featuring a rich custard filling and a complex heady rush of spices like cinnamon and clove and a layer of crunchy toasty pistachio frangipane. Now that I've got the idea, I am enchanted and can't wait to begin!

Theme or themeless, it's totally up to you. After all, it's your party. But sometimes giving a party a theme can help narrow down your menu and inspire your décor choices. If you're the type of person who can be overwhelmed by unending possibility, making a definite decision like "it's going to be an Asian-inspired patio party"

WHEN THE PARTY IS PORTABLE

If you're planning a picnic or tailgate, you'll have some special requirements:

TRANSPORTING TABLEWARE TO THE LOCATION

Whether you're using paper, plastic, or the real deal, you need to get it there. Think about picnic baskets (you can even buy specially designed picnic backpacks), large plastic storage bins, large canvas bags, or even carts with wheels.

KEEPING FOOD COOL

There are all sorts of coolers, including ones on wheels, and insulated backpacks and carry-alls available from a variety of sources including stores that offer housewares or camping supplies.

KEEPING FOOD HOT

Check out tailgating supply sites on the Internet for electric "hotbags" that will keep food prepared at home hot until you are ready to serve it. Use thermal containers to keep hot drinks warm. You can find specially outfitted tea and coffee thermal backpacks sold on Web sites that carry picnic supplies.

COOKING FOOD ON SITE

If you would rather cook food on site instead of carrying it hot there, there are numerous portable grills, both gas and charcoal that are available at specialty tailgating Web sites that will also work well for picnics. Camping supply sites and sporting good stores also sell a wide selection of portable grills. Before deciding to grill away from home, always check your location's specific rules and regulations. You may need a permit in some cases, and there is always a chance that extreme weather conditions may have forced a ban on outdoor fires.

Five Comforts You'll Miss in the Great Outdoors:

RUNNING WATER

REFRIGERATOR

TRASH CANS/DUMPSTER

HEAT OR AIR CONDITIONING

INDOOR RESTROOMS

LEFT: The hardest part of hosting a picnic is remembering to bring everything you'll need. The best way to keep organized is to make a detailed checklist ahead of time and to keep it handy as you pack up.

RIGHT: An important consideration when you're packing food to eat outdoors is storing it at a safe temperature.

Goodie bags are a terrific opportunity to reinforce the party's theme.

will provide you with a very useful filter when you're doing things like looking for recipes or thinking about how you want the table to look.

INVITATIONS

An invitation can be formal or informal. Today, there are plenty of socially appropriate ways to send them. You can call, send an e-mail or a message on a social network like Facebook, send a text, or extend the invitation in person.

When to Send Invitations

A good rule of thumb is: the more formal the event, the earlier the invitations should be extended. Invitations to

more casual get-togethers can usually wait until 2 to 4 weeks before, while invitations to formal events, such as weddings, should be sent out 6 to 8 weeks before, in order to give plenty of time for guests to RSVP. Always give a little more lead time if your party falls during a holiday season, because guests will have more tightly packed calendars.

How to Invite

The formality of the event will usually dictate the manner in which you extend the invitations. Just remember that the invitations often set the tone for the party. You may choose to write e-mail "e-vites," to send professionally printed invitations by mail, or simply to extend a phone call to each guest. No matter which method you choose, the most important thing is that the information about the party is very clearly and accurately communicated. An invitation should include the following details:

THE TYPE OF PARTY, IF IT IS CASUAL OR FORMAL

THE DATE

THE START AND END TIMES

THE LOCATION

RSVP INFORMATION

THE HOST'S CONTACT INFORMATION

DRESS EXPECTATIONS, IF NECESSARY

WHETHER CHILDREN ARE WELCOME

WHETHER GIFTS ARE EXPECTED (AND GIFT REGISTRY INFO, IF AVAILABLE)

AN INDICATION OF THE SIZE OF THE EVENT

Even for smaller get-togethers, it's best to ask guests to RSVP and to include a specific date by which they need to accept or decline the invitation. As the host, having a firm guest count a week or more before the event will help with virtually every aspect of the final party preparations by eliminating guesswork about how much food, drink, dinnerware, table space, etc., you will actually need.

SPECIAL CONSIDERATIONS WHEN THROWING KIDS' PARTIES

My seven-year-old son, Robbie, has spent the last six months totally obsessed with the *Pirates of the Caribbean* movies, so it came as little surprise when he asked for a pirate-themed birthday party this year. I was happy to oblige since the theme would not only thrill Robbie and his friends, but also give this stay-at-home mom an opportunity to flex her creative muscle.

ADULT SUPERVISION

If you're thinking of single-handedly hosting a party for twenty five-year-old kids, you'd better call in reinforcements. Invite a friend or two over to help you supervise or ask some of the guests' parents if they'd like to stay for the party.

ACTIVITIES

The younger the children, the more you need to keep them entertained. It's essential to plan a full schedule of age-appropriate games and other structured activities to avoid boredom-induced whining, fighting, or general chaos.

DÉCOR

Kids' parties are the best time to pick a theme and run with it. Over-the-top decorations will have your young guests' excitement piqued the minute they walk in the door and will help keep up the merry mood.

KID-FRIENDLY FOODS

Parties for children (even teenagers) are not the time to have a sit-down dinner of spaghetti and meatballs. Instead, go with one-bite snacks or more substantial foods that are still easy to grab-and-go, like mini pizzas or sandwich pockets. And just because it's a special occasion, doesn't mean that you have to serve a buffet composed solely of junk food. Try tempering the amount of sugary treats you serve with more healthful options: fruit cut into fun shapes, homemade trail mix, veggie sticks with natural peanut butter, or frozen yogurt.

KID-PROOFING

You should take precautions to make your home as kid-safe as possible. Depending on the ages of the children, that may mean relocating the dog for the day or stashing away that breakable family heirloom. You may also need to delineate areas of the house that are off limits—you can turn off the lights, close doors, or make some sort of other physical barrier.

FIRST AID KIT

Whenever kids are running around, you should always have a first aid kit handy.

Before the party, check that it's fully stocked with antiseptic wipes, hydrocortisone cream, antihistamine, ipecac, tweezers, non latex gloves, a cold compress, and bandages of all sizes.

CLEANUP

No matter how many precautions you take, spills are still going to happen (hey, it happens at adult parties, too). Use disposable or washable tablecloths wherever possible and be sure to stock up on plenty of paper towels. A mop and portable vacuum are good to have on hand for bigger messes.

The key to a successful kids' party spread is to choose foods that are easy to eat while keeping it fun with a mix of different colors, flavors, and textures.

HOW MANY GUESTS?

The number of guests you decide to invite ought to be determined by four factors: First, who do you want to invite? Second, how many people are you comfortable with entertaining? That means cooking, providing seating, and dealing with the group dynamics. Third, what's your budget? And last, how many people can your party space accommodate?

Another thing you want to consider as you are deciding on the number of guests is whether or not you want children at this get-together. If your soiree is emphatically meant to be sans kinder, decide that now and be upfront about it from the beginning to avoid any misunderstandings. If you're cool with kids, then as the planning process progresses, be sure you get an accurate accounting of how many children are coming and their ages, so you can factor them into your meal planning, which includes deciding where and what they will be eating.

WHERE TO HOLD THE PARTY?

If it's indoors, in your home or apartment, do a quick check of space versus the number of guests you plan to have over. Can your living room really hold forty people? If not, you might want to edit your guest list down to a manageable level or consider moving the party outdoors, if that is an option for you.

For anything other than a sit-down party that you can accommodate around your dining room table, you need to think through what your needs will be regarding tables, chairs, and drink and food setup for a bar area or buffet, if appropriate. It's best to deal with such things up front to avoid party-day panic attacks. If it's a backyard barbecue, do you have the outdoor furniture to seat everyone at mealtime? If the answer is no, but you don't want to change the location or guest list, you're going to have to go shopping, borrow from friends, or bring some indoor furniture outside to make up the deficit. If you're serving a large gathering family-style, do you need an extra table to extend your dining room table

into a banquet-size table, or would you prefer to break your guests into groups seated at a number of smaller round tables? In either case, where will these tables be located? Is your dining room large enough to accommodate them or will you need to use another, larger room or your backyard, weather permitting? For what you're planning, do you have sufficient tables and chairs? If you don't, can you borrow them, or would you prefer to buy or rent them from a party rental store?

Below follow other operational issues to consider.

Coats

If it's a cold-weather season, where will the coats go? Forty guests will mean forty coats. Is your front closet large enough to accommodate them if you clean it out? If not, is there any such closet on your first floor that might work? If yes, make sure to clear it out in advance of the party and fill it with more than enough hangers. If this is a large gathering and the closet isn't by the front door, you might want to set up signage to direct people to its location. If closet storage isn't a possibility and you have the space for outerwear in a spare room, you might want to consider renting coat racks from a party rental store. If that's not in your budget or you don't have the space, coats-on-a-bed is still a time-honored and perfectly acceptable practice. Just have a plan in place before your guests start streaming through the front door.

Parking

If your party is held in a suburban setting, how will you handle parking? Is there enough room in your driveway? Can guests park on the street? Can they park in front of your neighbors' houses? Will your neighbors be upset if there are suddenly thirty cars parked along their street? Does is make sense to give them a heads-up? Do you need to address the issue of parking in your invitation? Again, a little advance planning can prevent aggravation and your local police from showing up.

THE SPECIAL CHALLENGES OF ENTERTAINING OUTDOORS

There's truly nothing like entertaining friends in the open air but it can add an unwanted element of surprise. To enjoy your al fresco dining experience as much as possible, here are some things you might want to plan for:

Weather

This includes both good and bad. Whether your get-together is during the day or evening, have a back-up plan if it begins to rain. This could mean a tent, table umbrellas, or an attractive overhead tarp, or moving the whole shebang indoors or into the garage, where you can set up the outdoor tables and leave the door open for a semi–open air experience. If your party is during the day, you need to provide shade from the sun. Again, this means table umbrellas or tarps and setting up tables in the shade of trees considering how the shade will move with the sun. On a whimsical note, you could set up a sprinkler for grown-ups, or equip your tables with water pistols for a quick and spirited cooldown. You want your guests to go home with happy memories, not heat stroke.

Mosquitoes

Be prepared. Nothing will end a party quicker than an onslaught of mosquitoes. You have the option of citronella candles and bug zappers, which many of us have tried with varying success. If you're having an evening outdoor get-together, make sure you have bug spray on hand, both with and without DEET, so your guests can choose whichever they prefer (plus, full-strength DEET isn't recommended for children).

Lighting

If your eating area is any distance from well-lighted areas, and especially so if the ground is at all uneven, make sure there is adequate lighting for your guests to find their way without tripping or falling. You can do this by lighting the way with candles, solar-powered lights, lanterns, torches, or by having a quantity of flashlights on hand.

Keeping Drinks Cool and Close By

When you're entertaining outdoors, as a host, you want to minimize the number of times you have to go inside. To that end, you need to devise a cooler for your drinks that will reside out at the eating area. This could be a regular large cooler or something improvised, like a small children's pool or wheelbarrow filled with ice.

Keeping Food at a Safe Temperature

Take every precaution to make sure that hot foods stay hot and cold foods stay cold. If a food has been sitting at the room temperature for more than 2 hours, it can start making people sick. That is the last thing you want to happen. If you're serving al fresco on your home patio, wait until the last possible minute to serve the food and promptly return it to the refrigerator after service. Hot food should be kept above 135°F, and cold food should be below 40°F.

When entertaining outdoors in warm weather, keep the drinks in plenty of ice and, if possible, place the cooler in a shady spot to help keep the drinks colder longer.

Bathroom Facilities

For most gatherings, access to a single bathroom is likely sufficient, but make sure your fallback bathroom is also in good shape should an emergency require its use. In advance of the party you'll want to make sure both bathrooms are clean, well stocked with toilet paper that is easy to find and access, and fitted out with either cloth or paper hand towels. Make sure both bathrooms have wastebaskets. For large outdoor gatherings, you might want to consider bringing in portable restrooms. There are plenty of companies that cater to private events.

WHAT TYPE OF FOOD SERVICE TO OFFER?

Once you've settled on the number of people on the guest list and decided where to host the party, the next question is: How will the food be served? Do you want a sit-down dinner, presented either family style or plated in courses, or a buffet? Deciding this up front will guide you as you choose your menu, as well as inform a lot of the other decisions you'll need to make.

The number of people you're inviting is going to have a big influence on this decision. Unless you've got an enormous dining room table, once you get over fourteen guests, a buffet may be the way to go. And you probably won't want to attempt formal plated service for more than ten guests—it's just too difficult in the typical home kitchen to plate that many individual servings and get them to the table at the right temperature. Opt for family-style service.

CREATE A MASTER PLAN

The bigger and more involved the get-together, the more lists and timelines will be your friends. First, make a list of everything you plan to serve at your party, whether you'll be preparing it from scratch or buying it. For instance, include that you'll be serving a selection of cheeses after the meal, along with walnuts and sliced pears, or that one of your appetizers will be a smoked whitefish spread you'll be getting from a local store. Also include all the beverages you plan to serve. What you want is to create a master menu list that becomes a reference for building your master timeline and from that, your shopping lists.

Menu Planning

If the mere idea of entertaining creates a certain level of stress for you, plan a party that is well within your comfort zone in terms of the menu, the number of guests invited, and the type of service; a sit-down dinner versus buffet. Long-range planning as well as prepping as much as you can in advance will be key to your having a good time at your own get-together. If you're having a good time, your guests will have a good time.

A large part of pulling off a successful get-together is knowing your own comfort level as a host and then planning a party that takes it into consideration. For instance, if you love entertaining friends and family but don't have lots of experience cooking for a crowd, keep that in mind while you select recipes. Choose recipes that can be made well in advance and refrigerated or frozen or that make use of convenience products. Selecting recipes that acknowledge instead of challenge your skills, and tackling the cooking in steps will make the cooking much more manageable.

Below follow other considerations when selecting recipes for your event:

1. **DO ANY OF YOUR GUESTS HAVE FOOD ALLERGIES?** If someone is violently allergic to peanuts, for heaven's sake, don't tempt fate and serve a dish garnished with peanuts, thinking "I just won't put it on that person's plate." Some people are so allergic that just being in the proximity of the said food will cause them to break out into a rash or worse.

Is anyone on a special diet? If you know you have vegetarians or vegans coming, that doesn't mean you have to eighty-six the meat, poultry, and seafood all together. Just make sure you have a few dishes that are appropriate for people on those diets and that served together would make a satisfying meal. Also make sure you've got at least one appropriate appetizer selection for these groups of guests. Given advance warning, you want all your guests to be able to partake of each course.

2. **ARE YOU GOING TO BE FEEDING CHILDREN?** If you are, you might do well to check with the various parents to find out what they eat. What you think kids ought to be willing to eat might not line up with their reality. And this isn't the time to take a stance of "kids just shouldn't be so picky." If children are invited, then, as host, it's your duty to make sure you are offering something that they will eat, even if you have to make them a peanut butter sandwich. The reality is that if your adult guests' children are fussing, your guests will not be at ease. Avoid this situation by being forewarned. In many cases, when asked, the parents of smaller children will offer to bring food for their kids so you won't have to worry about it—if they offer, let them.

3. **WHAT TIME OF YEAR IS IT?** It's a nice idea to have your menu reflect seasonality whenever possible. It also makes budget sense too, as produce is cheaper in season. For example, if it's spring, you might plan to serve asparagus—chilled as a first course with lemon aïoli, as part of a composed salad, or grilled as a side dish. Or opt for sugar snap peas or ripe luscious strawberries. Throughout the summer, take your pick of melons, stone fruits, and berries. And don't just think of these fruits in terms of dessert. Wrap slices of melon with prosciutto, stuff fresh figs with goat cheese, or highlight juicy peaches in a green salad. In the fall, you might serve thin slices of apple and pear as part of a cheese board. In winter, opt for root vegetables, hearty greens, and squashes.

HOW SERVICE STYLE AFFECTS MENU OPTIONS

Before you make your recipe selection, decide whether you will be serving plated courses or family-style—on platters so your guests can serve themselves.

PLATED SERVICE

For plated courses, select dishes you can prepare in their entirety or almost entirely ahead of time. For first courses, look for cold composed dishes that can be prepared in advance and assembled right before serving, or warm dishes that can be cooked in advance and reheated or require only quick cooking before service. For warm-weather soirees, think of cold soups waiting in the refrigerator to be ladled into individual serving cups and topped with a pre-prepped garnish; in cold weather, your soup should be ready and simmering on the stovetop when guests arrive. You should be able to prep salad components entirely in advance, including the dressing, so that you can toss them together in a matter of minutes.

For your main dish, depending on your comfort level, you can choose a recipe that is essentially worry-free, like a roast or a ham or individual game hens, which can be in the oven finishing up when your guests arrive, or, if you are more confident in your skills, this can be your wow dish, cooked *à la minute*; if this is the case, make sure all your ingredients are prepped in advance and ready to go.

Select side dishes that can be made ahead and reheated or that can be cooked with little effort or time at the last minute, like roasted vegetables, braised or stewed vegetables, or gratins.

For some, dessert will be the moment of whip-it-up-at-the-last-minute glory. For most, though, dessert can be prepared entirely in advance. Plated service is a nice opportunity to look for recipes that can be prepared as individual servings, like crème brûlée, pots de crème, colorful parfaits featuring fresh whipped cream and summer fruit, or mini cakes that can be baked up in any of the wide array of individual-portion cake pans now available.

FAMILY-STYLE SERVICE

If you'll be serving family style, with all the platters put down all at once, have a selection of help-yourself appetizers that you have prepared in advance set out when guests arrive.

A lot of the advice for plated service applies to family-style service, though you have a bit more leeway on how much final cooking you're doing as you don't have to worry about multiple courses and all the individual plating. You may want to stick with larger cuts of meat that are carved at the table, as opposed to individually cooked pieces of meat or poultry, which run the risk of overcooking or cooling off too quickly once they're transferred to a platter. Others options for family-style courses are braises seafood dishes such as paella, bouillabaisse, and gumbo, and baked pastas.

BUFFET SERVICE

If you're serving buffet style, you'll want to take a two-step approach, setting out appetizers first, then your main event, and finally dessert and coffee. If you're going to be serving a lot of people, pre-prep should be your greatest concern when selecting recipes. Avoid recipes that have to be put together at the last minute.

Another consideration in buffet recipe selection is to pick dishes that will still taste good once they start cooling down. If this is a large party, an open house, for instance, remember that people will be picking over the food for an hour or more, so you want to stay away from side dishes that lose a lot of their yumminess once they get cold, like mashed potatoes, unless you have access to chafing dishes or hotel pans that can keep them hot. For appetizers, choose options that can be assembled on a platter and set out, like antipasti or crudités. If you are serving hot and cold appetizers in addition to these platters, remember to make it easy for guests to pick them up and eat them in a single bite; the same holds true of dessert options. For the main course, large cuts of meat that can be carved and served hot or cold are always a good choice. Dishes like gumbo or chili can be kept warm on the buffet table in a large slow cooker, as can rice.

For accompaniments, think of dishes with flavors and textures that will combine well with your main course. Possibilities include a mixed green salad with a piquant dressing and lots of delicious add-ins like toasted nuts, dried cranberries, and cherry tomatoes; toothsome wild rice and other grain-based salads; or a platter of marinated blanched green beans topped with shavings of Parmesan. Each of these could be prepared almost entirely ahead.

When it comes to dessert for a buffet, it's all about do-ahead. Cakes, pies, cookies, parfaits, trifle, whatever you choose, you want it all prepared and ready to go no later than noon the day of your party, if it's in the evening.

FINAL SELECTION AND REVIEW OF RECIPES

When you're choosing recipes for entertaining, read each one all the way through before deciding to include it. The name of a recipe can be absolutely beguiling, but if you don't take the time to read the recipe through, you may not find out in time that you have to start the recipe three days before you plan to serve it. When picking recipes, you will want to consider several other factors:

BUDGET

If finances are an important consideration for you, evaluate ingredients list for each recipe for cost. Does it include an expensive ingredient? Is it an ingredient that sometimes goes on sale in your area? If you are planning ahead, is there a good chance you could pick it up on sale and then freeze it until your party? Could you possibly substitute a less expensive ingredient with equally delicious results (say, using shiitake mushrooms instead of morels)?

AVAILABILITY OF INGREDIENTS

Sometimes you find a recipe that sounds wonderful but it includes an ingredient you've either never heard of, or you know with great certainty you won't be able to find easily, if at all, in your area. Read through the recipe carefully; with what you know, do you think you could substitute something else for this ingredient? Could you leave it out without substantially changing the taste of the dish? If you have enough planning time, could you special order the ingredient? If the answer to all of these questions is "no," you'd do well to look for another recipe instead. Remember that when an ingredient is in season, it is generally more affordable, so if a recipe calls for asparagus and you want to make it in January, consider substituting green beans or broccoli. For more information on seasonal produce, see the chart on page 237.

TIME AND EFFORT

How time-consuming, intricate, challenging is the recipe? If the answer is "very," but you still want to make it, ask yourself one more question and answer it honestly: Are your culinary skills truly up to the task of preparing this dish? If you think they are, and you're really excited about being able to serve it to your friends, go for it, but in selecting the other dishes to accompany it, make choices that are much simpler, so you can devote the appropriate time and effort to this showpiece recipe. There is a reason that most entertaining experts recommend a practice run with any recipe you've never made before. Practice gives you confidence, and also gives you the opportunity to make an alternate selection if necessary.

PREPARE IN ADVANCE

As you read through each recipe you are seriously considering, think whether you can prepare any part of it in advance and how far in advance. We make it easy for you: All of the recipes included in this book tell you which components of the dish can be prepared ahead, how far ahead, and whether they can be refrigerated or frozen. You'll need this information later on when you begin to build your party timeline (see page 18).

YIELD

Another consideration is how much the recipe makes and whether that will be sufficient for your get-together. If you decide you will need to scale the recipe up, this is explained in the following section.

MULTIPLYING RECIPES

You may find that you need to increase the number of servings for some or all of the recipes you have selected for your menu. In such cases, recipes like soups, sauces, stews, braises, grain dishes, or pastas are generally simple to increase. You can easily double a recipe's yield by multiplying each ingredient by two.

There are some ingredients that may require special handling, however, including spices, herbs, and other strong flavoring ingredients. For example, if you're doubling a paella recipe that calls for 2 teaspoons of saffron, you will not actually need 4 teaspoons of saffron (that would most likely overpower the dish); add the original 2 teaspoons then, from there, adjust the saffron to taste.

For several reasons, we generally advise against tripling, quadrupling (and beyond) recipes. First, home kitchens are normally not equipped to make quantities of food that large. For example, before you decide to quadruple that French onion soup recipe, stop to consider: Do you have a pan large enough to caramelize all those onions? How about a pot large enough to accommodate that much simmering soup? Rather than struggling to make one enormous, quadruple batch, make two double batches instead.

Another argument against tripling (or more) is that the original recipe's guidelines for cooking or baking times will no longer apply. Going back to the French onion soup example, using a larger cooking vessel might result in a higher rate of evaporation, so you may find that you need to either cover the soup as it cooks or increase the liquid to offset the evaporation, even if original soup recipe specifies that it be cooked uncovered.

Recipes for baked goods are a special consideration and we do not recommend multiplying them at all. We suggest that you make the recipe as written, as often as necessary to get the number of servings you need.

COMPILING A RECIPE DO-AHEAD LIST AND RECIPE SHOPPING LIST

Once you've compiled a master menu, pull out the individual recipes for all the dishes you plan to make. Read them through again and, recipe by recipe, note what portions of the dish you can make ahead and how long you can hold it in the refrigerator or freezer at that point. It's possible that with some recipes, there will be several make-ahead points; for instance, for a marinated leg of lamb, the marinade could be prepared a week ahead of time and then the lamb could be marinated up to two days ahead in the refrigerator. Once you compile all this do-ahead information, you can then decide what works with your own personal schedule.

At the same time you are gathering this information, review the ingredients lists of each recipe and start a shopping list of ingredients you are missing. If you think you have something in your cupboard, like beef broth, get up from your chair and go physically check to see whether you have it. Now is the time to discover whether your memory is faulty, not on the day of the party when that beef broth is the final thing you need to finish the sauce for your beef tenderloin.

Take a Tabletop Inventory

Next up is an inventory of serving pieces, including plates, glasses, flatware, and serving utensils as well as your table textiles. Take the following factors into consideration and then make your decision:

1. The type of party you are throwing (casual versus formal, sit-down versus buffet, and the particular theme you might have chosen).

2. How many people you have invited.

3. How many dishes and courses you will be serving.

4. The types of drinks you will be serving.

DINNERWARE

If you are throwing a formal dinner party, you might consider:

CHARGERS

DINNER PLATES

SOUP BOWLS

SALAD PLATES

BREAD AND BUTTER PLATES

PLATES FOR A FIRST COURSE

PLATES FOR A CHEESE COURSE

DESSERT PLATES OR BOWLS

CUPS AND SAUCERS

If your china set is missing serving pieces that you need, think about whether you can mix and match patterns and pieces. If the First Lady is doing it, so can you—as long as the pieces look good together. You can also try borrowing from friends and family, or you can rent pieces from a local party rental store. If you are having a large, formal gathering, such as (a wedding reception, for instance), whether it is a sit-down meal or buffet, and you want to use real plates, rather than disposables, a party rental store is going to be the only way to go for your tabletop needs.

If you are having a buffet, depending on what you're serving, you may need any of the following items:

PLATES FOR HORS D'OEUVRE

SALAD PLATES

DINNER PLATES

DESSERT PLATES OR BOWLS

CUPS AND SAUCERS

If you are throwing a more casual party or buffet, it's perfectly acceptable to choose to use disposable pieces. In that case, don't let price alone be your guide when purchasing them. Think about whether the plate you are considering will stand up to the weight placed upon it. You want to spare your guests the embarrassment of having the contents of their plate spill onto your floor because you bought cheap paper plates. An alternative to paper plates are reusable plastic plates, which, available in a dizzying array of colors and patterns, are a more economical choice than real plates and will add to the pizzazz of your table décor.

GLASSWARE

When inventorying glassware, think about what types of beverages you will be serving and how many guests you will be serving. Real glass is always the nicest choice but not always economically possible when you're planning a big event. It isn't a crime, but you probably won't want to mix disposal glassware if you are opting for china and linen.

For a formal dinner party, you may want or need:

MARTINI OR OTHER COCKTAIL GLASSES

PILSNER GLASSES OR MUGS FOR SERVING BEER

CHAMPAGNE FLUTES

WATER GOBLETS

RED WINEGLASSES

WHITE WINEGLASSES

SNIFTERS OR SMALL GLASSES APPROPRIATE FOR SERVING SHERRY, PORT, DESSERT WINE, OR OTHER AFTER-DINNER DRINKS

THE SILVERWARE POUCH

1. Lay the napkin facedown in front of you, fold the napkin in half, and orient the open end toward you.
2. Fold the napkin into quarters, and orient the napkin so that the open corner is facing away and to the left.
3. Fold only the topmost layer of the napkin in half and press it down firmly to crease. Turn the napkin over so that the open corner is now facing away and to the right.
4. Fold the right side back about one-third of the way and press firmly to crease. Then fold the left side back about one-third of the way and press firmly to crease.
5. Flip the napkin over and place your silverware into the pocket you've created.

LEFT: Rolling sets of silverware into napkins is a quick and easy option for casual buffets.

RIGHT: Folding the napkins into "silverware pouches" is an impressive touch for more formal buffets.

Any or all of these items might also be appropriate for a more casual affair or a buffet. If you can't afford to stock your shelves with enough glassware, try to get quality reusable plastic cups. And for serving coffee or other hot drinks, be sure what you buy is heatproof.

FLATWARE

For a formal get-together, this might be the time to pull out the good silver. Take a look at your menu and see what you need:

FORKS AND KNIVES FOR A FIRST COURSE

SOUP SPOONS

SALAD FORKS

DINNER FORKS AND KNIVES

STEAK KNIVES

DESSERT FORKS

SPOONS FOR COFFEE OR TEA AND FOR DESSERT

For a more casual party or buffet, you'll most likely choose to go with disposable flatware; you still need to make sure you have what you need for appetizers, the main meal, and dessert. Do not assume your guests will hold onto their fork throughout the meal, so be sure you have enough flatware for each wave of food you serve.

SERVING PIECES

If you are going to be serving family style or are planning on a buffet setup, think through your menu and decide how each preparation is going to be served. Do you have enough bowls that are big enough? If you don't, are there cooking vessels you own that could fit the role, like a brightly colored enameled cast-iron Dutch oven? If you're going to be serving a casserole, do you have the right size dish, and is it presentable? If you are going to be serving a carved meat, do you have a large enough platter? If you don't, do you have a large carving board or roasting pan that could be pressed into service? Will you need to keep

Hosting a family-style dinner may require condiment bowls, gravy boats, platters, and any number of other serving dishes and utensils. In order to avoid scrambling for dishes at the last minute, think about all of the serving dishes you'll need as you are finalizing your menu and then make a complete inventory list.

any of the food warm at service time? Do you have chafing dishes or slow cookers you can put to use, or might you want to rent chafing dishes from a party rental service? Do you have all the spoons, ladles, forks, and other serving utensils you'll need? Make a list of what you don't have, and see if you can borrow what you're missing from family and friends; otherwise, make sure to leave time to shop for them before the party, or consider renting these items.

TABLE TEXTILES

When you've decided on a theme or décor color scheme, take an inventory of your tablecloths and see if what you have will work with the tabletop decoration you have in mind. Remember you will also need cloths for your buffet table and bar areas, if appropriate—no matter what you are serving, there will inevitably be spills in the beverage area. If you are using a wooden table that you care about, consider either using a plastic underliner beneath a cloth covering, or use a patterned plastic covering.

Check ahead of time that all the cloths are presentable. If they need to be laundered or ironed, get all of that done before the day of the party. And if what you have doesn't suit your needs, be sure to allow yourself time to shop for something appropriate.

If you don't have cloth napkins (or enough of them that match), now is the time to decide whether you will go with cloth or paper. If you are setting a nice table with china and glassware, cloth is the best choice, but quality paper napkins are a perfectly fine alternative, especially for buffet service, and there are plenty of color and pattern choices to match your décor.

YOUR PARTY TIMELINE AND HELPFUL LISTS

Making a Timeline

Any type of get-together you plan, no matter how many people are coming, has a lot of moving parts: making planning decisions, shopping, cleaning, cooking, setting up. Compiling a list of absolutely everything that needs to get done (down to defrosting the shrimp to clearing out the front hall closet to ordering the birthday cake), then turning it into a specifically scheduled timeline will eliminate a lot of stress, as you will now have a very detailed checklist that will guide you through what you need to accomplish on a day-to-day basis.

How far out your timeline stretches is up to you and also depends on how much food prep you intend to do in advance. Most beverages, as well as paper and plastic goods, can be bought weeks in advance. If your supermarket is running a sale on the cut of meat you intend on serving, buy it and freeze it. If you need to rent items for your party, lock that in as soon as you have a concrete date in hand. As the date gets closer, you can always change the exact number of tables, chairs, etc. If you intend to have someone clean the house for you, get on their calendar as soon as possible. It's all about planning ahead.

If your schedule extends more than a week out, you have some maneuverability in terms of when you get

things done. Once you are down to a week, and counting, stick to your timeline; it will save your sanity and radically decrease your stress level the day before and the day of the party.

By referring to your completed timeline, you should know:

1. **WHEN YOU INTEND TO BUY, PREP, AND FINISH EVERY ITEM ON YOUR INTENDED MENU.** This includes listing every bit of food that needs to be served and when; it's remarkably easy, in the press of everything you need to get done, to forget about food you have waiting in the back of your refrigerator—cheese or spreads to put out, asparagus that needs to go into the oven for roasting right before serving, or a cold salad to be served as a side dish.

2. **WHEN AND HOW YOU WILL SET UP FOR THE PARTY.** This could include, but is not limited to: cleaning the house, renting and/or borrowing items, including arranging for their delivery and/or pick-up, setting up buffet and beverage tables, cleaning silver and service pieces and/or buying or borrowing pieces you need, contacting neighbors to warn them about increased traffic and parking on the street the night of the get-together, arranging for entertainment, if necessary, and having your septic tank pumped or renting portable restrooms.

3. **YOUR TIMING FOR COOKING.** This includes deciding what to make ahead and when, as well as how to manage the various courses or stages of the party. Consider when foods need to go into the oven, come out of the freezer, move from the kitchen to the buffet. If you are thoughtful as you do this, you may find that you've averted a potential bottleneck that can be resolved by making some adjustments to the menu, arranging to "borrow" a neighbor's stove, or similar changes. It will also remind you to set up the coffeemaker and turn it on so that coffee is ready when you serve dessert or to take the cheeses out of the refrigerator when you serve the first course so they are at the perfect temperature for serving.

Movie Night Potluck Dinner

TWO WEEKS AHEAD	Set party date and time	☐
	Make menu plan	☐
	Create shopping list	☐
	Invite guests	☐
	Suggest potluck dishes to bring	☐
	Prepare and freeze lasagnas	☐
ONE WEEK AHEAD	Confirm menu and "potluck" dishes with guests	☐
	Buy nonperishable goods, decorations, wine, beer, and cordials	☐
TWO DAYS AHEAD	Buy all perishable items	☐
	Trip to deli for salumi platter	☐
	Buy flowers	☐
THE DAY BEFORE	Make dips	☐
	Vinaigrette	☐
	Artichoke stuffing	☐
	Do advance prep work	☐
	Take lasagnas from freezer to thaw in refrigerator	☐
THE MORNING OF	Pick up breads and pastries	☐
	Set up area to serve drinks	☐
	Set dining room table	☐
	Organize big tray and coffee table for dessert and coffee service in dining room	☐
	Check that TV, DVD player, and stereo are working properly	☐
	Queue up movie	☐
	Chill prosecco	☐
	Run and empty dishwasher	☐
	Take out compost	☐
	Take out recycling	☐
	Clear counters and refrigerator space for guest contributions to meal	☐
ONE HOUR BEFORE GUESTS ARRIVE	Prepare salumi platter and garnish	☐
	Bake lasagnas	☐
THIRTY MINUTES BEFORE GUESTS ARRIVE	Light candles	☐
	Turn on theme music	☐

Sit-Down Thanksgiving Dinner

ONE MONTH AHEAD	Make up menu	☐
	Call the guests to offer invitations and assign dishes	☐
	Prepare shopping list	☐
	Call to reserve a 20-pound turkey to pick up the week of Thanksgiving	☐
THREE WEEKS AHEAD	Buy nonperishable goods	☐
	Make and freeze appetizers, pies, base for gravy	☐
ONE WEEK AHEAD	Locate all serving pieces, table linens, flatware, china, silver, platters, and bowls	☐
THREE DAYS BEFORE	Shop for all perishable goods and pick up turkey	☐
	Prepare cranberry compote	☐
	Make cornbread for stuffing	☐
TWO DAYS BEFORE	Sharpen carving knife	☐
	Peel chestnuts	☐
	Toast pecans	☐
	Make dough for soft rolls	☐
THE DAY BEFORE	Make vinaigrettes and dips	☐
	Cut vegetables for crudités	☐
	Rinse and spin dry lettuces and greens	☐
	Prepare garlic whipped potatoes	☐
	Assemble side dishes	☐
	Set and decorate the dining room table and area for drinks	☐
	Chill any cold beverages	
THE MORNING OF	Bake pies and rolls	☐
	Whip heavy cream for pies	☐
FOUR HOURS BEFORE GUESTS ARRIVE	Prep the turkey and get it into the oven (to allow 3–3¾ hours to cook and 30 minutes to rest)	☐
TWO HOURS BEFORE GUESTS ARRIVE	Dish up and place cranberry compote on table	☐
	Set up carving station at head of table	☐
ONE HOUR BEFORE GUESTS ARRIVE	Bake cornbread stuffing	☐
	Finish vegetable side dishes and transfer to serving dishes	☐

THIRTY MINUTES BEFORE GUESTS ARRIVE	Take turkey from oven and transfer to platter to rest	☐
	Bake phyllo appetizers	☐
	Finish the gravy	☐
	Set out crudités and dips	☐

The Master Shopping List

A master shopping list will include everything you need to buy, including the ingredients you need and the prepared foods and specialty items like cheeses and coffees you plan to serve.

FOOD Keep a running shopping list indicating how much of each ingredient you need to get, as it's likely that some ingredients will be called for in several of your recipes. Be specific in your notations; don't assume you'll remember that you need six onions—write it down. This is also the time to add the store-bought foods you will be serving at your party. Referring to that master menu list will prevent you from getting so focused on your recipes and the dishes you'll be preparing that you forget about the ready-made items you intend on offering.

BEVERAGES Refer to your master menu for the beverages you intend to serve. Again, make an inventory of what you do and don't have—and don't forget the accompaniments. If you'll be serving a specialty cocktail, does it require a particular garnish, like a maraschino cherry or an olive? If it does, then that goes on the list. If you plan to offer pitchers of ice water or bottles of sparkling water at the table, it might be nice to have a plate of lemon or lime wedges on the table for your guests, or to have them already floating in the pitcher. Add lemons or limes to your shopping list. If you're serving coffee and tea, make sure you have cream and milk on hand, milk alternatives if you know you'll have guests who are lactose intolerant or vegan, as well as sugar and a sugar substitute. If appropriate, make sure you have enough coffee filters. You should plan on serving both caffeinated and decaffeinated coffee, as well as offering your guests several tea choices, at least one of which should be decaffeinated. All of these items go onto the shopping list, as does the most crucial beverage item of all—ice. (For more information on serving beverages, see page 26).

PAPER AND PLASTIC GOODS Now look back at the decisions you made regarding the tabletop. If you're going with disposable or plastic goods, add all of these items to your shopping list, with the quantity of each item you need. If you'll be serving appetizers and dessert, you'll need enough small plates to accommodate both courses, as well as larger plates for the main portion of the meal. The same applies to paper napkins; cocktail or luncheon-size napkins for appetizers and desserts, larger ones for the meal. You'll likely need a double dose of forks. Assume that guests will not hold onto one plastic cup throughout the party and make sure you have more than enough, as well as heatproof cups if you'll be serving warm beverages. Also add to your list: paper towels, toilet paper, and garbage bags.

OTHER ITEMS TO BUY Add anything else to your list that you found you needed when doing your tabletop inventory, as well as items you will need for decorating. This includes: serving utensils, bowls, platters, tablecloths and napkins, napkin rings, place cards, candles, lights, tiki torches, bug spray.

MAKING THE MOST OF YOUR REFRIGERATOR
AND FREEZER SPACE

When throwing a big party, one of the biggest challenges can be fitting everything into your refrigerator, particularly if you want to prepare dishes in advance. Here is some advice, gleaned from experienced party-throwers, on using your refrigerator and freezer most effectively:

If you will be serving a hot appetizer that can be fully prepped in advance and frozen (like our Empanadas on page 87), arrange the individual pieces in a single layer on a baking sheet in the freezer until they are frozen solid, then transfer them to a ziplock bag. This makes for much more efficient storage than trying to accommodate baking sheets or muffin pans full of an assembled appetizer in the refrigerator.

For appetizers that can't be frozen, try to prep them as far as you can before they go onto a baking sheet or platter. For stuffed mushrooms (page 70), for instance, the mushrooms can be cleaned, the stems removed, and the filling prepared. At this point the mushrooms can still go into a ziplock bag in the refrigerator.

If you're making Deviled Eggs (page 40), don't store the hard-cooked eggs in a bowl; put them back into their cartons, which can be neatly stacked, making sure to label the cartons clearly (so that they can't be confused with raw eggs in other cartons).

Ziplock plastic bags are your friends. Because they aren't rigid, you have a lot more flexibility in fitting an item into whatever space it is that you have left in your fridge. When you must use a rigid container, choose the smallest container possible for the given item, and use containers with lids, since they can be easily stacked.

LEFT: Keep your refrigerator organized, and avoid spills and odors, by storing all the food in airtight, stackable containers, and clearly label every container with the contents and the date it was made to avoid confusion.

RIGHT: Any food you freeze should be clearly labeled with the name of the dish and the date it was made.

If you're going to be grilling, that would include a back-up tank of propane or charcoal and lighter fluid, if appropriate, as well as matches. Also, do a check of your pantry for other items you may need for cooking or storage, if you're prepping in advance, like plastic wrap, aluminum foil, ziplock plastic bags in both large and small sizes, and plastic storage containers.

ORGANIZE YOUR SHOPPING LIST

To improve the chances that you don't overlook anything you've included on your list, make sublists, organizing them by several different criteria. First, put like items together: vegetables, greens, and fresh fruits together; baking ingredients together; meats/poultry together; fish; deli items; dairy items; etc. You can also break your list down into sublists of stores you are likely to buy the items in: supermarket, specialty food store, price club, etc. Your goal in doing this is to decrease the likelihood of having to make several trips to the same store as well as to identify nonperishable items that you can buy a week or more in advance and perishable foods that you'll want to buy a day or two before the event.

PLANNING THE PARTY SPACE: TABLES, CHAIRS, AND THE ROOM SETUP

If you're planning a buffet, you must be sure that you have an appropriate-size table or counter that can handle the number of dishes you plan to serve. If you're going to be serving a large number of people buffet style, consider whether you will be able to set your table up so that you can have guests approaching on both sides of the table or whether it might be best to have two separate tables. For smaller parties, you might like to have hors d'oeuvre set out on several smaller tables throughout your party room to start, and then go to one large table for the main course. Consider also where your guests will actually eat. Will they sit and eat off their laps

(a perfectly fine option for an open house)? Or, do you need to have tables and chairs set up to accommodate everyone?

You will also want to decide whether you are going to have a bar setup and what you will need in the way of coolers, pitchers, and table space to accommodate what you will be serving at the bar. Is one bar sufficient or are two or more appropriate to the number of people you are inviting? Does it make sense to hire a bartender or will guests serve themselves?

For both the meal and bar area, you would do well to decide upon their location early on, particularly if this is an indoor party. This will help you realistically think through the placement of the food and beverage tables as well as the tables for your guests (and also double-check that the party space you've chosen is the appropriate size for all the tables). You want your guests to be able to easily move around the entire buffet table, which will speed up the time it takes your guests to serve themselves. Don't situate either a buffet table or bar area so that it or the guests trying to serve themselves end up blocking doors or doorways. You also don't want either setup placed anywhere near a bathroom (there's hygiene and privacy to consider). And you don't want either of these areas backing up into your kitchen area.

For a sit-down dinner, guests should be able to maneuver around the entire table, to pull their chairs out easily, and have plenty of elbow room at their place setting.

SETTING YOUR TABLE FOR A SIT-DOWN AFFAIR

If your party is a sit-down meal (and you've decided on the seating arrangement—see page 29), it's time to set the table. If it is possible, set your table, including your tablescape, the night before. For a formal sit-down dinner party during which you'll be serving multiple courses, check out the diagram below for the setup of dishes, glassware, and utensils you might possibly be using. Keep in mind, in a formal setting, all of the pieces should be equidistant from one another.

PLATES

For a formal setting, set the table using chargers, also called service plates. The service plate will remain on the table until you exchange it for the guest's plated dinner plate. First course plate, soup bowl, and salad plate are all set upon the charger for service.

For formal service, if you are serving bread, provide a separate bread and butter plate, with a butter knife set across the top of the bread and butter plate. Place this plate to the left of the charger, directly above the forks.

A table set for brunch.

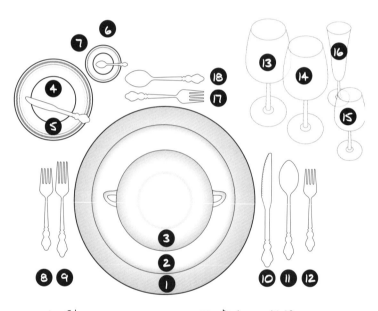

1	Charger	10	Dinner Knife
2	Dinner Plate	11	Soup or Fruit Spoon
3	Soup Bowl	12	Oyster Fork
4	Butter Plate	13	Water Goblet
5	Butter Knife	14	Red or White Wine Glass
6	Salt Dish	15	Sherry Glass
7	Salt Spoon	16	Champagne Flute
8	Salad Fork	17	Dessert Fork
9	Dinner Fork	18	Dessert Spoon

An individual place setting for a formal, sit-down dinner.

A table set for a formal dinner party.

UTENSILS

The dinner fork is set to the left of the setting. If you are serving a first course, the first course fork is set to the left of the dinner fork. The salad fork, if needed, is set to the right of the dinner fork. Then, the dinner knife is set to the right of the charger.

The first course knife, if needed, is set to the right of the dinner knife. The soup spoon is set to the right of the knives.

The dessert fork or spoon (or both) can either be brought in with the dessert plate, or can be set, spoon topmost and pointing left, fork pointing right, above the charger or at the top of the setting.

GLASSES

The glassware is arranged in order of use, set above the knives and angled slightly, left to right, towards the edge of the table. The water goblet is furthest left, followed by the champagne flute, white wineglass, red wineglass, and a glass for sherry, port, or dessert wine.

Finally, there is the napkin, which can be set to the left of the forks or arranged on the charger.

BUFFET TABLE SETUP

A buffet doesn't have to make use of just a single table. In addition to the primary table(s), you could have smaller stations, which can help break up the line and make it flow more smoothly if you'll be serving a large number of people. For instance, you could have your guests go to a smaller table to pick up their plates and cutlery. Or, you could have a smaller separate station for salad—as salad always seems to be a preparation that slows guests down at a buffet when they serve themselves. You could also have a separate table for carved meat that has a special accompaniment, or any other type of dish that a guest might need take time to personalize, like a burger bar, for instance.

In addition to table placement, think about configuration. If you're a traditionalist, you can simply use a single large table, positioned so that guests serve themselves along both sides of the table at the same time. If you will be serving a large number of dishes to a large group, you can set up a horseshoe configuration of tables. Other options would be T- and L-shaped configurations. Just figure out what will work best for your space and your party.

The day before the party, decide the placement of dishes on the buffet table. Pull out the serving pieces you plan to use and set them out on the tables. Your goal is to create a setting for your food that is attractive and that makes it easy for guests to serve themselves. Some guidelines you might want to keep in mind include:

- If plates and cutlery are placed on the same buffet line with the food, place the plates at the beginning of the line where they are easy to reach. It's best to place cutlery and napkins at the end of the line, so guests don't have to juggle them as they serve themselves food.

- Use pedestals and other devices (it could be as simple as an overturned bowl) under your tablecloth to elevate some platters. This adds visual interest to the table and is especially effective when you need to save space.

- Set foods that might drip or spill closest to the edge of the table.

- Group the foods in a logical manner: entrées first, then side dishes and salad.

- Place sauces and condiments directly with the foods they accompany so guests understand how to use them. Make sure each has an appropriate serving tool.

- It's best to pre-dress your salad for a buffet, but if you'd prefer to serve the dressing separately, put it in a squeeze bottle, so it's easier for guests to prepare their salad one-handed. For the same reason, provide a salad server that guests can use one-handed. If you use two separate salad servers, guests will have to put their plates down to serve themselves, causing a back-up on your buffet line.

There are countless ways to present fruit. Here, the mixed fruit kebabs are skewered into a decoratively carved watermelon.

Sliced fruit arranged on a platter is a classic buffet presentation.

- If you are setting up your buffet table so guests can serve themselves from both sides, provide two servers for each dish, to keep the line moving.

- Once you've decided on dish placement, set up your buffet table, complete with linens, serving pieces tagged with the name of the dish they'll be holding, and tablescape. While a beautiful tablescape can make a party memorable, the more important goal in buffet setup is to make it easy for your guests to serve themselves. A well-designed buffet line allows guests to get their food fast and to enjoy it while it's still hot and delectable, the way you intended it.

THE BEVERAGE AREA SETUP

If you are planning a get-together with more than eight people, you may find it easiest to let your guests serve themselves their own drinks. For more details about setting up a bar for your party, see chapter 9. Beverage self-serve area(s) should be kept separate from the food line(s). Your beverage area can take several different forms, depending on the type of party you are throwing. In the case of a brunch, for instance, you might set up a separate table or a counter with coffee urns or thermal carafes filled with decaffeinated and caffeinated coffee, as well as a thermal carafe containing hot water for tea. A basket might be set out with several selections of different breakfast teas, including at least one that is decaffeinated. You might also be offering pitchers of juices—orange, grapefruit, cranberry—as well as a celebratory alcoholic libation, like a Mimosa or Bellini (see page 309 and 315 for recipes).

If possible, set up your beverage area the night before. In this case, set out the urns or carafes and label them with what they will be containing. You'll need to do it the day of the party anyway, and this way you don't run the risk of forgetting which pot holds the decaffeinated before you get around to writing the label for it. You can also get your coffee pots ready to run, filling the filters with coffee. Don't fill the urn with water, however, until just before you run it; you want to make coffee with fresh water. Set out all of your cups and mugs, as well as the empty creamers, sugar bowl, artificial sweetener, and plates for lemon wedges for tea and discarded tea bags.

For the juices, set out small glasses or goblets, whatever you plan to use, as well as the pitchers that will hold the juices and plates to set the pitchers on to catch any drips. If you intend on keeping your pitchers cold by setting them in ice, also pull out the bowls you'll be using to set the pitchers in. If you will be serving an alcoholic beverage, set out those glasses, as well as the container you'll be using to serve from. In the instance that you might be serving a cocktail that bears a striking resemblance to a nonalcoholic drink you'll also be serving, you would do well to make abundantly clear which drink is which, by labeling them, by putting them in distinctive pitchers, by serving them in distinctive glasses (like a champagne flute). The last thing you want is for a guest (or a child) to take a big swig of a Mimosa thinking that it's orange juice.

If you are serving sangria or a punch (alcoholic or not) or a warm drink, like spiced wine or mulled cider (see the recipe on page 331), you might set that up on its own separate table. Drinks like sangria and punch are a wonderful opportunity to pull out your grandmother's punch bowl and cups, but any large attractive glass bowl will do. You'll need a decorative serving ladle (using your everyday soup ladle is probably not appropriate), and you'll want to make sure that the glasses you decide to use are large enough to easily use with the ladle. Those pretty little retro juice glasses may seem like a good idea, but if you can't get the

A selection of fresh juices presented in glass pitchers can be a delightful alternative to the traditional buffet fruit spread.

punch into it without spilling half a ladlefull you ought to think about using something else instead.

For a warm drink, consider putting it out in a slow cooker. Warm it up on the stovetop, then transfer it to the slow cooker, plug it in, set it to "keep warm," and put the lid on until guests arrive. Slow cookers are available in a wide range of styles and for the most part are reasonably priced.

In either case, set the punch bowl or slow cooker out the night before and arrange your cups, glasses, or mugs attractively around it. Set out small napkins as well, so guests can wipe away any drips. You might also want to set out a small plate to rest the bowl of the ladle on when it's not in use. For more about setting up to serve mixed drinks and cocktails, see chapter 9.

DECIDING ON DÉCOR

Décor is where you can really develop the theme you have chosen. Have some fun thinking about possible decorations, as well as ways to create the perfect overall ambience for your gathering, whether it's indoors or out.

When it comes to tablescapes, anything is possible, from bouquets of fresh flowers to artful arrangements of seasonal fruits and vegetables to thematically appropriate still life centerpieces. Just keep in mind that table arrangements should never interfere with conversation or service; you don't want your guests struggling to see each other over or around a centerpiece and you don't want the table so busy with things that there's no room for the dishes. Nor do you want fragrant flowers that overpower or clash with the aroma of the food.

If you've planned an event for the evening, the lighting can make it magical. Candles are appropriate both indoors and outdoors. When setting them outside,

When choosing flowers for your tabletop, always consider fragrance, height, and seasonality.

SPECIAL CONSIDERATIONS OF A LARGE GET-TOGETHER

If you're throwing a party for a lot of people, forty or more, planning truly becomes paramount. Your goal in planning is to eliminate as much uncertainty from the event as possible. That doesn't mean that something unexpected may not occur, it just lessens the chances of it and puts you in a place where you'll be better able to handle it.

All the issues we have discussed in this chapter pertain to a big event, just on a grander scale. You've got that many more people to meet, greet, and seat; that much more food to prepare and serve; that many more coats to deal with; that many more cars to figure out where to park; that much more garbage to dispose of, and that much more party cleanup afterwards.

Think it through as early in the process as you can. Keep it as simple as you can. Select dishes that are easy to prepare and that can be made entirely ahead of time. Do not pick fussy food that is not

going to taste so great if it is not served at just the right temperature. Understand that you don't have to do it all yourself. You can enlist guests to help out with the cooking—ask a handful of friends to each bring an appetizer or maybe put the call out for desserts. If that's not appropriate (for instance, at a wedding reception at home), then think about bringing in professional help. If you're set on doing all the cooking, then hire a crew to come in and clean your house top to bottom, or a bartender, or servers, or people who will do all the cleanup once the party is over.

Early on, determine what your needs are going to be regarding seating and serving. A party rental service may be your biggest and best resource. For a price, they will rent out almost everything, from tents, tables, chairs, tablecloths and napkins, to tabletop, flatware, and glassware, to chafing dishes and electric heaters for outdoor events. The beauty of renting plates and glasses is that, usually, you're not responsible for returning them to the company clean, just rinsed off. You will be responsible for any items that are lost or damaged, however.

THE SEATING ARRANGEMENT

If your get-together is a sit-down affair, whether it's formal or casual, at one table or multiple tables, you ought to give some thought to the seating arrangement. If it's a very casual affair with friends, many of whom already know each other, you may choose to leave the seating up to your guests. If it's a smaller soiree and includes a number of people who are not acquainted with one another, you might want to guide the seating, either by setting out place cards or suggesting seating to your guests as you approach the dining table. Some hosts are adamant in splitting up couples at the table, wanting their guests to make new connections as they enjoy their meal. This is certainly an option, but you don't have to split couples up in order to place people together who you think will enjoy one another; you can accomplish this equally well by seating people across from one another. If you have invited a couple for the first time who are on the quiet side, you might not want to split them up; as much as you want to promote conversation and new friendships at your table, you don't want to make any of your guests palpably uncomfortable.

If you have invited a guest who is particularly sociable or charismatic, you might want to place them in the middle of the table, as they will be able to shift about in all directions in their conversation-making, igniting the entire get-together. In addition, if you also have a guest who is either new to everyone else at the table or who is shy, you can sit him or her next to the social dynamo, or sit them next to you or your significant other, where you can concentrate your attention on them and perhaps involve them in conversations around the table.

Traditionally, the host sits at one end of the table, his or her significant other, if there is one, at the other end. Alternatively, you may wish to seat the guest of honor (say, if the party is to celebrate a birthday, anniversary, Mother's Day, a graduation, etc.) at the head of the table.

If your party is a large get-together with multiple tables, such as a wedding reception, you might want to consider providing a seating list or place cards set on a table or counter with the guest's table number indicated. This will prevent guests from having to go from table to table looking for their seats.

though, make sure they're in containers that will prevent them from being blown out by the wind and that will keep them from accidentally setting fire to anything. Indoors, you can create ambience galore with lit tapers throughout the room (always out of the way so that guests can enjoy the flickering light but you don't have to worry about anyone inadvertently backing up against one and lighting their hair on fire). For the tabletop, attractive votive candles are always your best bet, as they won't interfere with conversation or make it difficult to pass dishes.

But candles aren't your only option when it comes to mood lighting; there are all sorts of lovely battery-run paper lanterns and twinkle lights that can be used indoors and out to make your gathering more festive. If it's a cold-weather soiree and you have a fireplace, get it going. Nothing welcomes a guest more than a cheery fire and glass of champagne. Outdoors you can achieve the same effect with a chiminea, fire pit, or an old-fashioned bonfire.

THE ROLE OF HOST

If you are throwing this soiree on your own, try to enlist a friend to come early to help you with any last-minute tasks and to greet guests at the door, if you are still involved in the kitchen. If you are throwing this party with a friend, spouse, or significant other, you need to discuss the hosting responsibilities ahead of time. Whoever is not cooking should largely take on the role of host. That means greeting guests as they come through the door, taking their coats or indicating where they can leave them, pointing out where the food and drink tables are. Once most of your guests have arrived, the host should circulate, introducing people, making sure people have drinks, and checking back with the cook to see if he or she is in need of help. It's a good idea to make the bar the host's job: buying the ice and doing the final setup before the guests arrive, while the cook is at work in the kitchen. During the party, it will also be the host's responsibility to periodically check on the bar and replenish stock as needed.

DON'T FORGET WHY YOU ARE DOING THIS

The most important reason for planning any get-together is to have a good time. No matter the challenges, no matter the amount of work involved, no matter any frustrations you might have encountered along the way, once guests are in your home, make sure you take the opportunity to mingle, chat, and bask in the glow of their compliments on your food, your lovely house, the wonderful company. There is truly no more satisfying sound to a host than the happy roar of a room full of people eating, talking, laughing, and delighting in this moment that you have created for them.

WHEN SOMETHING GOES WRONG DURING YOUR PARTY

No matter how much planning and preparation you put into a party, unforeseen issues still may arise. Here are few common entertaining disasters:

LOSS OF POWER

INCLEMENT OR SEVERE WEATHER

SUDDEN REVELATION OF A GUEST'S FOOD ALLERGY OR PREFERENCE (I.E. VEGAN)

AN INVITED GUEST BRINGS EXTRA FRIENDS WITHOUT ASKING

THE PARTY RENTAL STORE DOESN'T DELIVER GOODS ON TIME

A FOOD DISASTER (I.E. YOU REALIZE THAT THE TURKEY IS STILL FROZEN THE MORNING OF THE PARTY OR THAT THE CULINARY CENTERPIECE OF A MEAL IS A COMPLETE FLOP FOR SOME REASON)

If something like this happens to you, *do not panic!* Assess the issue and begin looking for a practical solution. If you keep your cool and tend to the situation with a smile on your face, your guests will likely respond in kind.

> *The hostess must be like the duck—calm and unruffled on the surface, and paddling like hell underneath.*
>
> —ANONYMOUS

CLASSIC HORS D'OEUVRE ARE TECHNICALLY SMALL, BITE-SIZE ITEMS TO BE SERVED AS AN APPETIZER BEFORE A MEAL, BUT IT IS BECOMING MORE AND MORE COMMON TO SERVE A MENU COMPOSED ENTIRELY OF FINGER FOODS FOR AN EVENT LIKE A RECEPTION OR COCKTAIL PARTY. THESE "STANDING MEALS" CAN ACTUALLY BE QUITE EXTENSIVE, RUNNING THE GAMUT FROM COLD SOUPS, MEATS, FISH, CHEESES, VEGETABLE DISHES, AND PASTAS TO DESSERTS AND CONFECTIONS.

When my daughter Rita asked to hold her wedding reception at our home, her father and I were both honored and overwhelmed. The first step was to decide on the formality and style of the reception. We decided to have a cocktail reception immediately after the ceremony on the lawn near the gardens so the catering staff could set out the first course while we greeted the new couple. Since my husband and I wanted to make the hors d'oeuvre ourselves, we concentrated on do-ahead options that could be frozen well in advance. The dinner menu was easy to figure out, compared to determining how many things and how much of each item we needed to prepare.

SELECTING HORS D'OEUVRE AND FINGER FOODS FOR A MENU

When you choose hors d'oeuvre selections for a menu, you should keep in mind a few points. If these foods are meant to stand in as full meal, you'll need a good variety of options, and will most likely want to include some protein-rich foods. If there is a meal to follow, the number of different offerings can be kept to a minimum. If you are simply having a cocktail before a full dinner, you may want to set out a few types of nuts or a bowl of olives so your guests can enjoy the entire meal.

Most caterers calculate that you should have about 6 pieces per person for the first hour of a cocktail reception that is followed by a full meal. If the reception doesn't include a meal, that number is often doubled. If the reception lasts more than 1 hour, calculate that you'll need an additional 3 or 4 pieces for each additional hour that the reception goes on. A typical recommendation is to serve a varied selection that includes 6 to 8 hot hors d'oeuvre and 4 to 6 cold options.

To fine-tune your selections and the quantities you need to prepare even more, consider the following:

THE AGE AND GENDER OF YOUR GUESTS

THE TIME OF DAY AND THE TIME OF YEAR

THE LENGTH OF THE EVENT (FOR INSTANCE, IF YOU ARE HOLDING A 4-HOUR OPEN HOUSE, IT IS LIKELY THAT EACH GUEST WILL STAY ONLY 1½ HOURS)

THE TYPE OF SERVICE YOU ARE PLANNING

RECEPTION FOOD SERVING STYLES

When it comes to reception food, you essentially have two serving options: buffet-style (stationary) service or butler-style (circulating) service. For buffet-style service, the food is arranged on platters that are placed on a table so that guests can walk up to the platter and serve themselves. For butler-style service, servers carry trays of food around the party to the guests; they may help themselves to items on the tray or the servers may place the items onto the guests' plates.

PRESENTATION

Whether you choose buffet or butler service, presentation is all-important. Guests will select an item based on eye appeal (and possibly aroma), so you want to create interest by introducing a variety of visual elements. A certain amount of repetition is comfortable and appealing, but too much of anything becomes monotonous—whether it's an ingredient, color, shape, flavor, or texture.

Color is an important tool when building a presentation. We all have associations with certain colors: greens give the impression of freshness and vitality; browns, golds, and maroons are warming, comforting, and rich; and, orange and red are intense, powerful colors. The main concern when creating a buffet presentation is avoiding the overuse of one color.

Likewise, too much of the same shape or texture can be dull. The surface of a food can look glossy or matte, smooth or highly textured. Shapes can be rounded and organic or sharp and linear, tall or wide. Introducing contrasting elements adds energy and motion to your presentation. The natural shape of a food can be altered by cutting or slicing it. To give extra height to foods, arrange them in piles or pyramids, roll or fold them, or use display pieces like pedestals, columns, or baskets to raise them.

A buffet spread of hors d'oeuvre that are easy to eat and bite size.

A buffet table should contain platters of many different sizes and shapes.

ADAPTING RECIPE PRESENTATION TO YOUR SERVICE STYLE

Most reception food recipes can be made to suit any service style simply by adapting the plating or orientation
of the components. You can even take recipes that aren't traditionally served as hors d'oeuvre and reassemble them.
Miniaturize sandwiches like Reubens or club sandwiches. Arrange foods on skewers. Serve foods in unusual "containers"
such as endive leaves or even spoons. Present a traditional salad as a canapé or as a topping for crostini.
Here are two examples of dishes that have been modified to be served three different ways:

Scallop ceviche, butler-style service.   Scallop ceviche, individually plated.   Scallop ceviche, buffet service.

Platter of individual
melon and prosciutto
hors d'oeuvre.

Melon and prosciutto
skewers, buffet service.

The items on platters for circulating service may be arranged either symmetrically or asymmetrically. Symmetrical arrangements tend to look formal, whereas asymmetrical arrangements tend to look more natural. In order to have strong, clean lines, arrange the food logically. Lines can be straight, curved, or angled. When a line is repeated, a pattern is created. When two lines meet, they create a shape, and within it is the focal point. Lines can move away from or toward this point and, thereby, introduce a sense of flow or motion.

If your menu includes both hot and cold items, you need to plan ways to keep foods at the correct temperature. For a buffet presentation, chafing dishes are a great way to keep hot foods hot—but be certain that anything that can burn easily like linens, paper goods, or dried flowers, is kept away from open flames. Ice beds can be a dramatic way to keep seafood and caviar cold, but be sure to set them in a pan or other container that can hold water as the ice melts.

NEATNESS COUNTS

The neatness of your platters or trays will contribute greatly to the overall impact of an arrangement. Consider the accessibility of each item placed on a platter. Position taller items in the rear and shorter items in the front. Pay attention to the spacing among food pieces, because no one will want to take an item that has already been touched by another guest. If serving butler-style, the guest taking the last piece off the platter should not have to sift through discarded garnishes. The garnishes you choose should add something to the dish—contrasting texture, complementary color, etc.—rather than simply being a space filler.

Using interesting or handcrafted plates and containers makes for a unique buffet presentation. However, an uneven surface, such as that of a handmade platter, does require special attention to keep the food looking neat. Arrange items in such a way that they do not roll out of place. Uncooked rice, small beans, or grains will help

When hosting an open house or another event where guests will not all be eating at the same time, you want to put the food out in stages so that the buffet looks as full and beautiful for the last guests as for the first.

keep individual pieces from moving around on a platter and also add touches of texture and contrast to your buffet table.

ANTIPASTI, HORS D'OEUVRE VARIÉS, AND SALUMI PLATTERS

Literally translated from Italian, antipasto means "before the meal," just as hors d'oeuvre is French for "outside the main work (meal)." While hors d'oeuvre can be any of a number of things, hors d'oeuvre variés (various hors d'oeuvre) is typically understood to include marinated salads, pickles, pâtés, and terrines. Salumi platters feature the cured meats and sausages of Italy. Generally you should include three elements: meats, cheeses, and marinated or roasted vegetables. You could easily substitute seafood for the meats, or feature an array of grilled or roasted vegetables instead of sliced meats on an antipasti or hors d'oeuvre variés platter. Good, crusty bread is an important accompaniment, but crackers are equally suitable.

Opting for these platter presentations helps keep your work manageable, since the foods that go onto the platter are ready to serve: cured and preserved meats, sausages, pâtés, terrines, and cheeses purchased from your favorite deli. Arrange the sliced meats and cheeses attractively: for instance, shingle slices or roll slices up to make it easy to stack them for height. Cut pâtés and terrines into slices. Add a few jarred marinated or pickled items like roasted peppers, olives, peperoncini, giardiniera (mixed vegetables), pickled beets or mushrooms, or marinated artichokes or beans that you can keep on hand in your pantry, and your platter is ready to serve.

To make a traditional salumi platter, offer a few of these items, along with some cheese (cubed or sliced):

SOPRESSATA

GENOA SALAMI

MORTADELLA

PROSCIUTTO

BRESAOLA

CAPICOLLA (COPPA)

There are hundreds of Italian-style cured meats that could be selected as part of a salumi tray or antipasti platter. Shown here are, from upper right, dried chorizo, mortadella, capicolla, peppered salami, and sopressata, served with provolone cheese and cornichons.

INSTANT HORS D'OEUVRE

While some finger foods certainly involve a lot of effort and cooking time, the preparation of some require nothing more than slicing the components and arranging them on a platter. The following are a few low-maintenance options:

HARD-COOKED EGGS

NUTS (TOASTED, SMOKED, SPICED, CURRIED, OR MIXED)

PLAIN OR MARINATED OLIVES

DIPS AND SPREADS WITH CRACKERS OR CHIPS

SAUSAGES AND SMOKED MEATS AND FISH

PÂTÉS AND TERRINES

CHEESES

CAVIAR (FEATURED ON ITS OWN IN AN ICED CONTAINER)

To select cheeses for your platter, pick one or more favorite cheeses no matter their country of origin. Here is a selection of Italian cheeses for an antipasti platter:

SOFT OR FRESH CHEESES INCLUDING MARINATED MOZZARELLA

FIRM CHEESES SUCH AS ASIAGO OR RICOTTA SALATA

CREAMY, SOFT-RIPENED CHEESES INCLUDING ROBIOLA AND TALEGGIO

BLUE-VEINED CHEESES SUCH AS GORGONZOLA

HARD CHEESES INCLUDING PECORINO-ROMANO AND PARMIGIANO-REGGIANO

Antipasti generally contains three elements: meats, cheeses, and marinated or roasted vegetables. It may also include crusty Italian bread, fish or seafood, nuts, and fresh or dried fruits.

CRUDITÉS

Crudités is the French term for raw vegetables served with a dip, such as a vinaigrette or a bagna cauda. They could also be served with ranch dressing, flavored oil, yogurt sauce, or hummus. The vegetables may be served whole, as with asparagus or baby corn, or cut into pieces, as with celery, carrots, bell peppers, and broccoli. You may wish to very briefly blanch some vegetables to improve their colors and textures (see sidebar Blanching Vegetables, page 39). When selecting vegetables for a crudités spread, choose a variety of textures, shapes, and colors to create an attractive display of bold complementary colors or a monochromatic spread of, for example, all green vegetables. The vegetable cuts found on a crudités platter can range from simple celery sticks to intricately cut radish rosebuds. You just need to choose a presentation that suits your style and skill level.

For a party with circulating service, crudités may be prepared as individual cups.

A crudités platter for buffet service.

BLANCHING VEGETABLES

Blanching can make some vegetables served as part of a crudité arrangement look and taste better including tough or woody veggies like asparagus, cauliflower, green beans, artichokes, and broccoli. To blanch vegetables, cut them into bite-size pieces and cut away any tough stems or fibers. Bring a large pot of salted water to a rolling boil and add the vegetables. If you have a lot of vegetables to blanch, work in batches so the water temperature doesn't drop too much. Most vegetables are properly blanched in 20 to 30 seconds; any longer and they will lose too much texture. They should have bright colors and a crisp texture. Use a wire basket to get them into and out of the water quickly and then immediately transfer the blanched vegetables to a container filled with ice water to stop the cooking. Once they are cool, drain them well so they don't get soggy.

Use this technique to parcook vegetables to make sautéed side dishes easy to finish during dinner parties; just let the vegetables cook until they are tender-crisp.

EGGS

A CLASSIC HORS D'OEUVRE is a hard-cooked egg with a deviled filling. Hard-cooked eggs can be pickled for another popular option, as well as sliced or crumbled to garnish a salad or another dish, or made into a salad filling for tea sandwiches (see photo page 64).

To make hard-cooked eggs, fill a deep pot with enough water to hold the eggs comfortably. Lower the eggs gently into the pot of cold water so they don't crack. Heat the pot over high heat until the water comes to a full simmer. Immediately pull the pot off the heat, cover, and let the eggs cook in the hot water for 20 minutes. Remove the hard-cooked eggs.

Place hard-cooked eggs under cold running water until they are cool enough to handle. Gently press down and roll the egg over a countertop to crack the shell before peeling. Peel the shell and membrane away with your fingers. The best way to prevent the green ring around the yolk is to avoid overcooking and then cool and peel the eggs as quickly as possible.

Deviled Eggs

You can vary the presentation of deviled eggs. Instead of cutting them in half lengthwise, you can cut them into quarters to make wedges, or you can make a slice from the wide end so they stand flat and cut away enough of the top to pop out the yolks and then present them as whole eggs, standing upright, as shown in the photo (opposite).

MAKES 20 PIECES

10 hard-cooked eggs, peeled, cold

¾ cup mayonnaise

1 tbsp Dijon mustard

Kosher salt and freshly ground black pepper, as needed

1. Slice the eggs in half lengthwise. Separate the yolks from the whites. Reserve the whites separately until ready to fill. They can be held in the refrigerator in a covered container for up to 3 days.

2. Rub the yolks through a sieve or place them in a food processor bowl. Add the mayonnaise, mustard, salt, and pepper. Mix or process the ingredients into a smooth paste. This filling mixture may be prepared in advance and held in a covered container in the refrigerator for up to 2 days.

3. Just before serving the deviled eggs, pipe or spoon the yolk mixture into the egg whites, garnish as desired, and serve.

TOMATO, GARLIC, AND BASIL DEVILED EGGS

3 garlic cloves, minced

2 plum tomatoes, peeled, seeded, and minced

5 large basil leaves, minced

1 tbsp olive oil

Heat the oil in a small pan over medium heat. Add the garlic, tomatoes, and basil and sauté until very hot and tender, about 3 minutes. Most of the liquid should cook away from the tomato. Let the mixture cool, then add it to the separated egg yolks. Proceed to fill the egg whites and garnish as desired.

DEVILED EGGS WITH SPINACH *Add ½ cup blanched minced spinach to the egg yolk mixture. If you wish, you can use chopped frozen spinach that has been thawed and squeezed before mincing.*

PARMESAN DEVILED EGGS *Add 2 tbsp grated Parmesan to the yolk mixture.*

Deviled Eggs

MARINATED SNACKS

A SELECTION OF SALTY, SAVORY SNACK FOODS are the perfect accompaniment to cocktails. Choose briny options, like olives or fresh goat cheese that you've marinated in a good olive oil and plenty of herbs, or a refreshing ceviche made from scallops that "cook" in a bath of lime juice.

Herbed Marinated Olives

MAKES 1 POUND MARINATED OLIVES; ABOUT 3 CUPS

1 lb mixed brine-packed olives

2 tbsp dried oregano

1 tbsp dried rosemary

1 tbsp dried thyme

1 tbsp dried marjoram

1 tsp red pepper flakes

Finely grated zest from 2 lemons or oranges

½ cup extra-virgin olive oil, or as needed to cover olives

1. Spread out the olives on paper towels and blot dry to remove most of the brine.

2. Put the olives, herbs, and pepper flakes in a medium bowl and sprinkle with the zest. Sprinkle with extra-virgin olive oil to moisten the mixture and toss to mix well. Add more oil, if needed, to just barely cover the olives.

3. Let the olives marinate in a covered container in the refrigerator for at least 24 hours before serving. They will last up to 2 weeks in the refrigerator. Serve at room temperature on their own or as part of a antipasti or hors d'oeuvre variés platter.

Grilled Herbed Goat Cheese Wrapped in Grape Leaves

You could simply marinate the goat cheese in herbs and olive oil, without wrapping it in grape leaves or grilling it. It makes a great spread for canapés, or it can be served as is.

SERVES 8

1 log fresh goat cheese (about 9 oz)

¼ cup fresh herbs, minced (combination of parsley, tarragon, chives, chervil, tarragon, and a bit of fresh lavender)

1 tsp kosher salt, or as needed

½ tsp freshly ground black pepper, or as needed

1¼ cups extra-virgin olive oil, or as needed to cover goat cheese

8 jarred grape leaves, rinsed

1. Cut the goat cheese log into 8 pieces. Place the herbs, salt, and pepper in a shallow plate and roll the goat cheese in the herbs, pressing them into the surface. Transfer the herbed goat cheese to a jar or a dish. Pour the olive oil over the cheese and let marinate in the refrigerator for at least 12 and up to 48 hours.

2. Preheat a grill to medium-high or use a broiler. Lift the goat cheese from the oil, letting the oil drain away and set each piece in the center of a grape leaf. Wrap the leaf around the goat cheese. Grill or broil the grape leaves about 3 inches from the heat source until slightly charred, 2 to 3 minutes.

3. Serve immediately accompanied with bread or crackers.

NOTE *The size of jarred grape leaves can vary quite a bit, so you may need to overlap a couple of them to get the correct amount of area to wrap around the cheese. If the stems are very coarse, cut them out before wrapping the cheese.*

Escabèche of Tuna

Esabèche is a traditional pickled fish preparation. It is similar to ceviche, but unlike ceviche, which is best served an hour or two after it is prepared, you can make escabèche the day before you intend to serve it.

SERVES 8

1 lb tuna steak

Kosher salt and freshly ground black pepper, as needed

¼ cup olive oil

3 tbsp fresh lime juice

½ cup peeled, seeded, small-dice tomato

3 tbsp small-dice red onion

½ serrano, minced

1 green onion, white and green portions, thinly sliced on the diagonal

½ tsp minced garlic

1 tsp chopped cilantro

1. Cut the tuna into 1-inch cubes. Place in a bowl, season with salt and pepper, and drizzle with 1 tablespoon of the oil. Toss to coat the cubes evenly. Heat 1 tablespoon of the oil in a sauté pan over high heat, and add the tuna. Cook, turning as necessary, until all sides are seared, about 2 minutes; it should be cooked "black and blue"—colored on the exterior but still extremely rare inside.

2. Remove the tuna from the heat and transfer to a bowl.

3. To make the marinade: Mix the remaining olive oil with the lime juice, tomato, onion, chile, green onion, garlic, and cilantro in a medium bowl.

4. Pour the marinade over the tuna (it should still be warm) and turn or gently toss to coat evenly. Cover and refrigerate at least 12 and up to 36 hours before serving.

5. Serve as part of an hors d'oeuvre platter or in cucumber cups (see Scallop Ceviche, step 3, recipe follows) as a hors d'oeuvre or as a first course accompanied with a small salad.

Scallop Ceviche in Cucumber Cups

While you can prepare the cucumber cups and the vegetables for the ceviche a few hours ahead of time, ceviche tastes best when it marinates no more than an hour or two before you serve it.

MAKES 30 PIECES

8 oz scallops, finely diced

1 peeled and seeded tomato, finely diced

1 tsp minced chives

1 tbsp chopped cilantro

½ jalapeño, minced

¼ green bell pepper, seeded and finely diced

1 tbsp olive oil

5 drops Tabasco sauce

3 tbsp fresh lime, (1 or 2 limes)

Kosher salt and freshly ground black pepper, as needed

Thirty ½-inch-thick slices cucumber

Sour cream, as needed (optional)

2 tsp whole cilantro leaves (optional)

1. In a medium bowl, combine the scallops, tomato, chives, chopped cilantro, jalapeño, bell pepper, oil, and Tabasco.

2. Add the lime juice and toss to coat the scallops. Season with salt and pepper. Cover and marinate in the refrigerator for at least 1 and up to 2 hours, stirring occasionally.

3. Trim the cucumber slices with a round cutter to remove the rind. With a melon baller scoop out a shallow pocket in the middle of the cucumber slices—do not cut all the way through the slice.

4. Just before serving, fill the cucumber cups with the ceviche. Garnish each ceviche cup with a small dot of sour cream and a cilantro leaf, if desired.

Chili-Roasted Peanuts with Dried Cherries

NUTS, CHIPS, AND CRACKERS

FRESHLY ROASTED NUTS, whether served plain, lightly salted, or seasoned with one of the blends we offer below, are a classic companion for cocktails. They also find their way onto cheese boards or salads. They can be served as is or made into "cocktail" blends that include one or more varieties of nut as well as dried fruits like raisins or cherries. Making your own bagel, pita, or tortilla chips is easy, and they store well in airtight containers at room temperature.

To toast nuts evenly without scorching, use the oven. The nuts can be seasoned with one of the seasoning blends (recipes follow) before putting them in the oven. Spread out the nuts on a dry baking sheet and toast just until they develop a deeper brown color and pleasant aroma. Stir frequently during toasting to ensure even browning. Immediately pour the toasted nuts onto a cool baking sheet to avoid scorching.

Oven Temperature and Roasting Times for Nuts

TYPE OF NUT	TEMPERATURE	APPROXIMATE ROASTING TIME
Peanuts	325°F	5–7 minutes
Walnuts, pecans, pistachios, cashews	325°F	8–10 minutes
Almonds, hazelnuts (filberts)	300°F	10–12 minutes
Macadamia nuts	250°F	up to 15 minutes

Seasoned Nuts

Freshly roasted nuts are a classic companion for cocktails. They are also perfect on cheese boards or tossed into salads.

MAKES 1 POUND ROASTED NUTS

2 tbsp olive oil

1 tbsp Worcestershire sauce (optional)

1 lb unsalted, raw mixed or single whole nuts

½ tsp salt or 2½ tsp seasoning blend (recipes follow)

1. Preheat the oven (see chart for temperature).

2. Heat the oil in a medium sauté pan over medium heat. Add the Worcestershire sauce, if using, and bring to a simmer. Add the nuts and toss well to coat evenly. Sprinkle the salt or the seasoning mix over the nuts and toss or stir to coat evenly.

3. Pour the nuts onto a baking sheet and spread them out into an even layer. Bake until evenly browned, stirring occasionally to brown evenly (see chart for times). Immediately pour the nuts onto a cool pan and let them cool completely before serving or storing. The nuts can be made up to one week in advance and stored in an airtight containers at room temperature for up to 1 month or in the refrigerator for 6 months.

CHILI-ROASTED PEANUTS WITH DRIED CHERRIES *Season plain peanuts with 2½ teaspoons chili powder and add 5 ounces of unsweetened tart dried cherries.*

Seasoning Blends for Nuts

MAKES 2½ TEASPOONS; ENOUGH TO SEASON 1 POUND OF NUTS

Basic Blend

½ tsp kosher salt

½ tsp garlic powder

½ tsp chili powder

¼ tsp ground cumin

¼ tsp celery seed

Pinch of cayenne pepper

Curry Blend

¾ tsp kosher salt

1 tsp curry powder

¼ tsp garlic powder

½ tsp onion powder

Pinch of cayenne pepper

Pimiento Blend

2 tsp ground pimiento

½ tsp kosher salt

Bagel Chips

Add some fresh or dried herbs to the olive oil before you brush it on the chips. Rosemary is a great choice.

SERVES 12

3 bagels

½ cup olive oil

4 garlic cloves, minced

Kosher salt and freshly ground black pepper, as needed

1. Preheat the oven to 325°F. Combine the olive oil and the garlic in a small bowl.

2. Slice the bagels into thin slices, about ⅛ inch thick. Place the bagel slices on a baking sheet, brush with the garlic-scented olive oil, and season lightly with salt and pepper.

3. Bake, turning once to brown the chips evenly, just until crisp and light brown, about 15 minutes. Store in an airtight container at room temperature for up to 1 week. Serve with your choice of dips or spreads.

   PITA CRISPS *Use a pizza cutter or a sharp knife to cut 4 pitas into wedges. Place the wedges on a baking sheet and brush with the garlic oil. Bake until crisp, about 10 minutes.*

   TORTILLA CRISPS *Use a pizza cutter or a sharp knife to cut 6 corn tortillas, 6 inches in diameter, into wedges or strips. Toss the wedges or strips in the oil until coated and then transfer to baking sheets. Bake until crisp, about 10 minutes.*

Cheddar and Walnut Icebox Crackers

These rich crackers are tender and very satisfying. Choose an aged cheddar for the best flavor. You may wish to omit the salt in the dough and sprinkle the tops of the crackers with a little sea salt before baking.

MAKES ABOUT 4 DOZEN CRACKERS

½ cup (1 stick) unsalted butter, softened

2 cups grated aged cheddar (about 8 oz)

1⅓ cups all-purpose flour

¼ tsp kosher salt

½ cup finely chopped walnuts (about 2 oz)

1. In the bowl of an electric mixer fitted with the paddle attachment, cream the butter until fluffy, about 2 minutes. Add the cheese and mix well. Add the flour and salt and mix on low speed until evenly blended, scraping down the sides of the bowl to mix evenly. Add the nuts and continue to mix until just incorporated, about 1 minute.

2. Divide the dough into 3 equal pieces and shape each piece into a log about 1½ inches in diameter. Wrap well and chill for at least 1 hour or overnight. The dough can be held for up to 1 week in the refrigerator or frozen for up to 2 months.

3. Preheat the oven to 350°F. Line 2 baking sheets with parchment paper. Cut the dough into ¼-inch slices and place on the baking sheets. Bake until crisp and golden, about 15 minutes. Cool on wire racks and store in an airtight container for up to 2 weeks. Serve as a cocktail snack.

   BLUE CHEESE AND PECAN ICEBOX CRACKERS *Substitute an equal amount of blue cheese for the cheddar and pecans for the walnuts. If your blue cheese is very salty, you may wish to omit the added salt.*

Cheddar and Walnut Icebox Crackers

DIPS AND SPREADS

WHETHER YOU SERVE CREAMY DIPS, dips made from chunky vegetables, or bean-based dips, these versatile offerings are easy to make and easy to serve. Most dips are perfect for making ahead and store well in the refrigerator for a few days. Some even improve in flavor and texture if they have the chance to mellow for a day or two. Serve dips in crocks or bowls, hollowed out round bread loaves, or vegetable containers to add some color to your presentation.

CREATIVE DIP CONTAINERS

To make an already beautiful crudités platter more striking, be creative with what you use as the dip container. Hollowed out vegetables make excellent containers that will add color and interest to any presentation. Select a vegetable of the appropriate size to accommodate the volume of your dip recipe—an overflowing container makes it difficult for guests to help themselves, and a container that's only half-full looks unappealing. Vegetables commonly used as containers for dips and spreads are:

LARGE ENDIVE OR RADICCHIO LEAVES

SMALL RED CABBAGES, HOLLOWED OUT

ONIONS, CUT IN HALF AND THE INNER PORTIONS REMOVED

TOMATOES, CORED AND SCOOPED OUT

ARTICHOKES, INNER LEAVES REMOVED

EGGPLANTS, CUT IN HALF AND SCOOPED OUT TO MAKE "BOATS"

SMALL HARD-SKINNED SQUASHES AND PUMPKINS, TOPS CUT AWAY AND SEEDS SCOOPED OUT

BELL PEPPERS, TOPS SLICED OFF, SEEDS AND RIBS REMOVED

Eggplant Caponata

This eggplant relish can be served as a spread for bruschetta or on crackers, or as an accompaniment to roasted or grilled meats.

MAKES ABOUT 3 CUPS RELISH

2 tbsp olive oil

2¾ cups diced eggplant

1 red bell pepper, seeded and diced

2 garlic cloves, minced

4 canned plum tomatoes, diced

1 tbsp chopped basil

1 tsp chopped marjoram (or ½ tsp dried)

2 tsp balsamic vinegar

¼ lb piece Parmesan for shaving

1. In a large sauté pan, heat the olive oil over medium heat. Add the eggplant and sauté until it is lightly brown and tender, 4 to 5 minutes.

2. Add the bell pepper, and continue to sauté until it is tender, about 3 minutes more. Add the garlic and sauté until fragrant, about 1 minute.

3. Add the tomatoes and cook for 1 minute more. Stir in the basil, marjoram, and balsamic vinegar. The caponata is ready to serve warm or at room temperature now, or it may be stored in a covered container in the refrigerator for up to 4 days.

4. Present the caponata in a bowl or crock, topped with thin strips of Parmesan cheese. Serve with crusty bread, flatbreads, or crackers.

Hot Spinach and Artichoke Dip

Make a bread bowl from a small round loaf of sourdough or pumpernickel: Cut a slice from the top to make a lid, then pull out enough of the bread's interior to create a bowl. You can reserve the bread to make bread crumbs to use in another recipe.

MAKES 3 CUPS DIP

¼ cup (½ stick) unsalted butter

2 tbsp canola oil

¼ cup all-purpose flour

2 cups whole milk

1 cup grated Parmesan (about 4 oz)

½ cup grated Monterey Jack (about 2 oz)

Kosher salt, as needed

Freshly grated nutmeg, as needed

2 tbsp olive oil

1 cup small-dice onions

One 10-oz bag fresh spinach, stemmed, rinsed, and chopped

2 tbsp chopped garlic

Two 15-oz cans artichoke hearts, drained and chopped

Cayenne pepper, as needed

1. Preheat the oven to 400°F. Heat the butter and oil in a medium saucepan over medium heat. When the butter stops foaming, add the flour all at once and stir until smooth. Continue to cook until the mixture is golden brown and has a light, nutty aroma, about 5 minutes.

2. Using a whisk, incorporate the milk into the flour mixture. Bring the liquid to a boil and reduce to a simmer. Simmer for 5 to 6 minutes until it is thick and coats the back of a spoon. Remove the sauce from the heat and stir in half of both cheeses. Season with salt and nutmeg.

3. In a large sauté pan, heat the olive oil over medium heat. Add the onions and sauté until tender, about 4 minutes. Add the spinach and stir with a wooden spoon, coating all the leaves with the oil.

4. Add the garlic and artichokes and sauté until the garlic is aromatic, about 2 minutes. Season the vegetables with salt and cayenne.

5. Remove from the heat and turn into a large mixing bowl. Fold in the cheese mixture. The dip is ready to bake now, or it can be stored in a covered container in the refrigerator for up to 3 days.

6. Pour into a casserole dish. Top with the remaining ½ cup Parmesan. Bake until the top is golden brown, 10 to 15 minutes. If reheating the dip in a chilled dish, increase the baking time by 8 to 10 minutes. Serve the dip with chips, crackers, toasted pita, or sliced warm bread.

Bagna Cauda

Bagna cauda is a hot dip made with olive oil, garlic, and anchovies, traditionally served with a selection of vegetables. Keep it warm in a fondue pot or a small slow cooker, if you have them. If not, an earthenware bowl or an enameled cast-iron pot also hold the heat well.

MAKES 1½ CUPS DIP

1 cup extra-virgin olive oil

⅓ cup minced garlic

½ cup (1 stick) unsalted butter, cut into pieces

8 to 10 canned anchovy fillets, chopped

½ tsp fresh lemon juice

½ tsp finely grated lemon zest

¼ tsp kosher salt

⅛ tsp freshly ground black pepper

1. Heat ¼ cup of the oil over medium heat in a small sauce pot. Add the garlic and cook, until fragrant and soft, about 1 minute. Add the remaining ¾ cup oil and the butter and cook gently, stirring, to melt the butter. Lower the heat, add the anchovies, and cook until they dissolve, about 2 minutes.

2. Remove from the heat and stir in the lemon juice and the zest. Season with salt and pepper.

3. Transfer the bagna cauda to an earthenware pot, or fondue pot with a flame underneath, and place in the middle of the vegetables on a platter. Serve warm with forks for dipping vegetables or bread.

SUGGESTED ITEMS FOR DIPPING

Red or yellow bell pepper strips

Fennel strips

Steamed asparagus spears

Artichoke hearts

Green beans (haricots verts)

Cubes or slices of rustic bread

Curry Dip

MAKES ABOUT 1 CUP DIP

¾ cup mayonnaise

¼ cup sour cream

1 tsp curry powder

1 tbsp fresh lemon juice

1 tsp freshly grated lemon zest

1 tsp minced garlic

2 tbsp grated onion

Combine all of the ingredients in a small bowl. Cover with plastic wrap and chill for at least 3 hours before serving. The dip can be prepared up to 3 days in advance. Serve the dip in ramekins accompanied with vegetables for dipping.

Tapenade

You can find prepared tapenade in many markets, but making your own is very simple and the results are more than worth the effort. We prefer capers packed in sea salt instead of in brine, but either will work.

MAKES ABOUT 1 CUP TAPENADE

- 1 cup pitted Kalamata or other cured black olives
- 2 canned anchovy fillets, drained
- 1 tbsp capers, rinsed
- 1 garlic clove, minced
- 2 tbsp extra-virgin olive oil
- 1 tbsp fresh lemon juice
- 1 tbsp chopped flat-leaf parsley, rosemary, or basil

1. Put the olives, anchovies, capers, and garlic in the bowl of a food processor fitted with a steel blade. Pulse on and off in short blasts until a coarse paste forms. There should still be distinct pieces of olives in the mixture.

2. With the machine running, drizzle in the olive oil until the paste is smooth enough to spread, though it should be slightly chunky.

3. Transfer the mixture to a small bowl and stir in the lemon juice and fresh herbs. The tapenade can be stored in a covered container for up to 1 week in the refrigerator; bring to room temperature before serving. Serve at room temperature with crostini, sliced baguettes, or use as a topping on canapés.

Cannellini Bean Purée

This is a great dip to serve with pita or bagel chips. It also make a good spread for canapés.

MAKES ABOUT 2 CUPS PURÉE

- 2 cups cooked or canned cannellini beans, drained and rinsed
- ¼ cup extra-virgin olive oil, plus more as needed for serving
- ¼ cup vegetable broth or water, use as needed
- 2 garlic cloves, minced
- 5 tsp fresh lemon juice
- 1 tbsp chopped flat-leaf parsley
- 1 tsp chopped rosemary
- 1 tsp kosher salt, or as needed
- ½ tsp hot pepper sauce
- ½ tsp ground white pepper

1. Place the beans and the olive oil in a food processor and purée the beans until smooth, adding enough of the broth or water to achieve a spreadable consistency. Add the garlic, lemon juice, parsley, rosemary, salt, hot sauce, and pepper and purée until evenly blended. The dip is ready to serve now, or it may be stored in a covered container in the refrigerator for up to 4 days.

2. Serve the dip at room temperature in a bowl or other container, drizzled with a swirl of extra-virgin olive oil.

Hummus

Serve this with strips of fresh bell peppers in as many different colors as you can find and a basket of freshly made pita chips for a simple and satisfying hors d'oeuvre.

MAKES ABOUT 2 CUPS HUMMUS

⅓ cup tahini

2 cups cooked chickpeas, drained and rinsed

3 tbsp fresh lemon juice, plus more as needed

1 tbsp minced garlic

1 tsp kosher salt, plus more as needed

¼ tsp cayenne pepper, plus more as needed

Combine all of the ingredients in a food processor and process to a smooth paste. Adjust the consistency with a little water, if necessary; the hummus should be light and creamy. Taste and adjust the seasoning with additional lemon juice, salt, and cayenne, as needed. The hummus is ready to serve now, or it can be stored in a covered container in the refrigerator for up to 4 days.

Baba Ghanoush

This recipe calls for the eggplant to be roasted. You could, however, grill the eggplant over medium heat to give this dip a rich, smoky flavor.

MAKES ABOUT 3 CUPS BABA GHANOUSH

1 large eggplant

3 garlic cloves , minced

¼ cup tahini, plus more as needed

¼ cup fresh lemon juice , plus more as needed

¼ tsp ground cumin

Kosher salt, as needed

1 tablespoon extra-virgin olive oil

1 tablespoon chopped flat-leaf parsley

1. Preheat the oven to 400°F. Lightly grease a baking sheet. Place the eggplant on the baking sheet and pierce the skin in several places with a fork or paring knife. Roast, turning the eggplant occasionally, until it is very soft and tender, 30 to 40 minutes. Remove from the oven and cool to room temperature. Cut the eggplant in half lengthwise and scoop the flesh into a blender or food processor.

2. Add the garlic, tahini, lemon juice, and cumin and purée until blended. The baba ghanoush can be made very smooth or left somewhat chunky, depending upon your preference.

3. Taste and season with salt and additional lemon juice, as needed. Transfer to a bowl, cover, and refrigerate for at least 3 and up to 12 hours.

4. To serve: Drizzle the olive oil over the baba ghanoush and sprinkle the parsley on top. Accompany with pita, crackers, or fresh vegetables.

Baba Ghanoush and Hummus with Pita Crisps (page 46)

Guacamole

You can chop the tomatoes, onion, jalapeño, and garlic an hour or two ahead of time, but wait for the last possible moment to mash the avocados for the best flavor and color. Make a dramatic and colorful crostini with a combination of Guacamole and Papaya and Black Bean Salsa (page 55).

MAKES ABOUT 3 CUPS GUACAMOLE; SERVES 16

2 avocados

2 tomatoes, chopped

½ red onion, cut into small dice

1 jalapeño, finely minced, or as needed

1 garlic clove, minced

Juice of 1 lime, or as needed

1 tsp kosher salt, or as needed

¼ tsp freshly ground black pepper, or as needed

1. Peel the avocados, remove the pits, and scoop the flesh into a medium bowl. Use a table fork to mash the avocados (you can leave it rather chunky or mash it to a smooth paste). Add the tomatoes, red onion, jalapeños, and garlic and mix well to combine. Taste the guacamole and season with additional jalapeño, lime juice, salt, and pepper, as needed. The guacamole is ready to serve now, or it can be stored in a covered container in the refrigerator for up to 4 hours; to prevent browning, press plastic wrap directly on the surface.

2. Serve the guacamole with toasted tortilla chips or use to top crostini.

Tomato Salsa

A classic salsa is perfect to serve with tortilla chips and it is also a great topping for a variety of other dishes, including grilled flank steak or chicken, burritos, and tacos.

MAKES ABOUT 3 CUPS SALSA

3 cups chopped tomatoes

4 green onions, white and light green portions, thinly sliced

½ cup minced red onion

1 garlic clove, minced

2 tbsp chopped cilantro

1 jalapeño, seeded and finely chopped

4½ tsp fresh lemon juice, or as needed

Kosher salt and freshly ground black pepper, as needed

1. Combine the tomatoes, green onions, red onion, garlic, cilantro, and jalapeño. Taste the salsa and add the lemon juice, salt, and pepper as needed.

2. Let the salsa rest at room temperature for at least 15 and up to 30 minutes before serving in order to develop flavor. The salsa is ready to serve now, or it can be stored in a covered container in the refrigerator for up to 2 days. Serve the salsa with tortilla chips.

Papaya and Black Bean Salsa

This is a striking salsa with bright colors. Substitute mango for the papaya, if you prefer.

MAKES ABOUT 3 CUPS SALSA

1 cup cooked black beans, rinsed and drained

1 ripe papaya, peeled and cut into small dice

2 red bell peppers, seeded and cut into small dice

1 red onion, cut into small dice

1 jalapeño, seeded and minced

¼ cup chopped cilantro

¼ cup olive oil

3 tbsp fresh lime juice

2 tsp kosher salt, or as needed

1. In a large bowl, combine the black beans, papaya, bell peppers, onion, jalapeño, cilantro, and olive oil. Taste and add the lime juice and salt as needed.

2. Let the salsa rest at room temperature for at least 15 and up to 30 minutes before serving in order to develop flavor. The salsa is ready to serve now, or it can be stored in a covered container in the refrigerator for up to 2 days. Serve the salsa with tortilla chips

Tomatillo Salsa

Instead of simmering the tomatillos as we do here, you can roast them, along with the jalapeño and garlic, under the broiler or in a very hot (450°F) oven until they become tender and slightly charred, about 10 minutes, before puréeing them with the green onion and cilantro.

MAKES ABOUT 3 CUPS SALSA

1¼ lb tomatillos

½ cup water

1 jalapeño, seeded and minced

4 garlic cloves, crushed

4 green onions, white and light green portions scallions, thinly sliced

½ cup chopped cilantro

Kosher salt and freshly ground black pepper, as needed

1. Pull off the papery husk from the tomatillos and cut the tomatillos into wedges. In a medium saucepan, combine the tomatillos, water, jalapeño, and garlic. Place over medium-high heat and bring to a boil. Reduce the heat to low and simmer until the tomatillos are tender and have turned an olive green color, about 20 minutes.

2. Purée the tomatillo mixture in a blender or food processor until smooth. Add the green onions and cilantro and purée for a few more seconds. Taste the salsa and adjust as needed with salt and pepper.

3. Let the salsa rest at room temperature for at least 15 and up to 30 minutes before serving in order to develop flavor. The salsa is ready to serve now, or it can be stored in a covered container in the refrigerator for up to 2 days. Serve the salsa with tortilla chips.

From front to back: Papaya and Black Bean Salsa, Tomatillo Salsa, and Salsa Fresca

Salsa Fresca

This salsa has a fresh, mild flavor, but you can add some heat with a jalapeño or two if you wish.

MAKES ABOUT 3 CUPS SALSA FRESCA; SERVES 16

3 cups chopped tomatoes

1 green bell pepper, seeded and minced

½ cup minced sweet or red onion

2 garlic cloves, minced

2 tbsp chopped cilantro

Juice of 1 lime, or as needed

Kosher salt and freshly ground black pepper, as needed

1. In a medium bowl, combine the tomatoes, bell pepper, onion, garlic, and cilantro. Taste the salsa and add the lime juice, salt, and pepper as needed.

2. Let the salsa rest at room temperature for at least 15 and up to 30 minutes before serving in order to develop flavor. The salsa is ready to serve now, or it can be stored in a covered container for up to 4 days. Serve the salsa with tortilla chips.

Other ingredients, such as parsley, chopped celery, jícama, celery root (or celeriac), and red, yellow, or orange bell peppers may also be added.

CROSTINI AND BRUSCHETTA

THESE APPETIZERS ARE THE VERY SOUL OF INGENUITY. At their simplest, they are nothing more elaborate than a slice of bread brushed with oil and seasoned with garlic. Crostini are typically toasted and bruschetta is more often grilled or broiled for a rich, smoky taste. Although both are at their best when they aren't made too far in advance, you can hold them for up to 2 days in an airtight container at room temperature, that you broil or grill until richly toasted.

Basic Crostini

Crostini are the perfect vessel for any of your favorite spreads or toppings. They can be topped and garnished creatively or served as is for guests to enjoy with various dips and spreads.

MAKES 24 PIECES

1 baguette

¼ cup extra-virgin olive oil

2 garlic cloves, minced

Kosher salt and freshly ground black pepper, as needed

1. Slice the baguette into rounds ½ inch thick.

2. In a small bowl, combine the olive oil and garlic. Brush both sides of the bread with the garlic oil, and season lightly with salt and pepper.

3. Preheat the oven to 400°F.

4. Toast the baguette slices until golden, turning once if necessary, about 12 minutes total. The crostini are ready to top or serve now, or they can be stored in an airtight container at room temperature for up to 2 days.

Bruschetta

Bruschetta is a grilled or broiled slice of bread, typically a little larger than a crostini. For a classic bruschetta topping, recipe follows. Tomato and basil are also typical toppings for bruschetta. Serve bruschetta fresh from the grill, or prepare it in advance and serve at room temperature.

MAKES 24 PIECES

1 baguette

¼ cup extra-virgin olive oil

2 garlic cloves, peeled and halved

Kosher salt and freshly ground black pepper, as needed

1. Slice the baguette on a slight angle into pieces about ½ inch thick.

2. Preheat the broiler or a grill to medium-high heat.

3. Grill the baguette slices until deep brown, turning once to grill on both sides, about 6 minutes total. While the bruschetta are still warm, brush them with oil and rub them with the garlic, cut side down. The bruschetta are ready to top or serve now, or they can be stored in an airtight container at room temperature for up to 2 days.

Classic Bruschetta Topping

This is the most familiar topping for bruschetta. Making your own fresh topping takes only a few minutes.

MAKES ABOUT 2 CUPS TOPPING; ENOUGH FOR ABOUT 30 PIECES

1½ cups peeled, seeded, and diced tomatoes

¼ cup chopped basil

½ tsp minced garlic

¼ cup extra-virgin olive oil

Kosher salt and freshly ground black pepper, as needed

Combine all of the ingredients in a medium bowl and let the mixture rest at room temperature for at least 30 minutes before serving. The spread is ready to use now, or it can be stored in a covered container in the refrigerator for up to 24 hours. Bring to room temperature before serving. Serve with bruschetta.

FAVORITE TOPPINGS

SUN-DRIED TOMATO AND SWEET ONION (PAGE 62)

BABA GHANOUSH (PAGE 52)

GOAT CHEESE SPREAD (PAGE 62) AND ROASTED PEPPER TOPPING (PAGE 59)

TAPENADE (PAGE 51)

FRESH MOZZARELLA AND SHREDDED BASIL

WILD MUSHROOM RAGOUT

FIG PRESERVES WITH FRESH MOZZARELLA, HONEY, AND PINE NUTS

MUSSELS (PAGE 60)

EGGPLANT CAPONATA (PAGE 48)

LOBSTER (OR SHRIMP) AND PROSCIUTTO (PHOTO ON PAGE 61)

CANNELLINI BEAN PURÉE (PAGE 51)

Roasted Pepper Topping

Use a combination of bell peppers for a more colorful topping. This recipe makes a good marinated pepper salad to serve as part of an antipasti platter.

MAKES ABOUT 2 CUPS TOPPING; ENOUGH FOR ABOUT 30 PIECES

3 medium bell peppers (red, yellow, and green), left whole with stems

¼ cup olive oil, plus more as needed

2 tbsp golden raisins

2 tbsp dry sherry wine

2 tbsp balsamic vinegar

1 tsp Dijon mustard

Kosher salt and freshly ground black pepper, as needed

½ cup diced, seeded tomato

½ red onion, thinly sliced

5 Kalamata olives, pitted and cut into strips

2 tbsp minced cilantro, plus leaves for garnish

½ jalapeño, seeded and minced

1 garlic clove, minced

1. Preheat the oven to 350°F.

2. Rub the peppers with a little olive oil and place them in a baking pan. Roast the peppers, turning them every 15 to 20 minutes, until they are very soft, about 45 minutes. When they are cool enough to handle, pull out and discard the stems and seeds, Pull off the skin and cut the peppers into thin strips. You can roast as many peppers as you wish and store any that you don't need for this dish in a covered container in the refrigerator for up to 10 days.

3. In a small bowl, combine the raisins with the sherry and let the raisins soften for about 10 minutes.

4. In a medium bowl, whisk together ¼ cup olive oil, vinegar, and mustard. Add the tomato, onion, olives, cilantro, jalapeño, and garlic and stir to combine.

5. Add the raisins and any of the sherry they have not absorbed to the mixing bowl. Add the roasted pepper strips and toss well to coat them evenly. Set aside to marinate in a covered container in the refrigerator for at least 1 hour or up to 3 days.

6. Serve as a topping for crostini or bruschetta, or include as part of an hors d'oeuvre or antipasto platter.

Mascarpone Spread

Mascarpone is a rich, mild cheese with a soft, spreading consistency.

MAKES ABOUT ½ CUP SPREAD; ENOUGH FOR 24 CANAPÉS

4 oz mascarpone

1 tsp Dijon mustard

4 or 5 drops Tabasco sauce

Kosher salt and freshly ground black pepper, as needed

1. In a small bowl, combine the mascarpone, mustard, and Tabasco and mix until well blended. Season with salt and pepper. The spread is ready to use now, or it can be stored in a covered container in the refrigerator for up to 3 days

2. Spread or pipe the mixture onto bread for canapés or tea sandwiches.

Mussel Topping

This recipe is shown as a crostini variation on page 61, but it would be perfect to serve in a mussel shell or a spoon as well.

SERVES 8

½ cup dry white wine

½ cup water

3 garlic cloves, minced

1 dried bay leaf

3 to 4 lb mussels, cleaned and debearded

¼ cup minced shallots

1 tbsp olive oil

2 plum tomatoes, peeled, seeded, and chopped

½ tsp red wine vinegar

1 tbsp chopped flat-leaf parsley

¼ tsp kosher salt, or as needed

Pinch of freshly ground black pepper, or as needed

1. In a large pot, combine the wine, water, garlic, and bay leaf and bring to a simmer.

2. Add the mussels, cover, and cook over high heat for 5 minutes, or just until the mussels open.

3. Remove the mussels and cool them. Discard any mussels that do not open. While the mussels are cooling, bring the cooking liquid back to a simmer and cook until reduced by three-quarters, about 5 minutes. Reserve. The mussels are ready to assemble into canapés now, or they can be stored in a covered container in the refrigerator for up to 12 hours.

4. In a medium sauté pan, sauté the shallots in the olive oil until translucent, 3 to 4 minutes. Add the tomatoes and the reduced liquid and cook for 3 minutes, or until the mixture simmers and the aroma of the mussels is apparent. Remove from the heat and allow to cool completely before stirring in the vinegar and parsley.

Season with salt and pepper. This mixture is ready to use in the assembly of a crostini or to top the mussels now, or it may be stored in a covered container in the refrigerator for up to 12 hours.

5. To serve: Place 3 to 4 mussels on each crostini and garnish with 1 teaspoon of the tomato mixture.

MUSSELS

Fresh mussels, like clams, have a tightly closed shell, moist plump flesh, and a sweet smell. Before steaming, clean the mussels and remove and discard any with cracked or broken shells. They should be debearded and steamed as close to your service time as possible. To steam mussels, flavor the steaming liquid, bring the mixture to a boil, add the mussels, cover, and steam until just open.

Mussels often have a dark, shaggy beard. Use your fingers to pull the beard away from the shell. Removing the beard kills the mussel, so perform this step as close to cooking as possible.

From top to bottom: Mussel Crostini, Lobster and Prosciutto Crostini, Goat Cheese and Sweet Onion Crostini

Goat Cheese Spread

Adding a bit of sour cream to the goat cheese makes it easier to spread.

MAKES ABOUT ¾ CUP CHEESE SPREAD; ENOUGH FOR 24 CANAPÉS

½ cup crumbled fresh goat cheese

¼ cup sour cream

Kosher salt and freshly ground black pepper, as needed

1. In a small bowl, combine the cheese and sour cream and mix until well blended. Season with salt and pepper. The spread is ready to use now, or it can be stored in a covered container in the refrigerator for up to 3 days.

2. Spread or pipe the mixture onto bread for canapés or tea sandwiches.

LOBSTER AND PROSCIUTTO CROSTINI *For an elegant hors d'oeuvre, spread toasted crostini with the goat cheese spread and top with a small piece of thinly sliced prosciutto, a chunk of lobster, and a bit of sage, as shown in the photo on page 61.*

GOAT CHEESE AND SWEET ONION CROSTINI *Spread crostini with the goat cheese spread and top with a spoonful of the Sun-Dried Tomato and Sweet Onion Topping (recipe follows).*

Sun-Dried Tomato and Sweet Onion Topping

Roasting the onions gives them a deep flavor and lessens the chance that they might scorch. This recipe doubles or triples easily, so you can make a large batch to serve with crostini or to use as a relish for burgers or other grilled foods.

MAKES 1½ CUPS TOPPING

2 cups medium-dice Vidalia onions

3 tbsp olive oil

Kosher salt and freshly ground black pepper, as needed

2 tbsp chopped sun-dried tomatoes

1 tsp chopped garlic

1½ tsp granulated sugar

2 tsp red wine vinegar

1. Preheat the oven to 350°F. In a small baking dish, toss the onions with 2 tablespoons of the oil and season with salt and pepper. Roast the onions until soft and fork-tender, about 25 minutes, stirring occasionally.

2. Heat the remaining olive oil in a small saucepan over medium heat, add the sun-dried tomatoes and cook, stirring frequently, until softened about 3 minutes. Add the garlic and the prepared onions and continue to cook over low heat until the ingredients are warm. Add the sugar and vinegar, and season with salt and pepper. Cook, stirring occasionally, until flavorful and very hot, about 3 minutes. The topping is ready to serve now, or it can be stored in a covered container in the refrigerator for up to 3 days. Serve hot, warm, or chilled with crostini.

CANAPÉS AND TEA SANDWICHES

THERE ARE PRACTICALLY UNLIMITED ingredient combinations for making delicious and beautiful tea sandwiches and canapés. Tea sandwiches are delicate items made on fine-grained breads that are trimmed of their crusts and usually cut into small, special shapes to be eaten in one bite; they may be closed, with both a top and bottom slice of bread, or open-face, with only one slice of bread. Canapés are small open-face sandwiches. Cut tea sandwiches as close to serving time as possible. If you must hold sandwiches that have been prepared ahead of time, use airtight containers or cover the sandwiches with damp towels.

BUTTER SPREADS

Easily made ahead and refrigerated until needed, compound, or flavored, butters are a quick way to dress up all types of meats, fish, vegetables, and breads. Just vary the flavoring to suit the dish and your taste. Here are some popular compound butters:

TARRAGON	SUN-DRIED TOMATO AND OREGANO
PIMIENTO	
CAPER	BASIL
GREEN ONION	ROSEMARY-MUSTARD
DILL	JALAPEÑO-CILANTRO
CAYENNE PEPPER	

Garlic and Parsley Butter

In addition to making a spread for canapés and tea sandwiches, it is an easy and elegant topping for broiled or grilled chicken and steaks.

MAKES ABOUT ½ CUP COMPOUND BUTTER; ENOUGH FOR 24 CANAPÉS

6 tbsp (¾ stick) unsalted butter, softened

2 tbsp chopped flat-leaf parsley

½ tsp minced garlic

½ tsp fresh lemon juice

Kosher salt and freshly ground black pepper, as needed

In a small bowl, combine the butter, parsley, garlic, and lemon juice and mix until well blended. Season with salt and pepper. Store in a covered container in the refrigerator for up to 2 days or in the freezer for up to 4 weeks. Let the butter soften to a spreading consistency before assembling canapés or tea sandwiches.

Closed tea sandwiches filled with egg
salad (back) and smoked salmon (front)

Dill and Lemon Butter

The flavors in the butter pair well with salmon and other fish in a canapé.

MAKES ABOUT ½ CUP COMPOUND BUTTER; ENOUGH FOR 24 CANAPÉS

6 tbsp (¾ stick) unsalted butter, softened

2 tbsp chopped dill

½ tsp fresh lemon juice

½ tsp finely grated lemon zest

Kosher salt and freshly ground black pepper, as needed

In a small bowl, combine the butter, dill, lemon juice, and lemon zest and mix until well blended. Season with salt and pepper. Store in a covered container in the refrigerator for up to 2 days or in the freezer for up to 4 weeks. Let the butter soften to a spreading consistency before assembling canapés or tea sandwiches.

Prosciutto and Melon Canapés

This canapé is a reinterpretation of a popular, classic first course. Choose a variety of melons for additional color. If you don't have a tiny melon baller, just cut the melon into small cubes instead.

MAKES 24 PIECES

24 white bread canapé bases (see page 63)

8 very thin slices prosciutto (about 5 oz), cut into thirds

½ cup Mascarpone Spread (page 59)

48 cantaloupe melon balls (the size of small peas)

24 honeydew melon balls (the size of small peas)

6 mint leaves, cut into fine shreds

1. Toast the canapé bases if desired. Spread each base with about ½ teaspoon of the mascarpone spread and top with a piece of prosciutto.

2. Pipe or spoon a small dollop of the mascarpone spread in the center and top with the melon balls and a few shreds of mint. Serve immediately.

Mint Butter

Use this butter to make delicate tea sandwiches filled with cucumber and watercress.

MAKES ABOUT ½ CUP COMPOUND BUTTER; ENOUGH FOR 24 CANAPÉS

6 tbsp (¾ stick) unsalted butter, softened

2 tbsp chopped mint leaves

Kosher salt and freshly ground pepper, as needed

In a small bowl, combine the butter and mint and mix until well blended. Store in a covered container in the refrigerator for up to 2 days or in the freezer for up to 4 weeks. Let the butter soften to a spreading consistency before assembling canapés or tea sandwiches.

Horseradish Butter

Horseradish is a natural companion to roast beef, but it would be a good partner for chicken, turkey, or pork as well.

MAKES ABOUT ½ CUP COMPOUND BUTTER; ENOUGH FOR 24 CANAPÉS

6 tbsp (¾ stick) unsalted butter, softened

1 tbsp drained prepared horseradish

Kosher salt and freshly ground pepper, as needed

In a small bowl, combine the butter and horseradish and mix until well blended. Season with salt and pepper. Store in a covered container in the refrigerator for up to 2 days or in the freezer for up to 4 weeks. Let the butter soften to a spreading consistency before assembling canapés or tea sandwiches.

Roquefort Butter

Substitute other blue cheeses, such as Gorgonzola or Maytag Blue. Some blue cheeses are creamier than others. If the variety you like is a bit dry, compensate by adding a tablespoon or two of cream cheese.

MAKES ABOUT ¾ CUP COMPOUND BUTTER; ENOUGH FOR 24 CANAPÉS

6 tbsp (¾ stick) unsalted butter, softened

6 tbsp crumbled Roquefort or another blue cheese

Kosher salt and freshly ground pepper, as needed

In a small bowl, combine the butter and Roquefort and mix until well blended. Season with salt and pepper. Store in a covered container in the refrigerator for up to 2 days or in the freezer for up to 4 weeks. Let the butter soften to a spreading consistency before assembling canapés or tea sandwiches.

Radish and Poppy Seed Spread

Grated radishes add color and poppy seeds add crunch to this spread.

MAKES ABOUT ¾ CUP SPREAD; ENOUGH FOR 24 CANAPÉS

4 oz cream cheese, soft

½ cup minced radishes

1 tsp poppy seeds

Kosher salt and freshly ground pepper, as needed

In a small bowl, combine the cream cheese, radishes, and poppy seeds and mix until well blended. Season with salt and pepper. Store in a covered container in the refrigerator for up to 3 days. Let the spread soften to a spreading consistency before assembling canapés or tea sandwiches. Spread or pipe the mixture onto bread for canapés or tea sandwiches.

Smoked Trout Canapés

Smoked trout is flavorful and moist, but feel free to substitute other smoked fish in this canapé.

MAKES 24 PIECES

24 rye bread canapé bases (see page 63)

2 fillets smoked rainbow trout

½ cup Horseradish Butter (page 66)

6 pimiento-stuffed green olives, sliced into rounds

1. Toast the canapé bases if desired. Remove the skin from the trout and flake it into pieces about the same width as your canapé base, following the natural striations.

2. Spread each canapé base with 1 teaspoon of the horseradish butter, top with a piece of trout, and garnish with a slice of olive. Serve immediately.

Roasted Pepper and Goat Cheese Canapés

MAKES 24 PIECES

24 whole wheat bread canapé bases (see page 63)

½ cup Goat Cheese Spread (page 62)

1½ cups Roasted Pepper Topping (page 59)

24 small cilantro leaves

1. Toast the canapé bases, if desired. Pipe about 1 teaspoon of the goat cheese spread in a ring around the edges of toasted canapé rounds or spread it in a thin layer.

2. Mound about 1 tablespoon of the roasted pepper topping in the center of each canapé and top with a cilantro leaf. Serve immediately.

Cucumber and Mint Tea Sandwiches

MAKES 24 PIECES

½ cup Mint Butter (page 66)

12 thin slices white sandwich bread, crusts removed

1 cucumber, peeled and thinly sliced

Salt and pepper, as needed

1. Lay out the slices of bread on the work surface and spread the top side of each with a thin layer of mint butter mixture, about 1½ teaspoons.

2. Lay the cucumber on 6 slices of the bread and sprinkle with the remaining salt and pepper. Cover with the remaining 6 slices of bread and cut each sandwich into 4 squares. Arrange the sandwiches on a platter and keep covered with plastic wrap until ready to serve.

Arugula Radish Poppy Seed Tea Sandwiches

A nice variation on the classic watercress sandwich, this tea sandwich has a bold flavors, textures, and colors.

MAKES 24 PIECES

¾ cup Radish and Poppy Seed Spread (page 67)

Twelve ¼-inch-thick slices seedless rye bread

12 leaves arugula, watercress, or radicchio

1. Spread each slice of bread with about 1 tablespoon of the spread.

2. Top half of the bread slices with arugula, watercress, or radicchio and cover with the remaining slices of bread, spread side down.

3. Cut the crusts off the sandwiches and cut each sandwich into 4 triangles. Arrange on a platter and serve. If the tea sandwiches are made in advance, store them in a covered container in the refrigerator for up to 6 hours.

Cheese and Herb–Stuffed Mushroom Caps

Look for mushrooms that are firm and that are all approximately the same size. Mushrooms that are about the same diameter as a quarter are a good size for this hors d'oeuvre.

MAKES 16 PIECES

14 to 16 white mushrooms

1 tbsp unsalted butter

3 tbsp extra-virgin olive oil

2 tbsp minced shallots

Kosher salt and freshly ground pepper, as needed

2 tbsp Madeira

1¼ tsp chopped thyme

½ cup fresh bread crumbs

¼ cup crème fraîche or sour cream

2 tbsp minced flat-leaf parsley

2 tbsp water

1. Remove the stems from the mushrooms and chop them finely; there should be about 1¼ cups. Reserve the whole caps and chop the stems separately.

2. Melt the butter and 1 tablespoon of the olive oil in a medium skillet over medium-high heat. Add the shallots and cook, stirring frequently, until softened, about 2 minutes.

3. Add the chopped mushrooms and a pinch of salt. Cook, stirring occasionally, until all the liquid from the mushrooms has evaporated, about 3 minutes. Add the Madeira and thyme and cook until nearly dry. Transfer the mushroom mixture to a medium bowl and let cool slightly.

4. Add the bread crumbs, crème fraîche, and parsley to the mushroom mixture and stir to combine thoroughly. Season with salt and pepper. The stuffing mixture can be made up to 2 days in advance. Store in a covered container in the refrigerator.

5. Preheat the oven to 375°F. Lightly oil the bottom and sides of a baking dish that is just large enough for the mushroom caps to fit snugly in a single layer. Pour the water into the baking dish.

6. Brush the outside of the caps with 1 tablespoon of olive oil. Set the caps, smooth side down, in the baking dish. Divide the filling evenly among the caps. Drizzle the tops with the remaining 1 tablespoon olive oil. Bake until the mushroom caps are soft and cooked and the filling is browned, about 35 minutes. Remove from the oven and serve hot or at room temperature.

MEATBALLS

MEATBALLS ARE A TIME-HONORED FAVORITE among reception foods. A meatball is exactly what its name implies: ground meat that is mixed with a binding ingredient, such as eggs or bread crumbs, and pressed into a ball shape. You may choose beef, lamb, chicken, turkey, or pork; any meat can make wonderful meatballs, as long as it's properly ground and seasoned. For the best flavor, sear the shaped meatballs on all sides and then finish them by roasting or broiling them in the oven or simmering them in a sauce until they're cooked through.

Thai Meatballs with Green Curry Sauce

Turkey is a good substitute for the pork and beef called for in this recipe.

MAKES 20 PIECES

Thai Green Curry Sauce

1½ tsp Thai green curry paste

1½ cups coconut milk

Meatballs

1 lb ground pork

1 lb ground beef

4 green onions, white and green portions, finely minced

½ cup chopped cilantro

8 garlic cloves, finely minced

1 tsp finely grated orange zest

2 tsp oyster sauce

2 tsp Asian chili sauce

½ tsp freshly grated nutmeg

2 large eggs

1 cup cornstarch

½ cup canola oil

1. To make the sauce: In a small bowl, combine the curry paste with the coconut milk. Reserve.

2. To make the meatballs: In a large bowl, combine the pork, beef, green onions, cilantro, garlic, orange zest, oyster sauce, Asian chili sauce, nutmeg, and eggs. Mix well with a wooden spoon. Roll chunks of the mixture in your hands to form meatballs about 1 inch in diameter.

3. Place the cornstarch in a shallow medium bowl. Roll the meatballs in the cornstarch to coat them thoroughly.

4. Heat the oil in a sauté pan over medium-high heat until it is almost smoking. Sauté the meatballs, turning occasionally, until they are golden brown and no longer pink in the center, approximately 8 minutes. The meatballs can be combined with the sauce at this point, or both the meatballs and the curry sauce can be stored separately in covered containers in the refrigerator for up to 3 days.

5. Add the green curry sauce to the meatballs and bring to simmer. Serve the meatballs in a warmed bowl or on picks.

Meatballs with Almond Sauce

Adding green peas to the almond sauce makes a lovely presentation.

MAKES 24 MEATBALLS

Meatballs

½ cup fresh bread crumbs

3 tbsp dry white wine

6 oz ground beef

½ lb ground pork

½ lb ground veal

1 large egg

2 tbsp minced flat-leaf parsley

2 garlic cloves, finely minced

Kosher salt and freshly ground black pepper, as needed

2 tbsp olive oil, or as needed

Almond Sauce

½ cup minced onion

½ cup minced carrot

2 garlic cloves, thinly sliced

9 tbsp dry white wine

15 whole blanched almonds

1 cup beef broth

Finish

⅓ cup peas, fresh or frozen

2 green onions, white and green portions, minced

2 tbsp minced flat-leaf parsley

Kosher salt and freshly ground black pepper, as needed

1. To make the meatballs: In a large bowl, combine the bread crumbs with the wine and let them soak for 15 minutes.

2. Add the ground meats, egg, parsley, garlic, ½ teaspoon salt, and ¼ teaspoon pepper. Mix with a wooden spoon until the ingredients are evenly blended. Make a small meatball and cook it in a little hot olive oil. Taste the meatball and adjust the seasoning with salt and pepper, if needed. Shape the remaining mixture into 24 small meatballs, about 1 ounce, or 1½ tablespoons each.

3. Heat the oil in a large skillet or flameproof casserole over medium-high heat. Add the meatballs to the hot oil and cook, turning from time to time, until all sides are evenly browned, 6 to 7 minutes. Work in batches to avoid overcrowding the pan, and add more oil as necessary to keep the pan generously filmed with oil as you work. Transfer the meatballs to rest on a platter while preparing the sauce.

4. To make the sauce: Add the onion and carrot to the same pan used to brown the meatballs and sauté over medium-high heat, stirring frequently, until the onions are translucent, about 10 minutes. Add the wine and stir well to dissolve any flavorful bits stuck to the pan. Add the sliced garlic and continue to cook until most of the wine has cooked away, about 4 minutes.

5. Grind the almonds to a fine paste in a food processor. With the processor running, add the broth in a gradual stream. Once all of the broth has been added, pour this mixture into the pan with the onions and carrots. Bring to a simmer and return the meatballs to the sauce. Continue to simmer until the meatballs are completely cooked and the sauce is thickened and flavorful, about 45 minutes. The meatballs are ready to finish now, or they may be cooled and stored in a covered container for up to 3 days in the refrigerator or up to 2 months in the freezer.

6. Add the peas, green onions, and parsley to the sauce and adjust the seasoning with salt and pepper. Serve the meatballs in the sauce. If the meatballs were made ahead, reheat them either over low heat in a saucepan or in a covered pan in a 325°F oven until the sauce and the meatballs are hot all the way through. When the sauce is simmering and the meatballs are hot, add the finishing ingredients.

Swedish Meatballs

The addition of cream makes these meatballs very tender, and a hint of nutmeg gives them their classic flavor.

MAKES 24 MEATBALLS

Meatballs

1 tbsp unsalted butter

½ cup finely chopped onion

1 cup fresh white bread crumbs

¼ cup heavy cream

6 oz ground beef

½ lb ground pork

½ lb ground veal

1 large egg

¼ cup minced flat-leaf parsley

½ tsp kosher salt

¼ tsp ground white pepper

Pinch of ground ginger

Small pinch of freshly grated nutmeg

2 tbsp olive oil, or as needed

Sauce

2 tbsp unsalted butter

2 tbsp all-purpose flour

1½ cups beef broth

½ cup strong brewed coffee

½ cup heavy cream

Finish

2 tbsp minced flat-leaf parsley or snipped chives

1. To make the meatballs: Heat the butter in a sauté pan over medium heat. When the butter stops foaming, add the onions and sauté, stirring frequently, until the onions are translucent, about 5 minutes. Transfer the onions to a large bowl and let them cool to room temperature.

2. In a small bowl, combine the bread crumbs with the heavy cream and let them soak for 15 minutes.

3. Add the ground meats, egg, parsley, salt, pepper, ginger, and nutmeg to the bowl with the onions. Add the bread crumbs and mix with a wooden spoon until the ingredients are evenly blended. Make a small meatball and cook it in a little hot olive oil. Taste the meatball and adjust the seasoning with salt and pepper if needed. Shape the remaining mixture into 24 small meatballs, about 1 ounce, or 1½ tablespoons each.

4. Heat the oil in a large skillet or flameproof casserole over medium-high heat. Add the meatballs to the hot oil and cook, turning from time to time, until all sides are evenly browned, 6 to 7 minutes. Work in batches to avoid overcrowding the pan and add more oil, as necessary, to keep the pan generously filmed with oil as you work. Transfer the meatballs to a platter while preparing the sauce.

5. To make the sauce: Add the butter to the same pan used to brown the meatballs and heat the butter over medium-high heat. When the butter is melted, add the flour and stir well with a wooden spoon until smooth. Add the broth, coffee, and heavy cream and stir until there are no lumps. Simmer the sauce over low heat until it thickens and is very flavorful, about 10 minutes.

6. Return the meatballs to the sauce and continue to simmer, partially covered, until the meatballs are completely cooked and very tender, about 30 minutes. The meatballs are ready to finish now, or they may be cooled and stored in a covered container for up to 3 days in the refrigerator or up to 2 months in the freezer.

7. Transfer the meatballs to a warmed serving dish and sprinkle the parsley or chives over the top. If the meatballs were made ahead, reheat them either over low heat in a saucepan or in a covered pan in a 325°F oven until the sauce and the meatballs are hot all the way through. When the sauce is simmering and the meatballs are hot, they are ready to serve, sprinkled with the parsley or chives over the top.

SKEWERED FOODS

SKEWERS AND SMALL PICKS can be used to serve a wide array of foods from fresh fruits (see photo, page 26) to grilled meats. They make it easy for guests to handle the food without the hassle of forks and plates. Place an attractive bowl or container on the tables for guests to deposit used skewers. You may want to place a couple of skewers inside the container at the beginning of the party as a hint that it's the trash receptacle.

Single-use wood and bamboo skewers come in a variety of lengths and, if necessary, can be snipped to the exact length you need for a specific dish. If you are cooking foods on the skewers, soak them in cool water for about 20 minutes before using. You may also wish to provide smaller picks for guests to pick up an hors d'oeuvre neatly.

Chicken Satay with Peanut Sauce

Satays are an Indonesian dish. The addition of both turmeric and curry powder to the marinade gives the grilled meat its characteristic golden yellow color.

MAKES 24 PIECES

1½ lb boneless, skinless chicken thighs

Satay Marinade

¼ cup peanut oil

½ stalk lemongrass, tender white and light green portions only, shredded

3 garlic cloves, minced

¼ tsp red pepper flakes

2 tsp curry powder

½ tsp ground turmeric

2 tsp honey

1 tsp minced ginger

¾ tsp fish sauce

24 bamboo skewers, soaked in water

Peanut Sauce for Satays (recipe follows)

1. Slice the chicken into finger-size strips, about 1 ounce each.

2. To make the marinade: Combine all of the ingredients in a medium bowl or ziplock bag. Add the chicken pieces and turn to coat in the marinade. Cover the bowl or close the bag and marinate in the refrigerator for at least 4 and up to 12 hours.

3. Lift the chicken pieces from the marinade with a slotted spoon to allow the excess marinade to drain away and thread the chicken pieces onto the skewers. The recipe can be made ahead up to this point, with the chicken skewered and held in a pan or dish in the refrigerator for up to 4 hours before grilling.

4. Preheat a grill to medium-high or use a broiler. Grill the chicken until the meat is cooked through and golden, turning, as necessary, to cook evenly, about 5 minutes total, or broil 4 inches from the heat source.

5. Serve with the peanut sauce. If desired, garnish the sauce with chopped cilantro.

BEEF SATAY WITH PEANUT SAUCE *Substitute 1½ pounds boneless beef (top round or sirloin) for the chicken thighs and cut the meat into thin strips about ½ inch wide, ¼ inch thick, and 2 or 3 inches long.*

Peanut Sauce for Satays

MAKES ABOUT 1½ CUPS SAUCE; ENOUGH FOR 24 SERVINGS

1 cup creamy peanut butter

½ cup water

¼ cup fresh lime juice

1 tbsp soy sauce

1 tbsp peanut oil

2 tbsp chopped dry chile peppers (include the seeds, if desired)

2 tbsp chopped cilantro

1 tbsp minced garlic

1 tbsp granulated sugar

1 tsp cayenne pepper

Combine the peanut butter, water, lime juice, soy sauce, peanut oil, chili peppers, cilantro, garlic, sugar, and cayenne in a saucepan. Bring the mixture to a slow boil over medium heat and simmer until flavorful and very smooth, about 2 minutes. Set aside. The sauce can be made up to 2 days in advance and stored in a covered container in the refrigerator. Just before serving, reheat the sauce over low heat or in a microwave until hot, but not boiling.

Beef Negimaki

These Japanese beef rolls are very flavorful with a lot of texture from the green onion tops.

MAKES 30 PIECES

1¾ lb beef strip loin, well trimmed

Marinade

¾ cup water

⅔ cup soy sauce

⅓ cup honey

2 tbsp grated ginger

1 tbsp dark sesame oil

1 tbsp minced garlic

1 or 2 bunches green onions, green tops only, left whole

1 tsp cornstarch

2 tbsp sesame seeds

1. Wrap the beef well in plastic wrap and freeze just until very firm, but not frozen solid, about 2 hours.

2. To make the marinade: In a small saucepan combine the water, soy sauce, honey, ginger, oil, and garlic. Simmer over low heat until flavorful, about 5 minutes. Strain the marinade. The marinade can be made up to 2 days in advance. Cool before storing in a covered container in the refrigerator.

3. Using a very sharp slicer, slice the semifrozen beef into thin slices. Arrange the slices on a piece of parchment paper or plastic wrap, overlapping them slightly, to make an 8-inch square. Lay the scallion greens along one end of the square, and then roll the beef slices around the green onions, using the parchment paper or plastic wrap to roll as tightly as possible. Place the beef rolls in a shallow baking dish, seam side down. Add 1 cup of the marinade, cover, and marinate for at least 4 and up to 12 hours in the refrigerator.

4. In a small bowl, combine the cornstarch with 2 teaspoons cool water. In a small saucepan, bring the remaining ¾ cup marinade to a simmer, and add the

Beef Negimaki

cornstarch mixture, stirring if the cornstarch has settled. Continue to simmer until the glaze is thick enough to cling to a spoon and has a coating consistency. Remove it from direct heat but keep it warm.

5. Preheat the broiler to high heat. Gently drag the beef rolls against the rim of the baking dish they were marinating in to remove the excess marinade. Arrange them, seam side down, on a greased broiler pan or baking sheet.

6. Broil the beef rolls about 4 inches from the heat source until the beef is browned and cooked through, about 5 minutes. Remove from the broiler and brush lightly with the glaze. Cut the beef rolls into bite-size pieces, arrange on a platter, sprinkle with the sesame seeds, and serve at once. Serve the remaining glaze on the side as a dip, if desired.

Lamb Brochettes with Mint Pesto

The mint pesto gives these grilled lamb a bright flavor. If you prefer, you can use a more traditional basil pesto as well.

MAKES 24 PIECES

Lamb Marinade

¼ cup extra-virgin olive oil

2 tbsp fresh lemon juice (about ½ lemon)

2 tbsp chopped mint

3 large garlic cloves, crushed

1 tsp kosher salt

½ tsp freshly ground black pepper

1¾ lb boneless lamb, trimmed and cut into ¾-inch cubes

24 bamboo skewers, soaked in water

8 pancetta slices (thin), cut into thirds

2 cups Mint Pesto (recipe follows)

1. Combine all of the ingredients for the marinade in a large bowl or ziplock bag. Add the lamb and turn to coat in the marinade. Cover the bowl or close the bag and marinate in the refrigerator for at least 4 and up to 12 hours.

2. Thread 2 pieces of the marinated lamb and 1 piece of the pancetta onto skewers as shown in the photo [left]. The recipe can be made ahead up to this point. The assembled brochettes can be held in a pan or dish in the refrigerator for up to 4 hours before grilling.

3. Preheat a grill to medium-high or use a broiler. Grill until the lamb is cooked through and golden, turning as necessary to cook evenly, about 8 minutes total. Or broil 4 inches from the heat source. Serve immediately with the pesto as a dipping sauce.

Mint Pesto Sauce

MAKES 1 CUP PESTO SAUCE

¾ cup coarsely chopped mint leaves

½ cup coarsely chopped flat-leaf parsley

⅓ cup grated Parmesan

¼ cup extra-virgin olive oil

¼ cup chopped walnuts

1 tbsp fresh lemon juice

1 garlic clove, chopped

¼ tsp kosher salt, or as needed

⅛ tsp freshly ground black pepper

¼ cup plain Greek-style yogurt or sour cream

1. Combine the mint, parsley, cheese, olive oil, pine nuts, lemon juice, garlic, salt, and pepper in a food processor or blender.

2. Purée until a coarse paste forms. Transfer to a bowl, add the yogurt or sour cream, and stir until blended. Adjust the seasoning with salt and pepper if needed. The sauce is ready to serve now, or it may be stored in a covered container in the refrigerator for up to 3 days.

Barbecued Shrimp and Bacon Skewers

You can substitute other barbecue sauces for the one we recommend here, but we love the smoky sweet flavors of apricot and ancho paired with smoky bacon and briny shrimp.

MAKES 30 PIECES

15 strips bacon

30 shrimp, peeled and deveined

30 bamboo skewers, soaked in water

1 cup Apricot-Ancho Barbecue Sauce (recipe follows)

1. Heat a skillet over medium heat and add the bacon strips. Cook, turning them once or twice, until they are limp and translucent, but not browned, about 3 minutes. Transfer to a plate to cool and then cut the strips in half across the width.

2. Wrap each shrimp with a bacon strip. Thread each wrapped shrimp on a small bamboo skewer.

3. Place the skewers on a wire rack set into an aluminum foil–lined sheet pan. The assembled shrimp skewers are ready to finish now, or they may be covered and stored in the refrigerator for up to 24 hours.

4. Preheat the broiler and position a rack 4 inches from the heat source. Broil the shrimp 1 to 2 minutes on the first side. Turn and broil another 1 to 2 minutes, or until the bacon gets crispy and the shrimp are just cooked through.

5. Remove from the broiler and baste with the barbecue sauce. Arrange on a platter and serve immediately.

Apricot-Ancho Barbecue Sauce

MAKES 2 CUPS SAUCE

2 tbsp canola oil

¾ cup chopped onion

1 tbsp minced garlic

⅓ cup ketchup

½ cup orange juice

⅓ cup packed dark brown sugar

⅓ cup chopped dried apricots

3 tbsp malt vinegar

1 ancho chile, diced

1 tsp dry mustard

½ tsp Tabasco sauce

½ tsp cayenne pepper

1 tsp kosher salt, plus more as needed

½ tsp freshly ground black pepper, plus more as needed

1. Heat the oil in a medium saucepan over medium heat. When it is hot, add the onions and sauté, stirring frequently, until golden, about 5 minutes. Add the garlic and sauté until aromatic, about 1 minute.

2. Add all the remaining ingredients and simmer until the apricots are very soft, about 10 minutes. Taste the sauce and season with additional salt and pepper, if needed.

3. Transfer the mixture to a blender and purée until relatively smooth. The sauce is ready to use now, or it can be cooled and stored in a covered container in the refrigerator for up to 1 week.

PHYLLO DOUGH

PHYLLO DOUGH COMES FROZEN in thin, delicate sheets that must be handled very gently. Before using, allow at least 12 hours for frozen phyllo to thaw in the refrigerator, or 5 hours to thaw at room temperature. Before unwrapping the phyllo sheets, have at hand: your prepared filling, a pastry brush, a bowl of melted butter, a sharp knife, and parchment paper–lined baking sheets to hold the finished pastries. Follow these steps for working with phyllo:

1. Remove the sheets from the package and lay them out flat on a clean work surface.

2. To keep the phyllo flexible while you work, cover the stack of sheets with plastic wrap and then a lightly dampened towel.

3. Lift one sheet at a time from the stack and re-cover the unused sheets to keep them from drying out. Place the sheet flat on a work surface.

4. Brush the melted butter over the surface of the phyllo sheet. Continue adding phyllo sheets on top of the buttered sheet, and brushing each additional sheet with butter; until you have a stack with the correct number of sheets. Some recipes call for 3 or 4 sheets, others may require 5 or 6.

For added texture and crunch, sprinkle plain dry bread crumbs over the butter between the buttered sheets.

TO MAKE PHYLLO CUPS Butter and stack 3 sheets of phyllo as described above. Cut the dough into 2-inch squares. Press the squares into mini muffin pans and refrigerate long enough for the butter to firm up before baking (or freeze them, carefully wrapped, at this point for up to 4 weeks.) Bake at 375°F until golden brown, about 4 minutes (or 6 minutes if you are baking them directly from the freezer).

TO MAKE PHYLLO PURSES, ALSO KNOW AS BEGGAR'S PURSES Butter and stack 3 sheets of phyllo as described above. Cut the dough into 3-inch squares. Place about 2 teaspoons of a filling into the center of the square. Gather the corners of the dough and twist them to close the "purse." Place the filled purses on a parchment paper–lined baking sheet and refrigerate long enough for the butter to firm up before baking (or freeze them, carefully wrapped, at this point for up to 4 weeks.) Bake at 375°F until golden brown, about 8 minutes, or 10 to 12 minutes if you are baking them directly from the freezer.

TO MAKE PHYLLO TRIANGLES Butter and stack 3 sheets of phyllo as described above. Cut the dough lengthwise into thin strips. Place about 2 teaspoons of a filling on each strip, near a narrow end. Pick up the right-hand corner of the strip and fold it over the filling to make a triangle. Bring the tip of triangle up to align with the left side of the strip. Fold the left-hand corner over to align with the right side of the strip; this is a flag fold. Continue folding in this sequence. Place the filled triangles on a lined baking sheet and refrigerate long enough for the butter to firm up before baking (or freeze them, carefully wrapped, at this point for up to 4 weeks.).

Spanakopita

Instead of making bite-size pieces, you can use the filling mixture to prepare a larger spinach pie. Line a baking dish with 3 buttered sheets of phyllo, add the spinach mixture in an even layer, and top with three more sheets of buttered phyllo. Bake for about 40 minutes and then cut into pieces.

MAKES 40 PIECES

2 tbsp olive oil

1 cup small-dice onions

1 tbsp minced garlic

1 lb fresh spinach, blanched, squeezed dry, and chopped (or ¾ lb frozen spinach, thawed, squeezed dry, and chopped)

5 oz feta cheese, crumbled

3 oz cream cheese

1 large egg, beaten

¼ cup chopped dill

Kosher salt and freshly ground black pepper, as needed

24 sheets phyllo dough, thawed

2 cups (4 sticks) unsalted butter, melted

1. Heat the oil in a skillet over medium-high heat. Add the onions and garlic and cook, stirring frequently, until the onions are tender and translucent without any browning, about 5 minutes. Add the spinach and stir together with the onions. Sauté until any moisture from the spinach has cooked away, about 3 minutes.

2. Transfer the spinach mixture to a bowl and stir in the cheeses, egg, and dill. Season with salt and pepper.

3. Brush a phyllo sheet with the melted butter, place another on top and brush the surface with butter again, then add a third sheet and brush with butter. Cut the dough lengthwise into 5 equal strips.

4. Place a spoonful (about 2 teaspoons) of the spinach mixture at base of each phyllo strip and fold like a flag to make triangles .

5. Place the spinach triangles on buttered parchment and brush their tops with the melted butter. Chill the spanakopita for 30 minutes before baking, or wrap them well and freeze for up to 4 weeks.

6. Preheat the oven to 375°F. Bake until the phyllo is golden brown and crisp, about 20 minutes. Keep warm until ready to serve.

Forest Mushroom Strudel

You can shape this mushroom filling into triangles as described on page 81, if you prefer.

MAKES 24 PIECES

2 tbsp unsalted butter

2 tbsp minced shallots

1 garlic clove, minced

8 oz assorted mushrooms (such as shiitake, cremini, button), roughly chopped

3 tbsp dry white wine

¼ cup crumbled fresh goat cheese

1 tsp chopped flat-leaf parsley

1 tsp chopped chives

¾ cup (1½ sticks) unsalted butter, melted

6 sheets phyllo dough, thawed

1. In a medium sauté pan over medium heat, melt the 2 tablespoons of butter, and cook the shallots and garlic until soft and translucent, about 3 minutes. Add the mushrooms and wine and continue to cook until the mushrooms are cooked through, 8 to 10 minutes. Remove from the heat and allow the mixture to cool thoroughly.

2. When the mushroom mixture is cool, add the cheese and fresh herbs and mix well to form a paste.

3. Lay out a phyllo sheet on a work surface and brush with warm melted butter. Top with the second and third sheets, brushing the surface with butter each time. Spoon half of the mushroom mixture down the length of the phyllo and roll the phyllo around the mushrooms to make a log. Butter the entire outside of the roll. Transfer the strudel to a lightly oiled or parchment paper–lined baking sheet.

4. Make small slits in the phyllo to make it easier to slice the strudels after they are baked. Repeat with the remaining phyllo and mushroom mixture to make a second strudel. Chill the strudels for 30 minutes, or they may be wrapped and frozen for up to 4 weeks.

5. Preheat the oven to 375°F. Bake the strudels until golden brown, about 15 to 20 minutes. Allow to cool slightly and cut all the way through the strudels to make slices. Serve warm.

PREPARED PUFF PASTRY

THE MOST IMPORTANT THING TO REMEMBER when using prepared puff pastry is to work quickly to prevent the dough from getting too warm.

1. Thaw frozen puff pastry as directed on the package, letting the dough soften just until it becomes pliable but is still cool to the touch.

2. Keep the dough chilled, taking out only the amount you will be able to work with in a short amount of time.

3. Roll out the dough using gentle, even pressure. Avoid running your rolling pin over the edges of the dough.

4. Use a sharp knife when cutting and shaping the dough. Clean cuts will ensure even rising.

5. Refrigerate the shaped or filled puff pastry item after forming and before baking to ensure the best rise in the oven and a flaky texture in the finished pastry.

Classic Cheese Sticks (Paillettes)

Add some flavor by including a Cajun spice blend, cayenne pepper, poppy seeds, or sesame seeds instead of, or in addition to, the paprika.

MAKES 35 TO 40 PIECES

1 large egg yolk

1 tbsp whole milk

1 sheet puff pastry (about 8 oz)

½ cup grated Parmesan

Sweet paprika, as needed

1. Preheat the oven to 400°F.

2. In a small bowl, beat the egg yolk with the milk to make an egg wash. Brush the top side of the puff pastry sheet with the egg wash. Sprinkle the cheese and paprika evenly over the puff pastry. Cut the pastry lengthwise into ¼-inch strips.

3. Line two baking sheets with parchment paper and transfer the pastry strips to the baking sheets, leaving ½ inch between each strip to allow for expansion. Bake until golden brown, about 10 minutes. Let the cheese sticks cool before serving. They may be held in an airtight container at room temperature for up to 3 days.

Palmiers with Prosciutto

Palmiers, sometimes known in the United States as "elephant ears," are crunchy pastries made from double-rolled puff pastry. Substitute pesto for the tomato paste in this recipe, if you have it available.

MAKES 20 PIECES

1 sheet puff pastry (about 8 oz), thawed

¼ cup tomato paste

6 prosciutto slices, very thin

¾ cup finely grated Parmesan

1. Line a baking sheet with parchment paper.

2. Lay the puff pastry sheet on a work surface and roll lightly with a rolling pin to even the thickness. Brush the tomato paste evenly over the surface of the sheet.

3. Lay the prosciutto slices over the puff pastry and dust with cheese. Roll the long sides of the sheet in toward the center.

4. Cut into slices about ¼ inch thick and transfer to a baking sheet lined with parchment paper. Refrigerate the palmiers until the dough is firm, at least 15 minutes. The palmiers are ready to bake now, or they may be covered and stored in the refrigerator for up to 2 days or frozen for up to 3 weeks.

5. Preheat the oven to 400°F. Lay a second sheet of parchment on top of the palmiers (this will help them rise evenly) and bake until golden brown, about 10 minutes. Transfer to wire racks and cool before serving. The baked palmiers can be stored in an airtight container at room temperature for up to 2 days.

Gougères

These little tidbits are best served warm. If you make them in advance, reheat them for a few minutes in a 325°F oven.

MAKES ABOUT 40 PIECES

1 cup whole milk

½ cup (1 stick) unsalted butter

½ tsp kosher salt

1 cup bread flour

4 large eggs

Pinch of cayenne pepper

½ cup grated Gruyère

1. Preheat the oven to 350°F. Line two baking sheets with parchment paper.

2. In a medium saucepan, bring the milk, butter, and salt to a boil over medium heat, stirring constantly. Remove from the heat, add the flour all at once, and stir vigorously to combine. Return the pan to medium heat and cook, stirring constantly, until the mixture pulls away from the sides of the pan, about 3 minutes.

3. Transfer the mixture to the bowl of a stand mixer fitted with the paddle attachment and beat on medium speed to release some of the heat, about 2 minutes. Add the eggs, one at a time, beating until smooth after each addition. Add the cayenne and cheese and mix until blended.

4. Fill a pastry bag fitted with a medium plain tip and pipe ¾-inch domes of batter onto the baking sheets, leaving about 1½ inches between them. Bake until the pastries are puffed and golden brown, about 30 minutes. The gougères can be made in advance and stored in a container in the refrigerator for up to 3 days or frozen for up to 3 weeks; reheat until hot in a 325°F oven. Serve warm.

Clockwise from top left: Classic Cheese Sticks, Palmiers with Prosciutto, and Gougères

Pork Picadillo Empanadas

Substitute beef, turkey, or chicken for the pork in this recipe. Serve with sour cream flavored with fresh lime juice and a bit of lime zest, if you like.

MAKES 30 PIECES

Pork Filling

2 tsp olive or canola oil

¾ lb ground pork

1 tbsp minced jalapeño

2 tsp chili powder

1 tsp ground cumin

1 tsp ground cinnamon

Pinch of ground allspice

⅓ cup golden raisins, plumped in warm water for 30 minutes

3 tbsp chopped toasted almonds

3 tbsp fresh lime juice, or as needed

Kosher salt, as needed

Freshly ground black pepper, as needed

2 tbsp sour cream

Empanada Dough (recipe follows)

Egg wash: 1 whole egg blended with ¼ cup water

Canola oil, as needed for frying

1. To make the filling: Heat the oil in a medium sauté pan over medium heat. Add the pork and sauté, breaking up the meat, until it is no longer pink, about 10 minutes. Stir in the jalapeño, chili powder, cumin, cinnamon, and allspice. Continue to sauté until most of the liquid has evaporated, 5 to 6 minutes more.

2. Transfer the pork mixture to a large bowl and fold in the raisins and almonds. Season with lime juice, salt, and pepper. Fold in the sour cream, adding just enough to gently bind the filling. Let cool, cover, and refrigerate until ready to assemble the empanadas, for up to 2 days.

3. To assemble the empanadas: Place 2 or 3 teaspoons of the filling on each dough circle. Brush the edges with the egg wash, fold in half, and seal the seams. The filled empanadas can be made ahead up to this point and refrigerated for up to 24 hours, or frozen for up to 1 month.

4. In a deep fryer (or use a straight-sided skillet and fill it with oil to a depth of 2 inches) heat the oil to 350°F. Add the empanadas to the hot oil in batches and fry until golden brown and crisp, turning, if necessary, to brown both sides evenly, about 5 minutes. Drain the empanadas briefly on paper towels. Keep them warm in a 200°F oven while you finishing frying the remaining empanadas. Transfer to a serving platter. Serve very hot.

Empanadas can be filled with pork, beef, lamb, or chicken to add variety to a buffet spread.

Empanada Dough

MAKES ABOUT 1¼ POUNDS DOUGH; ENOUGH FOR 30 EMPANADAS

- 1¾ cups all-purpose flour
- ¾ cup masa harina
- 1 tbsp baking powder
- 1 tsp kosher salt
- 4 oz lard, melted and cooled
- ½ cup water, or as needed
- 1 large egg

1. To make the dough: In a large bowl, blend the flour, masa harina, baking powder, and salt. Add the lard and mix by hand or with an electric mixer fitted with the dough hook on low speed until evenly moistened.

2. In a small bowl, blend the water and egg together and add gradually to the dough, stirring or blending with the dough hook. Knead the dough until it is pliable, about 3 minutes. If the dough seems very stiff, add additional water, a teaspoon at a time.

3. Roll out the dough to a thickness of $1/16$ inch and cut into circles 3 inches in diameter to make at least 30 circles. If necessary, gently knead the dough scraps together and roll out the dough again to make enough circles.

Sun-Dried Tomato and Goat Cheese Tartlets

If you have already prepared the tartlet shells, these hors d'oeuvre are quick to assemble. An alternative is to roll out the dough in a large rectangle and use it to line a jelly roll pan. Then, add the filling mixture, bake for about 30 minutes, and then cut the tart into small squares, rectangles, or diamond shapes.

MAKES 30 TARTLETS

- ¾ cup whole milk
- ¼ cup dry sherry
- 3 tbsp chopped basil
- 1 tbsp minced garlic
- 1 tsp ground white pepper
- 3 large eggs
- 1 tbsp all-purpose flour
- 4 oz fresh goat cheese, crumbled
- ⅓ cup minced green onions, white and green portions
- ½ cup minced sun-dried tomatoes
- 30 Tartlet Shells (recipe follows)

1. Preheat the oven to 325°F. Combine the milk, sherry, basil, garlic, and pepper in a food processor. Add the eggs and flour and process until just blended.

2. In a small bowl, toss together the goat cheese, green onions, and sun-dried tomatoes. Place the tartlet shells on a baking sheet. Add a scant tablespoon of the goat cheese mixture into each tartlet and pour enough of the egg mixture into the shell to fill it to about two-thirds.

3. Bake the tartlets until the filling is set but still moist, about 15 minutes.

Tartlet Shells

1 lb puff pastry dough or Quiche Shell (page 233)

1. Preheat the oven to 425°F. Roll out the dough, if using, to ⅛ inch in thickness. Cut 30 rounds from the dough using a 2-inch round cutter. Press the rounds gently into tart molds or mini muffin pans. Use a fork to prick a few holes in the dough, and top with a second empty tartlet or muffin pan, or line with a small piece of foil and fill with dry beans or rice—this is to prevent the dough from rising.

2. Bake until the tartlet shells are dry but have no color, about 5 minutes. Allow to cool completely in the pans and then remove the weights. The shells can be stored at room temperature for up to 3 days.

Sun-Dried Tomato and Goat Cheese Tartlets

Vegetable Samosas

Samosas take a little time to assemble, but they are worth the effort. You can opt to bake the filled samosas, either right after filling or straight from the freezer.

MAKES 24 PIECES

Samosa Wrappers

2½ cups all-purpose flour

1 tsp kosher salt

½ cup water, as needed

¼ cup canola oil

Potato and Pea Filling

3 tbsp canola oil

½ tsp coriander seeds

1 tsp cumin seeds

1 onion, minced

1 piece ginger (about 1 inch long), peeled and minced

1 jalapeño, seeded and minced

1 tsp cayenne pepper

2½ cups diced boiled yellow-flesh potatoes, peeled

½ cup green peas, fresh or thawed frozen

Kosher salt, as needed

1 tbsp chopped cilantro

⅓ cup all-purpose flour

2 tbsp water

Canola oil, as needed for frying

1. To make the wrappers: In a medium bowl, sift the flour and salt together. Add ½ cup water and the oil and mix until a soft, pliable dough forms. Cover and set aside for 30 minutes.

2. To make the filling: In a medium skillet or saucepan, heat the oil on medium-high heat. Add the coriander and cumin seeds. When they stop sizzling, add the onions and cook, stirring frequently, until the onions turn brown, about 6 minutes. Add the ginger and jalapeño. Sauté until aromatic, about 1 minute, then stir in the cayenne. Cook for 1 minute more. Remove from heat and allow to cool.

3. Place the potatoes in a medium bowl and use a wooden spoon or a fork to lightly mash the potatoes. Stir in the peas and the onion mixture. Season with salt, add the cilantro, and mix well. The filling should be lumpy.

4. Divide the dough into 24 balls, each about 1 inch in diameter. Working on a floured surface, use a rolling pin to roll out each ball into a 3- to 4-inch circle, dusting the dough and the rolling pin with additional flour as needed to keep the dough from sticking.

5. To assemble the samosas, place a spoonful of the potato-pea filling in the center of each dough circle. Brush the edges of the dough lightly with water, fold the dough in half to enclose the filling, and crimp the edges to seal. The filled samosas can be refrigerated for up to 24 hours before frying or baking, or frozen for up to 1 month.

6. In a deep fryer (or use a straight-sided skillet and fill it with oil to a depth of 2 inches) heat the oil to 350°F. Add the samosas in batches and deep-fry until golden brown, turning, if necessary, to brown both sides evenly, about 4 minutes. Drain the samosas briefly on paper towels. Keep them warm in the oven preheated to 200°F while you finish frying all of the samosas. (If you prefer, you can bake the filled samosas as follows: Preheat the oven to 425°F and bake the samosas until light golden brown, about 15 minutes. Reduce the heat to 350°F and finish baking until a rich golden color, another 10 minutes. Turn the samosas as they bake to brown them evenly, if necessary.)

7. Serve the samosas hot or warm on a platter accompanied with a chutney or a Cucumber Raita (page 192).

SEAFOOD BAR

A SEAFOOD BAR is a sure way to make any party look and feel more extravagant. A typical seafood bar includes freshly shucked clams and oysters as well as a selection of cooked seafood such as mussels, shrimp, and crab.

To ensure the safety of your seafood bar, when shopping, ask for "depurated" oysters, clams, and mussels—this means that the shellfish have been purged of sand and other impurities. It is also advisable to buy "cultivated" oysters, clams, and mussels. Since cultivated shellfish are raised in a controlled environment, they are generally cleaner and safer to eat.

Before serving, all the shellfish should be thoroughly scrubbed and held on a bed ice in the refrigerator, between 35 to 40°F, for no more than a day in advance. You can set up a seafood bar either as an "action station" with an attendant shucking the shellfish and creating plates for the guests or as a self-serve bar with all the shellfish shucked ahead of time and held on ice.

Shellfish on a raw bar should be served with accompaniments. Popular accompaniments include: lemon wedges, cocktail sauce, hot sauce, vinegars, salsas, seaweed salad, and mignonette sauce.

A raw bar is a sure way to impress even the most sophisticated guests

Oysters on the Half Shell

There are four varieties of oyster that are commonly eaten raw: Atlantic, Pacific, European, and Kumamoto, and each species has a distinct flavor. It is sometimes difficult to determine the freshness of an oyster from the outward appearance, because they do not open and close as readily as clams do; the best indicators are moist plump flesh and a fresh smell.

For safety, wear a wire mesh glove to hold the oyster when opening it. Work the tip of an oyster knife into the hinge while holding the upper and lower shells together and twist it to break open the hinge.

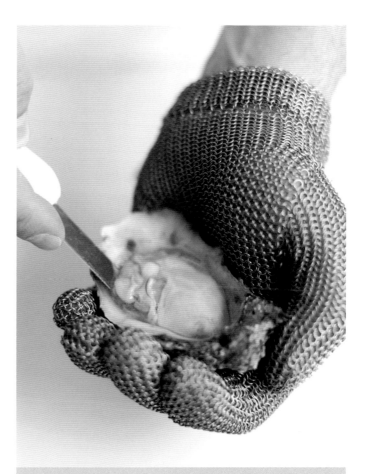

Once open, slide the knife over the inside of the top shell, then make a similar stroke inside the bottom shell to release the oyster.

CAVIAR

CAVIAR, A DELICACY MADE FROM the roe of a sturgeon, is among the most expensive and exclusive of all preserved foods. The best caviar needs no special accompaniments. It should be served in an iced container and, if possible, with mother-of-pearl, bone, horn, or glass spoons to avoid any flavor change that might occur from metal spoons. Toast points, brioche, or blinis are often served as a base for a caviar canapé. Lesser quality caviar may be appropriate for garnishing other items, like potato crêpes with crème fraîche (see photo, page 94). Just remember that caviar should never be added to a food during cooking.

There are many different ways to present caviar on a buffet table. Here, spoons are filled with bluepoint oysters and topped with beluga caviar.

Purchasing caviar can be intimidating if you aren't familiar with the terminology and grading system. Below are some of the basics.

Caviar Terminology

Classic caviars include beluga, sold in containers with blue labels, osetra, sold in yellow jars or tins, and sevruga, in red jars or tins, are the most famous types of caviar and come from the sturgeon.

American caviars include salmon, bowfin, hackleback, and paddlefish caviars.

Tobiko caviar is made from the roe of the flying fish and may be flavored with wasabi. It is available as black, red, or orange as well.

Malassol indicates that the fish eggs have been processed with the least possible amount of salt.

Pressed caviar, also known in Russian as pajusnay, is made from mature, broken, or overripe eggs. The salted eggs are pressed into a marmalade-like substance that is usually spread on bread. The flavor is more intense than other caviars.

The individual eggs, or "berries," are graded for color, with "000" indicating the lightest color and finest-quality caviar and "0" denoting the darkest color and lesser-quality caviar.

Caviar served on bite-size potato crepes.

The best caviar needs no special accompaniments. Here, it is served in iced bowls with mother-of-pearl spoons.

three | THE FIRST COURSE

A S THE NAME SUGGESTS, THE FIRST COURSE IS A SMALL SERVING THAT STARTS A MEAL BY TAKING THE EDGE OFF THE GUEST'S APPETITE TO ALLOW FOR THE THOROUGH ENJOYMENT OF THE MAIN COURSE. OTHER THAN THAT, THERE ARE FEW HARD-AND-FAST RULES GOVERNING THE FIRST COURSE. CLASSIC HORS D'OEUVRE ARE OFTEN SERVED AS A FIRST COURSE, AND PERENNIAL FAVORITES INCLUDE SHRIMP COCKTAIL, SMOKED FISH, ESCARGOT, PÂTÉS, AND TERRINES. HOWEVER, SALADS, SOUPS, PASTAS, BROILED OR GRILLED MEAT, SEAFOOD OR VEGETABLES, AND SAVORY SOUFFLÉS, TURNOVERS, OR TARTS ARE ALL VIABLE FIRST-COURSE OPTIONS IF SERVED IN THE PROPER PORTION.

SELECTING A FIRST COURSE

The idea of "building" a menu calls for a logical connection between the first course and all the courses to follow, but for every rule you read about what should or should not constitute a first course, you will find at least one good exception. What all successful first courses have in common is proper portioning, careful attention to execution, and deliberate plating. The first course is your guests' first impression, and they may judge the entire meal by its presentation; so, you need to select a dish that is full of flavor, visually appealing, and in keeping with the dishes that fill out the rest of your menu.

PLATING AND COMPOSITION

The shape and portion of the first course is crucial. You should offer just enough food on the plate to make it appealing, but not so much that the guest could feel overwhelmed by the portion. You should also select plates that are the correct size and shape to suit the food—the food shouldn't look cramped, but there shouldn't be too much blank space left on the plate either. The color of the plate is another consideration. White is always a safe choice, but it is okay to go with a bright color or bold pattern, as long as it complements the food and doesn't distract from it.

Also, be mindful of the temperature at which the food is served. Chill or warm the plate accordingly, because it makes a bigger difference than you might think. And be sure to provide guests with all the items necessary to eat the dish, such as cups for dipping sauces or soup spoons.

Once you've chosen the appropriate serving pieces, decide how the food will be arranged. Some first courses will feature several components of contrasting colors, flavors, textures, and sizes, while others are based on a single motif that holds all the components together. The bottom line is that the components should be arranged in the way that the textures and colors of the food are most attractive to the eye. This is somewhat subjective, but you can follow basic principles of design.

A good visual design also serves a function. The design of a plate should combine all the dish's components in the best possible way. Yes, the flavor of each of the components on the plate should be able to stand alone; however, the arrangement on the plate should enhance the flavor of each component by its being combined with the others. This makes for a more intriguing eating experience for your guests.

Likewise, the plate's garnish should serve a function. The garnish element can identify an ingredient that is found in the food, such as citrus zest or nuts, or can suggest the style or region where the food originated, such as Thai basil or a Greek olive. Garnishes are most effective, and attractive, when they offer some information about the food instead of simply adding a spot of color.

SOUPS

FROM LIGHT, CLEAR BROTHS AND CREAMY PURÉES to cool fruit soups, there is a soup to suit every season and every occasion. Soups make good starters for nearly every menu, from an elegant dinner party to a backyard picnic.

Chilled Cream of Asparagus Soup

A chilled soup is a great choice for a dinner party. You can replace the heavy cream with crème fraîche or Greek-style yogurt for a little additional tang.

SERVES 8

3 lb asparagus, ends trimmed

¼ cup olive oil or canola oil

1 yellow onion, chopped

1 leek, white and light green parts, chopped

1 celery stalk, chopped

¼ cup all-purpose flour

6 cups chicken or vegetable broth

½ cup heavy cream, warmed

1 tsp fresh lemon juice

Kosher salt and freshly ground black pepper, as needed

1. Slice off 16 of the best-looking asparagus tips, about 2-inch-long pieces, and reserve them for garnish, then coarsely chop the rest of the asparagus.

2. Heat the oil in a soup pot over medium heat. Add the onion, leek, celery, and chopped asparagus. Cook, stirring frequently, until the onion is translucent, 6 to 8 minutes. Add the flour and cook, stirring frequently with a wooden spoon, until thoroughly blended, about 5 minutes.

3. Gradually, add the broth to the pot, whisking well to work out any lumps. Bring the soup to a simmer and cook until flavorful and thickened, about 45 minutes, stirring frequently and skimming as needed.

4. Meanwhile, bring a large pot of water to a boil. Have a large bowl of ice water ready to chill the asparagus quickly. Add the reserved asparagus tips and parboil, cooking until just tender, 3 to 4 minutes. Remove the tips with a slotted spoon and plunge into ice water. Once cool, drain and reserve.

5. Strain the soup, reserving both the solids and the broth. Purée the solids, adding broth as needed to facilitate puréeing.

6. Combine the purée with enough of the reserved broth to achieve the consistency of heavy cream. Strain the soup through a fine-mesh sieve, if desired. Transfer the soup to a container and refrigerate for at least 3 hours and up to 2 days.

7. When ready to serve, add the cream and lemon juice. Taste and season with salt and pepper. Garnish each serving of the soup with the reserved asparagus tips.

Chilled Gazpacho

The flavor of gazpacho improves if allowed to chill overnight.

MAKES 2 QUARTS SOUP; SERVES 8 TO 10

28 oz canned plum tomatoes, with their liquid

1 green bell pepper, seeded and sliced into eighths

6 green onions, white and green portions, roughly chopped

1 cucumber, peeled, seeded, and sliced

1 jalapeño, diced

3 tbsp chopped basil

1 tbsp chopped tarragon

2 tbsp extra-virgin olive oil

1 tbsp balsamic vinegar

1 tbsp fresh lime juice, or as needed

1 tsp Worcestershire sauce, or as needed

½ tsp Tabasco sauce, or as needed

Kosher salt and freshly ground black pepper, as needed

Croutons

2 tsp extra-virgin olive oil

1 garlic clove

2 bread slices, cut into ¼-inch cubes

1. Combine the tomatoes, pepper, onions, cucumber, jalapeño, basil, and oregano in a food processor or countertop blender and purée until relatively smooth. Add the olive oil, vinegar, lime juice, Worcestershire, and Tabasco and blend briefly. Chill in the refrigerator for at least 1 and up to 24 hours before serving.

2. To make the garnish: Heat the olive oil in a medium saucepan over medium heat, add the garlic and sauté until aromatic, about 1 minute.

3. Remove the garlic clove from the oil and add the bread cubes. Sauté on medium-high heat, turning frequently, until crisp and lightly browned, 3 to 4 minutes. The croutons can be prepared up to 24 hours in advance; store them in an airtight container at room temperature.

4. Just before serving the soup, taste and season with lime juice, Worcestershire, Tabasco, salt, and pepper. Garnish each serving of the soup with a small amount of the croutons.

Cream of Mushroom Soup

So-called exotic varieties of mushrooms, such as cremini and oyster, work well in this soup, as do regular white mushrooms. Use a combination or a single variety, depending on your taste and what's available.

MAKES 2 QUARTS SOUP; SERVES 8

2 tbsp unsalted butter

2 garlic cloves, chopped

1 cup chopped onions

½ cup chopped celery root (celeriac)

8 cups sliced mushrooms (about 1½ lb)

¼ cup all-purpose flour

¼ cup sherry

6 cups vegetable broth, plus more as needed

¾ cup heavy cream

Kosher salt and freshly ground black pepper, as needed

Chives, sliced, as needed

⅛ tsp freshly grated nutmeg (optional)

1. In a large soup pot, melt the butter over medium heat. Add the garlic, onions, and celery root and cook, stirring frequently, until translucent, 5 to 7 minutes. Add the mushrooms and cook until tender, about 5 minutes. Sprinkle the mixture with the flour and mix well.

2. Add the sherry and vegetable broth and simmer, covered, until the mushrooms are completely tender, about 25 minutes. Remove the soup from the heat and let cool for 5 to 10 minutes.

3. Purée the soup with a handheld blender, or in batches in a food processor or countertop blender. Strain the puréed soup through a colander or sieve. The soup is ready to finish and serve now, or it may be cooled and held in a covered container in the refrigerator for up to 2 days.

4. When ready to serve, reheat the soup, if necessary. In a small saucepan, gently simmer the heavy cream, then add it to the soup. Adjust the consistency of the soup with a little more broth, if needed. Season with salt and pepper.

5. Serve the soup in warmed soup cups or bowls. Garnish with the sliced chives and nutmeg, if using.

Thai Fresh Pea Soup

This soup adds a subtle twist to the delicate taste of peas. It is a great starter course for an evening of Thai cuisine.

MAKES 2 QUARTS SOUP; SERVES 8 TO 10

  1 cup diced onions

  4 garlic cloves, finely minced

  2 tsp green curry paste

  1½ quarts vegetable broth

  2½ lb shelled peas, fresh or thawed frozen

  Kosher salt and freshly ground black pepper, as needed

  1 tsp mustard seeds, lightly toasted

  ¼ cup chopped mint

1. Heat a small amount of the stock in a soup pot over medium heat. Add the onions, garlic, curry paste, and cook, stirring frequently, until the onions are tender, 2 to 3 minutes.

2. Add the remaining broth to the pot and bring to a boil. Add the peas, cover, and simmer for 10 minutes. Remove the soup from the heat and let cool for 5 to 10 minutes.

3. Purée the soup with a handheld blender, or in batches in a food processor or countertop blender. Season with salt and pepper. The soup is ready to serve and garnish now, or it may be held in a covered container in the refrigerator for up to 2 days.

4. Reheat the soup, if necessary. Serve the soup in warmed soup cups or bowls. Garnish each serving with a sprinkle of toasted mustard seeds and with some chopped mint.

Vichyssoise

This classic cold soup is also excellent served piping hot to introduce a fall or winter dinner menu.

MAKES 2 QUARTS SOUP; SERVES 8 TO 10

  2 cloves

  2 parsley stems

  2 black peppercorns

  ½ dried bay leaf

  2 cups finely chopped leeks, white part only

  ½ onion, minced

  2 tbsp canola oil

  1¼ lb potatoes, cut into small dice

  3½ cups chicken broth

  1½ cups heavy cream or half-and-half, chilled

  ¼ cup snipped chives

  Kosher salt and freshly ground black pepper, as needed

1. Put the cloves, parsley stems, peppercorns, and bay leaf in a cheesecloth pouch.

2. Heat the oil in a in a large soup pot over medium heat. Add the leeks and onions and cook, stirring frequently, until tender and translucent, about 5 minutes.

3. Add the potatoes, broth, and the prepared cheesecloth pouch. Bring the mixture to a boil, then reduce the heat and simmer until the potatoes begin to fall apart, about 15 minutes.

4. Remove the soup from the heat and let cool for 5 to 10 minutes. Remove and discard the cheesecloth pouch. Purée the soup with a handheld blender, or in batches in a food processor or countertop blender. Let the soup cool completely and then refrigerate for at least 2 hours and up to 2 days.

5. When ready to serve, add the heavy cream or half-and-half, fold in the chives, and season with salt and pepper.

SALADS

SALADS ARE EASY TO PREPARE IN STAGES AND THEN assemble at the last minute. The salads we've assembled here are considered "composed salads," which means that the individual elements are arranged on the plate, instead of being simply tossed together. In addition to the salads in this chapter, you can create a composed salad plate that includes small portions of a variety of salads such as those found on pages 239–249 of this book.

Most salads can be served either chilled or at room temperature, giving you the option of having the first course already set on the table before your guests gather at the table.

Prosciutto and Summer Melon Salad

This simple composed salad can be prepared as a platter for a buffet or individual cubes or spears of melon may be wrapped with a bit of prosciutto and skewered as an hors d'oeuvre (see photo on page 34).

SERVES 8

2 lb mixed melons, peeled and sliced or diced (cantaloupe, honeydew, casaba, etc.)

8 oz prosciutto, thinly sliced

3 tbsp aged balsamic vinegar

4 tsp cracked black pepper

16 thin bread sticks (grissini)

1. For each serving, arrange ¾ cup melon on the plate. Fold 1 ounce prosciutto and arrange it next to the melon.

2. Just before serving, drizzle a few drops of the balsamic vinegar on the melon. Scatter ½ teaspoon pepper on the plate and serve with two grissini.

Mushrooms, Beets, and Baby Greens with Robiola Cheese and Walnuts

This recipe is a great option for a fall or winter menu. We like the contrast of red and green beets. To keep their colors bright, keep the two colors separated until you are ready to assemble the salads.

SERVES 8

10 oz medium red beets

10 oz medium golden beets

Kosher salt and freshly ground black pepper, as needed

1 cup Apple Cider Vinaigrette (recipe follows)

2 tbsp extra-virgin olive oil

1 lb assorted mushrooms, such as button, cremini, shiitake, chanterelle, or oyster

16 baguette slices, cut ¼ inch thick, on the diagonal

6 oz Robiola cheese

4 oz frisée hearts

4 oz arugula

4 oz mesclun greens

½ cup roughly chopped toasted walnuts

Truffle oil, as needed (optional)

1. Remove the tops from the beets. Place the beets in separate pots and add enough cold water to cover them by about 2 inches. Add a few pinches of salt and cook over medium heat until they are tender, 30 to 40 minutes. Drain the beets and let them cool until they can be handled easily.

2. Peel the beets with the back of a paring knife and cut into medium dice. Place each beet variety in a separate bowl. Add 1 tablespoon of the vinaigrette to each bowl, season with salt and pepper, and reserve. The beets can be covered and stored in the refrigerator for up to 2 days.

3. Heat the oil in a large sauté pan over medium heat. Add the mushrooms and sauté them until golden brown and tender, 4 to 5 minutes. Work in batches, if necessary, to avoid overcrowding the pan. Transfer the mushrooms to a bowl and toss the mushrooms with 4 tablespoons of the vinaigrette and reserve. The mushrooms can be covered and stored in the refrigerator for up to 2 days.

4. Cut each baguette slice in half lengthwise. Brush each slice with olive oil, place on a sheet pan, and bake at 400°F until golden brown on the first side, about 2½ minutes. Turn the croutons over to brown the opposite sides, about 2½ minutes. The croutons can be covered and stored in an airtight container at room temperature for up to 12 hours.

5. Preheat the broiler. Spread 1 or 2 tablespoons of cheese on each crouton. Season with salt and pepper, place on a baking sheet or a broiling pan, and broil until the cheese is just starting to melt. The croutons can be spread with the cheese up to 3 hours ahead of time, but they should be broiled at the last possible moment.

6. Combine the frisée, arugula, and mesclun in a large bowl and toss together with the remaining vinaigrette. Mound the greens on 8 salad plates, top with the beets, mushrooms, and walnuts. Add 2 broiled croutons and serve at once. Drizzle with a little truffle oil, if desired.

Apple Cider Vinaigrette

MAKES 1½ CUPS

¾ cup apple cider

¼ cup apple cider vinegar

¼ small-dice Granny Smith apple

½ cup peanut oil

1 tbsp chopped tarragon

Kosher salt and freshly ground black pepper, as needed

To make the vinaigrette: In a medium bowl, whisk together the cider, cider vinegar, diced apple, and oil by hand. The vinaigrette can be made up to 12 hours ahead and stored in a covered container in the refrigerator.

Greek Salad

Greek Salad

Simple Mediterranean flavors come together in this easy-to-make salad. The time needed is mostly for vegetable preparation, which will make an elegant presentation a cinch.

SERVES 8

1½ lb romaine lettuce hearts

1 cup Greek olives, pitted and sliced in half lengthwise

1 seedless cucumber, peeled, sliced ⅛ inch thick

1 lb cherry tomatoes, halved

1 yellow bell pepper, seeded and thinly sliced

1 red onion, peeled, sliced ⅛ inch thick

½ cup Lemon-Parsley Vinaigrette (recipe follows)

4 whole wheat pitas, toasted, cut into 16 wedges

¾ lb feta, crumbled

16 purchased stuffed grape leaves

1. Remove about a third of the stem from the romaine lettuce. Wash and spin dry. Slice the romaine or tear it into bite-size pieces. Place the lettuce in a large serving bowl.

2. Add the olives, cucumber slices, cherry tomatoes, bell peppers, and red onions. Toss with the vinaigrette. Top the salad in a serving dish or each individual serving with the feta cheese and garnish with pita wedges and the stuffed grape leaves.

Lemon Parsley Vinaigrette

MAKES ¾ CUP VINAIGRETTE

3 tbsp fresh lemon juice

1 tbsp white wine vinegar

6 tbsp extra-virgin olive oil

2 tbsp chopped flat-leaf parsley

Kosher salt and freshly ground black pepper, as needed

Combine the lemon juice and vinegar in a bowl. Add the oil in a thin stream, whisking continuously. Stir in the parsley and season with salt and pepper. The vinaigrette can be stored for up to 2 days in the refrigerator. Whisk to recombine before serving.

Frisée with Walnuts, Apples, Grapes, and Blue Cheese

Frisée, a light green variety of endive with very curly leaves, is the base for a delicious combination of early autumn produce, crunchy walnuts, and pungent blue cheese.

SERVES 8

1½ lb frisée lettuce

2 tsp fresh lemon juice, as needed (optional)

2 Granny Smith apples, or other tart apples

½ cup Apple Cider Vinaigrette (page 102)

1 cup seedless red grapes, cut in half lengthwise

½ cup coarsely chopped walnuts, toasted

1 cup crumbled blue cheese

1. Clean and thoroughly dry the frisée. Core the apples and slice them ⅛ inch thick. If you wish to slice the apples in advance, hold them in water with a splash of lemon juice; this can be done up to 1 hour in advance.

2. Just before serving, bring the vinaigrette to room temperature, if necessary. Whisk the vinaigrette vigorously, taste, and reseason with salt and pepper, if necessary. Toss the frisée with the vinaigrette.

3. To serve: Arrange the frisée on chilled plates and top each portion with the apple slices, about 2 tablespoon of the grapes, 1 tablespoon of the walnuts, and 2 tablespoons of the blue cheese. Serve immediately.

NOTE *Mesclun lettuce mix may be mixed with the frisée.*

Romaine and Grapefruit Salad with Walnuts and Stilton

For additional flavor, you could add one of the seasoning blends on page 45 to the walnuts before you toast them.

SERVES 8

2 white or pink grapefruit

¼ cup ruby port

2 tbsp red wine vinegar

2 tbsp grapefruit juice

4 tsp olive oil

Kosher salt and freshly ground black pepper, as needed

1 lb romaine lettuce, cut into bite-size pieces

1 cup crumbled Stilton

½ cup chopped walnuts, toasted

1. Peel the grapefruit and break them into sections. For a more elegant presentation, make suprêmes as follows: Cut away the skin and the white pith from the grapefruit and then cut the flesh of the grapefruit away from the membranes. Pick out any seeds and discard them.

2. In a small bowl, whisk together the port, red wine vinegar, grapefruit juice, and olive oil. Season with salt and pepper.

3. In a large bowl, toss the romaine with the dressing and divide evenly among 8 plates. Arrange the grapefruit sections, Stilton, and walnuts on top of each portion.

Baked Goat Cheese with Mesclun, Pears, and Toasted Almonds

The rich and creamy texture of the cheese contrasts nicely with its crispy, baked crust. The almonds add a deep, rich flavor to the dish. The backdrop of the mesclun mix pulls all the elements together.

SERVES 8

1¼ lb fresh goat cheese, well chilled

1 cup dry bread crumbs

1½ lb mesclun lettuce mix

¾ cup extra-virgin olive oil

¼ cup fresh lemon juice

Kosher salt and freshly ground black pepper, as needed

2 pears, cored, sliced into thin wedges

1 cup sliced almonds, toasted

1. Preheat the oven to 400°F. Slice the cheese into ½-inch-thick disks. Gently press the bread crumbs onto the cheese and place on a baking sheet. Bake until lightly browned, about 10 minutes. Allow the cheese to cool slightly while assembling the salads.

2. In a large bowl, toss the mesclun mix with the olive oil, lemon juice, salt, and pepper. Divide the lettuce evenly among 8 plates, mounding each portion on the plate. Top each portion with 3 to 4 pear slices, about 2 tablespoons of the almonds, and 2 of the goat cheese rounds.

Balsamic Vinaigrette

MAKES 1½ CUPS VINAIGRETTE

1/3 cup balsamic vinegar

2 tbsp red wine vinegar

2 tsp Dijon mustard

¼ tsp sugar or honey

¾ cup extra-virgin olive oil

Kosher salt and freshly ground black pepper, as needed

Whisk together the vinegars, mustard, and sugar or honey. Add the oil in a thin stream, whisking continuously. Season with salt and pepper. Store in a covered jar in the refrigerator for up to 5 days.

Spinach Salad with Marinated Shiitakes and Red Onions

You can double or triple the quantity of marinated shiitakes. They make a great topping for burgers or an inclusion in a griddled panini sandwich.

SERVES 8

Marinated Shiitakes

2 tbsp peanut oil

3 cups sliced shiitake mushrooms

2 tsp soy sauce

4 tsp apple cider vinegar

Dash of Tabasco sauce

Kosher salt and freshly ground black pepper, as needed

½ cup diced red onion

2 tsp olive oil

½ cup Balsamic Vinaigrette (this page)

6 cups fresh spinach, trimmed, washed, and torn

2 cups radicchio, cut into fine shreds

1. Heat the peanut oil in a medium sauté pan over medium-high heat. Add the mushrooms and sauté for 2 minutes. Add 2 tablespoons of water and the soy sauce and cook until dry, about 5 minutes. Remove from the heat and add the vinegar and Tabasco sauce. Season with a little salt and pepper. Cool completely and store for up to 2 days in a covered container in the refrigerator.

2. Heat the olive oil in a skillet over medium heat. Add the onion and cook, stirring frequently, until translucent, about 3 minutes. Add the marinated shiitakes and the vinaigrette and bring to a simmer. Keep warm.

3. In a large bowl, toss the spinach, prepared red onion, radicchio, and the prepared mushrooms with the warm vinaigrette. Adjust the seasoning with salt and pepper. Serve at once.

VEGETABLES FOR THE FIRST COURSE

A FIRST COURSE THAT FEATURES VEGETABLES is a perfect way to celebrate the season. You can opt to lightly blanch or steam vegetables and then dress them with a pungent vinaigrette or grill them to serve with a sauce. Letting vegetables stand on their own as a first course gives you a chance to capitalize on their fresh flavors, bright colors, and interesting textures.

Haricots Verts with Prosciutto and Gruyère

This is a stunning addition to any meal and it requires minimal preparation. This dish can be served in individual portions or on a large platter for a beautiful presentation.

SERVES 8

Lemon and Shallot Dressing

3 tbsp fresh lemon juice, or as needed

1 tbsp white wine vinegar

2 tbsp minced shallots

6 tbsp olive oil

Kosher salt and freshly ground black pepper, as needed

1 lb haricots verts

¼ lb prosciutto, thinly sliced

¼ lb Gruyère

1. Combine the lemon juice, vinegar, and shallots. Gradually whisk in the oil to make a dressing. Season with salt and pepper. The dressing can be prepared up to 12 hours in advance and stored in a covered container in the refrigerator. Let the dressing return to room temperature before combining it with the haricots verts.

2. Trim the haricots verts and rinse. Bring a pot of salted water to a rolling boil. Add the haricots verts and cook until barely tender to the bite and bright green, about 3 minutes. Rinse the haricots verts under cold water, drain, and blot dry with paper towels.

3. Toss the haricots verts with the dressing and let marinate at room temperature for 10 minutes.

4. Arrange the haricots verts on individual plates or a platter. Drape with the prosciutto. Or, for a more elegant look, roll the prosciutto into a cone, making one end of the cone tight and leaving the other loose so that they look like roses. Using a vegetable peeler, shave curls of the Gruyère on top to garnish.

Asparagus with Morels

Celebrate spring with this delectable combination of fresh morels and asparagus. Morels have an intense smoky, earthy, nutty flavor that is prized among wild mushrooms. If they are not available, substitute portobello mushrooms.

SERVES 8

2 lb asparagus

4 oz morel mushrooms

1 tbsp canola oil

2 tbsp minced shallots

1 tbsp minced chives

Kosher salt and freshly ground black pepper, as needed

2 tbsp unsalted butter

1 tsp fresh lemon juice

1. Rinse the asparagus, trim the ends, and cut on the diagonal into 1-inch-long pieces. Wipe the mushrooms clean, trim the stems, and, if necessary, cut into quarters or thinly slice.

2. Heat the oil in a large skillet over medium heat. Add the shallots and cook until aromatic, about 1 minute. Add the morels, season with a pinch of salt, and sauté, stirring frequently, until the morels are very hot, 4 to 5 minutes. Remove the mushroom mixture from the skillet and fold in the chives.

3. Heat ½ cup water in the same skillet over high heat. Add the asparagus, salt, and pepper. Cover the skillet and pan steam over high heat until the asparagus are tender and bright green, 6 to 7 minutes. There should now be about ⅓ cup of liquid in the bottom of the pan. Pour off if there is too much or add a bit of water if there is too little.

4. Add the mushroom mixture to the asparagus and sauté, stirring until evenly blended and very hot. Add the butter and continue to cook, swirling the pan over the heat, just until the butter melts and thickens the liquid enough to cling to the vegetables. Taste and adjust the seasoning with salt and pepper, if needed. Drizzle the lemon juice over the asparagus. Serve immediately.

Grilled Vegetable Appetizer with Balsamic Vinaigrette

Use a variety of tomatoes, if available, for extra color in this dish. This appetizer would be nice served with grilled French bread sliced on the diagonal and brushed with the olive oil mixture.

SERVES 8

1 cup extra-virgin olive oil

½ cup chopped basil

1 tsp kosher salt, or as needed

¼ tsp freshly ground black pepper, or as needed

1 medium eggplant, sliced into ½-inch-thick rounds

1 medium zucchini, sliced on the diagonal into ½-inch-thick slices

1 medium yellow squash, sliced on the diagonal into ½-inch-thick slices

2 red bell peppers, seeded and cut into eighths

2 yellow bell peppers, seeded and cut into eighths

½ lb portobello mushrooms, stems and gills removed, sliced

2 red tomatoes, quartered

2 yellow tomatoes, quartered

8 green onions, including green tops, root ends trimmed

½ cup Balsamic Vinaigrette (page 107)

1. Preheat a grill to medium-high. In a small bowl, combine the oil with the basil, salt, and pepper. Brush the vegetables with this mixture.

2. Grill the vegetables over direct heat about 5 minutes per side, until they are tender and very hot.

3. To serve: On each of 8 serving plates, arrange 2 to 3 slices each of eggplant, zucchini, and yellow squash. Add 2 strips of red bell pepper, 2 strips of yellow bell pepper, a tomato quarter, a yellow tomato quarter, and a green onion.

4. Drizzle with the balsamic vinaigrette and serve warm or at room temperature.

PASTA AND RISOTTO

PASTA AND RISOTTO ARE A GOOD CHOICE for a first course, especially when the main course is a longer-cooking roast or braise. Served in small portions, they are a good way to introduce the meal without overwhelming the appetite. You can make "nests" from long pastas by twirling them around the tines of a kitchen fork and then sliding the pasta nest into the plate for a more elegant presentation. Risotto is traditionally served on flat plates and eaten from the outside in, so that as you eat from the outer edges to the center, it cools very slightly.

Orecchiette with Ricotta, Peas, and Lemon Zest

Look for good-quality ricotta that is freshly made and quite soft and moist. For a richer flavor you may add some fine strips of prosciutto or pancetta to cook with the green onion.

SERVES 8

2 lb fresh garden peas in the shell (about 1 cup unshelled)

½ cup extra-virgin olive oil

2 green onions, thinly sliced, white and green portions (about ½ cup)

½ cup chopped flat-leaf parsley

¾ cup chicken or vegetable broth, or as needed

1 lb orecchiette, preferably artisanally made

1½ cups ricotta

Kosher salt and freshly ground black pepper, as needed

½ cup grated Parmigiano-Reggiano

Finely grated zest of ½ lemon

1. Shell the peas and set aside.

2. Heat the olive oil in a large skillet over medium heat. Add the green onion and cook, stirring frequently, until tender, about 2 minutes. Add the parsley and cook for 2 minutes longer. Add the shelled peas and the broth and bring to a simmer, stirring well. Reduce the heat to medium-low or low and continue to cook, covered, until the peas are tender but not mushy, 4 to 5 minutes; the time may vary depending upon the size of your peas. Take the pan with the peas off the heat and set them aside.

3. Fill a deep 5-quart pot two-thirds full with cold water and place over high heat. Add about 1 tablespoon of salt; the water should taste just barely salty. Bring the water to a rolling boil over high heat. Add the orecchiette all at once and stir a few times to separate the pasta and submerge the pieces. Cook, uncovered, at a boil until the pasta is just tender to the bite but still al dente, 8 to 10 minutes.

4. Immediately drain the orecchiette through a colander. Shake well to remove any water clinging to the pasta. Transfer the drained pasta into the peas and return the pan to low heat. Gently stir the orecchiette into the peas until well combined, without too much moisture in the pan. If there is a lot of liquid, continue cooking for a minute or two to cook it away.

5. Remove the pan from the heat, add half of the ricotta to the orecchiette and fold together. Fold in the remaining parsley, the cheese, and lemon zest.

6. Serve the orecchiette at once in a warmed serving bowl or pasta plates topped with spoonfuls of the remaining ricotta and drizzled with some extra-virgin olive oil.

Spaghetti with Black Pepper and Pecorino

Choose the pecorino for this dish carefully, as it makes all the difference. Some varieties are saltier than others, so taste it before you decide how much salt you will need. You may not need any, except for salting the pasta water.

SERVES 6

1 lb dried spaghetti

Kosher salt, as needed

4 tsp freshly ground black pepper, or as needed

4 oz grated Pecorino-Romano (about 1 cup), plus more for serving

6 tbsp extra-virgin olive oil, or as needed

1. Bring a large pot of salted water to a rolling boil over high heat. Add the spaghetti all at once and stir a few times to separate the pasta. Cook, uncovered, at a boil until the pasta is just tender to the bite, 10 to 12 minutes. Transfer a few ladlefuls of pasta water from the the pot to a bowl or cup to have ready for finishing the sauce; you may need up to ½ cup.

2. Drain the spaghetti immediately through a colander. Shake well to remove any water clinging to the pasta.

Pour the spaghetti back into the pot. Add the cheese, olive oil, and black pepper. Stir the pasta until the cheese and pepper are evenly distributed. Add about ¼ cup of the pasta cooking water to the spaghetti to moisten the pasta slightly. It should appear creamy, not oily. If necessary, add a bit more of the pasta water. Taste and add salt, if necessary.

3. Serve at once, passing additional cheese on the side.

Capellini with Grilled Vegetables

Serve this pasta dish very hot, straight from the pan, or enjoy it as a cold or room-temperature salad. To make it a salad, prepare the vegetables through step 4 and chill them well. Combine the vegetables with the drained, cooled pasta and top with the Gorgonzola just before serving.

SERVES 8

½ cup balsamic vinegar

⅔ cup plus 1 tbsp olive oil

2 tsp kosher salt, plus more as needed

1 tsp freshly ground black pepper, plus more as needed

2 red onions, cut into ½-inch-thick slices

2 zucchini, cut into ½-inch-thick slices

2 yellow squash, cut into ½-inch-thick slices

1 fennel bulb, cut into ½-inch rings

1 shallot, minced

2 garlic cloves, minced

2 cups grape tomatoes, halved lengthwise

½ cup white wine

1 tbsp chopped flat-leaf parsley

1 tbsp chopped basil

1 lb dried capellini

6 oz Gorgonzola, broken into small pieces

1. Preheat a grill to medium-high or use a broiler. Bring a large pot of salted water to a boil for the pasta.

2. In a large bowl, combine the vinegar, ⅔ cup of the olive oil, 2 teaspoons salt, and 1 teaspoon pepper. Add the onions, zucchini, squash, and fennel and toss with the vinaigrette.

3. Grill the vegetables on both sides until tender, about 8 minutes total. Remove from the grill or broiler and let cool slightly. When the vegetables are cool enough to handle, cut them into 1½-inch dice. The vegetables may be prepared up to 2 days in advance and stored in a covered container in the refrigerator.

4. Heat the remaining tablespoon of the oil in a sauté pan on medium-high heat. Add the shallot and garlic and sauté until aromatic, about 3 minutes. Add the grilled or broiled vegetables, the tomatoes, and the wine. Heat thoroughly and season with the fresh herbs, salt, and pepper, as needed.

5. Bring a large pot of salted water to a rolling boil over high heat. Add the cappellini all at once and stir a few times to separate the strands. Cook, uncovered, at a boil until the pasta is just tender to the bite, 6 to 8 minutes. Immediately drain the cappellini through a colander. Shake well to remove any water clinging to the pasta and transfer to a large bowl.

6. Toss the cooked capellini with about half of the cheese. To serve: Mound the pasta in warmed pasta bowls. Top each portion with some of the vegetable mixture and garnish with the remaining cheese.

Risotto with Asparagus

Top individual servings of risotto with a few pieces of pan-seared, broiled, or poached seafood for an elegant first course. Shrimp, scallops, or lobster are all great choices.

SERVES 8

   4 cups chicken broth

   2 cups dry white wine

   ¼ cup olive oil

   1 cup finely chopped yellow onion

   2 cups Arborio rice, uncooked

   ¼ tsp freshly ground black pepper, plus more as needed

   4 tbsp (½ stick) unsalted butter

   ½ cup grated Asiago

   24 thin asparagus spears, cut on the diagonal into 1-inch pieces

   Kosher salt and freshly ground black pepper, as needed

1. In a medium saucepan, bring the broth and the wine to a simmer over medium heat and keep warm.

2. Heat 2 tablespoons of the oil in a large saucepan over medium heat. Add the onion and sauté, stirring frequently, until tender, about 1 minute. Add the rice and cook, stirring, until it is coated with oil and the rice has a toasty smell, about 2 minutes.

3. Add 2 cups of the hot broth-wine mixture to the rice and cook, stirring constantly, until the rice absorbs all the liquid, 5 to 6 minutes. Add another 2 cups of the broth and simmer, stirring, until the rice absorbs the second addition, 5 to 6 minutes. The risotto can be finished at this point (step 4), or it may be transferred to a shallow pan and cooled. Once cool, it can be covered and stored in the refrigerator for up to 24 hours. Store the remaining 2 cups of the wine-broth mixture separately.

4. Add the remaining 2 cups of the broth-wine to the rice. If completing the risotto after cooling it, reheat the broth in the pan and then add the partially cooked rice. Simmer over medium to low heat, stirring constantly, until the risotto has a creamy consistency and the rice is tender, 6 to 8 minutes more. Remove the pan from the heat and stir in the butter and Asiago until well blended and creamy. Taste and season with salt and pepper, if needed.

5. While completing the risotto, bring about ½ inch of water to a rolling boil in a shallow pot. Add the asparagus and a pinch of salt. Cover the pan and steam the asparagus until it is just tender, about 3 minutes. Drain well in a colander. Fold the asparagus into the risotto.

6. Spoon portions of the risotto on warmed flat plates and serve at once.

SEAFOOD

A CLASSIC STANDBY OPTION for a visually appealing first course is a seafood cocktail. We've included some options here that go beyond a shrimp cocktail. Most seafood cooks quickly and is delicious served hot, warm, or chilled, making it easy to adapt to the season and your menu.

Salad of Crab and Avocado

We like presenting this salad in a glass to let the layers show. The salsa and the guacamole can be prepare a few hours in advance. The salad can be assembled and held in the refrigerator for an hour or two. The layering keeps the guacamole from turning color.

SERVES 8

Salsa

½ cup small-dice red bell pepper

2 plum tomatoes, cored and chopped

2 green onions, white and green portions, thinly sliced on the diagonal

1 garlic clove, minced

2 tbsp coarsely chopped cilantro

2 tsp minced jalapeño, seeds and ribs removed

Kosher salt and freshly ground black pepper, as needed

Guacamole

2 ripe Hass avocados, peeled, pitted, and cut into small dice

3 tbsp fresh lime juice

Kosher salt and freshly ground black pepper, as needed

2½ cups lump crabmeat, picked over to remove cartilage and shell

¼ cup sour cream

1. In a medium bowl, toss together the bell pepper, tomatoes, green onions, garlic, cilantro, and jalapeño to form a salsa. Season with ¼ teaspoon salt and a pinch of black pepper and let the mixture sit at room temperature for about 20 minutes. The salsa can be prepared in advance and held in a covered container in the refrigerator for up to 24 hours.

2. Meanwhile, in a small bowl, gently toss together the avocado, lime juice, ½ teaspoon salt, and a pinch of black pepper.

3. To serve: For each portion layer in a 6-ounce glass or a small dish ¼ cup of the tomato salsa, about 5 tablespoon of the crabmeat, and 2 tablespoons of the avocado mixture. Spoon approximately 1 teaspoon of the sour cream on top of the avocado layer and garnish with a little bit of the salsa.

Crab Cakes with Creole Honey-Mustard Sauce

For a smoky flavor, you can add a few slices of cooked crumbled bacon to the crabmeat mixture in step 1.

MAKES 24 CRAB CAKES; SERVES 8

1 lb lump crabmeat, picked over to remove cartilage and shell

2 green onions, white and green portions, minced

2 garlic cloves, minced

1 cup fresh bread crumbs

¼ cup minced celery

2 tsp Dijon mustard

2 tsp dry mustard

1 tsp salt

Pinch of cayenne pepper

Mayonnaise, as needed

2 tbsp fresh lemon juice

1½ cups Japanese-style bread crumbs (panko)

1 cup canola oil

1 cup Creole Honey-Mustard Sauce (recipe follows)

1. In a large bowl, combine the crabmeat, green onions, garlic, bread crumbs, celery, Dijon mustard, dry mustard, salt, cayenne, and just enough mayonnaise to hold the mixture together. Toss gently until combined. Add the lemon juice and stir to combine.

2. Portion the crab cakes into 24 balls, each about 2 inches in diameter. Flatten the balls slightly and roll in the Japanese-style bread crumbs. The crab cakes can be made in advance to this point and stored, individually wrapped, in the refrigerator for up to 24 hours or in the freezer for up to 2 weeks. Thaw frozen crab cakes before panfrying them in step 3.

3. Heat the oil in a sauté pan over medium heat. Add the crab cakes and panfry until heated through and golden brown on both sides, about 4 minutes total. Work in batches to avoid overcrowding the pan. Drain briefly on paper towels. Serve immediately with the honey-mustard sauce.

Creole Honey-Mustard Sauce

MAKES 1 CUP SAUCE; SERVES 8

1 tbsp canola oil

2 tbsp minced shallots

1 tsp crushed green peppercorns (brine-packed)

¼ tsp cracked black peppercorns

3 tbsp dry white wine

3 tbsp Dijon mustard

3 tbsp Creole mustard

¼ cup mayonnaise

⅓ cup sour cream

4 tsp honey

Kosher salt, as needed

1. Heat the oil in a small saucepan over medium heat. Add the shallots and the green and black peppercorns and cook, stirring frequently, until the shallots are tender and translucent, about 2 minutes. Add the white wine and cook, stirring occasionally, until the wine has almost completely cooked away. Transfer to a small mixing bowl and let the mixture cool.

2. Add the mustards, mayonnaise, sour cream, and honey and stir to mix well. Taste and adjust the seasoning with salt as needed. The sauce is ready to serve now, or it may be stored in a covered container in the refrigerator for up to 4 days.

Mussels in Saffron and White Wine Sauce

As the mussels cook, they release their own aromatic juices into the simmering white wine, creating a flavorful broth.

SERVES 6

2 tsp butter

2 garlic cloves, minced

⅔ cup dry white wine

⅔ cup heavy cream

½ tsp lightly crushed saffron threads

⅓ cup thinly sliced green onions, white and green portions

⅔ cup tomatoes, peeled, seeded, and chopped

1 tbsp fresh lemon juice

60 mussels, cleaned and debearded

1 tbsp chopped chives

1. Heat the butter in a large soup pot over medium heat. Add the garlic and sauté until aromatic, about 1 minute. Add the wine, cream, and saffron and simmer over medium-low heat for about 5 minutes more.

2. Add the green onions, tomatoes, lemon juice, and continue to simmer until the sauce is thickened and very flavorful, about 5 minutes.

3. Add the mussels and cover the pot. Steam the mussels until their shells open, about 4 minutes. Discard any mussels that do not open. Serve the mussels with the sauce in heated soup plates and garnish with the chives.

Mussels in Saffron and White Wine Sauce

Classic Shrimp Cocktail

Instead of a classic cocktail sauce, you could opt for a pesto-flavored mayonnaise, aïoli, or a lemon vinaigrette. Fresh shrimp with the heads on are a real treat, and if you can find them, will make a memorable first course. In that case, be sure to break out the finger bowls!

SERVES 6

- **1 lb extra-large shrimp (26/30 count)**
- **1 tsp kosher salt, or as needed**
- **1 lemon, unpeeled and thickly sliced**
- **1 dried bay leaf**
- **1 sprig thyme**
- **4 or 5 whole black peppercorns**
- **1 cup Cocktail Sauce (recipe follows)**

1. Before cooking, fully defrost the shrimp, if necessary. Peel and devein the shrimp.

2. Add about 2 inches of water to a large pan. Bring the water to a simmer over medium-high heat and add the lemon slices, bay leaf, thyme, and peppercorns. Reduce the heat to low and add the shrimp, cover the pan, and poach the shrimp until they are cooked through and firm, 6 to 8 minutes (see table below for cooking times for sizes other than extra-large).

3. Drain the shrimp and let cool to room temperature. The shrimp can be stored in a covered container for up to 2 days. To serve, arrange the shrimp around the cocktail sauce.

Cocktail Sauce

MAKES 1 CUP SAUCE; SERVES 6

- **½ cup prepared chili sauce**
- **½ cup prepared ketchup**
- **1 tbsp fresh lemon juice**
- **2 tsp sugar**
- **½ tsp Tabasco sauce**
- **½ tsp Worcestershire sauce**
- **2 tbsp prepared horseradish**

In a small bowl, stir together all of the ingredients until evenly combined. The sauce is ready to serve now, or it can be stored in a covered container in the refrigerator for up to 5 days.

TYPES OF SHRIMP

MARKET NAME	SHRIMP COUNT (NUMBER) PER POUND	TYPICAL NUMBER SHRIMP PER POUND	AVERAGE COOKING TIMES (POACHING AND STEAMING)
Extra Colossal	U10	5	10–12 minutes
Colossal	U15	14	8–10 minutes
Extra Jumbo	16/20	18	8–9 minutes
Jumbo	21/55	23	7–8 minutes
Extra Large	26/30	28	6–7 minutes
Large	31/35	33	5–7 minutes
Medium Large	36/40	38	4–5 minutes
Medium	41/50	45	3–4 minutes
Small	51/60	55	2–3 minutes
Extra Small	61/70	65	2 minutes

PURCHASING AND PREPARING FRESH SHRIMP

Shrimp are available both fresh and frozen in a variety of sizes. You may be able to buy them with the heads on in some parts of the country, although you are most likely to find them with the heads removed. If you purchase shrimp uncooked (whether fresh of frozen) the shell is typically left on. You can opt to remove the shell either before or after steaming or poaching shrimp. Be sure to remove the dark vein running along the back of the shrimp for the best flavor and texture. If there is a great deal of grit in the vein, you should rinse the shrimp after removing the vein and before either cooking or serving it. Fresh shrimp will smell sweet and be free of any ammonia odor, slimy feel, or residue.

Shrimp are properly cooked when the flesh is no longer translucent and it changes color and turns a bright pinkish orange. Before cooking frozen shrimp, allow them to fully defrost, otherwise the shrimp will cook unevenly and some will overcook before the entire batch is done.

To poach them, whether you have peeled them or not, bring a large pot of salted water along with any seasonings you like (for instance, bay leaf, lemon slices, whole peppercorns, or wine) to a rolling boil. Add plenty of salt to bring out the flavor in the shrimp. Add the shrimp all at once, cover the pot, and reduce the heat to low. Once they are properly cooked. drain them in a colander and let them cool. If you want to chill the shrimp, let them cool in the refrigerator for at least 3 hours before serving.

To devein shrimp, lay the shelled shrimp on a work surface, with the curved outer edge of the shrimp on the same side as your cutting hand. Make a shallow slice into the shrimp with a paring knife.

Use the tip of the knife to scrape out the "vein," or intestinal tract.

As an alternative, to remove the vein without cutting the shrimp, hook the vein with a toothpick or skewer and pull it out completely.

Clams Casino

Serve theses clams in gratin dishes, or make a bed of salt in a pasta or soup plate for a dramatic presentation.

SERVES 8

Casino Butter

¼ cup diced bacon

¼ cup minced onions

⅓ cup minced green bell peppers

⅓ cup minced red bell peppers

1 cup (2 sticks) unsalted butter

Kosher salt and freshly ground black pepper, as needed

Worcestershire sauce as needed

48 littleneck or cherrystone clams

8 strips bacon, blanched and cut into 6 pieces

1. To make the casino butter: Heat a small skillet over medium heat. Add the diced bacon and cook gently until the fat has melted and the bacon bits are crisp. Add the onions and peppers and cook, stirring frequently, until the onions are tender and translucent, about 4 minutes. Transfer to a mixing bowl and let the mixture cool completely.

2. Add the butter to the onion-pepper-bacon mixture and stir with a wooden spoon until the ingredients are combined. Add salt, pepper, and Worcestershire sauce to taste. The butter can be used to top the clams now, or it may be stored in a covered container in the refrigerator for up to 3 days.

3. Scrub the clams and discard any that are open. Open the clams and loosen the meat from the shells. Replace the clam in one-half of the shell. Top each clam with about 1 teaspoon of the casino butter and a piece of blanched bacon.

4. Preheat the broiler. Broil the clams 3 or 4 inches from the heat source until the bacon is crisp and the clams are just barely cooked through. Serve immediately.

CLAMS

Certain varieties of hard-shell clams are served raw, with littlenecks, top necks, and cherrystones being the most popular. Clams are often named for the place in which they were harvested. The location has a great deal to do with the flavor of the clam. Fresh clams should have a tightly closed shell, moist plump flesh, and a sweet smell.

LEFT: Wearing a mesh glove, place the clam in your hand so that the hinged side is toward the palm of your hand. Twist the blade slightly, like a key in a lock, to pry open the shell.

RIGHT: Once the shell is open, slide the knife over the inside of the top shell, then make a similar stroke inside the bottom shell to release the clam.

Seared Sea Scallops with Artichokes and Peperonato

If you want a great color on your seared scallops, be sure to blot them dry with a paper towel before adding them to the pan and don't salt them before adding them to the pan. If you prefer, you can broil the scallops instead of searing them.

SERVES 8

1½ lb sea scallops

2 tbsp olive oil, or as needed

1½ cups Peperonata (recipe follows)

8 cooked artichoke hearts (see page 122)

Kosher salt and freshly ground black pepper, as needed

1. Remove and discard the muscle tab from the scallops. Blot them dry with paper towels.

2. Heat the oil in a heavy skillet over medium-high heat until it is almost smoking. Add the scallops to the pan, working in batches, if necessary, to avoid overcrowding the pan. Add more oil as needed to keep the pan generously filmed with oil as you work. Sauté on the first side until deep brown, about 2 minutes. Turn the scallops once and cook just long enough to color the second side, about 1 minute.

3. Mound the warm peperonato on warmed appetizer plates and arrange the artichoke and scallops on top of the peperonata. Serve immediately.

Peperonato

MAKES ABOUT 1½ CUPS; SERVES 8

2 tbsp extra-virgin olive oil

1 small onion, thinly sliced

2 garlic cloves, thinly sliced

½ tsp dried Italian oregano

¼ tsp red pepper flakes

1 red bell pepper, seeded and cut into thin strips

1 yellow bell pepper, seeded and cut into thin strips

1 green bell pepper, seeded and cut into thin strips

¼ cup chopped flat-leaf parsley

½ tsp chopped thyme leaves

Kosher salt and freshly ground black pepper, as needed

1. Heat the olive oil in a sauté pan over medium heat. Add the onions and sauté, stirring occasionally, until tender and translucent with no color, about 8 minutes. Add the garlic, oregano, and red pepper flakes and sauté until aromatic, about 1 minute. Add the bell peppers and continue to cook, stirring from time to time, until the peppers are soft and tender, 5 to 6 minutes more.

2. Add the parsley and thyme. Taste and adjust the seasoning with salt and pepper. Simmer over low heat until flavorful, stirring as necessary to avoid browning the mixture, about 15 minutes.

3. Serve immediately or cool, cover, and refrigerate for up to 5 days.

CLEANING, COOKING, AND SERVING ARTICHOKES

Artichokes are a great option for a first course. You can steam them whole and serve with a vinaigrette or a garlicky mayonnaise. Your guests pull off the leaves, dip them in the sauce, and scrape away the bit of flesh as the base of each leaf, and then enjoy the tender, flavorful heart and bottom.

If you want to feature just the tender hearts or bottoms, either on their own or in a salad, you'll need to remove the tough outer leaves, the stem, and the fuzzy choke. Artichokes can turn brown or black when the cut surfaces are exposed to air, so rub them with a lemon. Artichoke hearts usually include some of the tender inner leaves. Artichoke bottoms don't have any leaves and look a bit like a bowl or a mushroom cap without the stem.

Cook artichokes in salted water with added lemon juice. To keep whole artichokes and artichoke hearts submerged as they cook, put a plate on top of them. Check for doneness by piercing the artichoke at its base with a paring knife. It should slide in easily.

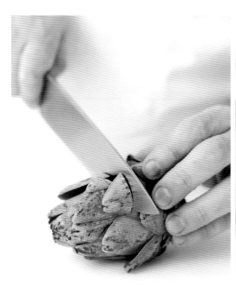
Pull away the leaves from around the stem and trim off the stem. Make a cut through the artichoke at its widest point.

Use a paring knife to trim the tough outer leaves away from the artichoke bottom.

Scoop out the center of the artichoke bottom, known as the choke.

SAVORY SOUFFLÉS

THE PREPARATION AND BAKING OF SOUFFLÉS are not difficult tasks on their own. The tricky part is getting the timing right; your guests need to be at the table as the soufflés come out of the oven. Soufflés, like omelets and quiches, are not strictly for breakfast; in fact, they are more typically the first course of a dinner menu.

Soufflés are usually baked in ceramic or glass soufflé dishes or ramekins. For the best rise in the soufflé, the sides of the dish should be straight. To prepare the baking dishes, butter them lightly but thoroughly and coat the sides and bottom with bread crumbs or grated Parmesan, if desired.

The oven should be set to the appropriate temperature, generally 400 to 425°F for individual ramekins. For a larger soufflé, the temperature should be slightly lower, about 375°F.

TOP ROW, LEFT: For the best rise in a soufflé, have the base at room temperature and gently fold the flavoring ingredients just until evenly blended. TOP ROW, RIGHT: Whip the egg whites to soft peaks and very carefully fold them into the base.

BOTTOM ROW, LEFT: Immediately spoon the batter into molds prepared with a film of butter and a dusting of flour. For even cooking and a good rise, bake the molds on a cookie sheet. BOTTOM ROW, RIGHT: Do not disturb the soufflés as they bake. Merely opening the oven door can be enough to affect the finished product. When fully risen and browned, remove the soufflés from the oven; a toothpick carefully inserted into the side of the soufflé should come out clean.

Spinach Soufflé

Individual soufflés cook in about 16 minutes. It takes about 4 minutes to do the last-minute assembly. Don't be shy about telling your guests it is time to come to the table so that your soufflés get all the attention they deserve.

SERVES 8

¼ cup (½ stick) unsalted butter

⅓ cup all-purpose flour

2½ cups whole milk

Kosher salt and freshly ground black pepper, as needed

8 large egg yolks

½ cup grated Parmesan, plus more as needed

3 cups chopped spinach (blanched or thawed, squeezed well before chopping, about 8 oz)

8 large egg whites

1. To make the soufflé base: Heat the butter in a pan over medium heat and stir in the flour. Cook over medium heat, stirring frequently, until it is golden in color and has a lightly toasted aroma, 6 to 8 minutes.

2. Add the milk, whisking well until the mixture is very smooth. Add salt and pepper. Bring to a full boil, reduce the heat to low, and simmer, stirring constantly, until very thick and smooth, 15 to 20 minutes.

3. In a small bowl, blend the yolks with about 1 cup of the hot soufflé base. Return the warmed egg yolks to the pan with the soufflé base and continue to simmer 3 to 4 minutes, stirring constantly. Do not allow the mixture to boil.

4. Adjust the seasoning with salt and pepper, and strain the mixture through a sieve, if necessary. The base is ready to use now, or it can be cooled and stored in a covered container in the refrigerator for up to 3 days. If you have refrigerated the soufflé base, let it warm to room temperature before combining it with the spinach in step 6.

5. Preheat the oven to 425°F. Prepare eight 8-ounce soufflé molds by brushing them liberally with soft butter. Lightly dust the interior of each mold with grated Parmesan cheese. Set the prepared molds on a baking sheet.

6. Blend the soufflé base with the spinach, the ½ cup of cheese, salt, and pepper until the spinach is evenly distributed.

7. In a large bowl, whip the egg whites to soft peaks. Fold about one-third of the beaten egg whites into the soufflé base. Add the remaining egg whites in one or two additions.

8. Spoon the soufflé batter into the prepared molds to within ¼ inch of the rim. Wipe the rim carefully to remove any batter. Sprinkle the soufflé tops with a little grated cheese.

9. Place the soufflés on the baking sheet pan and bake, undisturbed, until puffy and a skewer inserted in the center comes out relatively clean, 16 to 18 minutes. Serve immediately.

SAVORY CHEESE SOUFFLÉ *Replace the spinach with 3 ounces of grated Gruyère or Emmentaler.*

O FTEN, A MEAL'S CROWNING GLORY IS A PERFECT SERVING OF MEAT, BUT NO MATTER WHAT TYPE OF MAIN COURSE YOU PLAN, IT IS IMPORTANT TO THINK ABOUT THE ENTIRE MENU. THE OTHER COURSES YOU PLAN TO SERVE CAN MAKE A BIG DIFFERENCE IN HOW SUCCESSFUL THE MAIN COURSE WILL BE. IF YOU HAVE PLANNED A FIRST COURSE, YOU MAY NEED TO ALLOW TIME TO ASSEMBLE, PLATE, GARNISH, OR EVEN FINISH PREPARING THE DISH. IN THAT CASE, YOU'LL WANT TO SELECT A MAIN COURSE AND ACCOMPANIMENTS THAT CAN BE MADE IN ADVANCE OR THAT ARE FORGIVING WHEN IT COMES TO TIMING. ON THE OTHER HAND, IF YOUR FIRST COURSE AND SIDE DISHES ARE CHOSEN TO SIMPLIFY YOUR WORK, YOU MAY BE ABLE TO HANDLE A SLIGHTLY MORE ADVENTUROUS DISH LIKE A SAUTÉ.

FIRST COURSE:	MAIN DISH:	ACCOMPANIMENTS:	LAST COURSE:
Greek Salad (page 105)	Roast Leg of Lamb (page 140)	Vegetable Gratin (page 261) / Tabbouleh Salad (page 243)	Yogurt Parfait
Chilled Cream of Asparagus Soup (page 97)	Glazed Ham (page 138)	Potato Gratin (page 270) / Roasted Carrots with Parsnips and Herbs (page 250)	Angel Food Cake (page 294)
Baked Goat Cheese with Mesclun, Pears, and Toasted Almonds (page 106)	Crown Roast of Lamb Persillade (page 142)	French Lentil Salad (page 242) / Grilled Belgian Endive (page 254)	Crème Caramel (page 278)
Risotto with Scallops and Asparagus (page 112)	Pesto-Stuffed Chicken Breasts with Tomato Relish (page 145)	Panzanella (page 239) / Mushrooms, Beets, and Baby Greens with Robiola Cheese and Walnuts (page 102)	Ricotta Cheesecake (page 278)
Frisée with Walnuts, Apples, Grapes, and Blue Cheese (page 105)	Roast Turkey with Pan Gravy (page 147)	Potato Purée (page 266) / Haricot Verts with Walnuts (page 256)	Cranberry Pecan Tartlets (page 288)
Crêpes with Zucchini and Mushrooms (page 220)	Red Snapper en Papillote (page 156)	Pan-Steamed Lemon Asparagus (page 256) / Wild Rice Pilaf (page 264)	Strawberries Shortcakes with Clabbered Cream (page 300)

FIRST COURSE:	MAIN DISH:	ACCOMPANIMENTS:	LAST COURSE:
Spinach Soufflé (page 124)	Sautéed Duck Breast with Pinot Noir Sauce (page 152)	Potato Gratin (page 270)	Bittersweet Chocolate–Orange Tart (page 288)
		Brussels Sprouts with Mustard Glaze (page 258)	
Asparagus with Morels (page 108)	Sole Vin Blanc (page 153)	Tarragon Green Beans (page 252)	Berry Napoleon (page 290)
		Basic Rice Pilaf (page 263)	
Thai Fresh Pea Soup (page 100)	Tofu with Red Curry, Peas, Green Onions, and Cilantro (page 166)	Coconut Rice with Ginger (page 264)	Chilled orange slices topped with grated fresh coconut
		Sautéed Snow Peas with Sesame Seeds (page 254)	
Chilled Gazpacho (page 98)	Grilled Soft-Shell Crab (page 174)	Barley and Wheat Berry Pilaf (page 265)	Mixed fresh berries over French-Style Ice Cream (page 297)
		Corn, Pepper, Jícama Salad (page 241)	
Green Salad (page 237)	Guava-Glazed Pork Ribs (page 173)	Coleslaw (page 269)	Lemon Champagne Sorbet (page 299)
		Warm Potato Salad (page 249)	
Capellini with Grilled Vegetables (page 111)	Eggplant alla Parmigiana (page 164)	Creamed Swiss Chard with Prosciutto (page 262)	Cannoli
Greek Salad (page 105)	Muffaletta (page 184)	Mediterranean Salad (page 239)	Almond Anise Biscotti (page 275)
		Greek-Style Orzo Salad (page 245)	
Grilled Vegetable Appetizer with Balsamic Vinaigrette (page 109)	Goat Cheese-Stuffed Turkey Burger (page 178)	Asian Vegetable Slaw (page 240)	Brownies
		Red Pepper-Apricot Relish (page 178)	
Cheese Plate with Olives (page 37)	Eggplant and Havarti Sandwiches (page 185)	Mediterranean Salad (page 239)	Rice Pudding with Golden Raisins
		Couscous (page 265)	
Seared Scallops with Artichokes and Peperonato (page 120)	Moroccan Chicken Pita Sandwiches with Carrot Salad (page 187)	Moroccan-Style Roasted Vegetables (page 250)	Mango Mousse (page 280)
		Coconut Rice with Ginger (page 264)	
Salumi Platter (page 36)	Pizza Margherita (page 196)	Green Salad (page 237)	Chocolate Gelato
		Sautéed Swiss Chard (page 253)	
Vegetarian Nachos	Whole Wheat Quesadillas with Chicken, Jalapeño Jack, and Mango Salsa (page 188)	Black Bean Salad with Lime-Cilantro Vinaigrette (page 243)	Apple Cinnamon Dessert Empanadas
Crab Cakes with Creole Honey-Mustard Sauce (page 113)	Duck, Shrimp, and Andouille Gumbo (page 198)	Cornbread	Berry Napoleon (page 290)
		Basic Rice Pilaf (page 263)	

COOKING, PRESENTING, AND SERVING WITH STYLE

Planning your menu around your main dish makes good sense. The ingredients you want to feature may suggest the cooking style you will use. The seasons can help determine what to serve before, alongside, and after the main course. Keep in mind not only the flavors of the foods in the main course, but also the textures, shapes, and colors you will have at your disposal. And finally, be sure to consider how your kitchen and serving options translate to a successful dinner party or celebration. You want to be a part of the event.

Cooking Style

The cooking technique you choose can have a definite impact on the overall success of your meal. Large roasts are great for holiday meals, since they cook untended while you finish up or reheat side dishes. Braises and stews can be made almost completely in advance, and they often improve in flavor and texture if they sit overnight. Poached foods may be kept warm without overcooking, giving you a little leeway in between courses or in case your guests are delayed. Composed dishes are a perfect way to make meatless dishes part of an entertaining menu, and since they are assembled then baked, they are great for do-ahead cooking.

ROASTING

Whether you are planning on a gorgeous glazed ham or an herb-crusted medallion of beef, roasted foods are a great choice for party menus. Large cuts of meat and whole birds generally produce enough rich, savory drippings for a pan sauce. Smaller pieces like chicken breasts or fish steaks develop a delicious outer layer. The key to success is choosing the foods, preparing them well by techniques such as adding seasonings or coatings, and cooking foods to the perfect point of doneness. Roasted and baked foods should come out of the oven at least 10 minutes before you want to serve them. If the roast

is quite large, for instance a whole turkey or a sirloin roast, it can rest for even longer. We've provided a roasting timetable (page 135) with doneness temperatures for various cuts of meat.

This resting period gives you a chance to finish the sauce, if you are making one. It also gives the meat enough time to settle so that they are easier to carve.

BRAISING AND STEWING

Braising and stewing are gentle, slow cooking methods that will transform large, tough cuts of meat such as shanks or short ribs into tender morsels in a rich, flavorful sauce. It is a perfect choice for entertaining, since you can make the dish well in advance. Letting it rest overnight in the refrigerator does something magical to the flavor and texture of braised dishes. It also means that there is virtually no work or mess on the day of your party.

The meat should be seasoned with any spice blends or marinades before searing.

The first step in most braises is to sear, or brown, the surface of the meat or poultry quickly in fat over high heat to develop flavor and a rich color.

Remove the seared meat from the pan and cook any accompanying vegetables to a deep golden brown. (Acidic ingredients, like tomatoes or wine, should be added last.)

Add enough broth to cover the browned vegetables by one-third to one-half. Bring the liquid to a simmer and add the meat back to the pan. Finish cooking the braise in a moderate oven.

Braised meat should slide easily from a kitchen fork and may be cut with the side of a fork.

Foods that are braised on the bone have a wonderful flavor and texture but may be a challenge for your guests to eat gracefully. To remove the bones from braised shanks, short ribs, or similar cuts, let them cool until they are easy to handle, and then simply pull out the bone or pull the meat in large pieces away from the bones. Transfer the boneless meat to a baking dish or casserole. Moisten with a little of the sauce, cover, and refrigerate the meat. Cool and store the sauce separately in a covered container. When ready to serve, reheat the sauce in a saucepan over medium-high heat and simmer for about 5 minutes. Taste the sauce and add seasonings like salt, pepper, fresh herbs, fortified wines, if you wish. Ladle enough sauce over the meat to coat it well, and then reheat the shanks in a 325°F oven until they are very hot, about 30 minutes.

When deep poaching fish, chicken, or meat, the liquid should be warm but not simmering when you lower the food into the pan.

POACHING AND SHALLOW POACHING

Poaching food by submerging it in liquid and cooking it at a constant, moderate temperature highlights the texture and flavor of naturally tender foods like fish, shellfish, or poultry breast meat. The great advantage of this cooking technique is that you can keep the food very warm right in the poaching liquid until you are ready to serve it, for up to 2 hours with the heat kept very low, or even turned off. There is no danger that the food will overcook, even if it has to stand while you tend to other duties or wait for your guests to arrive at the table. Poached foods can be served hot or cold, making them a versatile option no matter what the season.

There are two different poaching techniques: deep poaching and shallow poaching. Deep poaching is ideal for whole fish, seafood including lobster and shrimp, and other boneless skinless cuts of poultry. You can wrap whole fish in cheesecloth to help retain its shape during cooking, an especially nice touch for a buffet.

Shallow poaching combines the delicate heat of a deep poach with the speed of a sauté, plus the poaching

To ensure even cooking, the pan should not be overcrowded and the food should all be fully submerged in the liquid. Make sure the poaching liquid does not boil. Adjust the heat to maintain a temperature of 160 to 185°F; even a few degrees can make a difference in the final texture, so a thermometer is useful.

liquid may be used to create a flavorful pan sauce. You place the foods in a buttered pan, add a rich broth, wine, and aromatic ingredients like shallots or mushrooms. Top the pan with a loose "hat" of parchment paper and bring the liquid just up to a simmer, then put the pan into a preheated oven to finish cooking. The liquid in the pan makes a great broth to serve with the main item, or you can enrich the liquid with some cream or butter to make a sauce. This is an excellent method for cooking shellfish and smaller pieces of fish, and a great choice for entertaining. You can have the dish assembled in a baking dish or ovenproof skillet up to 4 hours before you plan to prepare it. Then it is ready to cook while you and your guests are enjoying your first course.

When shallow poaching, the liquid should never be higher than halfway up the food. If too much liquid is used, either a great deal of time will be needed to reduce it properly or only a part of it will be usable in the sauce.

It's best to finish poaching foods in the oven because oven heat is more even and gentle, so cover the fish with buttered parchment paper and put it into the oven.

Cook shallow poached foods until just done. Fish and shellfish should appear opaque and feel slightly firm, as seen here.

Presentation Style

Our dining room is small, so I try to plan a series of smaller dinner parties, rather than large get-togethers. This gives me the chance to experiment with different menus. Over the years, I've learned that I can only swing one course with last-minute finishing touches. Otherwise, I miss out on the conversation at the table. A main dish of a quickly cooked piece of fish with a simple sauce does require a bit of time in the kitchen, but meanwhile my husband clears the first course away and opens the wine for the main course. With a group of just six, I have enough room in the kitchen to make individual plates. And that keeps our tabletop from becoming jammed with bowls and platters!

The way you serve the meal has an impact on many aspects of the menu. Sit-down dinners can be served family style. Large cuts of meat to carve at the table are a nice touch and give the host a chance to show off his or her knife skills, but, if carving is not your strong suit, you can carve in the kitchen and serve on a platter. If you are preparing portion-size pieces of meat, fish, or poultry, you might opt to plate the food in the kitchen, as long as you have enough counter space to hold the plates and a willing helper to dish out the food and carry the plates to the table.

Take advantage of some restaurant techniques to make the most of your foods. Add some sheen by including a sauce. Introduce some contrasting colors and textures. Experiment with shapes by using molds to create a little height on the plate. If there is an herb in the dish, add a small sprig of the same herb to the plate for color and freshness.

Serving Style

Thanksgiving is my family's favorite holiday, so we love to bring lots of friends, family, and neighbors around the table. It takes some doing to get the tables all arranged and set. We like to bring everything to the table at once while Dad sharpens the carving set he inherited from his father. Then, we all sit down and enjoy the show while he asks each of us in turn which part of the bird we want.

Sometimes, a celebration meal involves some tried-and-true traditions. Family style is a perfect option when you have a lot of guests. You can fill the table with bowls and platters and condiments and relishes and let everyone pass the food around the table. Plated meals are a little more elegant, but demand space in the kitchen and some willing hands to carry the plates to the dining room. Buffet service is a bit like family service, with all the food laid out and ready to enjoy, but instead of passing food around the table, the guests carry a plate down the buffet line, helping themselves. Lap service can be the answer when you don't have enough space at your table. Guests serve themselves from a buffet and then find a comfortable seat. You can make this style of service easier on your guests if you choose foods that don't require a lot of cutting.

MEATS

Beef, pork, lamb, game, poultry, and seafood demand good technique from the cook. They also require a certain level of adaptability. As a host, the more you prepare meats, poultry, and seafood using your favorite techniques, the less wedded you are to recipes and the more you can open yourself up to opportunities for creativity.

Purchasing and Handling Meats

A fairly common menu-planning standard calls for 6 ounces of cooked meat per person. Since these foods tend to lose weight as they cook, you may want to buy about 8 ounces per person. On top of that, you should account for any bones or skin that you don't plan on serving to your guests. If you aren't sure about how much of a specific cut to buy, ask the butcher at your market. They will be able to help you find the right cut and the right size.

To start, cut several lengths of string; each piece should be long enough to wrap completely around the meat with sufficient additional length to knot it. Place the strings at even intervals along the length of the meat and tie each string with a series of double knots.

The medallions on the right are just cut, while the medallions on the left have been molded and are of a more uniform size and shape.

Once you've brought the meat home, you can extend the life of fresh meats by wrapping them in coated paper (either butcher's paper or freezer wrap) or plastic wrap. Properly wrapped and refrigerated meats, most meats will last for 3 to 5 days without a noticeable loss of quality.

TYING A ROAST

Tying a roast helps it hold its shape, cook more evenly, and holds in any stuffing during roasting. Take care to tie secure knots that have the right tension; tight enough to hold the meat in place, but not too tight.

TRIMMING MEATS AND REMOVING SILVERSKIN

Cutting away the fat and gristle on the exterior of a cut of meat before cooking is a good practice. This fat covering does not really "moisturize" the meat as it cooks, unlike the fat that is distributed throughout the meat itself. To cut away exterior fat, use a sharp knife and follow the meat's grain as much as possible. Angle the knife's blade slightly away from the meat as you cut to avoid cutting into the meat. Look for pockets of gristle and use the tip of your knife to cut them away, removing as little meat as possible. Some meats have a tough membrane known as "silverskin." If silverskin is left on the meat as it cooks, it tends to toughen and shrink. To remove silverskin, work the tip of a boning knife, sharp edge facing away from you, under the silverskin to loosen a flap. Grip the flap and hold it taut at a low angle over the meat. Glide the knife just underneath the membrane, using a smooth stroke and angling the blade away from the meat.

Shaping Medallions, Noisettes, and Mignons

Boneless cuts prepared from the tenderloin or loin may be referred to as medallions, noisettes, or mignons. After the cuts are portioned, you can be wrap them in cheesecloth as shown here, which gives the meat a more attractive appearance and also as helps the meat to cook more evenly. Place a meat on a piece of cheesecloth, gather the cheesecloth together and twist to tighten the cheesecloth around the piece of meat. As you twist the cloth with one hand, use the broad side of a chef's knife to press down on the top of the meat firmly, with even pressure.

MAKING A CROWN ROAST

A crown roast is an impressive way to present pork or lamb. You can order the pork or lamb from your butcher already made into a crown roast, but it is also easy to make it yourself. Two prepared sections of rib (known as "racks" for lamb) are tied together with butcher's twine to create a round shape that resembles a king's crown. Traditionally, the ends of the ribs are adorned with paper frills after cooking, although this is not essential.

You can stuff the open space in the crown roast with a ball of crumpled aluminum foil to retain the shape of the crown while the roast cooks. Fill the center of the roast with a selection of beautiful vegetables before you present the roast at the table. Carving is usually very simple. Just slice between the bones to separate the roast into single or double chops.

To help your crown roast keep the round shape, wrap the frenched racks around a ball of aluminum foil.

Use three lengths of string to firmly tie the racks around the foil.

Cut between the chops of the finished crown roast to create individual portions of the desired size.

Doneness Temperatures for Meat

TYPE OF MEAT	DESIRED DEGREE OF DONENESS	FINAL DONENESS TEMPERATURE (AFTER RESTING FOR LARGE CUTS)	VISUAL CUES
Beef, Lamb, or Veal	Rare	120–125°F	Interior is shiny
	Medium-rare	125–130°F	Deep red or deep pink
	Medium	130–135°F	Pink
	Well done	150°F (after resting for large cuts)	No traces of red or pink; moist but no juices
Pork	Fully cooked	145°F (after resting for large cuts)	Slight touch of pink at the bone (for bone-in cuts), juices
Poultry (includes whole birds, pieces, and ground poultry)	Fully cooked	165°F (after resting for whole birds)	Legs move easily in sockets, juices run clear with no trace of pink

BEEF

WHEN YOU ARE PLANNING YOUR MENU, you'll want to take the type of cut into account that you plan to prepare. Beef cuts from the rib, loin, and the top round include a variety of roasts and steaks in all different sizes. Because they are naturally tender, they match well with dry-heat cooking techniques like sautéing, roasting, grilling, and broiling.

Shoulder cuts (also known as the chuck or arm), as well as the bottom round, brisket, shank, and oxtail, are best for long, slow cooking methods like braising or stewing.

Flank, skirt, hanger, and tri-tip steaks (also known as butcher's cuts) have enough intramuscular fat to ensure that the meat stays tender even when grilled or roasted, as long as it's not overcooked.

Tenderloin of Beef with Blue Cheese and Herb Crust

Simple and elegant, this dish is a sure winner. Whether serving an intimate dinner for two or a number of guests, the delicious flavors of Madeira and blue cheese are a perfect choice with the beef tenderloin.

SERVES 6

Madeira Sauce

3 tbsp unsalted butter, softened

3 tbsp all-purpose flour

3 cups beef broth

6 tbsp Madeira

2¼ lb beef tenderloin

¼ cup fresh bread crumbs

6 tbsp crumbled blue cheese

¼ cup chopped flat-leaf parsley

¼ cup chopped chives

¼ tsp crushed black peppercorns

1 tbsp olive oil

1. Using a fork, blend the butter and flour together to make beurre manié. In medium saucepan, bring the broth and Madeira to a boil over medium-high heat. Add the beurre manié in small pieces, whisking until it is completely dissolved. Simmer over medium heat until the sauce is thickened and reduced by half, 15 to 20 minutes. This sauce can be cooled and stored in a covered container in the refrigerator for up to 3 days.

2. In a small bowl, combine the bread crumbs, blue cheese, parsley, chives, and peppercorns to form a paste. This mixture can be prepared in advance and stored in a covered container in the refrigerator for up to 3 days.

3. Slice the tenderloin into 6 portions, each about 3 inches in diameter and 1½ inches thick. Shape into neat rounds as described on page 133. Optional: Tie butcher's twine around the beef to maintain their shape while cooking, if desired.

4. Preheat the oven to 350°F. Spray the rack of a roasting pan with cooking spray and place in the pan.

5. Heat the oil in a skillet over high heat. Sear the medallions until just browned, 2 to 3 minutes on each side. Arrange the medallions on the rack in the roasting pan. Coat the top side of each medallion with 3 tablespoons of the blue cheese-and-herb paste.

6. Roast until the crust is golden brown and the meat is cooked as desired (see chart on page 135), about 6 to 8 minutes for medium-rare, depending on the thickness of the medallions. If butcher's twine was used, be sure to remove it.

7. Serve the medallions in a pool of the warm Madeira sauce.

Beef Tenderloin with Pizzaiola Sauce

Try this dish with pork cutlets or medallions, pork chops, or chicken breast instead of beef.

SERVES 8

Pizzaiola Sauce

1 cup dry white wine

4 tsp minced flat-leaf parsley

2 tsp chopped basil

2 tsp chopped oregano

1 dried bay leaf

1 peperoncini pepper, chopped

2 tbsp olive oil

1 small yellow onion, minced

2 garlic cloves, minced

1½ cups canned crushed tomatoes

8 beef tenderloin steaks (5–6 oz each)

Kosher salt and freshly ground black pepper, as needed

2 tbsp olive oil, plus more as needed

1½ cups sliced white, oyster, or porcini mushrooms (or a combination)

1. To make the sauce: Simmer the wine in a small saucepan over medium-high heat until reduced by half, 4 to 5 minutes. Remove from the heat and add the parsley, basil, oregano, bay leaf and pepperoncini. Set aside to steep for 30 minutes before preparing the rest of the sauce.

2. Heat the oil in a medium saucepan over medium-high heat. Add the onion and garlic and sauté, stirring often, until light golden, about 5 minutes. Add the crushed tomatoes and simmer for 5 minutes more.

3. Remove the bay leaf from the wine mixture and discard it. Add the wine mixture to the pan with the tomatoes and simmer for 5 minutes. Remove from the heat and set aside. The sauce is ready to finish with the mushrooms (step 6) or it may be cooled and stored in a covered container in the refrigerator for up to 3 days.

4. Blot the beef dry with paper towels and season with salt and pepper. Heat the oil in a heavy sauté pan over high heat. Add the beef and sauté to the desired doneness (see chart on page 135), 3 to 4 minutes per side for medium-rare. Transfer the steaks to a warmed platter and cover to keep warm while completing the sauce.

5. Return the sauté pan to medium-high heat and add enough oil to coat the bottom of the pan. Add the mushrooms and sauté until browned and any juices they have released cook away, about 4 minutes.

6. Add the pizzaiola sauce and any juices released by the steaks. Reduce the heat to medium and simmer until the sauce develops a good flavor and consistency, about 5 minutes. Taste and season with salt and pepper. Serve the steaks at once with the sauce.

PORK AND HAM

PORK HAS A NATURAL AFFINITY FOR BOLD FLAVORS including mustard, tarragon, and fresh herbs. The latest USDA standards for doneness mean that you can easily avoid serving pork that is dry. Most cuts of pork are naturally tender enough to prepare using dry-heat methods such as roasting or sautéing, but we also enjoy braises and stews made with pork, especially from the shoulder. Pork tenderloins are a classic choice for entertaining since they are easy to find, simple to prepare, and have a great flavor.

Mustard-Glazed Ham

If you think of baked ham only in terms of a shiny glazed roast with pineapple rings and maraschino cherries, this will be a revelation. The sauce has a delightful chunky texture. Its piquant flavors set off the smoky ham beautifully.

SERVES 10 TO 12

Spicy Mustard Glaze

1 tbsp olive oil

1 cup minced onion

1 tbsp minced garlic

½ cup white wine vinegar

⅓ cup spicy brown mustard

2 tbsp granulated sugar

½ tsp celery seed

Kosher salt and freshly ground pepper, as needed

1 shank end ham (about 7 lb)

1. Preheat the oven to 350°F. Spray the rack of a roasting pan with cooking spray and place in the pan.

2. To prepare the glaze: Heat the oil in a medium sauté pan over medium heat. Add the onion and garlic and cook, stirring from time to time, until the onion becomes soft and translucent, about 5 minutes.

3. Add the vinegar, mustard, sugar, and celery seed. Bring to a simmer over low heat, stirring to completely dissolve the sugar. Simmer until flavorful and very hot, about 3 minutes. Taste the glaze and season it with salt and pepper.

4. Score the ham with a wide crosshatch pattern, making incisions about ¼ inch deep. Place the ham on the rack in the roasting pan and spoon enough sauce over the ham to coat it evenly and lightly.

5. Bake the ham uncovered, spooning a little additional glaze over it every 10 to 15 minutes, until the ham is heated through and registers 140°F on an instant-read thermometer, about 1½ hours.

6. Remove the ham from the oven and allow it to rest for 5 to 10 minutes. Carve the ham into slices and serve with the remaining glaze as a sauce.

Pork Crown Roast with Rosemary Jus Lié

You can use this basic recipe to prepare a pork loin roast, either bone-in or boneless.

SERVES 8 TO 10

1 pork crown roast or 1 whole bone-in pork loin (about 9 lb)

4 tbsp olive oil

3 garlic cloves, minced fine

½ tsp rosemary

1 tsp thyme

Kosher salt and freshly ground pepper, as needed

½ cup coarsely chopped yellow onion

¼ cup sliced carrot

¼ cup sliced celery

2 cups chicken broth

1 dried bay leaf

½ cup dry white wine

Cornstarch slurry (optional): 2 tbsp cornstarch blended with 2 tbsp cold water or chicken broth

1. Preheat the oven to 325°F. Spray the rack of a roasting pan with cooking spray and place in the pan. If you are making the crown roast from a whole pork loin, trim the heavy layer of fat, scrape the meat from the bones, and bend into a round. Tie with butcher's twine to make a crown roast (see page 134).

2. In a small bowl, combine 2 tablespoons of the oil with the garlic, rosemary, and thyme. Season the roast with salt and pepper, and rub with the herb mixture.

3. Place the roast the rack in the roasting pan. Roast, basting with pan juices occasionally, until the meat registers 145°F on an instant-read thermometer, 2½ to 2¾ hours.

4. Meanwhile, heat the remaining 2 tbsp oil in a sauté pan over medium heat. Add the onion and sauté until golden brown, 5 to 6 minutes. Add the carrot and celery and cook until the celery becomes translucent, 3 to 4 minutes more. Add the chicken broth and bay leaf and simmer slowly over low heat until the broth is very flavorful and slightly reduced, 10 to 12 minutes.

5. When the roast is ready, transfer it to a platter, tent loosely with aluminum foil, and keep warm while finishing the sauce.

6. Add the wine to the roasting pan and stir to deglaze the pan, scraping up any browned bits from the bottom. Add this mixture to the simmering broth and return the broth to a simmer, skimming to remove excess fat and other impurities. If the sauce is not thick enough, add just enough of the cornstarch slurry while stirring to thicken the sauce slightly. Strain the sauce into a sauceboat. Carve the pork roast into slices and serve with the sauce.

Roasted Pork Tenderloin with Honey-Mustard Sauce

Delicate and lean, pork tenderloin is an excellent cut that can be roasted whole or sliced into medallions. This recipe will allow you to prepare the rest of the meal while the tenderloin is roasting in the oven.

SERVES 8

3 lb whole pork tenderloin

Kosher salt and freshly ground black pepper, as needed

2 tbsp olive oil

2 garlic cloves, minced

2 tbsp minced shallots

1 tbsp tomato paste

2 tbsp whole-grain mustard

2 tbsp honey

3 tbsp red wine vinegar

1½ tsp chopped thyme

½ tsp crushed black peppercorns

1⅓ cups vegetable or chicken broth

1. Preheat the oven to 425°F. Spray the rack of a roasting pan with cooking spray and place in the pan.

2. Remove any excess fat or silverskin from the tenderloins. Season with salt and pepper.

3. Heat the oil in a large sauté pan over medium-high heat. Cook the tenderloins in the hot oil, turning as necessary to color and stiffen the meat on all sides, about 5 minutes total.

4. Place the tenderloins on the rack in the roasting pan. Roast until an instant-read thermometer inserted in the center registers 145°F, 15 to 20 minutes. Remove the tenderloins from the oven and let rest for 5 to 10 minutes before slicing.

5. While the tenderloin is roasting, return the sauté pan to medium heat. Add the garlic and shallots and cook, stirring frequently, until fragrant, about 1 minute. Add the tomato paste and cook until slightly browned, about 1 minute. Add the mustard, honey, vinegar, thyme, peppercorns, and broth. Bring the sauce to a boil, then reduce the heat to low and simmer until lightly thickened, about 5 minutes.

6. Pour the pan juices from the roasting pan into the honey-mustard sauce and return to a simmer. Use a serving spoon to skim any fat from the sauce, if necessary. Taste the sauce and season with salt and pepper. Carve the tenderloins into slices and serve with the warm honey-mustard sauce.

LAMB

LAMB IS A CLASSIC CHOICE FOR ENTERTAINING, whether you choose to prepare a roast leg of lamb, a crown roast, or succulent braised shanks. Lamb, like beef, can be prepared to a range of doneness. It all depends upon your preference. Lamb pairs well with bold flavors and makes a good match with a wide array of sides. Although lamb is traditionally thought of as a springtime food, you can find good-quality domestic and imported lamb throughout the year.

Mustard and Tarragon Roast Leg of Lamb

This recipe can also be used to prepare a leg of venison. If you prefer using a boneless lamb roast, the cut will weigh about 5 pounds, instead of 7. Reduce the cooking time to about 1½ hours total roasting time.

SERVES 8

1 semiboneless leg of lamb, trimmed (about 7 lb)

½ cup dry white wine

3 tbsp Dijon mustard

6 garlic cloves, minced

2 tbsp minced fresh tarragon or 1 tsp dried

Kosher salt and freshly ground black pepper, as needed

1 small yellow onion, minced

¾ cup diced tomatoes, with their juices

1 cup chicken or beef broth

1. Cut small slits in the fat covering the leg. In a small bowl, combine 2 tablespoons of the wine, the mustard, garlic, tarragon, salt, and pepper and rub the mixture evenly over the lamb. Cover loosely with aluminum foil and let it marinate at least 30 minutes at room temperature or up to 4 hours in the refrigerator.

2. Preheat the oven to 400°F. Spray the rack of a roasting pan with cooking spray and place in the roasting pan.

3. Place the lamb on the rack in the roasting pan and roast until the exterior is colored, about 20 minutes. Reduce the heat to 325°F and continue to roast to the desired doneness (see the chart on page 135), another 1½ to 1¾ hours for medium, or until an instant-read thermometer inserted in the center registers 135°F.

4. Transfer the lamb to a platter, cover loosely with aluminum foil, and let it rest for 10 to 15 minutes before carving.

5. While the lamb is resting, pour off or spoon off the fat that has accumulated in the roasting pan, leaving behind as many of the juices from the roast as possible. Heat the roasting pan on the stovetop over high heat.

6. Add the onion and tomatoes and cook, stirring constantly, until the onion turns golden brown, about 10 minutes. Add the remaining wine and cook, scraping up the browned bits from the bottom of the pan, until the wine has cooked away, about 4 minutes. Add the broth and bring the sauce to a boil. Reduce the heat and simmer until the sauce is reduced and flavorful, about 15 minutes.

7. Carve the lamb (see sidebar below). Serve the sauce on the side or spoon it over the slices as you carve.

NOTE *You can roast the lamb up to 1 hour before you plan to serve it. Remove it from the oven when it reaches about 10 degrees below the doneness you like and hold it, loosely tented with foil, in a warm spot in the kitchen. Carve the leg right before serving.*

CARVING A LEG OF LAMB

All roasts need a resting period before they are carved, and lamb is no exception. Note that the same basic steps used to carve a leg of lamb apply to a ham or venison leg.

Before you start carving, cut a small piece from one side of the leg to create a flat surface that rests on the platter or carving board.

Hold the shank bone firmly in one hand with a clean cloth or napkin. Cut out a narrow wedge of meat down to the bone, near the shank end, to give yourself room for carving slices. Leave a 1- to 2-inch-thick piece of meat intact at the shank bone to shield your hand as you hold the leg. Begin carving large, even slices, usually about ¼ inch thick, by making parallel cuts from the shank end down to the bone. Always cut against the grain of the meat, to keep the slices as tender as possible. As you carve each slice, make the cut almost perpendicular to the bone, then turn the knife parallel to the bone to free the slice. When the slices become very large, begin to cut the meat at a slight angle, first from the left side, then from the right side, alternating until the leg is entirely carved. If you begin to see long fibers in the slices, reposition the knife to cut at a sharper angle or at another side of the leg.

Crown Roast of Lamb Persillade

The persillade topping featured in this recipe can be used to top salmon, catfish, or chicken breasts. It can be prepared in advance and held for up to 3 days.

SERVES 8

Persillade

1 cup fresh white bread crumbs

2 tbsp unsalted butter, melted

1 tbsp chopped flat-leaf parsley

2 garlic cloves, crushed and minced fine

Kosher salt and freshly ground black pepper, as needed

2 lamb racks (about 2 lb), trimmed

1 tsp chopped rosemary

1 tsp chopped thyme

Olive oil, as needed

1 small yellow onion, diced

1 celery stalk, diced

1 small carrot, diced

1 cup beef broth

Cornstarch slurry (optional): 1 tbsp cornstarch blended with 1 tbsp cold water or broth

1. Preheat the oven to 400°F. Spray the rack of a roasting pan with cooking spray and place in the pan.

2. To make the persillade: In a medium bowl, mix together the bread crumbs, butter, parsley, garlic, and salt and pepper, as needed to make an evenly moistened mixture. Set aside.

3. Season the lamb with salt and pepper and rub with the rosemary, thyme, and oil. Place the lamb on the rack in the roasting pan. Roast for 15 minutes, basting occasionally . Scatter the onion, celery, and carrot around the lamb in the roasting pan. Reduce the oven temperature to 325°F and continue to roast until an instant-read thermometer inserted in the center of the meat registers 140°F for medium-rare, 15 to 20 minutes more.

4. Transfer the lamb to a platter, cover loosely with aluminum foil, and set aside. The lamb may be roasted up to 1 hour in advance and held at room temperature, loosely covered with foil.

5. To make a pan sauce: Place the roasting pan on the stovetop over medium-high heat and cook until the vegetables are browned and the fat is clear, about 5 minutes. Pour off or spoon away any fat.

6. Add the broth and stir to deglaze the pan, scraping up any browned bits from the bottom. Simmer until flavorful and lightly thickened, about 20 minutes. Add any juices released by the roast as it rests. If needed, add just enough of the cornstarch slurry while stirring to thicken the sauce slightly. Strain through a fine-mesh sieve, if desired. The sauce can be prepared up to 1 hour in advance.

7. Increase the oven temperature to 425°F. Transfer the lamb to a baking sheet. Carefully pack the persillade on the top of the lamb rack. Return the lamb to the oven and roast until the bread crumbs are lightly browned, about 10 minutes.

8. Let rest for 8 to 10 minutes, then cut the rack into chops. Return the pan sauce to a simmer and taste and season with salt and pepper. Serve with the lamb chops.

Braised Lamb Shanks

We like to pair the mellow flavor of roasted garlic with lamb in this dish. To roast garlic, simply rub a whole head of garlic with a little oil, place in a small baking dish, and roast at 350°F until the juices turn brown and the garlic feels soft.

SERVES 10

Sachet d'Épices

3 or 4 parsley stems

1 sprig thyme or 1 tsp dried thyme

1 dried bay leaf

1 tsp cracked black peppercorns

1 garlic clove (optional)

10 lamb shanks (about 1 lb each)

1 tbsp kosher salt

1½ tsp freshly ground black pepper

¼ cup olive oil

1 medium yellow onion, cut into large dice

1 carrot, cut into large dice

1 celery stalk, cut into large dice

1 garlic head, roasted

2 tbsp tomato paste

½ cup all-purpose flour

2 cups dry red wine

8 cups beef broth

1. First make the sachet d'épices: Cut a square piece of cheesecloth, place the ingredients in the center of the square, and gather the edges to make a bag. Tie the sachet closed with a piece of butcher's twine.

2. Preheat the oven to 350°F. Season the shanks with salt and pepper. Heat the oil in a Dutch oven or flame-proof casserole over medium-high heat until it starts to shimmer. Place the shanks carefully in the oil and sear, turning the meat from time to time, until deep brown on all sides. Transfer the shanks to a platter or baking dish, cover loosely with aluminum foil, and set aside.

3. Add the onion to the pan and cook, stirring from time to time, until golden brown, about 6 minutes. Add the carrot and celery and cook until barely translucent, 4 minutes more.

4. Cut the head of roasted garlic in half, squeeze out the pulp, and add it to the vegetables along with the tomato paste. Cook, stirring frequently, until the tomato paste turns a deeper color and gives off a sweet aroma, about 1 minute. Stir in the flour and cook for 4 to 5 minutes.

5. Add the wine, stirring well. Whisk in the broth and bring to a simmer. Return the shanks to the pan along with any juices they may have released.

6. Bring to a gentle simmer over medium-low heat. Cover the pan, transfer it to the oven, and braise the lamb shanks for 45 minutes. Turn the shanks as they braise to keep them evenly moistened.

7. Add the sachet and spoon off any grease from the surface of the liquid, if necessary. Finish braising the lamb until fork-tender, about 45 minutes more. The lamb is ready to finish now, or it may be cooled in the braising liquid and stored in a covered container in the refrigerator for up to 3 days.

8. Transfer the shanks to a platter or a baking dish and moisten with some of the cooking liquid. Cover and set aside while finishing the sauce.

9. Continue to simmer the cooking liquid over medium heat until it has a good flavor and is slightly thickened, about 10 minutes. Skim thoroughly to degrease the sauce. Adjust the seasoning with salt and pepper and strain the braising liquid.

10. Pour some of the sauce over the shanks and warm them in a 300°F, if necessary. Serve the shanks immediately with the sauce.

POULTRY

POULTRY'S VERSATILITY IS ITS GREATEST ASSET. Reliable, familiar, and inexpensive, it is a great vehicle for mastering every basic cooking method, from broiling to braising. And poultry doesn't have to just mean chicken. Turkey, goose, duck, and even game birds are no longer just a treat for the winter holiday season. They are now available year-round in many supermarkets.

Whenever you buy poultry, take the time to read the label or talk to the butcher. "Fresh" means that the bird was never chilled below 26°F. Many cooks prefer organic or free-range poultry for a variety of reasons, including health, nutritional value, and perhaps most importantly, flavor. Birds bearing the organic symbol or the word "organic" are raised using organic management techniques and are certified by an entity such as the National Organic Program (NOP), which has a system for ensuring that those standards are met.

Doneness Temperatures for Poultry

	INTERNAL TEMPERATURE	VISUAL CLUES
Whole birds	165°F in the thigh	Legs will move easily in sockets. When the thigh is pierced, juices will run clear. Juices in a bird's cavity will no longer have a pink hue.
Breasts	165°F	Meat becomes opaque and firm throughout.
Legs, thighs, and wings	165°F	Meat releases easily from the bone.
Stuffing	165°F	Check the temperature of stuffing cooked inside a whole bird.

Walnut Chicken

Here, chicken is cooked along with a pilaf of bulgur and walnuts. Bulgur wheat—wheat kernels that have been steamed, dried, and crushed—is available in most supermarkets.

SERVES 8

2 tsp olive oil

3 lb boneless, skinless chicken breasts, cut into 1- to 2-inch chunks

Kosher salt and freshly ground black pepper, as needed

2 small yellow onions, chopped

4 carrots, chopped

1 tsp cumin seeds

1 tsp caraway seeds

2 cups chicken broth

2 tbsp chopped walnuts

½ cup golden raisins

1½ cups bulgur wheat

½ tsp ground cinnamon

1. Heat 1 teaspoon of the oil in a large skillet over medium-high heat. Season the chicken chunks with salt and pepper. Sauté the chicken until browned, about 5 minutes. Transfer to a plate and reserve.

2. Add the remaining 1 teaspoon oil to the skillet. Add the onions, carrots, cumin, and caraway. Sauté until the onions are translucent and the carrots are tender, 3 to 5 minutes.

3. Add the chicken broth, scraping any brown bits from the bottom of the skillet. Add the walnuts, raisins, and bulgur wheat. Bring to a boil, then lower the heat to medium-low.

4. Add the cinnamon, ½ teaspoon salt, and ¼ teaspoon pepper. Cover and cook for 10 minutes. Add the reserved chicken chunks and cook for 5 minutes more. Adjust the seasoning with salt and pepper, if necessary. This dish is ready to serve now, or it may be kept warm for up to 1 hour in a 180°F oven.

Pesto-Stuffed Chicken Breasts with Tomato Relish

Pesto, traditionally made from garlic, oil, pine nuts, basil, and Parmesan cheese, adds an exciting twist to simple boneless, skinless chicken breasts . Complement these flavors with a touch of tomato relish and you have a winner.

SERVES 6

Tomato Relish

4 plum tomatoes, seeded and chopped

1 tbsp extra-virgin olive oil

2 tsp balsamic vinegar

Kosher salt and freshly ground black pepper, as needed

Pesto

3 garlic cloves, peeled

2 packed cups basil

Zest and juice of 1 lemon

5 tbsp pine nuts, toasted

⅔ cup grated Parmesan

Kosher salt and freshly ground black pepper, as needed

¼ cup extra-virgin olive oil

2¼ lb boneless, skinless chicken breast

Kosher salt and freshly ground black pepper, as needed

2 tbsp olive oil

1. To make the relish: In a small bowl, combine the tomatoes, oil, vinegar, ¼ tsp salt, and pepper. This relish can be made in advance and stored at room temperature for up to 1 hour or in a covered container in the refrigerator for up to 2 days.

2. Preheat the oven to 400°F. Spray a shallow baking dish with cooking spray.

3. To make the pesto: Combine the garlic, basil, lemon juice and zest, pine nuts, cheese, salt, and pepper in a food processor. Pulse until finely chopped. Add the oil in a thin stream until fully incorporated and a thick paste forms. The pesto can be made in advance and stored at room temperature for up to 1 hour or in a covered container in the refrigerator for up to 2 days. Add a little additional olive oil on top of the pesto to keep it from losing its green color.

4. Place the chicken breasts, skinned side down, between 2 sheets of waxed paper. Pound the breasts with a meat mallet until they are reduced to ¼-inch thickness. Remove and discard the top sheet of waxed paper. The chicken is ready to stuff and cook now, or it can be stored in a covered container in the refrigerator for up to 24 hours.

5. Spread each chicken breast with about 2 tablespoons of the pesto mixture. Starting with the narrower end, roll each breast around the filling; discard the remaining sheet of waxed paper.

6. Tie each rolled breast with butcher's twine (see page 133) or secure with toothpicks to prevent it from unrolling. Season with salt and pepper.

7. Heat the oil in a large sauté pan over medium-high heat. Sauté the chicken breasts, turning from time to time, until golden brown on all sides, 8 to 10 minutes total. Place the chicken breasts in the oven and roast until cooked through, 10 to 15 minutes.

8. Remove the chicken from the oven and let stand 5 minutes. Remove and discard the twine or toothpicks, and slice each chicken breast on the diagonal into 4 pieces. Arrange the slices on 6 individual warmed plates, and garnish with some of the tomato relish. Serve immediately.

CARVING A TURKEY

After roasting a turkey and letting it rest, transfer the bird to a carving board, preferably a cutting board with an indentation around the edges that captures the juices released during carving. If you're carving the turkey at the table, you can carve on a serving platter, but make sure the platter's edges are not so high as to obstruct the blade of your knife. Have a separate platter or stack of plates ready for the meat as you carve. A carving fork will help you steady the bird as you cut. Cut away the trussing string before you begin carving.

A standard carving set, left to right: carving knife, honing steel, and carving fork.

First, make a cut between the leg and the breast, and remove the leg.

Make a cut down the keel bone that runs lengthwise down the center of the turkey.

Working perpendicular to the table, carve down the breast meat to make slices.

Using the carving fork to stabilize the slices against the knife, serve each guest a portion of turkey.

Classic Roast Turkey with Pan Gravy

This same recipe is a good blueprint for roasting any whole bird.

SERVES 10

1 turkey (about 15 lb)

1 apple, quartered and cored

1 dried bay leaf

1 large sprig thyme

½ bunch flat-leaf parsley

1 to 2 tbsp fresh lemon juice

Kosher salt and freshly ground black pepper, as needed

¾ cup diced yellow onion

½ cup diced carrot

½ cup diced celery

5 cups chicken broth

Cornstarch slurry: ⅓ cup cornstarch blended with ⅓ cup cold water or chicken broth

1. Preheat the oven to 450°F. Spray the rack of a roasting pan with cooking spray and place in the pan.

2. Stuff the turkey with the apple, bay leaf, thyme, and parsley. Rub the lemon juice over the entire bird and season with salt and pepper. Place the turkey, breast side up, on the rack in the roasting pan, transfer to the oven, and immediately reduce the oven temperature to 350°F. Roast for 3 hours, basting occasionally with accumulated pan drippings.

3. Remove the turkey from the oven and transfer it on its rack to a baking sheet. Skim the fat away from the pan drippings with a spoon.

4. Return the turkey and any juices that have accumulated on the baking sheet to the roasting pan and return to the oven. Roast until an instant-read thermometer inserted in the thickest part of the turkey's thigh registers 165°F, 30 to 60 minutes more. Remove the turkey and the rack from the roasting pan, cover the bird, and let rest for at least 30 minutes before carving.

5. While the turkey is resting, in a medium saucepan, combine the pan drippings, onion, carrot, and celery. Add ½ cup of the broth to the roasting pan and stir to deglaze the pan, scraping up any browned bits from the pan bottom. Add this to the saucepan along with the remaining broth.

6. Simmer over medium heat until slightly reduced and flavorful, skimming away any fat that rises to the surface, 20 to 25 minutes. Gradually add enough of the cornstarch slurry to the simmering broth, whisking constantly, until the gravy has thickened. Simmer 2 minutes more, strain, taste, and season with salt and pepper.

7. Remove and discard the apple, bay leaf, thyme, and parsley from the turkey cavity. Carve the turkey and serve immediately with the gravy.

Mole Poblano de Pollo

There are hundreds of traditional mole sauces featured in Mexican cuisine. This version is relatively simple to prepare and holds well in the refrigerator.

SERVES 8

Mole Sauce

2 tbsp olive oil

1 medium yellow onion, finely diced

2 green bell peppers, finely diced

2 jalapeños, finely chopped

½ cup blanched almonds, chopped

5 garlic cloves, crushed

3 tbsp chili powder

2 tsp grated ginger

1 tsp minced thyme

½ tsp aniseed

½ tsp ground cinnamon

5 plum tomatoes, peeled, seeded, and chopped

2 cups chicken broth, plus more as needed

¼ cup almond or peanut butter

2 tbsp olive oil

8 bone-in chicken breast halves

2 oz Mexican chocolate, chopped

Kosher salt and freshly ground black pepper, as needed

1. To prepare the mole sauce: Heat the olive oil in a heavy-gauge saucepan over medium heat. Add the onion and cook, stirring frequently, until light brown, 10 to 12 minutes. Add the bell pepper, jalapeño, almonds, and garlic to the pan and sauté until aromatic, 3 to 4 minutes.

2. Add the chili powder, ginger, thyme, aniseed, and cinnamon and sauté briefly until aromatic, being careful not to burn the mixture, about 30 seconds. Add the tomatoes. Pour in the broth and stir to deglaze the pan, scraping up any browned bits from the bottom of the pan. Whisk in the almond butter. The sauce is ready to use now, or it may be cooled and stored in a covered container in the refrigerator for up to 6 days.

3. Preheat the oven to 350°F. Heat the oil in a large Dutch oven over medium-high heat. Sear the chicken until browned on all sides, about 8 minutes total.

4. Add the mole sauce to the pan and bring to a bare simmer over low heat. Cover the pan and transfer to the oven. Braise the chicken until tender, about 1 hour. Throughout the cooking time, add a little more broth, as needed, to keep the liquid level constant.

5. Remove the chicken from the pot and cover to keep warm. Add the chocolate to the pan with the cooking sauce and stir until melted. Taste and season with salt and pepper.

6. Return the chicken to the sauce and turn to coat evenly. Bring the mixture to a simmer over medium heat and heat the chicken through. Serve at once.

Chicken Tagine with Preserved Lemons

Preserved lemons are easy to make yourself, however, they do need to be started at least one week before you plan to use them. You can find preserved lemons already prepared in markets that specialize in Middle Eastern foods.

SERVES 8

3 broiler or fryer chickens, each cut into 6 pieces

Kosher salt and freshly ground black pepper, as needed

¼ cup extra-virgin olive oil

30 cipollini onions, blanched and peeled

One ½-inch-long piece ginger, thinly sliced

5 garlic cloves, thinly sliced

1 tsp cumin seeds, toasted and ground

¼ tsp saffron threads

1¼ cups chicken broth or water, plus more as needed

¾ cup Picholine olives, pitted

2 preserved lemons (recipe follows, or use purchased)

¼ cup chopped flat-leaf parsley

1. Season the chicken pieces with salt and pepper. Heat the oil over medium-high heat in a tagine or cast-iron Dutch oven. Place the chicken pieces carefully in the oil and sauté until they turn golden brown, about 8 minutes. Transfer the chicken to a plate and reserve.

2. Add the onions to the tagine or Dutch oven and cook, stirring from time to time, until golden brown, 7 to 8 minutes. Add the ginger and garlic and cook until aromatic, 1 minute more. Add the cumin and saffron and cook until the mixture turns a deep golden color and gives off a sweet aroma, about 1 minute.

3. Return the chicken to the tagine or Dutch oven and add the broth or water. Bring to a gentle simmer over medium-low heat. Cover and braise until the chicken is cooked through, turning the pieces occasionally to keep them evenly moistened, 30 to 40 minutes. Add more broth or water, if necessary, but maintain only a small amount of liquid in the pot so the braising liquid will become concentrated.

4. During the last 15 minutes of cooking, add the olives, lemons, and parsley. Simmer the mixture until the olives are tender and the aroma of the lemons is apparent. Remove the lemons and serve the tagine immediately, or the tagine can be kept warm in a 180°F oven for up to 1½ hours.

Preserved Lemons

MAKES 6 LEMONS

6 lemons

¾ cup kosher salt

1¼ cups fresh lemon juice, or as needed

1. Wash the lemons very well. Cut each one into 6 wedges lengthwise and remove all the seeds. Place the lemon wedges in a very clean jar. Add the salt and enough of the lemon juice to just cover the lemons.

2. Cover the jar with a lid and refrigerate. Stir the lemons every day or two to help dissolve the salt. Allow the lemons to cure for at least 1 week. Rinse under cold water before using, as needed. Any lemons you do not use for the tagine can be stored in the refrigerator for up to 1 month.

Sautéed Duck Breast with Pinot Noir Sauce

Duck can be cooked rare, medium-rare, or well done, depending upon how you like it. If you want to make the presentation a bit more elegant, you can slice the breasts and shingle or fan them on the plate.

SERVES 6

One 750-ml bottle pinot noir

6 cups chicken broth

2 tbsp olive oil

1 medium yellow onion, diced

4 celery stalks, diced

2 carrots, diced

1 garlic clove, crushed

4 flat-leaf parsley stems

6 black peppercorns

¼ tsp dried thyme

1 dried bay leaf

3 tbsp tomato paste

½ tsp olive oil

Kosher salt and freshly ground black pepper, as needed

2¼ lb boneless, skin-on duck breasts, trimmed of excess fat

3 tbsp unsalted butter

1. In two medium saucepans, bring the wine and broth to a boil separately and reduce each by about one-third, about 10 minutes.

2. While the liquids are reducing, heat the oil in a large sauté pan over medium-high heat. Add the onion and cook until slightly translucent, about 5 minutes. Add the celery and carrots and sauté until lightly browned, about 10 minutes. Meanwhile, put the garlic, parsley stems, peppercorns, thyme, and bay leaf in a cheese-cloth pouch to make a sachet.

3. Add the tomato paste to the vegetables and cook to a deep red-brown color, stirring constantly, about 5 minutes. Deglaze the pan with the reduced wine, scraping up any browned bits from the bottom, and simmer until reduced by half, about 5 minutes. Add the reduced broth and the sachet and simmer until the sauce lightly coats the back of a spoon, 15 to 20 minutes. Remove and discard the sachet. The sauce may be prepared in advance to this point and stored in a covered container in the refrigerator for up to 5 days.

4. Preheat the oven to 400°F. Coat a roasting rack with cooking spray and place in a roasting pan. In a large sauté pan, heat the olive oil over medium heat. Season the duck with salt and pepper. Sauté the duck breasts, skin side down, until the fat has rendered and the skin is dark golden brown, 8 to 10 minutes.

5. Transfer the duck breasts, skin side up, to the rack in the roasting pan. Roast until cooked to the desired doneness, 5 to 6 minutes for medium-rare (125°F on an instant-read thermometer). Keep the duck hot until ready to serve.

6. Just before serving, return the sauce to a simmer, season with salt and pepper, and swirl in the butter. Serve the duck breasts immediately with the sauce.

SEAFOOD

FISH AND SEAFOOD ARE A GREAT CHOICE when entertaining. Fillets cut to portion size make it simple to buy the right amount. Look for fillets that appear moist and meaty. Ask your fishmonger for guidance if you want to substitute a regional or seasonal fish for the ones we suggest here. Seafood is quick-cooking but elegant. Dishes like Paella (page 160) or Cioppino (page 162) are a great choice when you are cooking for a crowd.

Sole Vin Blanc

To make preparing this dish more streamlined, you can butter the pan and add the shallots and fish paupiettes, then cover and refrigerate for up to 6 hours.

SERVES 4

¼ cup (½ stick) unsalted butter, softened, plus more as needed for coating the pan

1 tbsp minced shallot

4 sole fillets (about 6 oz each)

Kosher salt and freshly ground black pepper, as needed

½ cup dry white wine

¼ cup fish or chicken broth

1 tbsp fresh lemon juice

½ cup heavy cream

Tarragon sprigs for garnish (optional)

1. Preheat the oven to 300°F. Generously coat a baking dish with butter and sprinkle with the minced shallot. Cut a piece of parchment paper the same dimension as the baking dish.

2. Season the sole with salt and pepper. Roll the sole into a corkscrew shape, known in French as a paupiette. Place the sole paupiettes in the prepared dish, seam side down. At this point, you can cover the fish and keep refrigerated for up to 6 hours.

3. Combine the wine, broth, and lemon juice in a saucepan and bring to a simmer over medium heat. Pour over the fish, cover with the parchment paper, and transfer to the oven. Poach until the fish is firm and opaque, 15 to 16 minutes. Transfer the sole from the pan to warmed plates and cover to keep warm while completing the sauce.

4. To make the vin blanc sauce: Bring the poaching liquid to a boil in a saucepan over high heat and reduce by half, about 3 minutes. Add the cream and continue to reduce to a saucelike consistency. Whisk in the butter until melted. Season with salt and pepper. Serve the paupiettes on warmed plates or a platter with the hot sauce poured over the fish. If desired, garnish with tarragon sprigs.

Poached Salmon with Hollandaise Sauce

Use a wide, shallow pan to poach the salmon, or use a skillet with sides high enough to keep the salmon completely submerged as it cooks. To keep the salmon moist and to prevent it from separating as it cooks, keep the court bouillon at a bare simmer. You should see tiny bubbles forming around the sides of the pan, but no big bubbles breaking on the surface. Cold poached salmon is also delicious presentation option, served with a flavored mayonnaise.

SERVES 8

Court bouillon

2 qt cold water

1½ cups white wine vinegar

1 medium onion, thinly sliced

1 carrot, thinly sliced

1 celery stalk, thinly sliced

6 parsley stems

1 sprig thyme

1 dried bay leaf

1 tsp kosher salt

¼ tsp black peppercorns

8 pieces salmon fillet (about 6 oz each)

¼ tsp freshly ground black pepper, or as needed

2 cups Hollandaise Sauce (recipe follows)

1. To make a court bouillon for poaching the salmon: In a large pot, combine the water, the vinegar, onion, carrot, celery, parsley stems, thyme, bay leaf, 1 teaspoon of the salt, and the peppercorns. Bring to a simmer over high heat. Reduce the heat to medium and simmer until flavorful, about 20 minutes. Strain. The court bouillon is ready to use now or it may be cooled and stored in a covered container in the refrigerator for up to 3 days.

2. Season the salmon with the remaining salt and the pepper. Place the strained court bouillon in a wide saucepan or deep skillet and bring to a bare simmer. Add the salmon pieces using a slotted spoon or a poaching rack. Poach until the salmon is cooked through but still very moist, 8 to 10 minutes.

3. Lift the salmon from the court bouillon carefully and let drain briefly. Serve on warmed plates with the warm Hollandaise sauce.

Hollandaise Sauce

You can use either fresh or pasteurized eggs to make this classic sauce. If you need to make the sauce ahead of time, hold it in a Thermos for up to 3 hours

MAKES 2 CUPS SAUCE; SERVES 8

½ tsp cracked black peppercorns

¼ cup white wine or apple cider vinegar

4 large egg yolks, fresh or pasteurized

1½ cups (3 sticks) melted unsalted or clarified butter, warmed

2 tsp fresh lemon juice, or as needed

2 tsp kosher salt, or as needed

Pinch of ground white pepper

Pinch of cayenne pepper (optional)

1. In a small pan, combine the peppercorns and vinegar and reduce over medium heat until the peppercorns are nearly dry, about 5 minutes. Add ¼ cup water to the vinegar reduction and strain this liquid into a bowl.

2. Add the egg yolks to the reduction and set the bowl over a pot of simmering water. Whisking constantly, cook the mixture until the yolks triple in volume and fall in ribbons from the whisk, about 3 minutes. Remove the bowl from the simmering water and set it on a kitchen towel to keep the bowl stationary.

3. Gradually ladle the warm butter into the egg mixture, whisking constantly. As the butter is blended into the yolks, the sauce will thicken. If it becomes too thick and the butter is not blending in easily, add a little water or lemon juice to thin the egg mixture enough to be able to whisk in the remaining butter. Season the hollandaise with the lemon juice, salt, pepper, and cayenne, if desired.

Seared Salmon with a Moroccan Spice Crust

The impact of this bold spice mixture is a fantastic match for salmon, which has its own rich flavor. Easy to prepare, the spices are pressed onto the salmon steaks as a coating before they are seared in a very hot pan. The salmon should be cooked through without overcooking so that the texture is still tender inside and the spicy exterior is browned from the searing.

SERVES 8

Moroccan Spice Crust

1½ tsp curry powder

1½ tsp coriander seeds

1½ tsp cumin seeds

1½ tsp caraway seeds

1½ tsp aniseed

1½ tsp black peppercorns

8 salmon steaks (about 6 oz each)

1 tsp kosher salt, or as needed

½ tsp freshly ground black pepper, or as needed

¼ cup olive oil

1. In a small bowl, combine the curry powder, coriander, cumin, caraway, aniseed, and peppercorns. Coarsely grind the mixture in a spice grinder or mortar and pestle. This spice mixture can be stored in a tightly covered container at room temperature for up to 1 week.

2. Season the steaks generously with salt and pepper, then rub both sides of each salmon piece with a generous amount of the spice mixture.

3. Heat about 2 tablespoons of the olive oil in a skillet over medium-high heat. The oil should get very hot and should shimmer but not smoke. Add half the salmon and cook, turning once, until the fish is browned on the outside and opaque in the center, about 4 minutes per side. Transfer to a warmed platter and cover. Add the remaining olive oil to the skillet and cook the second batch of the salmon. Serve the fish at once.

Red Snapper en Papillote

You can replace the parchment paper with aluminum foil, although you will lose the dramatic "puff" that happens with paper. We've included some finely cut vegetables to add the moisture that turns into steam, as well as adding flavor, color, and texture to the finished dish.

SERVES 4

3 tbsp unsalted butter, softened, plus more for buttering baking sheet

2 tbsp minced shallot

2 cups asparagus tips

1 cup sliced white mushrooms

1 cup thinly sliced green onions, white and green parts

¾ cup heavy cream

½ cup dry white wine

Kosher salt and freshly ground pepper, as needed

4 skinless red snapper fillets (about 6 oz each)

1. Melt 2 tablespoons of the butter in a sauté pan over high heat. Sauté the shallot until translucent, about 2 minutes. Add the asparagus, mushrooms, and green onions. Continue to sauté until the asparagus turns bright green, about 1 minute more.

2. Add the cream and wine, and simmer until the asparagus is barely tender and the cream is reduced enough to coat the vegetables well, about 6 minutes. Taste and season with salt and pepper. The vegetable-and-cream mixture can be prepared up to 2 days in advance and stored in a covered container in the refrigerator.

3. Cut 4 pieces of parchment paper into heart shapes large enough to fit a fillet comfortably on one side with at least a 2-inch margin around the edges. Fold the hearts in half lengthwise to crease the paper. Use about 1 tablespoon of the butter to coat both sides of each parchment paper heart.

4. Season the fish with salt and pepper. Place ½ cup of the vegetable mixture on one side of each buttered parchment paper heart. Top each mound of vegetable mixture with a snapper fillet. Fold each paper heart in half over the food and align the edges. Starting at the top of the heart, make small, tight folds all along the edge of the paper; when you come to the bottom of the heart, give it a good twist to seal the packet. This will prevent steam from escaping. The packets can be assembled and then held in the refrigerator for up to 4 hours.

5. Preheat the oven to 375°F. Butter a baking sheet and preheat it by putting it in the oven for 5 minutes. Transfer the packets to the hot baking sheet. Bake until the parchment paper puffs up high and become brown, about 10 minutes. Serve immediately. For a dramatic presentation, carefully cut the packages open with scissors or a sharp paring knife at the table.

COOKING FISH EN PAPILLOTE

Cooking *en papillote*, which literally means "in paper," is a variation on steaming in which the fish and accompanying ingredients are wrapped in a parchment paper package and cooked in the oven in the steam produced by their own juices. The fish is then served to the guest still inside the package for a dramatic presentation.

To cook fish en papillote, cut a piece of parchment paper into a heart shape large enough to hold the food on one half, with an extra 1-inch margin of paper all the way around. Lightly oil or butter the wrapper on both sides to prevent it from burning. Arrange the fish, along with any sauce, vegetables, and aromatics, on one half of the wrapper. Fold the other half of the paper over, and crimp the edges tightly together to securely seal the package. Place the sealed package on a baking sheet and bake in a moderate oven, 400 to 425°F. Serve as soon as possible after you take the package from the oven; as the package cools, it will begin to deflate.

SPLITTING A LOBSTER TO BROIL

Purchasing live lobster for cooking guarantees the best flavor and texture. Look carefully at a split lobster; you may find a green tomalley or a pink coral. Both portions are not only edible, they are delicious.

Use the knife's tip to split the head.

Reverse the lobster and cut the tail section in half.

The first step in preparing a lobster to broil, bake, boil or steam is to kill it. Leave the bands on the lobster's claws and lay it, stomach side down, on a work surface. Insert the tip of a chef's knife into the base of the head. Pull the knife all the way down through the shell, splitting the head in half.

If you are making broiled or baked stuffed lobster, you need to cut the lobster in half. Split the tail by reversing the direction of the lobster and positioning the tip of the knife at the point where you made your initial cut. Then, cut through the shell of the tail section.

Broiled Lobster with Bread Crumb Stuffing

Use cornbread crumbs and a bit of spicy chorizo to vary this basic stuffing combination. The stuffing mixture can be made up to 2 days in advance and is easy to double or even triple if you want to serve this to a larger crowd. Remember to provide lobster crackers to your guests so they can enjoy the leg and claw meat.

SERVES 4

Stuffing

2 tbsp unsalted butter

1 small yellow onion, minced

1 celery stalk, minced

¼ cup minced red bell pepper

¼ cup minced green bell pepper

1 garlic clove, minced

2 cups fresh bread crumbs

¼ cup minced sun-dried tomatoes

2 tbsp minced basil

2 tbsp dry sherry

Kosher salt and freshly ground pepper, as needed

2 live lobsters (1½ to 2 lb each)

Lemon wedges, as needed

½ cup (1 stick) clarified butter, warmed

1. To make the stuffing: Heat the butter in a sauté pan over low heat. Sauté the onion, celery, bell peppers, and garlic, stirring frequently, until soft but not colored, 5 to 6 minutes. Remove from the heat. Add the bread crumbs, sun-dried tomatoes, and basil. Stir in the sherry and season with salt and pepper.

2. Preheat the broiler, positioning the rack about 3 inches from the heat source. Split the lobsters in half lengthwise. If the coral and tomalley are present, remove and reserve to add to the stuffing, if desired.

3. Place the lobster halves on a baking sheet, shell side up. Broil until the meat is opaque around the edges, 5 to 6 minutes. Cover to keep warm and set aside.

4. Preheat the oven to 400°F. Turn the lobsters cut side up. Stir the tomalley and coral into the stuffing mixture, if desired, and then spoon the stuffing into the body cavity of each lobster; do not place it over the tail meat. Put the lobsters in the oven and roast until the lobster meat is opaque in the center, about 10 minutes. Serve the lobsters on warmed plates or a platter with the lemon wedges and hot clarified butter.

Paella Valenciana

This paella version uses short-grain rice from the Valencia region, and fresh-grown vegetables. The seafood must always be fresh and ideally locally caught. If there is one unique attribute to true paella, it is the use of saffron.

SERVES 10

6 cups chicken broth

1 cup canned crushed tomatoes

1 tsp saffron threads

Kosher salt, as needed

¼ cup extra-virgin olive oil

2 lb boneless, skinless chicken (breasts or thighs), cut into 1-inch cubes

1 lb chorizo, cut into ½-inch pieces

2 lb boneless pork or beef, cut into 1-inch cubes

2 medium yellow onions, diced

2 green bell peppers, seeded and diced

2 red bell peppers, seeded and diced

3 carrots, cut into small dice

3 garlic cloves, minced

3 cups short-grain rice, such as Calasparra or Bomba

1 cup green peas, fresh or thawed frozen

10 mussels in their shells

10 clams in their shells

10 large shrimp in their shells, with tails and heads intact

4 lemons

2 roasted red bell peppers, seeded and cut into ¼-inch strips (see sidebar this page)

1. In a large saucepan, heat the chicken broth, crushed tomatoes, saffron, and a pinch of salt over medium heat. When the broth comes to a simmer, remove it from the heat, cover, and let steep for 15 minutes. This saffron-infused broth is ready to use, or it may be cooled and stored in a covered container in the refrigerator for up to 3 days.

2. In a paella or a large, wide, shallow skillet, heat the oil over medium-high heat and sauté the chicken, chorizo, and pork or beef until well browned, 3 to 5 minutes. Add the onions, diced bell peppers, carrots, and garlic and sauté for about 2 more minutes.

3. Add the rice and coat it slightly with the rest of the ingredients, about 3 minutes. Add the broth mixture and stir. Taste and add more salt, if necessary. Bring the mixture to a simmer and cook for 8 minutes.

4. Add the peas, mussels, clams, and shrimp to the pan, arranging the shellfish in a pattern, if desired. Cover the pan and continue cooking at a simmer until the clams and mussels have opened, about 5 minutes more. Discard any that do not open.

5. Remove the pan from the heat, squeeze 2 of the lemons over the top, cover, and let sit for 5 minutes. Garnish with the roasted peppers and the remaining 2 lemons cut into wedges. Serve immediately.

ROASTING BELL PEPPERS

You can buy good-quality jarred roasted peppers, but it is quite simple to make them yourself. To roast bell peppers, heat the oven to 350°F. Rub the whole peppers with a little olive oil and place them in a baking sheet. Roast, turning the peppers occasionally, until the flesh is very tender and the skin seems loose. Remove them from the oven and let them cool until they are easy to handle. Pull out the stem and seeds and peel the skin away; use a paring knife if the skin is stuck. The peppers are ready to use right away in a recipe or as a garnish for a dish, or store them in a covered container in the refrigerator for up to 2 weeks.

Cioppino

Cioppino is a classic fish stew from San Francisco. It is based on the fish stews popular throughout the Mediterranean region and may have arrived in San Francisco with Italians who flocked to California during the Gold Rush.

SERVES 10

2 tbsp olive oil

1 yellow onion, diced

10 green onions, white and green parts, diced

1 green bell pepper, diced

1 fennel bulb, sliced

8 garlic cloves, minced

1 cup dry white wine

One 32-oz can diced tomatoes

2 cups bottled clam juice

2 cups chicken broth

½ cup tomato purée

3 dried bay leaves

12 littleneck clams, scrubbed

3 blue crabs, disjointed

1½ lb swordfish fillet, coarsely diced

1 lb large shrimp, peeled and deveined

½ lb scallops (preferably bay scallops)

¼ cup chopped basil

10 Crostini (page 57)

1. To make the cioppino: Heat the oil in a soup pot over medium-high heat. Add the yellow onion, green onions, bell pepper, fennel, and garlic. Sauté until the onions are translucent, 6 to 8 minutes.

2. Add the white wine and reduce by half, about 5 minutes. Add the tomatoes, clam juice, broth, tomato purée, and bay leaves. Cover the pot, adjust the heat to a slow simmer, and cook until very flavorful but still brothy, about 45 minutes. Add a small amount of water, if

necessary, to adjust the consistency. Cioppino should be more of a broth than a stew. Remove and discard the bay leaves. The cioppino can be prepared to this point and then cooled and stored in a covered container in the refrigerator for up to 3 days.

3. Add the clams and crabs to the broth. Simmer until the crab shells are bright red and the clams have just started to open, about 10 minutes. Add the swordfish, shrimp, and scallops and simmer just until the fish is cooked through, 8 to 10 minutes more. The clams should be completely open. Discard any that are not.

4. Add the basil, taste, and season with salt and pepper, as needed. Ladle the cioppino into warmed soup bowls and garnish with the crostini.

COMPOSED ENTRÉES

WE'VE GATHERED A COLLECTION of meatless entrées that come from around the world. You can offer these dishes as the main course on their own or in combination with a simple roast or grilled main dish that features meat, fish, or poultry. Several of these composed dishes are perfect for do-ahead cooking since they can be assembled and stored in the refrigerator or freezer ready to bake. Choose your most attractive casserole dishes or bakeware, since they can usually go straight from the oven to the table. Or, if you have enough individual pieces, you can assemble some of them in smaller gratin dishes to create individual servings.

Savory Squash and Rice Tart

SERVES 8 TO 10

Tart Dough

2¼ cups all-purpose flour, sifted

10 tbsp (1¼ sticks) unsalted butter, cold, cut into small cubes

1 tsp kosher salt

Squash and Rice Filling

1¼ cups short-grain white rice

½ cup (1 stick) unsalted butter

2 cups chopped leeks (about 4), white and light green portions only

4 sage leaves

1⅔ cups butternut squash purée (see sidebar this page)

1½ cups grated Parmesan

Kosher salt and freshly ground black pepper, as needed

Small pinch of freshly grated nutmeg

1. To make the dough: Put the flour in the bowl of an electric stand mixer or in a large mixing bowl. Add the butter and salt. Using the paddle attachment of the mixer or a pastry blender, mix the butter into the flour until the dough resembles cornmeal.

2. Add 6 tablespoons of ice cold water and mix the dough briefly, just enough so that it will hold together when pressed into a ball. Wrap the dough in plastic wrap and chill it in the refrigerator for at least 4 hours and up to 2 days.

3. To make the filling: Fill a 3-quart pan about two-thirds full with cold water. Add salt to taste and bring to a full boil over high heat. Add the rice and stir to separate the grains; cook, uncovered, until tender, about 15 minutes. Lower the heat, if necessary, to keep the rice from boiling over. Drain the rice in a wire-mesh sieve.

4. Heat the butter in a skillet over medium heat. Add the leeks and sage and cook gently over low heat until the leeks are tender, about 5 minutes. Transfer to a mixing bowl and add the prepared rice, squash purée, and cheese. Stir until evenly blended. Season with salt, pepper, and nutmeg as needed. The filling mixture can be prepared ahead of time and stored in a covered container in the refrigerator for up to 2 days.

5. Unwrap the dough and set it on a floured work surface. Cut the dough into 2 almost equal-size balls; one should be slightly bigger than the other. Working with the large ball first, roll out the dough into a 14-inch-diameter round, about ⅛ inch thick. Lift the dough gently and place it into the tart pan.

6. Gently spread the filling in an even layer in the lined tart pan. Roll out the smaller ball of dough into an 11-inch-diameter round; it should be the same thickness as the bottom layer. Place the top dough round on top of the filling. Pinch the dough edges together with your fingertips or crimp them together with the tines of a fork. The assembled tart is ready to bake now, or it may be covered and refrigerated for up to 24 hours or frozen for up to 2 weeks before baking.

7. Preheat the oven to 350°F. Position a rack in the bottom third of the oven. Bake the tart until the crust is golden brown, about 40 minutes. Cool the tart at least 15 minutes, then cut and serve it warm on warmed plates.

BUTTERNUT SQUASH PURÉE

To make a butternut squash purée, you can opt to either peel the squash, cut it in cubes, and then boil or steam it until tender, or you can bake the squash until it is tender and then remove the seeds and scoop out the tender flesh. The cooked squash is easy to purée with a potato masher or by pushing it through a wire-mesh sieve.

Eggplant alla Parmigiana

This eggplant recipe includes a creamy ricotta layer for a moist dish with a lighter texture than a typical eggplant Parmesan. Assemble individual servings in ovenproof gratin dishes, if you wish.

SERVES 8

1¼ lb sliced eggplant (about 1 large or 2 medium), peeled first if desired

1½ cups ricotta cheese

1 cup grated Parmesan

½ cup minced flat-leaf parsley

Small pinch of freshly grated nutmeg, as needed (optional)

Kosher salt and freshly ground black pepper, as needed

4 large eggs

⅔ cup whole milk

2 cups all-purpose flour

2 cups dry bread crumbs, or as needed

Olive oil, as needed

3 cups Tomato Sauce (page 165), heated

2 cups grated mozzarella

1. Place the eggplant slices in a colander, salt generously, and let the eggplant rest for about 20 minutes; set the colander in a bowl or on a plate to collect any juices released by the eggplant. Rinse the slices well with cold water and blot them dry with paper towels.

2. In a shallow bowl, blend the remaining 3 eggs with the milk to make an egg wash. Put the flour in a second shallow bowl and season with a pinch of salt and pepper. Put the bread crumbs in a third shallow bowl.

3. Dip the eggplant slices, one at a time, into the flour, then the egg wash, and last, the bread crumbs, patting the crumbs evenly over all sides of the eggplant. Transfer the eggplant slices to a plate or baking sheet.

4. Pour about ½ inch of oil into a deep skillet and heat over medium-high heat until the oil shimmers. Add the breaded eggplant slices to the hot oil, a few pieces at a time, and fry on the first side until golden brown, about 2 minutes. Turn the eggplant and continue to fry until golden and crisp on the second side, about 2 minutes. Transfer to a plate lined with paper towels; continue to fry the eggplant in batches until all of it has been fried. The eggplant is ready to assemble into the finished dish, or it may be cooled and stored in a covered container in the refrigerator for up to 24 hours.

5. In a large bowl, blend the ricotta, ½ cup of the Parmesan, the parsley, nutmeg, if using, salt, pepper, and 1 egg until smooth. The ricotta mixture is ready to assemble into the finished dish, or it may be cooled and stored in a covered container in the refrigerator for up to 24 hours.

6. Spread about half of the tomato sauce in a lasagna pan, rectangular baking dish, or divided among individual gratin dishes. Assemble the dish in layers: half of fried eggplant, the ricotta mixture, the remaining half of the eggplant, and the remaining tomato sauce. Sprinkle evenly with the mozzarella and the remaining ½ cup Parmesan. The recipe can be made in advance up to this point, and the fully assembled dish can be frozen for up to 1 month.

7. Preheat the oven to 350°F. Cover and bake until the ricotta mixture is very hot and the mozzarella cheese has melted, 20 to 25 minutes; increase the baking time by 10 minutes if frozen. Remove the cover and continue to bake until the cheese is golden brown, another 10 minutes. Let the dish rest for 10 minutes, then cut and serve on warmed plates.

Tomato Sauce

Use fresh, ripe plum tomatoes for this sauce when they are season, and consider doubling or tripling this recipe to have on hand.

MAKES 4 CUPS; ENOUGH FOR 6 SERVINGS

3 tbsp olive oil

8 garlic cloves, minced

6 cups peeled, seeded, and chopped plum tomatoes, peeled, seeded, and chopped

2 tbsp chopped fresh basil

Kosher salt and freshly ground pepper, as needed

1. Heat the olive oil in a large saucepan over medium heat. Add the garlic and sauté, stirring frequently, until fragrant, about 2 minutes. Add the tomatoes, bring the sauce to a boil, reduce the heat, and simmer until thick and flavorful, 20 to 25 minutes.

2. Add the basil and simmer for 5 minutes more. Taste and season with salt and pepper, if needed. If you wish a very smooth sauce, push it through a wire-mesh sieve or a food mill, or purée it with a blender or food processor. The sauce is ready to use now or it may be cooled and stored in a covered container in the refrigerator for up to 1 week.

Chickpea and Vegetable Tagine

If you wish, try adding a few spoonfuls of dried currants and a handful of toasted slivered almonds as a final garnish.

SERVES 8

2 tbsp olive oil

4 cups chopped onions

3 garlic cloves, peeled and thinly sliced

1 tbsp ground cumin

¼ tsp ground cinnamon

Kosher salt and freshly ground black pepper, as needed

2 cups water

2 lb butternut squash, peeled, seeded, and cut into chunks

6 carrots, cut into chunks

2½ cups cooked chickpeas, drained and rinsed

2 lb diced tomatoes and their juices

2 sweet potatoes, peeled, cut into chunks

4 parsnips, cut into chunks

1 dried bay leaf

¼ cup chopped flat-leaf parsley

1. Heat the oil in a large saucepan over medium heat. Add the onions and sauté until soft and translucent, about 5 minutes. Add the garlic, cumin, cinnamon, and a pinch of salt and pepper and sauté until aromatic, about 1 minute.

2. Stir in the water, the squash, carrots, chickpeas, tomatoes, sweet potatoes, parsnips, and bay leaf. Bring to a boil over high heat. Reduce the heat to medium and simmer, partially covered, until the vegetables are tender, about 30 minutes. Discard the bay leaf. The dish can be cooled and stored in a covered container in the refrigerator for up to 2 days. Return to a simmer before serving.

3. Sprinkle the dish with the parsley and serve immediately.

Roasted Eggplant Stuffed with Curried Lentils

Small globe eggplants are the perfect size for this dish and can sometimes be found in the supermarket produce section or at farm stands. If you cannot find them, however, use a larger eggplant, leaving the same size "wall" but cooking for up to 10 minutes longer, and cut it into serving portions after baking.

SERVES 8

- **1 cup brown lentils**
- **4 cups vegetable broth or water**
- **4 small globe eggplants**
- **2 tbsp olive oil**
- **½ cup minced yellow onion**
- **2 garlic cloves, minced**
- **1 tsp grated ginger**
- **1 cup minced white mushrooms**
- **1 tsp kosher salt**
- **1 tsp finely grated lemon zest**
- **1 tsp curry powder**
- **¼ tsp ground cinnamon**
- **½ tsp ground turmeric**
- **Freshly ground black pepper, as needed**

1. In a small pot, bring the lentils and broth or water to a boil over high heat. Cover and reduce the heat to low. Simmer until the lentils are tender to the bite, 25 to 30 minutes. Remove from the heat and set the lentils aside in their cooking liquid.

2. Grease two 8 by 13-inch baking pans. Halve the eggplants lengthwise and scoop out some of the flesh, leaving a ½- to ¾-inch "wall." Mince the scooped flesh and set aside. Transfer the eggplant halves to the prepared baking pans, skin side down.

3. Heat a large nonstick skillet over medium heat. Swirl in the oil, then add the onion, garlic, and ginger. Sauté, stirring occasionally, until the onion is golden brown, 6 to 8 minutes. Add the minced eggplant, mushrooms, salt, lemon zest, curry powder, cinnamon, turmeric, and pepper. Sauté over medium heat, stirring occasionally, until the mushrooms begin to release some moisture, about 5 minutes.

4. Drain the lentils, reserving the cooking liquid, and add the lentils to the eggplant and mushroom mixture. Add enough of the cooking liquid (about ½ cup) to moisten the vegetables well, then simmer until the liquid is reduced, 6 to 8 minutes. Fill the hollowed eggplant halves with the vegetable mixture. The dish can be assembled and held in a covered container in the refrigerator for up to 8 hours before baking.

5. Preheat the oven to 375°F. Cover the dish with aluminum foil and bake until the eggplants are tender and cooked through, 35 to 40 minutes. Serve at once.

Tofu with Red Curry, Peas, Green Onions, and Cilantro

Here tofu is complemented by the bold and exciting flavors of Thai cuisine. Curry pastes come in a broad variety of flavor intensities from mildly spicy to very hot. Prepared Thai red curry paste can be found in jars in the Asian foods section of many supermarkets or in specialty food shops and Asian markets.

SERVES 8

- **2 cups brown rice**
- **2 tbsp grapeseed oil**
- **One 14-oz package firm tofu, drained, cut into 1-inch cubes**
- **2 tbsp fresh lime juice**
- **1 cup diced onion**

2 tbsp minced garlic

1 cup coconut milk

2 oz prepared Thai red curry paste

1 tbsp ground turmeric

Kosher salt and freshly ground black pepper, as needed

1½ cups peas, blanched

1 cup grape tomatoes, halved

⅓ bunch cilantro, chopped

½ bunch green onions, white and green portions, minced

1 cup pea shoots (optional)

4 cups cooked brown rice, hot

¼ cup black sesame seeds

1. Bring 3½ cups of water and the uncooked rice to a boil over high heat. Cover the pot tightly, turn the heat to low, and cook until the rice is tender, about 25 minutes.

2. Heat 1 tablespoon of the oil in a medium sauté pan. Add the tofu and cook until the moisture is evaporated and the tofu is a light golden brown. Remove the tofu from the pan and sprinkle with the lime juice. The tofu can be prepared in advance and stored in a covered container in the refrigerator for up to 2 days.

3. Heat the remaining 1 tablespoon oil in the pan over medium-high heat, add the onions and cook until translucent, about 5 minutes. Add the garlic and cook for 2 minutes more.

4. Add the coconut milk, curry paste, and turmeric. Season with salt and pepper. Reduce the heat to medium and simmer until the sauce has thickened slightly, 10 to 12 minutes. The sauce can be prepared ahead to this point and held in a covered container in the refrigerator for up to 2 days.

5. Return the sauce to a simmer, add the peas, tomatoes, and the prepared tofu and simmer just to combine and thoroughly heat the ingredients, about 3 minutes. Adjust the seasoning, if necessary. Toss the mixture with the cilantro and green onions.

6. Serve the tofu in the curry sauce with the cooked rice. Sprinkle the black sesame seeds on top of the rice and top with the pea shoots as a garnish, if desired.

Varying the heights of the food will add interest to any plate. Here, a mold was used to add height to the rice side dish served with the Tofu with Red Curry, Peas, Green Onions, and Cilantro.

Paella with Vegetables

The traditional way to prepare a paella is in a wide, shallow pan over an open fire.

SERVES 8 TO 10

6 cups vegetable broth

5 garlic cloves, peeled and crushed

2 tsp curry powder

½ tsp ground turmeric

1 tsp kosher salt

⅛ tsp freshly grated nutmeg

1 cinnamon stick

3 carrots, sliced ½ inch thick on the diagonal

2 cups cauliflower florets

1 cup pearl onions

5 brine-packed artichoke hearts, rinsed, drained, and quartered

1 cup canned chickpeas, drained and rinsed

⅓ cup raisins

2 medium zucchini, cut into 1-inch cubes

¾ cup roasted red pepper strips

1 cup peeled, seeded, diced tomatoes

One 10-ounce bag triple-washed spinach, rinsed and torn

2 cups couscous (see Notes)

3 tbsp chopped toasted peanuts

2 tbsp drained pickled caperberries (optional)

8 lemon wedges

Purchased harissa sauce, as needed

1. In a paella pan or a large, wide shallow skillet, bring 3 cups of the broth, the garlic, curry powder, turmeric, salt, nutmeg, and cinnamon stick, to a boil over high heat. Reduce the heat to medium and add the carrots, cauliflower, and onions. Simmer until the carrots are barely tender, about 12 minutes.

2. Add the artichoke hearts, chickpeas, and raisins and simmer until the artichoke hearts are very hot, about 5 minutes. Add the zucchini, roasted red pepper strips, and tomatoes and simmer until the zucchini is tender and translucent, about 5 minutes more. Add the spinach and simmer until it becomes deep green and wilted, about 5 minutes. Discard the cinnamon stick. The vegetable mixture can be cooled and stored in a covered container in the refrigerator for up to 2 days. Reheat over low heat while preparing the couscous, if necessary.

3. Bring the remaining 3 cups broth to a boil over high heat and add the couscous. Return to a boil, cover the pot tightly, and remove it from heat. Let the couscous sit for 5 minutes. Remove the cover and gently fluff the couscous with a fork.

4. To serve: Place the couscous in the center of a platter or individual, warmed plates. Arrange the vegetables around the couscous and add little bit of the broth from the vegetables around each serving. Garnish with the peanuts, caperberries, if using, and lemon wedges. Drizzle with a little harissa sauce.

NOTE *This recipe calls for couscous, which is actually a type of pasta. The couscous most often found in the store is Moroccan couscous that has been parcooked. It cooks in about 5 minutes. Large couscous varieties, such as Lebanese or Israeli, take longer to cook. Instead of removing it from the heat, let these large types of couscous simmer in a covered pot over low heat until tender, 10 to 12 minutes for Israeli couscous, or 40 to 45 minutes for Lebanese couscous. You could also use a Sardinian couscous for this dish; you may find it sold as "fregola." It cooks in 12 to 14 minutes.*

five CASUAL FOODS

OT EVERY PARTY CALLS FOR AN ELEGANT FOUR-COURSE MEAL. WE ALL HAVE CERTAIN COMFORT FOODS THAT MAKE OUR MOUTHS WATER AND JUST MAKE US FEEL GOOD. PATIO PARTIES, BARBECUES, SPORTS EVENTS AND TAILGATES, KIDS' PARTIES, AND PICNICS ARE THE PERFECT OPPORTUNITIES TO OFFER THESE TYPES OF CASUAL DISHES TO YOUR GUESTS. HOWEVER, JUST BECAUSE A FOOD IS SIMPLY PREPARED DOESN'T MEAN IT CAN'T BE BOTH BEAUTIFUL AND DELICIOUS.

Put the same effort and care you would pour into a more complicated meal into the casual foods on your menu. If you're making traditional Italian hoagies, try to build the most appealing, best-tasting Italian hoagie your guests have ever had. If you're serving pizza, come up with an unusual combination of toppings and arrange them on the crust in an interesting way. Instead of hamburgers with American cheese, create curried turkey burgers with a homemade seasoning blend. It can be fun to put your own signature on familiar foods to make them a little more special.

DO-IT-YOURSELF DISHES FOR CASUAL MEALS

Many casual foods lend themselves well to a "build-your-own" buffet; this means that the host provides all the components and condiments for a specific item, but the guests actually compose their own food. This can be a fun activity, especially for kids, and it allows your guests to eat exactly what they like. Here are some easy build-your-own foods:

BURGERS

SHISH KEBABS

SALADS

BAKED POTATOES

HOT DOGS

SANDWICHES, SUBS, WRAPS, OR HOAGIES

PIZZAS

TACOS, BURRITOS, OR NACHOS

ICE CREAM SUNDAES

The point is not to have every condiment imaginable but rather to have a nice assortment of different types of components. For example, if you decide to have "Build-Your-Own Submarine Sandwich" at your Super Bowl party, you may give your guests the option of:

WHITE, WHOLE WHEAT, AND SESAME SEED SUB ROLLS

SLICED ROAST BEEF, TURKEY, HAM, PEPPERONI, OR MARINATED MEATBALLS

AMERICAN CHEESE, PROVOLONE, OR CHEDDAR

**PESTO, YELLOW MUSTARD, SPICY
MUSTARD, MAYONNAISE**

**LETTUCE, TOMATO, ONIONS, OLIVES,
CUCUMBERS, GREEN PEPPERS, AND PICKLES**

When you're estimating the amount of food to buy for a build-your-own buffet, remember that every guest is not going to eat a full serving of every component. For example, if you have invited 20 guests for a Build-Your-Own Pasta party, you do not need enough marinara for 20 people, plus enough pesto for 20 people, plus enough alfredo for 20 people. Instead, you should estimate the total amount of sauce you'll need to feed 20 people and divide it by the number of sauces you'd like to serve. Following the same example:

**20 GUESTS X ¾ CUP OF SAUCE EACH =
15 CUPS OF SAUCE NEEDED**

**15 CUPS OF SAUCE ÷ 3 TYPES OF SAUCE =
5 CUPS OF EACH SAUCE**

Some build-your-own foods, such as shish kebabs and pizzas, will need to be cooked after they are assembled by the guests. If this is the case, be sure to devise a system to keep track of which food belongs to whom. That could mean using different colored trays or skewers or having guests make an identifying mark on the tray or food itself. You don't want the person with the shellfish allergy ending up with someone else's shrimp and garlic pizza, because the food got mixed up in the oven.

GRILLING

PATIO PARTIES, BARBECUES, AND TAILGATES are a great opportunity to cook outdoors, which most often means firing up the grill. Gas grills are easy to use and easy to care for. They cook foods consistently without the challenges of lighting and maintaining a fire. Charcoal grills require a little more skill but give the food a rich, smoky flavor that gas grills can't achieve.

A good fire will typically need to burn for at least 35 to 45 minutes before it's ready for cooking, and will burn evenly for long enough to cook all the food completely. To begin, open the vents in the grill to let air in, add a few sheets of crumpled newspaper, then add hardwood chips, charcoal briquettes, or kindling to the paper to make a mound. Light the paper on fire and let it burn without disturbing it. We strongly discourage the use of lighter fluid, because it can be very dangerous and also leave a distinct chemical flavor on foods. When the flames start to die down, carefully add more wood or briquettes until you have enough fuel to last for the cooking session.

You can position the wood or briquettes to create "heat zones" on different areas of the grill. For example, you may want to keep one area of the grill very hot to give chicken legs a good color, but then move them to a slightly cooler area to cook all the way through without burning. If you are cooking a variety of different foods on the grill, like steaks and vegetables, you can create separate zones to keep the raw meat from coming in contact with the vegetables.

A gas grill may have a gas tank or it may be set up to hook directly to a gas line. The BTU rating (British thermal unit) is a measure of how much gas can flow through the line. Almost as important as the BTUs of a particular grill is the number of burners. A good gas grill has at least two burners; large grills may have three or more. With more than one burner, you can control the heat more effectively. By turning one or more of the burners off after preheating the grill, you can create the indirect heat necessary to prepare long-cooking foods like a whole turkey or spareribs or delicate foods like breads or vegetables without charring the outside of the food.

Some grills have built-in thermometers to make it easy to monitor how hot the grill is. If you don't have a thermometer, there is a simple test you can do. Hold your hand palm-down just over the grill rack, and count how many seconds it takes before you have to move your hand away from the grill:

2 SECONDS EQUALS HIGH HEAT

3 SECONDS EQUALS MEDIUM-HIGH HEAT

4 SECONDS EQUALS MEDIUM HEAT

5 SECONDS EQUALS MEDIUM-LOW HEAT

6 SECONDS EQUALS LOW HEAT

When you're finished cooking, it's essential to let the coals burn out and cool completely before removing them from the grill. Hot coals and ashes can hold a lot of heat, so to be sure your coals won't cause a fire, transfer them to a metal bucket or wrap them in a double layer of aluminum foil when you're ready to dispose of them. Never dump the ashes into a trashcan or anywhere they might catch other garbage on fire.

Lighting charcoal in a chimney starter before putting it into the grill can help keep you from needing to use lighter fluid, a toxic and highly flammable chemical.

Strategically place the charcoal to create "heat zones" on the grill.

These hot dogs are cooking over direct heat, while indirect heat is warming the buns.

Guava-Glazed Grilled Pork Ribs

SERVES 8

2½ cups water

1½ cups red wine vinegar

1½ cups chopped oregano

1¼ cups chopped cilantro

1 cup chopped yellow onion

8 garlic cloves, minced

2 tsp ground cumin

1½ tsp freshly ground black pepper

8 lb pork baby back ribs

4 cups Guava Barbecue Sauce (recipe follows)

1. Make a marinade by puréeing the water, vinegar, oregano, cilantro, onion, garlic, cumin, and pepper in a blender.

2. Place the ribs in a large container and coat with the marinade. Cover and refrigerate for at least 24 and up to 36 hours.

3. Preheat a grill to medium-high; the coals should be glowing red with a moderate coating of white ash. To create zones, spread the coals in an even bed on one side of the grill or turn one burner on a gas grill off. Clean the cooking grate and rub lightly with a little vegetable oil. If desired, add wood chips to the grill, either directly onto the hot coals or in a small aluminum pan over one of the gas burners.

4. Grill the ribs over indirect heat, covered, until the ribs are browned on both sides, about 15 minutes per side.

5. In a medium saucepan, bring 2 cups of the barbecue sauce to a simmer. Brush the ribs with a light coating of the barbecue sauce and continue to barbecue over indirect heat, turning the ribs every 5 minutes and brushing with the sauce after each turn, until the ribs are very tender and a rich glaze has built up on the ribs, another 30 to 35 minutes.

6. Remove the pork ribs from the grill, let them rest for about 3 minutes, and cut into portions. Serve on a warmed platter or plates. Reheat the remaining 2 cups of barbecue sauce separately and pass on the side.

Guava Barbecue Sauce

MAKES 4 CUPS SAUCE

1½ cups guava marmalade

1 cup water

½ cup dry sherry

¼ cup tomato paste

2 tbsp dry mustard

4 tsp molasses

1 habanero chile, minced

5 tsp minced garlic

1 tbsp ground cumin

2 tsp kosher salt

1 tsp freshly ground black pepper

½ cup fresh lime juice

1. In a medium saucepan, combine the marmalade, water, sherry, tomato paste, powdered mustard, molasses, chile, garlic, cumin, salt, and pepper. Simmer the sauce until slightly thickened, about 30 minutes.

2. Remove from the heat and stir in the lime juice. The sauce is ready to use now, or it can be cooled and stored in a covered container in the refrigerator for up to 1 week.

Lemon-Ginger Grilled Chicken

We love the interplay of the smoky taste you get from grilling with the bright notes of lemon and ginger, but we also enjoy this as a broiled dish. To broil: Preheat the broiler. Put the chicken on a broiling pan or on a roasting rack in a baking sheet and place the pan about 4 inches from the heat source. Turn the chicken once as it broils to cook it evenly.

SERVES 8

Marinade

⅔ cup fresh lemon juice

¼ cup finely grated lemon zest

4 tsp minced ginger

4 tsp firmly packed light brown sugar

1 tbsp peanut oil

1 tbsp kosher salt, or as needed

4 Szechwan chile peppers, dried, seeds removed

3 lb boneless, skinless chicken thighs

1. In a ziplock plastic bag, combine the lemon juice, zest, ginger, brown sugar, oil, salt, and chiles. Add the chicken, squeeze out the air from the bag, and seal the bag. Turn to coat the chicken with the marinade. Marinate in the refrigerator, turning the bag occasionally, for at least 15 minutes and up to 8 hours.

2. Preheat a gas grill to medium-low; turn one burner off. If you are using a charcoal grill, build a fire and let it burn down until the coals are glowing red with a heavy coating of white ash. Spread the coals in an even bed on one side of the grill. Clean the cooking grate and rub lightly with a little vegetable oil.

3. Remove the chicken from the marinade, letting any excess drain away. Place the chicken on the grill, skin side down, over direct heat for 2 minutes on each side, then over indirect heat, until cooked through (165°F on an instant-read thermometer), another 4 to 5 minutes per side. Serve the chicken thighs straight from the grill or chill them to serve cold.

Grilled Soft-Shell Crab with Barley and Wheat Berry Pilaf

SERVES 8

Citrus Marinade

⅓ cup fresh lemon juice

¼ cup minced red bell pepper

1 cup red wine vinegar

1 cup dry white wine

¼ cup extra-virgin olive oil

⅓ cup minced green onions, white and green portions

1 roasted jalapeño, minced

2 tsp chopped basil

2 tsp chopped fennel fronds

2 tsp chopped tarragon

2 tsp chopped thyme

2 garlic cloves, minced

8 soft-shell crabs, cleaned (see page 176)

Barley and Wheat Berry Pilaf (page 265), warm

1. In a shallow dish, combine all of the ingredients for the crab marinade. Add the crabs and marinate in the refrigerator for at least 2 and up to 12 hours.

2. Preheat a gas grill to medium heat; turn one burner off. If you are using a charcoal grill, build a fire and let it burn down until the coals are glowing red with a coating of white ash. Spread the coals in an even bed on one side of the grill. Clean the cooking grate and rub lightly with a little vegetable oil.

3. Remove the crabs from the marinade, dragging them along the edge of the dish to scrape away any excess marinade.

4. Working in batches, grill the crabs over direct heat on the first side until bright red, 3 to 4 minutes. Turn the crabs once and grill over indirect heat until thoroughly cooked, about 4 minutes more. Serve at once with the pilaf.

PREPARING SOFT-SHELL CRAB

A seasonal favorite, soft-shell crab is not particularly difficult to clean and is considered a great delicacy. They are commonly prepared by sautéing or panfrying, and the shell may be eaten along with the meat.

First, peel back the pointed shell and scrape away the gill filament on each side.

Cut the eyes and mouth away from the head just behind the eyes, and squeeze gently to force out the green bubble, which has an unpleasant flavor.

Bend the tail flap back and pull with a slight twisting motion. This should draw the intestinal vein out of the body at the same time.

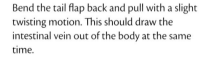

The cleaned crab with the gill filaments, head, and tail flap removed.

BURGERS

HAMBURGERS ARE A BELOVED AMERICAN TRADITION, but there's no reason to limit yourself to beef patties. Ground turkey, chicken, lamb, game, pork, and seafood all make flavorful burgers. Ground meat is readily available, but grinding your own meat, poultry, or fish ensures its freshness. Pulse 1-inch chunks in a food processor, being very careful not to overprocess the meat into a paste.

The ground meat may be seasoned and simply shaped into patties, or bread crumbs, egg, or a combination of the two, may be added to help keep the patties together. Patties should be shaped to ½ to 1 inch thick. Ground pork, game, and veggies cook best in patties ½ inch thick; poultry and lamb patties should be about ¾ inch thick; and beef patties may be up to 1 inch thick.

Burgers, especially those made with leaner meats, can burn very quickly, so never walk away from your burgers while they're cooking. Also, resist the temptation to press down on top of a cooking burger with a spatula, because you'll push out its flavorful juices. For the juiciest burgers, let them rest for a minute or two after cooking to allow the juices to redistribute.

Everybody loves a good cheeseburger, but why not opt for blue cheese, chèvre, or havarti instead of the usual American cheese? If you want a slice of cheese to melt onto the burger, place it on the burger 1 to 2 minutes before pulling the burger off the grill. For crumbly cheeses, like feta or queso fresco, let the cheese come to room temperature and then add it to the burger when it's done cooking.

Classic Burgers with Caciotta Cheese and Guacamole

You can substitute other cheeses, such as Monterey Jack, cheddar, or Swiss, for the caciotta if it is unavailable in your neighborhood grocery store.

SERVES 8

- 3 lb ground beef
- 6 tbsp Japanese-style bread crumbs (panko)
- 2 tbsp kosher salt
- 1 tbsp ground black pepper
- 2 tsp ground cumin (optional)
- 8 slices caciotta cheese
- 8 hamburger buns or Kaiser rolls
- 1 cup Guacamole (page 54)
- 8 Boston lettuce leaves (optional)
- 16 slices tomato (optional)
- 8 slices red onion (grilled, if desired) (optional)

1. Preheat a gas grill to medium-high. If you are using a charcoal grill, build a fire and let it burn down until the coals are glowing red with a moderate coating of white ash. Spread the coals in an even bed. Clean the cooking grate.

2. While the grill is heating, combine the ground beef with the bread crumbs, salt, pepper, and cumin. Shape into 8 patties about 4 inches in diameter and ¾ inch thick.

3. Grill the beef until well marked, 4 to 6 minutes. Flip the burgers over and grill until cooked through, about 4 minutes for medium, 6 minutes for medium-well.

4. Place the cheese on the burgers the last 2 minutes of grilling and allow it to melt. Place the burgers on the buns.

5. Serve the burgers dressed with the guacamole, lettuce, tomato, and onion.

Goat Cheese–Stuffed Turkey Burgers with Red Pepper–Apricot Relish

Try this shaping and filling technique for other burgers: beef burgers filled with Gorgonzola, or lamb burgers flavored with mint and filled with feta. Chilling the burgers before you grill them gives you the best results, so leave yourself time for that step.

SERVES 8

3 lb ground turkey

½ cup toasted bread crumbs

2 tbsp fresh lemon juice

2 tsp finely grated lemon zest

1 tsp chopped thyme

1 tsp kosher salt

½ tsp freshly ground black pepper

4 oz goat cheese

4 tsp vegetable oil

8 English muffins, toasted

2 cups Red Pepper–Apricot Relish (recipe follows)

1. Combine the turkey, bread crumbs, lemon juice, lemon zest, thyme, salt, and pepper. Blend well with a wooden spoon. Divide the mixture into 16 equal portions and press into 3-inch patties.

2. Top 8 of the patties with 1 tablespoon of the goat cheese each. Place a second patty on top and press down the edges to seal the patties together. Place the patties on a baking sheet, cover, and refrigerate for at least 30 minutes and up to 8 hours to firm.

3. Preheat a gas grill to high. If you are using a charcoal grill, build a fire and let it burn down until the coals are glowing red with a light coating of white ash. Spread the coals in an even bed. Clean the cooking grate.

4. Brush the burgers with the oil and place in a hand rack. Grill the burgers over direct heat until browned on the first side, 7 to 8 minutes. Turn the burgers and grill on the second side until browned and cooked through, 7 to 8 minutes more.

5. Serve the turkey burgers on the English muffins, topped with the relish.

Red Pepper–Apricot Relish

MAKES 2 CUPS RELISH

3 tbsp vegetable oil

1 cup dried apricots

1 cup diced red onion

1 tsp minced garlic

2 red bell peppers, roasted, cut into small dice (see page 160)

½ cup chicken broth

1 tbsp white vinegar

1 tsp Dijon mustard

2 to 3 drops hot sauce

½ tsp kosher salt

¼ tsp freshly ground black pepper

1 tsp chopped flat-leaf parsley

1. Heat the oil in a medium saucepan over medium heat. Add the apricots, onions, and garlic, and sauté until translucent, 4 to 5 minutes. Add the bell peppers and broth and simmer until most of the liquid has evaporated, 5 to 10 minutes.

2. Add the vinegar, mustard, and hot sauce. Cook until most of the liquid has evaporated, 1 to 2 minutes. Season the mixture with salt and black pepper. The relish is ready to serve now, or it can be cooled and stored in a covered container in the refrigerator for up to 4 days.

3. Serve the relish at room temperature or chilled. Add the parsley just before serving.

Greek-Style Lamb Burgers

Pine nuts, oregano, garlic, and lamb combine in these savory patties for a delicious Middle Eastern–inspired burger. Toast the pine nuts in a small, dry skillet over medium heat. Swirl the pan while the pine nuts toast. As they heat up, they'll become shiny, indicating that they will quickly start to turn brown. As soon as the nuts are just slightly paler than you like, pour them out of the pan into a cool bowl.

SERVES 8

6 tbsp fresh white bread crumbs

¼ cup cold water

2 tbsp vegetable oil

3 tbsp minced yellow onion

1½ tsp minced garlic

2½ lb lean ground lamb

2 large eggs, lightly beaten

3 tbsp toasted pine nuts

3 tbsp chopped flat-leaf parsley

2 tbsp tahini

2 tbsp grated ginger

2 tbsp ground cumin

¾ tsp ground coriander

¾ tsp ground fennel seeds

1½ tsp kosher salt

¾ tsp freshly ground black pepper

1. Soak the bread crumbs in the water until well moistened, about 2 minutes. Squeeze out any excess moisture. Transfer to a bowl.

2. Heat the oil in a sauté pan over medium-high heat. Add the onion and sauté, stirring frequently, until translucent, 4 to 5 minutes. Add the garlic and sauté until aromatic, about 1 minute. Remove from heat and transfer to a plate to cool.

3. Combine the bread crumbs and the onion-garlic mixture with the lamb, eggs, pine nuts, parsley, tahini, ginger, cumin, coriander, fennel, salt, and pepper. Mix gently until the ingredients are evenly blended.

4. Shape the mixture into 8 patties about 4 inches in diameter and ¾ inch thick, and chill them in the refrigerator for at least 30 minutes and up to 8 hours.

5. Preheat a gas grill to medium-high. If you are using a charcoal grill, build a fire and let it burn down until the coals are glowing red with a moderate coating of white ash. Spread the coals out into an even bed. Clean the cooking grate.

6. Grill the patties over direct heat until medium, 4 to 5 minutes on each side. Serve at once.

NOTE: *These burgers are great on a burger bun, but you could also serve them tucked inside a pita pocket with shredded lettuce and sliced tomatoes and cucumbers.*

SALADS

BIG BOLD SALADS ARE PERFECT FOR ENTERTAINING. They can be assembled ahead of time, leaving you free to spend time at the party instead of working in the kitchen. Most salads are at their best when they are served at room temperature.

You can wash and spin dry greens the day before, to cut down on the mess in the kitchen the day of the party. Most vegetables can be cut ahead too, and stored in ziplock bags or covered containers. Make the dressing the day before, too, and all you need to do is assemble the salad in a beautiful bowl or platter and add the main ingredient.

Grilled Parmesan Chicken Salad

This is a twist on the classic Caesar salad. Adding Parmesan as the coating for the chicken intensifies its flavor.

SERVES 8

8 boneless, skinless chicken breast halves

1 cup grated Parmesan, plus more for garnish

½ tsp kosher salt, or as needed

½ tsp freshly ground black pepper, or as needed

2 tbsp dried basil

½ cup olive oil

¼ cup fresh lemon juice

1 tsp anchovy paste

1 tsp Dijon mustard

2 garlic cloves, finely minced

1¼ lb romaine lettuce, washed, drained, and cut into bite-size pieces

4 cups Homemade Croutons (recipe follows)

Lemon slices for garnish (optional)

1. Preheat a gas grill to medium-low; turn one burner off. If you are using a charcoal grill, build a fire and let it burn down until the coals are glowing red with a heavy coating of white ash. Spread the coals in an even bed on one side of the grill. Clean the cooking grate and rub lightly with a little vegetable oil.

2. In a shallow bowl, combine the chicken, half of the cheese, salt, pepper, and basil. Turn the chicken breasts in the cheese mixture, making sure to coat it thoroughly.

3. Grill the chicken, turning occasionally, until cooked through (165°F on an instant-read thermometer), 10 to 12 minutes. Watch the chicken carefully because the cheese burns easily. If the outside is browning too rapidly, move the chicken to cook over indirect heat. Remove the chicken from the grill and let rest 3 or 4 minutes before slicing.

4. Meanwhile, in a large bowl, whisk together the oil, lemon juice, anchovy paste, mustard, and garlic. Add the lettuce, the remaining cheese, and the croutons. Toss to coat. Divide the salad among 8 individual plates, or mound it on a platter for buffet presentation.

5. Cut each chicken breast diagonally into 5 strips. Arrange the chicken over the salad, using one sliced breast half for each individual salad. Garnish with additional cheese and lemon slices, if desired.

Homemade Croutons

SERVES 8

4 cups cubed bread (rye, whole grain, peasant, or white)

3 tbsp olive oil, or as needed

Kosher salt and freshly ground black pepper, as needed

½ tsp dried rosemary, as needed

Preheat the oven to 350°F. In a large bowl, toss the bread with enough olive oil to coat, and season with salt, pepper, and dried rosemary. Spread the croutons in an even layer on a baking sheet. Bake until golden brown, stirring occasionally so the croutons bake evenly. Allow to cool. Use immediately or store in an airtight container for up to 5 days.

Grilled Steak Salad with Horseradish Dressing

Flank steak (as well as skirt steak and hanger steak) has long, coarse fibers that should always be sliced across the grain to create more tender slices.

SERVES 6

Horseradish Dressing

¼ cup sour cream

½ cup mayonnaise

1 to 2 tbsp prepared horseradish

1 tbsp fresh lemon juice

Kosher salt and freshly ground black pepper, as needed

Romaine and Blue Cheese Salad

6 cups romaine lettuce, washed and drained, cut into bite-size pieces

1½ cups cherry tomatoes, halved lengthwise

⅔ cup crumbled blue cheese

1 tsp freshly grated lemon zest

1½ lb flank steak

Kosher salt and freshly ground black pepper, as needed

½ cup thinly sliced red onion

1. In a small bowl, mix together the sour cream, mayonnaise, horseradish, and lemon juice. Season as needed with salt and pepper. This dressing is ready to use now, or it can be stored in a covered container in the refrigerator for up to 3 days.

2. Place the lettuce, tomatoes, and half the cheese in a salad bowl, sprinkle with the lemon zest, and set aside. The salad can be prepared to this point, covered, and stored in the refrigerator for up to 2 hours before serving.

3. Preheat a gas grill to medium-high. If you are using a charcoal grill, build a fire and let it burn down until the coals are glowing red with a coating of white ash. Spread the coals in an even bed. Clean the cooking grate and rub lightly with oil.

4. Season the beef generously with salt and black pepper. Grill the steak to the desired doneness (see chart, page 135, 3 to 4 minutes per side for medium rare.

5. While the steak is grilling, toss the salad with the horseradish dressing and place on a large platter or individual plates. Transfer the steak to a cutting board and let it rest for 3 minutes. Carve the steak across the grain and at an angle into thin slices. Arrange the steak slices on the salad, top with the onion slices and the remaining cheese, and serve.

When slicing flank steak, cut against the grain of the meat.

Traditional Cobb Salad

Cobb salad was originally created at the Brown Derby Restaurant in Hollywood, California. Various interpretations may call for either chicken or turkey. The garnish suggestions here are typical, but some versions include watercress, celery, cheddar cheese, hard-boiled eggs, black olives, or alfalfa sprouts.

SERVES 8

2 lb boneless, skinless chicken breasts

2 tsp kosher salt, or as needed

1 tsp freshly ground black pepper, or as needed

1 tbsp vegetable oil

16 bacon slices

1 lb romaine lettuce, washed, dried, and torn into bite-size pieces

½ cup Cobb Salad Vinaigrette (recipe follows)

1½ cups diced tomatoes

2 cups crumbled blue cheese

2 avocados, halved, peeled, and cut into ¼-inch slices

½ cup sliced green onions, cut on the diagonal

8 eggs, hard-boiled, quartered

1. Preheat the oven to 400°F. Season the chicken breasts with salt and pepper. Heat the oil in a large sauté pan over medium-high heat, add the chicken breasts, and sauté until golden brown, 2 to 3 minutes on each side.

2. Place the pan in the oven and bake until the chicken is cooked through; 165°F on an instant-read thermometer. Cool, then cut into ¼-inch-thick slices on the diagonal. The chicken can be baked up to 1 day in advance and stored in a covered container in the refrigerator.

3. In a skillet, sauté the bacon over medium-high heat until crisp. Drain on paper towels and crumble into small pieces.

4. In a large bowl, toss the romaine lettuce with the vinaigrette and arrange on a platter or individual plates. Top with the chicken slices, tomato, blue cheese, avocado, green onions, hard-boiled eggs, and crumbled bacon. Serve at once.

Cobb Salad Vinaigrette

This vinaigrette, while perfect for the Cobb Salad, is also versatile enough for most green salads.

MAKES 2 CUPS VINAIGRETTE

6 tbsp red wine vinegar

¼ cup water

½ tsp granulated sugar

2½ tsp fresh lemon juice

1¼ tsp kosher salt, or as needed

½ tsp freshly ground black pepper, or as needed

½ tsp whole-grain mustard

2 garlic cloves, minced

1¼ cups extra-virgin olive oil

In a medium bowl, whisk together the vinegar, water, sugar, lemon juice, salt, pepper, mustard, and garlic. Allow the flavors to marry for 5 minutes. Add the olive oil and whisk thoroughly. The dressing can be made in advance and stored in a covered container in the refrigerator for up to 2 days. It may be necessary to blend the dressing together again before serving.

SANDWICHES

WHEN CREATING A SANDWICH, you can select from an array of diverse culinary influences. You may choose to serve Scandinavian smørrebrød, Spanish bocadillas, American po'boys, Italian panini, French croques monsieur, or Vietnamese bahn mi. Sandwiches can be as elegant as foie gras on toasted brioche or as casual as a grilled Reuben on rye. They are one of the most adaptable foods, because the only thing that unifies the concept of a sandwich in all instances is a tasty filling served on or in bread or a similar wrapper.

Breads for making sandwiches run a similarly wide gamut. You might like a crusty baguette, the softness of a white Pullman loaf, or a flatbread like focaccia or pita. When building a sandwich, you should consider the characteristics of the bread and how they will fit in with the flavor and texture of the filling. Sandwich bread should be firm and thick enough to hold the filling, but not so thick that the sandwich is too dry to enjoy. Some sandwiches call for toasted bread; in that case, toast the bread immediately before assembling the sandwiches.

Many sandwiches call for a spread that is applied directly to the bread. Spreads can add moisture, help hold the sandwich together, and act as a barrier to keep the bread from getting soggy. Spreads can be very simple and subtly flavored, or they may themselves bring a special flavor and texture to the sandwich. The following list of spreads includes some classic options, as well as some that may not immediately spring to mind as sandwich spreads:

MAYONNAISE (PLAIN OR FLAVORED, SUCH AS AÏOLI OR ROUILLE)

CREAMY SALAD DRESSINGS

PLAIN OR COMPOUND BUTTERS

MUSTARD OR KETCHUP

SPREADABLE CHEESES, SUCH AS RICOTTA, CREAM CHEESE, OR MASCARPONE

TAHINI, OLIVE, OR HERB SPREADS (SUCH AS HUMMUS, TAPENADE, OR PESTO)

NUT BUTTERS

JELLY, JAM, COMPOTES, RELISHES, CHUTNEYS, OR OTHER FRUIT PRESERVES

MASHED AVOCADO OR GUACAMOLE

OILS OR VINAIGRETTES

Lettuce, slices of tomato or cheese, raw onion, and sprouts are used to garnish many sandwiches, but pickled or grilled vegetables, sliced fruits, and green salads are also possibilities. Garnishes like these become a part of the sandwich's overall structure, so consider the moisture level and texture of the garnishes and how they will complement or contrast with the sandwich's other components.

Reuben Sandwich

This classic combination of corned beef, Swiss cheese, and sauerkraut is reportedly named for the New York delicatessen owner who created it. Paired with a cup of hearty soup or a crisp, refreshing salad, it makes a satisfying meal.

MAKES 8 SANDWICHES

¼ cup (½ stick) unsalted butter, softened

16 slices rye bread

16 slices Swiss cheese

1¼ lb corned beef brisket, thinly sliced

1 lb sauerkraut

½ cup Russian Dressing (recipe follows)

1. Butter all the bread slices on one side. Place 8 of the slices, buttered side down, on a parchment paper–lined baking sheet. Top each bread slice with a slice of Swiss cheese, then divide half of the corned beef among the sandwiches.

2. Divide the sauerkraut among the sandwiches, and top each sandwich with 1 tablespoon of the Russian dressing. Add another layer of corned beef and a second slice of Swiss cheese to each sandwich. Finish with the remaining bread slices, buttered side facing up. The sandwiches can be assembled and then wrapped and held in the refrigerator for up to 8 hours.

3. Preheat a sandwich griddle or frying pan to medium heat. Cook the sandwiches on one side until the bread is golden brown, about 3 minutes. You may have to prepare the sandwiches in batches if your pan does not hold all of the sandwiches at once. Use a spatula to carefully flip the sandwiches over and finish cooking on the second side, 3 minutes more. If you are cooking the sandwiches in batches, keep the finished ones warm in a 200°F oven. To serve: Cut the sandwiches in half and place on a warmed platter or individual plates.

Russian Dressing

Russian dressing is a classic component of a Reuben sandwich, and it is equally at home in sandwiches featuring ham, turkey, or roast beef, as well as a dressing for an iceberg wedge salad.

MAKES 1 CUP DRESSING

⅔ cup mayonnaise

3 tbsp ketchup

1 tbsp prepared horseradish

1 tsp Worcestershire sauce

Kosher salt and freshly ground black pepper, as needed

In a small bowl, combine all of the ingredients thoroughly. The dressing is ready to use now, or it can be stored in a covered container in the refrigerator until needed, or for up to 3 days.

Muffaletta

The piquillo peppers in the olive spread give this sandwich a delightful heat. You can substitute other chiles, or leave them out entirely, if you prefer.

SERVES 12

¼ cup Kalamata olives, pitted

½ cup Picholine olives, pitted and chopped

½ cup extra-virgin olive oil

½ cup chopped flat-leaf parsley

⅓ cup jarred piquillo peppers, drained and chopped

2 anchovy fillets

1 tbsp red wine vinegar

1 tbsp fresh lemon juice

1 tsp dried oregano

2 muffaletta loaves or round focaccia, 1½ lb each

20 leaves romaine lettuce, trimmed, cleaned and left whole

12 oz mortadella, thinly sliced

12 oz sopressata, thinly sliced

12 oz provolone, thinly sliced

1. Combine the olives, olive oil, parsley, peppers, ancho-vies, vinegar, lemon juice, and oregano in the bowl of a food processor fitted with a blade attachment. Pulse un-til finely chopped. Transfer to a container, cover, and let the mixture mellow at least 6 hours in the refrigerator, or for up to 2 days.

2. Cut the loaves in half horizontally. Hollow out the top and bottom of each loaf slightly to make room for the filling. Line the hollows with romaine leaves. Spread the olive mixture evenly over the romaine on both sides.

3. Place the mortadella over the olive spread, the cheese over the mortadella, and the sopressata over the cheese. Top with the other half of bread, which is already lined with the lettuce and olive spread. Cut the loaf into 6 wedges and serve on a platter.

Eggplant and Havarti Sandwiches

Broiling the eggplant for this sandwich gives it a crisp texture on the outside while the inside stays smooth and creamy. The red onion adds a crisp bite to the sandwich and a slightly sweet flavor.

SERVES 6

¼ cup olive oil

½ cup balsamic vinegar

1 tsp minced garlic

⅓ tsp kosher salt, as needed

¼ tsp freshly ground black pepper, or as needed

1 medium Italian eggplant (about 1½ lb), cut into six ½-inch-thick slices

6 hard rolls, sliced in half horizontally

¾ cup roasted red pepper strips (page 160)

12 slices havarti (about 6 oz total)

6 thin slices red onion

1. Preheat the broiler, positioning the rack about 5 inches from the heat source. In a medium bowl, mix the olive oil, vinegar, garlic, salt, and pepper together until thor-oughly combined.

2. Dip the eggplant slices in the oil and vinegar mixture to coat, and reserve the remaining mixture. Place the eggplant on the rack of a broiling pan. Broil until lightly golden, 6 to 7 minutes per side. Reserve.

3. Meanwhile, spoon the remaining oil and vinegar mix-ture generously on both sides of the rolls. Toast the rolls under the broiler until lightly golden on one side, about 45 seconds.

4. For each sandwich, top one-half of each roll, oiled side up, with a slice of eggplant. Place a piece of roasted red pepper on top of the eggplant. Next layer 1 slice of the cheese.

5. Place the other halves of the rolls oiled side up and top them with a slice of red onion and 1 slice of cheese each. The sandwiches are ready to finish in the broiler at this point, or they can be wrapped and stored in the refrigerator for up to 8 hours.

6. Place the sandwiches under the broiler and heat until the cheese is melted, 1 to 1½ minutes. Assemble the sandwiches, cut in half, and serve immediately on a warmed platter or individual plates.

Moroccan Chicken Pita Sandwiches with Carrot Salad

SERVES 8

Chicken Marinade

2 tbsp fresh lemon juice

2 tsp kosher salt

1 tsp garlic powder

½ tsp Spanish paprika

½ tsp ground cumin

¼ tsp freshly ground black pepper

¼ tsp ground cinnamon

⅛ tsp ground cayenne

8 skinless chicken leg portions

3 tbsp extra-virgin olive oil

1 cup chicken broth

½ cup pitted chopped Kalamata olives

1 cup peeled, seeded, and diced tomato

½ cup diced roasted red peppers (page 160)

1 tbsp chopped cilantro

1 tbsp chopped flat-leaf parsley

1 tsp kosher salt

8 pieces pita, white or whole wheat

1. Combine the chicken marinade ingredients in a large ziplock bag. Add the chicken, seal the bag, and massage to coat evenly. Marinate, refrigerated, for at least 2 and up to 12 hours.

2. Heat the oil in a Dutch oven over medium heat. Remove the chicken from the marinade and place it in the hot oil. Brown the chicken on both sides, turning as needed to brown evenly, about 5 minutes total.

3. Add the broth and stir to release any brown bits in the pan. Add the olives, bring to a simmer, cover, and cook over low heat until the chicken is fork-tender, about 30 minutes. Remove the Dutch oven from the heat and let the chicken cool in the braising liquid. Remove the chicken from the liquid. Pull the chicken meat from the bones. Degrease the liquid and reserve. The chicken and the braising liquid can be prepared to this point and stored separately in covered containers in the refrigerator for up to 2 days.

4. Combine the chicken meat with the tomatoes, peppers, reserved braising liquid, cilantro, parsley, and salt and toss well.

5. Split the pitas to open up the pocket and fill with the chicken mixture. Serve at once.

Whole Wheat Quesadillas with Chicken, Jalapeño Jack, and Mango Salsa

SERVES 8

2 tbsp vegetable oil

3 lb boneless, skinless chicken breasts

2 tsp kosher salt, or as needed

1 tsp freshly ground black pepper, or as needed

4 mangoes, pitted, peeled, and diced

1 papaya, peeled, seeded, and diced

1 canned chipotle pepper, minced

¼ cup fresh orange juice

¼ cup fresh lime juice

4 cups pepper Jack, grated

6 cups green onions, white and green portions, thinly sliced

1 cup roughly chopped peanuts, toasted

16 whole wheat flour tortillas, 7 inches in diameter

3 tbsp peanut oil

1. Preheat the oven to 400°F.

2. Heat the oil in a large ovenproof sauté pan over high heat. Season the chicken breasts with the salt and pepper. Add the chicken breasts to the pan and sauté until golden brown on all sides, 8 to 10 minutes. Transfer the chicken in the oven and bake until cooked through; 165°F on an instant-read thermometer, 10 to 12 minutes.

3. While the chicken is baking, in a medium bowl, combine the mangoes, papaya, chipotle pepper, orange juice, and lime juice. Cover and reserve in the refrigerator until needed or for up to 24 hours.

4. Remove the chicken from the oven and allow it to cool for 5 minutes. Shred the chicken meat into bite-size pieces.

5. To assemble the quesadillas: For each portion, place ¾ cup chicken, ½ cup pepper Jack, ¾ cup green onions, and 2 tablespoons peanuts on a tortilla. Top with another tortilla. Repeat the process to make 8 quesadillas. The quesadillas can be assembled to this point and then wrapped and stored in the refrigerator for up to 24 hours.

6. Heat about 1 teaspoon peanut oil in a large sauté pan. Place 1 quesadilla in the pan and lightly brown on both sides, making certain that the cheese is melted in the middle before removing from the heat, about 6 minutes total. Repeat with remaining quesadillas, adding more peanut oil as necessary. Cut each quesadilla into fourths and serve with chilled the mango salsa on the side.

Open-Face Salmon and Red Onion Sandwich

Choose a fine-grained, whole grain or rye bread for this sandwich. These breads make a good match for a silken slice of smoked salmon.

SERVES 8

1 small red onion very thinly sliced

Caper-Dill Mayonnaise

½ cup mayonnaise

2 tbsp Dijon mustard

1 tbsp capers, rinsed and chopped

2 tbsp chopped dill

8 slices fine-grained whole wheat or rye bread

1 lb sliced smoked salmon

1 tbsp capers, rinsed

1 tbsp dill sprigs

1. Place the sliced onions in a small bowl and add enough cold water to cover completely. Let the onions soak in the cold water in the refrigerator for at least 20 minutes and up to 2 hours.

2. Stir together the mayonnaise, mustard, capers, and dill in a small bowl. Set aside.

3. Cut the bread slices in half. Spread with the caper-dill mayonnaise. Top with the smoked salmon.

4. Drain the red onion slices and blot dry with paper towels. Garnish each sandwich with red onion, whole capers, and a sprig of dill. Serve on a platter or individual plates.

Open-Face Salmon and Red Onion Sandwich

Pan Bagnat

Pan bagnat is the perfect do-ahead sandwich. It actually needs some time to rest to achieve the best flavor and texture.

SERVES 8

Dressing

6 tbsp red wine vinegar

2 tbsp chopped basil

¼ cup chopped flat-leaf parsley

4 anchovy fillets

1 jalapeño, roasted, peeled, seeded, and finely chopped

1 cup extra-virgin olive oil

8 ciabatta rolls or 2 baguettes

1 lb drained oil-packed tuna, flaked

1 cup peeled, seeded, and diced tomato,

½ cup Roasted Pepper Topping (page 59)

½ cup coarsely chopped pitted Kalamata olives

1 large seedless cucumber, peeled, seeded, and chopped

½ cup minced red onion

2 hard-boiled eggs, chopped

2 tbsp capers, rinsed

1. Combine the vinegar, basil, parsley, anchovies, and jalapeño in a blender and purée until smooth. With the motor running, slowly pour in the oil. This dressing can be made in advance and stored in a covered container in the refrigerator for up to 2 days. Let it warm to room temperature and stir or shake well to recombine before using.

2. Cut the rolls in half lengthwise and scoop out the insides. Crumble the bread that you've pulled out of the rolls into a medium bowl and add the tuna, tomatoes, roasted peppers, olives, cucumber, onion, eggs, capers, and garlic. Add enough dressing to moisten and bind the filling. Season to taste with salt and pepper.

3. Brush the inside of the rolls with some of the remaining dressing. Fill the roll with about ½ cup of the tuna mixture and firmly press the sandwich closed. Wrap each sandwich tightly with waxed paper and let it rest at room temperature for at least 1 hour before serving. You can hold the assembled sandwiches in the refrigerator for up to 8 hours.

Falafel in Pita Pockets

Falafel is traditionally served in a pita pocket, garnished with chopped fresh tomatoes, sliced cucumbers, shredded lettuce, and some Cucumber Raita.

SERVES 6

3 cups dried chickpeas

1 cup water

2 tbsp all-purpose flour, plus additional as needed for dredging

½ tbsp baking soda

3 garlic cloves, finely minced

1 large egg, beaten

2 tbsp minced flat-leaf parsley

2 tbsp minced cilantro

2 tsp ground cumin

½ teaspoon ground turmeric

½ tsp ground coriander

½ tsp kosher salt, as needed

Freshly ground black pepper, as needed

4 cups olive oil, or as needed

8 pitas, white or whole wheat

2 cups shredded lettuce

1 cup chopped tomatoes

½ cup thinly sliced, peeled seedless cucumbers

Cucumber Raita (recipe follows)

1. Rinse and pick over the chickpeas and soak them in a medium pot in cool water for at least 24 and up to 48 hours.

2. Drain the chickpeas, and place them in a food processor with the water, flour, baking soda, garlic, egg, parsley, cilantro, cumin, turmeric, coriander, salt, and pepper in a food processor. Process until the ingredients form a coarse paste.

3. Place some flour in a shallow bowl. Form the chickpea mixture into twenty-four 1-inch balls. The falafel can be prepared to this point and stored on a baking sheet for up to 24 hours before frying.

4. In a deep fryer, or use a straight-sided skillet and fill it with oil to a depth of 2 inches, heat the oil to 350°F. (The oil is about at that temperature, when a 1-inch cube of bread, when dropped in, browns in about 65 seconds.)

5. Dredge each falafel in flour and deep-fry them in batches in the oil until they are golden brown on both sides, 3 to 4 minutes total per batch. Drain on paper towels.

6. Split the pitas and fill with the lettuce, tomato, cucumber, and falafel patties. Spoon in some of the raita and serve them at once.

Cucumber Raita

MAKES 2 CUPS RAITA

2 cups plain yogurt

½ cup small-dice cucumber, peeled and seeded

2 garlic cloves, minced

1 tbsp chopped mint

½ tsp ground cumin

¼ tsp kosher salt, or as needed

¼ tsp freshly ground black pepper, or as needed

Dash of cayenne pepper

1. Line a wire-mesh sieve with a coffee filter or cheesecloth, add the yogurt and let it drain over a bowl for 30 minutes. For a thicker, creamier raita, opt for Greek-style yogurt or drain the yogurt overnight in the refrigerator.

2. In a medium bowl, combine all of the ingredients thoroughly. The raita is ready to use now, or can be stored in a covered container in the refrigerator for up to 2 days.

NOTES *A quick and easy way to prepare the cucumbers is to peel them and chop them in the food processor. Excess water can be drained before the cucumbers are added to the yogurt.*

To remove the sharp garlic "bite" and impart a more subtle garlic flavor, toss the garlic cloves in a small pot of boiling water for a minute and drain them. Then dip the garlic in the water one more time and drain again. The garlic can then be chopped in the food processor with the cucumber or minced separately.

PASTA

COOK PASTA IN A LARGE AMOUNT of boiling, well-salted water. Use a minimum of 4 quarts of water and 1 to 2 tablespoons of salt for every pound of pasta.

Pasta is cooked until al dente, literally "to the tooth," or "just yielding" when bitten into. Cooking times depend on whether the pasta is dried or fresh, as well as the size and shape. Fresh pasta cooks very quickly, often needing only 2 or 3 minutes to cook.

Drain the pasta well in a colander before combining it with a sauce. If you will not be using it immediately, rinse it with cold water to stop the cooking and prevent sticking.

Pasta Quattro Formaggi

Very easy to make, this pasta sauce is nothing more than heavy cream carefully reduced with a selection of four (quattro) cheeses added. The selection of cheeses can vary, but generally includes a soft blue cheese, such as Gorgonzola, and Parmigiano-Reggiano, among others. Choose your favorites and enjoy.

SERVES 6

2 cups heavy cream

1 cup grated Emmentaler

1 cup grated Gruyère

1 cup crumbled Danish blue (Danablu) cheese

¾ cup grated Parmigiano-Reggiano

1¼ lb dried fusilli (corkscrew pasta)

2 tsp freshly ground black pepper, or as needed

1. In a large sauté pan, bring the cream to a simmer over medium heat, watching carefully to avoid scorching. Reduce the cream by one-fourth. Add the cheeses. Stir continuously while the cheeses melt. Keep the sauce warm, or cool and store in a covered container in the refrigerator for up to 12 hours.

2. Bring a large pot of salted water to a boil. Add the pasta and stir once or twice to separate the pieces. Cook until it is tender to the bite, 8 to 10 minutes. Drain well. Reheat the sauce over low heat, if necessary. Add the cooked pasta to the cream sauce mixture, toss to coat, and season with pepper. (Salt will probably not be needed due to the saltiness of the water and the saltiness of the cheese.) Serve immediately in warmed pasta bowls.

Spinach and Escarole Lasagna

This delicious take on a classic lasagna is easy to make ahead of time. Assemble the lasagna (through step 6), then wrap well and freeze for up to 6 weeks. Let the lasagna thaw in the refrigerator for at least 12 hours before baking, and increase the baking time, if necessary, to get it piping hot all the way through.

SERVES 8

About 10 dried lasagna noodles

Cheese Filling

15 oz ricotta

1 cup grated Parmesan

⅓ cup minced flat-leaf parsley

½ tsp kosher salt, plus as needed

¼ tsp freshly ground black pepper, plus more as needed

¼ tsp freshly grated nutmeg, or as needed

2 large eggs, beaten

Escarole Filling

2 tbsp olive oil

1 tsp minced garlic

1 head escarole, well washed, trimmed, and chopped

Spinach Filling

2 tbsp olive oil

2 tsp minced garlic

1 bunch spinach, well washed, trimmed, chopped

4 cups Tomato Sauce (page 165)

2½ cups shredded mozzarella

½ cup grated Parmigiano-Reggiano

1. Bring a large, wide pot of salted water to a boil to cook the pasta. Add the lasagna noodles and stir to separate. Cook until tender to the bite, about 8 minutes. Drain the noodles and rinse with very cold water. Drain again and lay flat on clean kitchen towels.

2. Preheat the oven to 375°F. To make the cheese filling: In a large bowl, combine the ricotta, Parmigiano-Reggiano, parsley, salt, pepper, and nutmeg. Add the eggs and mix well. Set aside.

3. To make the escarole filling: Heat the oil in a large skillet over medium-high heat. Add the garlic and sauté for 15 seconds. Add the escarole and sauté, turning frequently, until the greens have wilted and cooked through, about 4 minutes. Season well with salt and pepper, transfer to a medium bowl, and set aside.

4. To make the spinach filling: Add the oil to the skillet and return to medium-high heat. Add the garlic and sauté for 15 seconds. Add the spinach and sauté, turning frequently, until the greens have wilted and cooked through, about 2 minutes. Season well with salt and pepper, transfer to another medium bowl, and set aside.

5. To assemble the lasagna: In the bottom of a 9 by 13-inch baking dish, spread 1 cup of the tomato sauce. Add a layer of cooked pasta, then spread half of the cheese filling evenly over the pasta, followed by all the escarole and its juices. Top with 1½ cups of the tomato sauce. Spread half of the mozzarella over the sauce and sprinkle with half of the Parmigiano-Reggiano.

6. Place another layer of pasta on top and spread with the remaining cheese filling, then add the spinach and its juices. Top with the remaining 1½ cups of tomato sauce. Tuck any long noodles into the pan to prevent them from curling and drying, scatter the remaining mozzarella on top, and sprinkle with the remaining Parmigiano-Reggiano. Cover with aluminum foil.

7. Preheat the oven to 375°F. Bake the lasagna until it is hot all the way through and the cheese has melted, 35 to 45 minutes. Remove the foil and continue to bake until the cheeses are bubbly and the top turns golden brown, about 10 minutes more. Remove the lasagna from the oven and let it stand for about 15 minutes. Cut into portions and serve in warmed pasta bowls.

PIZZA

MUCH LIKE BURGERS, pizza is a blank canvas for your culinary creativity. The crust can be thick or thin, classic white or whole wheat; the sauce may be marinara, pesto, alfredo, or none at all; the cheese may be nearly any variety, shredded, finely grated, or shaved; the toppings may be meat, poultry, seafood, veggies, fruits, nuts, herbs, or any combination thereof.

Excellent-quality pizza dough can be bought premade, fresh or frozen, at most grocery stores, but nothing beats a homemade crust. Pizza dough freezes beautifully, so you can mix the dough ahead, wrap it up, freeze it, and simply thaw and bake it on party day. If you're making the dough from scratch on the day of your party, remember to start at least 1½ hours before you plan to serve it, so that you can give the dough time to rise and rest properly.

Pizza Margherita

The dough for this pizza is perfect for a number of different toppings. This a classic option, but you can add whatever vegetables or meats you like.

MAKES TWO 12-INCH ROUND PIZZAS

Semolina Pizza Dough

3½ cups bread flour

½ cups semolina flour

1½ tsp instant dry yeast

1½ cups water

3 tbsp olive oil

2 tsp kosher salt

Toppings

2 cups Tomato Sauce (page 165)

12 oz shredded mozzarella

½ cup grated Parmesan

1. Place the flours and yeast in the bowl of a mixer (or a large bowl if you are mixing by hand). Add the water, olive oil, and salt; mix on low speed with the dough hook attachment for 2 minutes and then on medium speed until the dough is satiny and elastic, but is still a little sticky, another 4 minutes. (If you are mixing by hand, stir long enough to make a rough dough and then transfer the dough to a floured work surface and knead until satiny, about 10 minutes.)

2. Transfer the dough to a clean bowl, rub the surface with oil, cover with plastic wrap or damp towels, and let rise until nearly doubled, about 30 minutes, and gently fold the dough over on itself in two or three places. Allow the dough to relax another 30 minutes before cutting it into pieces. Cut the dough in half and shape each piece into a smooth round ball. At this point, the dough can be wrapped and held in the refrigerator for up to 24 hours or frozen for up to 6 weeks. Let the dough come to room temperature before shaping into pizza crusts.

3. Preheat the oven to 450°F. Scatter a thin layer of cornmeal on round pizza pans.

4. To shape pizza dough: Press each piece of dough into a disk, stretching and turning the dough as you work. You may finish stretching the dough by flipping it: With the dough resting on the backs of your hands, simultaneously spin the dough and toss it into the air. As it falls back down, catch it on the backs of your hands once more. Continue until the crust is an even thickness, ⅛ to ¼ inch. If you prefer, you can pull and stretch the dough directly on a lightly floured work surface until it is an even thickness.

5. Transfer the dough to the pizza pans. Top with tomato sauce, mozzarella, and Parmesan, leaving a 1-inch border without garnish.

6. Bake the pizzas until golden brown around the edges, 10 to 12 minutes. Serve at once.

STEWS

STEWS ARE A WONDERFUL OPTION for casual entertaining. Most can be prepared a day or two in advance. Many chefs feel that the flavor improves if the stew has a chance to mellow. These are the ideal choices for tailgates or cold-weather picnics. You can keep them warm in a thermos and serve them in cups.

New Mexican Green Chile Stew

Poblano chiles and jalapeños give this dish its color and flavor. Serve warm flour tortillas and a little grated Monterey Jack cheese to accompany the stew.

SERVES 8

2 tbsp canola oil

3 lb boneless pork shoulder, cut into 1-inch cubes

Kosher salt and freshly ground black pepper, as needed

2 large yellow onions, cut into medium dice

1 tbsp minced garlic

4 cups chicken broth

½ cup tomato purée

3 to 4 poblano chiles, roasted, seeded, peeled, and cut into medium dice

2 tbsp mild red chili powder

1 tbsp ground cumin

2 tsp ground Mexican oregano

2 jalapeños, seeded, finely minced

2 tbsp green Tabasco sauce

1 tsp white vinegar

3 cups cubed, unpeeled red-skinned potatoes

1. Heat the oil in a casserole or Dutch oven over medium heat until it shimmers. Season the pork with salt and pepper and sauté until lightly colored on all sides. Transfer the pork to a plate or dish using a slotted spoon, allowing most of the oil to drain back into the casserole. Return the casserole to the heat, add the onions and garlic, and sauté, stirring frequently, until translucent, 6 to 8 minutes.

2. Return the pork and any juices it may have released to the casserole. Add the broth, tomato purée, poblanos, chile powder, cumin, and oregano and bring to a boil. Immediately adjust the heat to establish a gentle simmer. Simmer the stew, covered, for 1 hour, stirring occasionally.

3. Add the jalapeños, Tabasco, vinegar, and potatoes. Continue to simmer, covered, until the potatoes and pork are very tender, about 20 minutes. Season to taste with additional salt and pepper. The stew can be cooled and stored in a covered container in the refrigerator for 2 days. Reheat before serving.

4. Serve in warmed bowls.

Duck, Shrimp, and Andouille Gumbo

Gumbo is a stewlike dish that was created in Louisiana and is now recognized and enjoyed in many varieties. It originally combined meat and shellfish, okra, tomatoes, bay leaf, and hot pepper sauce.

MAKES 2 QUARTS GUMBO; SERVES 8

2 tbsp unsalted butter

¼ cup all-purpose flour

2 tbsp vegetable oil

1½ onions, diced

3 celery stalks, diced

1 green bell pepper, diced

4 garlic cloves, minced

2 tbsp tomato paste

¼ cup white wine

1 quart chicken broth

1 cup tomato purée

1 ham hock

¾ cup okra, trimmed, cut into ¼-inch slices

½ lb andouille sausage, sliced into ¼-inch pieces

2 skinless duck breasts

2 tsp kosher salt, or as needed

1 tsp freshly ground black pepper, or as needed

½ lb shrimp, peeled and deveined

3 plum tomatoes, seeded, diced

½ tsp hot pepper sauce

1. In a small saucepan over medium heat, combine the butter and flour to make a roux. Cook until dark brown, stirring frequently, 8 to 10 minutes.

2. While the roux is cooking, heat the oil in a sauté pan over medium heat. Add the onions, celery, and bell pepper and cook, stirring occasionally, until golden brown, 12 to 15 minutes.

3. Add the garlic and cook until aromatic, about 2 minutes more. Add the tomato paste and cook to a rich reddish-brown color, stirring constantly, 3 to 4 minutes. Add the wine to the pan, stir well to release the brown bits in the bottom of the pan, and allow the wine to reduce by half, about 4 minutes more.

4. In a large pot, bring the broth to a simmer. Whisk the roux into the hot broth, making sure to break up any lumps, and then add the prepared vegetable mixture. Add the tomato purée, ham hock, and okra and simmer until thickened, 15 to 20 minutes.

5. While the gumbo is simmering, cook the andouille in a dry sauté pan over medium heat until some of the fat is released and the sausage is browned and cooked through, 4 to 5 minutes. Remove the andouille from the pan and reserve the rendered fat in the pan.

6. Season the duck breasts with ½ teaspoon of the salt and ¼ teaspoon of the pepper. Return the pan with the andouille fat to medium-high heat, and add the duck breasts. Sauté on both sides until cooked through; 165°F on an instant-read thermometer. Let the breasts rest for at least 3 minutes, or until cool enough to handle and then cut them into medium dice.

7. Season the shrimp with ½ teaspoon of the salt and ¼ teaspoon of the pepper. Add the shrimp, andouille, and duck to the gumbo along with the tomatoes. Continue to simmer until all of the ingredients are heated through, about 10 minutes. Season with the remaining salt, pepper, and hot pepper sauce, as needed. Serve in warmed soup bowls. The complete gumbo can be made in advance and stored in a covered container in the refrigerator for up to 2 days or in the freezer for up to 2 months.

Butternut Squash, Eggplant, Zucchini, and Fava Bean Stew

Packed with colorful vegetables, this hearty and warming stew is full of sweet and spicy flavors.

SERVES 8

1 tbsp olive oil

2 leeks, white portion only, well washed, sliced

2 tbsp minced garlic

1 tbsp red curry paste

½ lb butternut squash, peeled, diced

1 lb canned chickpeas, drained and rinsed

½ cup shelled fava beans

3 cups vegetable broth

2 cups diced zucchini

2½ cups peeled, diced eggplant

1½ cups diced carrots

¾ cup diced celery

⅓ cup dried currants

3 tbsp tomato purée

2 tsp fresh lemon juice

1½ tsp freshly grated lemon zest

Kosher salt and freshly ground black pepper, as needed

1. Heat the oil in a large pot over medium-high heat. Add the leeks and garlic and sauté, stirring frequently, until translucent, 3 to 5 minutes. Add the curry paste and sauté until fragrant, 1 minute more.

2. Stir in the squash, chickpeas, and fava beans. Add enough broth to cover the vegetables and simmer for 10 minutes. Add the remaining broth, zucchini, eggplant, carrots, celery, currants, and tomato purée. Simmer until the vegetables are tender, about 20 minutes. The stew is ready to serve now, or it can be cooled and stored in a covered container in the refrigerator for up to 2 days. Reheat before adding the final seasoning in step 3.

3. Add the lemon juice and zest and season with salt and pepper. Serve the stew on warmed plates over rice or couscous.

Southwest White Bean Stew

Try using a mix of colored bell peppers for this stew. Green peppers, which are unripened, will be less sweet than the fully ripened orange, red, or yellow peppers.

SERVES 6

3 cups cooked or canned navy beans, rinsed and drained

1 tsp safflower oil

½ cup diced red onion

½ cup diced assorted bell peppers

2 jalapeños, seeded, diced

3 garlic cloves, minced

2 tbsp sherry vinegar

⅓ cup peeled, seeded, and chopped plum tomato

2 tbsp chopped cilantro

1. In a blender or food processor, purée half of the cooked beans until smooth.

2. Heat the oil in a soup pot over medium heat. Add the onion, bell peppers, jalapeños, and garlic and sauté until the onions are translucent, 4 to 5 minutes.

3. Add the puréed and whole beans, stirring constantly, until the beans are heated through, 3 to 4 minutes.

4. Add the vinegar and tomato and remove from the heat when hot. The stew can be served now, or it can be cooled and stored in a covered container in the refrigerator for up to 3 days. Reheat before serving.

5. Stir in the cilantro just before serving. Serve at once in warmed bowls.

Traditional Swiss Fondue

A fondue pot keeps the fondue warm without letting it get too hot. If you don't have one, we strongly urge you to borrow one from a friend, and remember to ask for the dipping forks. If the cheese is getting too stringy as it melts, or even while you and your guests are enjoying it, you can save the day with a splash of wine or squeeze of lemon juice.

SERVES 8

1 garlic clove, peeled

1⅔ cups dry white wine

1 lb Gruyère, grated

2 tsp cornstarch

¼ cup kirsch

Ground white pepper, as needed

Freshly grated nutmeg, as needed

1 baguette, cut into 1-inch cubes

3 or 4 Granny Smith apples, cored and cut into 1-inch cubes

16 cornichons

16 pickled onions

1. Cut the garlic clove in half and rub the inside of the fondue pot with the cut sides. Turn the heat to medium under the pot.

2. Toss the grated cheese with the cornstarch and set aside.

3. Add the wine to the fondue pot, turn the heat to medium-high, and bring to a simmer. Add the cheese, a handful at a time, waiting for the previous bit to have melted. Stir in a figure-eight pattern rather than in a circle; this will help keep the cheese from becoming too stringy.

4. When all the cheese has melted, add the kirsch, white pepper, and a few gratings of nutmeg.

5. Serve with the bread, apple cubes, cornichons, and pickled onions. Keep the fondue steaming, but not boiling.

Traditional Swiss Fondue

Mu Shu Vegetables

Have all of your ingredients and stir-frying tools arranged in bowls and ready to go so you can stir-fry the vegetables and serve them sizzling hot from the wok. You can cut all the vegetables up to 4 hours in advance and store them, in the refrigerator, in ziplock bags. Combine the garlic, ginger, and scallions in one bag, but keep the other vegetables separate.

SERVES 8

- 3 tbsp peanut oil
- 1 tbsp minced garlic
- 1 tbsp peeled, minced ginger
- 1 tbsp green onions, white and green portions,, minced
- 1 red bell pepper, seeded and cut in 1-inch strips
- 4 celery stalks, cut in 1-inch strips
- 4 carrots, cut in 1-inch strips
- ½ head Napa cabbage, cut into thin strips
- 2 tbsp hoisin sauce
- 3 tbsp soy sauce
- 1 tbsp sesame oil
- 1 large egg, beaten
- 16 mu shu pancakes, warmed (recipe follows)

1. Heat the oil in a wok or a large sauté pan over high heat. Add the garlic, ginger, and green onions. Stir-fry until aromatic, about 1 minute.

2. Add the bell pepper, celery, carrots, and cabbage. Stir-fry until tender, about 2 minutes. Stir in the hoisin sauce, soy sauce, and sesame oil.

3. Make a well in the middle of the vegetable mixture, pour in the egg and let it cook, undisturbed, until it starts to set, about 30 seconds, then use large chopsticks to break it up into the vegetables.

4. Serve the hot vegetables immediately with mu shu pancakes.

Mu Shu Pancakes

The pancakes are not difficult to make, but you can certainly substitute purchased mu shu pancakes. You'll find them in refrigerated cases in the produce section of most stores. If not, use flour tortillas. Warm the purchased pancakes as described in step 5.

MAKES 16 PANCAKES

- 2 cups all-purpose flour
- ¾ cup boiling water, plus more as needed
- 3 tbsp light sesame oil, plus more as needed

1. Sift the flour into a large bowl, add the boiling water to the flour, and begin stirring it in immediately, adding a little additional water, as necessary, to make a soft firm dough. Knead the warm dough on a lightly floured surface until smooth, 3 or 4 minutes. Wrap the dough and let it rest at room temperature for 30 minutes.

2. Turn the rested dough out onto a floured surface. Cut the dough in half. Working with one piece of dough at a time, roll into a long rope and then cut into 8 equal pieces and roll each into a ball. Press the ball flat with the palm of your hand. Using a lightly floured rolling pin, roll the dough into a circle about ¼ inch thick and 3 inches in diameter.

3. Brush sesame oil lightly over the tops of 2 dough circles. Lay one pancake on top of another, so that the oiled sides are together. (The edges don't have to line up perfectly.) Roll out the pancakes to form a 6-inch circle. Repeat with the remaining the pancakes. Use a damp towel to cover the prepared pancakes, to keep them from drying out as you work.

4. Heat about ½ teaspoon oil to a skillet over low heat. Add one of the paired pancakes and cook until barely golden, dry, and blistered, about 1 minute. Turn and cook on the second side until barely golden, dry, and blistered, about 1 minute. Remove the paired pancakes from the pan, transfer to a dish, and cover with a cloth. Repeat with the remaining pancakes, stacking them on top of each other in the dish. Let them rest about 5 minutes, and then pull them apart. Serve immediately or wrap and hold at room temperature.

5. The pancakes can be cooled, stacked, wrapped well in plastic wrap, and stored in the refrigerator for up to 24 hours. Reheat the pancakes in a microwave for 30 to 45 seconds before serving.

Spicy Bell Pepper, Cheddar, and Red Onion Fajitas

Cutting this colorful mixture of vegetables into thin strips is the key to the quick cooking time. Canned pinto beans make the preparation even easier.

MAKES 16 FAJITAS; SERVES 8

2 tbsp olive oil

1½ cups red onion, cut into thin strips

1 tbsp minced garlic

1 lb red bell pepper, seeded and cut into thin strips

1 lb green bell pepper, seeded and cut into thin strips

1 lb yellow bell pepper, seeded and cut into thin strips

1 lb Napa cabbage, cut into fine shreds

One 15-oz can pinto beans, drained and rinsed

3 tbsp red chili sauce

16 flour tortillas, 12-inch diameter

2⅔ cups grated cheddar

1 tbsp chopped cilantro

1. Heat the oil in a large sauté pan over medium heat. Add the onions and garlic and cook, stirring frequently, until the onions are translucent, 5 to 7 minutes. Add the bell peppers and sauté just until they begin to soften, about 5 minutes.

2. Add the cabbage and cook until tender, about 5 minutes more. Stir in the beans and chili sauce and heat just until warmed through. The vegetable filling is ready to use now, or it can be cooled and stored in a covered container in the refrigerator for up to 2 days.

3. Fifteen minutes before serving the fajitas, preheat the oven to 250°F. Place the tortillas in a stack on a baking sheet, cover with a lightly dampened kitchen towel, and warm up in the oven, about 10 minutes. Reheat the filling, if necessary.

4. To assemble the fajitas: Place ½ cup of the hot vegetable mixture in the center of each tortilla and top with a few tablespoons of the grated cheese. Sprinkle with a little cilantro for garnish and roll the tortilla around the filling. Alternatively, serve the fajitas in the traditional manner: bring the tortillas, filling, and garnishes to the table, and let each individual assemble their own.

BRUNCHES AND, FOR YOU EARLY-RISING HOSTS, BREAKFASTS ARE IDEAL FOR FAMILY CELEBRATIONS, LIKE BIRTHDAYS, ANNIVERSARIES, AND BABY SHOWERS, ESPECIALLY WHEN THE MEAL IS PART OF A WEEKEND- OR EVEN WEEK-LONG CELEBRATION, LIKE A WEDDING. PLANNING A BREAKFAST OR BRUNCH MENU IS ALL ABOUT BALANCE. SALTY AND SMOKY FOODS, LIKE BACON, SAUSAGE, LOX, AND CHEESE, AND SAVORY HOT DISHES, LIKE HASH BROWNS, HOME FRIES, AND EGG CASSEROLES, FIND A BALANCE WITH TART FRUIT JUICES. SOFT AND CREAMY SPREADS CONTRAST WITH CRUNCHY, CRISPY, AND CHEWY.

A MORNING BUFFET

Most breakfast and brunch foods are well suited to buffet-style service, so you can accommodate everyone, from the early birds to the sleepyheads that roll out of bed at the last possible moment by making the meal as self-serve as possible. You can also ease the morning rush for yourself by making every effort to set up the party space the night before. Here are some do-ahead tips:

GET OUT ALL BOWLS, PLATES, PLATTERS, AND SERVING UTENSILS.

ROLL SETS OF SILVERWARE (KNIFE, SPOON, FORK) INTO NAPKINS AND PILE IN A BASKET. (FOR MORE ON FOLDING NAPKINS, SEE PAGE 16).

POSITION MUGS OR CUPS AND SAUCERS AND COFFEE SPOONS CLOSE TO THE COFFEE POT, ALONG WITH A CREAMER AND SUGAR BOWL.

SQUEEZE ALL FRESH FRUIT JUICES. SET OUT JUICE GLASSES ALONG WITH ANY GLASS PITCHERS.

PICK A PLACE TO SERVE THE FOOD THAT WILL STILL LEAVE YOU AMPLE COUNTER SPACE.

IF YOU'RE SERVING TOAST, PUT OUT A CUTTING BOARD, A BREAD KNIFE, AND BUTTER KNIVES TO SPREAD BUTTER, CREAM CHEESE, JAM, OR PEANUT BUTTER, AND MOVE THE TOASTER TO A SPOT NEARBY.

IF YOU'RE SERVING PANCAKES OR WAFFLES, MEASURE OUT THE DRY INGREDIENTS, COMBINE IN A BOWL, AND COVER WITH PLASTIC WRAP. COMBINE THE WET INGREDIENTS IN A SEPARATE BOWL AND HOLD IN THE REFRIGERATOR.

BREAKFAST CAKES AND PASTRIES

BAKED GOODS OF ALL SORTS are a perfect addition to any breakfast or brunch menu. Coffee cakes, muffins, and scones are classic offerings. If you have a great bakery in your area, you may want to include croissants, brioches, or a variety of Danish pastries.

Cornbread and biscuits are best served hot and fresh from the oven. We've also included a delicious sausage gravy to serve with your biscuits, to make them into a substantial main dish.

Honey Almond Crumb Cake

SERVES 12 TO 14

- 3⅓ cups pastry flour
- 1 tsp salt
- ½ tsp baking powder
- ¾ cup sour cream
- ½ cup canola oil
- 3 tbsp honey
- 1 tbsp pure vanilla extract
- ½ cup almond paste
- 6 large eggs, beaten
- 1¼ cups (2½ sticks) unsalted butter, softened
- 1¼ cups granulated sugar
- 2 cups Oatmeal Streusel (recipe follows)

1. Preheat the oven to 350°F. Prepare an 11 by 17-inch jelly roll pan by spraying it lightly with cooking spray or lining it with parchment paper. Dust it lightly with flour and shake out any excess.

2. In a large bowl, sift together the flour, salt, and baking powder. Set aside. In a small bowl, blend the sour cream, oil, honey, and vanilla. Set aside.

3. In the bowl of an electric mixer fitted with the paddle attachment, cream the almond paste with 2 tablespoons of the beaten eggs on medium speed until smooth and light, 2 to 3 minutes. Scrape down the bowl to blend evenly. Add the butter and sugar and continue to mix until very smooth and light, about 2 minutes more.

4. Add the remaining beaten eggs in three additions, mixing until smooth and scraping down the bowl after each addition. Scrape down the bowl to blend evenly.

5. Add the flour mixture to the creamed butter mixture and mix the batter until it is evenly blended, scraping down the bowl as needed. Fold in the sour cream mixture by hand with a rubber spatula until just combined.

6. Spread the batter in an even layer in the prepared jelly roll pan. Sprinkle the streusel evenly over the top of the cake. Bake until a toothpick inserted into center of the cake comes out clean and the cake edges are golden brown, about 30 minutes.

7. Cool the cake in the pan on a wire rack. When the cake is completely cool, slice it and serve, or wrap well in plastic wrap and store at room temperature for up to 3 days or in the freezer for up to 6 weeks.

Oatmeal Streusel

MAKES 2 CUPS STREUSEL

- ¾ cup pastry flour
- ⅔ cup rolled oats
- 6 tbsp granulated sugar
- 1 tsp ground cinnamon
- ¼ tsp kosher salt
- 3 tbsp unsalted butter, softened

In a large bowl, combine the flour, oats, sugar, cinnamon, and salt and stir until evenly blended. Add the butter and mix by hand or with an electric mixer fitted with the paddle attachment until crumbly, about 5 minutes. Refrigerate for up to 2 weeks or freeze for up to 3 months.

Ham and Cheddar Scones with Green Onions

The cheese gets nice and brown and bubbly on the outside, and the ham adds a lot of flavor. The green onions provide a nice counterpoint to the ham and cheese and give the scones a fantastic fresh flavor. These scones are so moist, they almost fall apart.

MAKES 10 SCONES

>   3 cups bread flour
>
>   ¼ cup granulated sugar
>
>   2 tbsp baking powder
>
>   ½ tsp kosher salt
>
>   1 cup medium-dice ham
>
>   ½ cup medium-dice cheddar
>
>   ½ cup sliced green onions, white and green portions
>
>   2 cups heavy cream

1. Cut two 10-inch circles of parchment paper. Use one to line a 10-inch round cake pan. Reserve the second piece.

2. In a large bowl, sift together the flour, sugar, baking powder, and salt. Add the ham, cheese, and green onions and toss together with the flour mixture until evenly distributed.

3. Make a well in the center of the flour mixture. Add the cream and stir by hand just until the batter is evenly moistened.

4. Place the dough in the prepared cake pan, dust your hands lightly with flour, and press into an even layer. Cover the dough with the second parchment paper circle. Freeze the dough until very firm, at least 12 hours and up to 4 weeks.

5. Preheat the oven to 350°F. Prepare a baking sheet by spraying it lightly with cooking spray or lining with parchment paper.

6. Thaw the dough for 5 minutes at room temperature. Turn it out of the cake pan onto a cutting board. Cut the dough into 10 equal wedges and place the individual wedges on the baking sheet, spacing them about 2 inches apart.

7. Bake the scones until golden brown, 30 to 40 minutes. Cool the scones on the pan for a few minutes, then transfer them to wire racks. Serve the scones warm or at room temperature. Scones should be served on the same day they are made, or they can be frozen for up to 4 weeks.

Dried Cherry Scones

Dried fruits give scones a magnificent flavor. A touch of salt in the dough is the perfect counterpoint to their sweetness. As the scones bake, the dried cherries plump up and take on a great jammy texture. Or try dried currants or apricots instead of cherries for a change.

MAKES 10 SCONES

>   3 cups bread flour
>
>   ½ cup granulated sugar
>
>   2 tbsp baking powder
>
>   1½ tsp kosher salt
>
>   1 cup dried cherries
>
>   2 cups heavy cream
>
> Sugar Glaze (optional)
>
>   2 tbsp whole milk
>
>   1 cup confectioners' sugar, sifted

1. Cut two 10-inch circles of parchment paper. Use one to line a 10-inch round cake pan. Reserve the second piece.

2. In a large bowl, sift together the flour, sugar, baking powder, and salt. Add the dried cherries and toss them together with the flour mixture until evenly distributed.

3. Make a well in the center of the flour mixture. Add the cream and stir by hand with a wooden spoon just until the batter is evenly moistened.

4. Place the dough in the prepared cake pan, dust your hands lightly with flour, and press into an even layer. Cover the dough with the second parchment circle. Freeze the dough until very firm, at least 12 hours and up to 4 weeks.

5. Preheat the oven to 350°F. Prepare a baking sheet by spraying it lightly with cooking spray or lining it with parchment paper.

6. Thaw the dough for 5 minutes at room temperature. Turn it out of the cake pan onto a cutting board. Cut the dough into 10 equal wedges and place the individual wedges on the baking sheet about 2 inches apart.

7. Bake the scones until golden brown, 30 to 40 minutes. Cool the scones on the pan for a few minutes, then transfer them to wire racks.

8. To make the optional glaze: In a small bowl, mix together the milk and confectioners' sugar until blended. Spoon the glaze evenly over the scones while they are still warm. Serve the scones warm or at room temperature. Scones should be served on the same day they are made, or they can be wrapped well in plastic wrap and frozen for up to 4 weeks.

Cornbread

This recipe produces a moist cornbread with a delicate crumb and is very versatile: try making it into cornbread muffins.

SERVES 6

1¼ cups all-purpose flour

¾ cup cornmeal

1 tbsp baking powder

1 tsp kosher salt

1¾ cups buttermilk

2 large eggs

3 tbsp corn oil

2 tbsp honey

1. Preheat the oven to 350°F. Lightly oil an 8-inch square baking pan,

2. In a large bowl, combine the flour, cornmeal, baking powder, and salt until mixed thoroughly.

3. In a medium bowl, combine the buttermilk, eggs, oil, and honey and whisk to mix thoroughly.

4. Add the egg mixture to the flour mixture and mix together just until evenly moistened. Pour the batter into the prepared pan and bake until a toothpick inserted in the center comes out clean and the top of the cornbread springs back lightly to the touch, 22 to 25 minutes.

5. Allow the cornbread to cool slightly, then cut into 2-inch-square pieces. Serve the cornbread warm or at room temperature. Cornbread should be served on the same day it is made, or it can be well wrapped in plastic wrap and frozen for up to 4 weeks.

Cheddar and Thyme Muffins

Add these muffins to your repertoire as a savory alternative for breakfast or brunch.

MAKES 12 MUFFINS

2 cups all-purpose flour

2 tbsp dry mustard

1 tbsp baking powder

1 tsp kosher salt

¼ tsp freshly ground black pepper

Pinch of cayenne pepper

1 cup grated sharp cheddar

1 tbsp chopped thyme

1½ cups whole milk

1 large egg

¼ cup (½ stick) unsalted butter, melted

¼ tsp hot pepper sauce, or as needed

1. Preheat the oven to 350°F. Prepare the muffin pans by spraying them lightly with cooking spray or lining them with paper liners.

2. In a large bowl, sift together the flour, mustard, baking powder, salt, black pepper, and cayenne. Add the cheese and thyme and toss together until evenly distributed. Make a well in the center of the flour mixture.

3. In a medium bowl, whisk together the milk, egg, melted butter, and hot sauce. Add the milk mixture to the flour mixture and stir by hand just until the batter is evenly moistened.

4. Fill the prepared muffin pans about three-quarters full with the batter. Bake until a toothpick inserted into the center of a muffin comes out clean, 20 to 25 minutes.

5. Cool the muffins in the pan for about 10 minutes before serving them. The muffins can be stored in an airtight container for up to 2 days or frozen for up to 6 weeks.

Buttermilk Biscuits with Sausage Gravy

MAKES 12 BISCUITS; SERVES 6

1¼ cups cold buttermilk

1 large egg

2 cups bread flour

1¾ cups all-purpose flour

3 tbsp granulated sugar

2 tsp baking powder

1¼ tsp kosher salt

¾ cup (1½ sticks) diced unsalted butter, cold

Egg wash: 1 egg yolk whisked with 2 tbsp heavy cream

Sausage Gravy (recipe follows)

1. Prepare a baking sheet by spraying it lightly with cooking spray or lining it with parchment paper.

2. In a small bowl, combine the buttermilk and egg and blend with a whisk until evenly mixed. Set aside.

3. In a large bowl, sift together the flours, sugar, baking powder, and salt. Add the butter, cutting it into the flour mixture with a pastry blender or 2 knives until the dough resembles coarse meal; you should still be able to see small pieces of butter.

4. Add the buttermilk mixture to the flour mixture and stir until barely combined. The dough will look coarse and shaggy at this point.

5. Transfer the dough to a lightly floured work surface, press into a ball, and knead once or twice. Press or roll out the dough to a thickness of ½ inch. Cut out the biscuits using a 2-inch cutter. Gather the scraps together, reroll, and cut out additional biscuits. Place the biscuits on the prepared baking sheet, spacing them about 1 inch apart, and lightly brush the tops with the egg wash. Refrigerate, uncovered, for 15 minutes. At this point, the biscuits can be wrapped well with plastic wrap and frozen for up to 3 weeks.

6. Meanwhile, preheat the oven to 425°F.

7. Bake the biscuits until they have risen and the tops are golden brown, 18 to 20 minutes (if you are baking frozen biscuits, add an additional 8 minutes). Serve the biscuits very hot, directly from the oven, and pour the gravy on top

Sausage Gravy

This simple and satisfying gravy may be also used as a topping for a plain omelet.

MAKES 2 CUPS GRAVY

8 oz bulk breakfast sausage

1 tbsp vegetable oil

2 tbsp all-purpose flour

2 cups whole milk, plus more as needed

1 tsp kosher salt, or as needed

½ tsp freshly ground black pepper, or as needed

1. Heat a large skillet over medium heat. Crumble the sausage into the pan and sauté, stirring frequently with a wooden spoon and breaking up the sausage as it cooks, until it is golden brown and thoroughly cooked, about 5 minutes. Transfer the sausage to a colander set over a bowl and let drain.

2. Add the oil and the flour to the same pan used to cook the sausage. Stir to blend and cook over medium heat, scraping up any brown bits on the bottom of the pan. Continue to cook, stirring constantly, until the mixture is a pale golden brown, about 3 minutes.

3. Add the milk, and stir constantly to remove any lumps. Simmer over low heat, stirring frequently, until the gravy thickens, about 20 minutes. Taste the gravy and add salt and pepper as needed. If the gravy is too thick, thin it with a little additional milk; use only enough to achieve a pourable consistency.

4. Return the cooked sausage to the gravy and stir to combine. Adjust the seasoning with additional salt and pepper, if necessary. The gravy can be cooled and stored in a covered container in the refrigerator for up to 2 days. Reheat over low heat and adjust the consistency with additional milk, if necessary, and season as needed.

PANCAKES, WAFFLES, AND FRENCH TOAST

PANCAKES REQUIRE A GENTLE TOUCH. First, the way you handle the dry ingredients has a direct effect on a pancake's texture. The more evenly the dry ingredients are blended, the fewer strokes it takes to blend the batter, and the less the batter is mixed, the more tender your pancakes will be.

Heat the pan over medium to medium-high heat until a few drops of water skitter over the surface and evaporate in a few seconds. Brush or rub a coating of oil on the pan once it's hot. Pancake batter will spread, so be sure to leave enough space between the pancakes to allow them to spread without touching. The pancakes are ready to flip when bubbles start to break over the top surface.

Waffles are made from a batter similar to pancake batter and then cooked on a special griddle, known as a waffle iron. Most waffle irons have adjustable thermostats. Read the instructions that came with your waffle iron for more details about what temperatures are best, as well as guidelines for how much batter to add to the iron. As a rule of thumb, you should add enough batter to cover the iron by not more than two-thirds. It will expand and fill in the entire iron once the lid is closed and as the waffles cook.

French toast is essentially a bread pudding in a slice, cooked on a griddle or in a skillet. It is best made from thick slices of brioche, but any fine-textured bread can be used. The bread should be somewhat stale and dry so that it soaks up the eggs and milk. The outside of French toast should be golden and very slightly crispy and the inside should be soft and creamy.

Three-Grain Waffles with Maple and Apple Butter Syrup

Oat flour is available in health food stores or in the natural foods section of some larger supermarkets. However, if you can't find it, you can make your own by grinding rolled oats in a blender or food processor until you have a relatively fine flour.

SERVES 6

1 cup nonfat buttermilk

1 large egg

1 large egg white

3 tbsp vegetable oil

⅔ cup all-purpose flour

½ cup whole wheat flour

¼ cup cornmeal

⅓ cup rolled oats

2¼ tsp baking powder

2 tbsp granulated sugar

Vegetable oil or cooking spray, as needed

Maple and Apple Butter Syrup

¾ cup maple syrup

¼ cup apple butter

2 tbsp unsalted butter

1. In a large bowl, whisk together the buttermilk, whole egg, egg white, and oil. In a medium bowl, combine the flours, cornmeal, oats, baking powder, and sugar.

2. Add the flour mixture to the buttermilk mixture and mix just until incorporated. The batter can be stored in a covered container in the refrigerator for up to 2 days. Stir well to recombine before using.

3. In a small saucepan, combine the maple syrup, apple butter, and butter and bring to a simmer over low heat. Keep warm.

4. Preheat a waffle iron to medium heat (or follow the instructions that came with your waffle iron). Lightly grease the iron with the oil or cooking spray. Ladle the batter into the waffle iron and cook until the waffles are golden brown, about 3 minutes. The amount of batter to add depends upon the size of your waffle iron; use enough to cover about two-thirds of the surface. Continue cooking the waffles, in batches, until all the batter is used up. Serve at once with the maple and apple butter syrup on the side.

French Toast

The French call this dish *pain perdu* because it is made from stale bread (*pain*) that would otherwise be lost (*perdu*).

SERVES 8

24 challah bread slices, cut ½ inch thick

4 cups whole milk

8 large eggs

¼ cup granulated sugar

Pinch of kosher salt

Pinch of ground cinnamon (optional)

Pinch of ground nutmeg (optional)

Unsalted butter or canola oil, as needed

Accompaniments and Garnishes (optional)

Unsalted butter, as needed

Maple syrup or honey

Confectioners' sugar

Cinnamon sugar: ½ tsp ground cinnamon mixed with ½ cup sugar

Toasted nuts

Fresh or dried fruit

1. Dry the challah slices on sheet pans at room temperature overnight, or in a 200°F oven for 1 hour.

2. In a large bowl, whisk together the milk, eggs, sugar, salt, cinnamon, and nutmeg, if using, and mix into a smooth batter. The batter is ready to use now, or it can be refrigerated for up to 24 hours.

3. Dip the bread in the batter, coating the slices evenly. Transfer to a wire rack set inside a baking sheet and let the coated bread slices rest at room temperature for 20 to 30 minutes to fully absorb the coating.

4. Preheat the oven to 300°F. Heat enough of the butter or oil in a large skillet or griddle over medium heat to grease it liberally, or use a nonstick pan over moderate heat. Fry the slices on the first side until evenly browned, 2 to 3 minutes, then turn and brown the other side, 2 minutes more. Work in batches, if necessary, and transfer the fried French toast to another rack set inside a baking sheet. Finish cooking the French toast in the oven, about 10 minutes.

5. Serve the French toast at once on warmed plates with butter and maple syrup or honey and any of the optional garnishes.

Banana Pancakes

A fine purée of sweet ripe bananas gives these pancakes a fine texture, but feel free to leave them a little coarser so that you get nuggets of tender banana in your pancakes.

SERVES 8

2 cups all-purpose flour

¼ cup granulated sugar

4 tsp baking powder

½ tsp baking soda

½ tsp kosher salt

1¾ cups buttermilk

4 large eggs

¼ cup (½ stick) unsalted butter, melted and cooled

¾ cup mashed ripe bananas

Vegetable oil or cooking spray, as needed

Confectioners' sugar, as needed

2 cups Blueberry Maple Syrup (recipe follows)

Blueberries, as needed

1. In a large bowl, sift together the flour, sugar, baking powder, baking soda, and salt. Make a well in the center of the flour mixture.

2. In another large bowl, blend together the buttermilk, eggs, and melted butter with a whisk. Add the buttermilk mixture to the flour mixture and stir by hand with a wooden spoon just until the batter is evenly moistened. The batter is ready to use now, or it can be stored in a covered container in the refrigerator for up to 12 hours.

3. Heat a large skillet or griddle over medium-high heat. Oil it lightly by brushing with the oil or spraying with cooking spray. Just before making the pancakes, fold the bananas into the batter. Drop the pancake batter into the hot pan by large spoonfuls, about ¼ cup each. Leave about 2 inches between the pancakes to allow them to spread and to make turning easier.

4. Cook on the first side until small bubbles appear on the upper surface of the pancakes and the edges are set, about 2 minutes. Using an offset spatula or a palette knife, turn the pancakes and finish cooking on the second side, 2 to 3 minutes more. Adjust the temperature beneath the skillet or griddle to produce a good brown color.

5. Serve the pancakes at once, dusted with the confectioners' sugar and with blueberry maple syrup on the side. Garnish with the blueberries.

Blueberry Maple Syrup

We've strained the syrup in this recipe for a smooth, pourable consistency. You may prefer to skip the straining step for a more rustic texture, similar to a fruit topping. In that case, simply add the maple syrup once the blueberries and their liquid have a soft, jam-like texture.

MAKES 2 CUPS SYRUP

4 cups blueberries, fresh or frozen

1 tsp finely grated lemon zest

1 cup maple syrup

1. In a medium saucepan, combine the blueberries and lemon zest. Simmer over medium heat, stirring occasionally, until most of the juice has been released and the mixture develops a saucelike consistency, about 10 minutes.

2. Strain the mixture through a fine-mesh sieve into a clean saucepan, making sure to press all of the juice out of the blueberry mixture. Return the juice to a simmer and add the maple syrup. Simmer over low heat until the syrup is slightly reduced and thickened, about 10 minutes. The syrup is ready to use now, or it can be cooled and stored in a covered container in the refrigerator for up to 10 days. To serve, reheat over low heat or in the microwave.

CRÊPES

THE SAYING "PRACTICE MAKES PERFECT" is definitely applicable to making crêpes. With each batch, you'll need to find the right amount of batter and level of heat for your particular pan. Unlike omelets, fillings are added to crêpes only after they are finished cooking, therefore hot fillings need to be prepared and cooked separately.

Crêpe batters have a more liquid consistency than pancake batters, because you're trying to achieve the thinnest crêpes possible. When preparing the batter, whisk well to remove any lumps, and let the batter rest at room temperature for 30 to 60 minutes or up to 12 hours in a covered container in the refrigerator to ensure a tender texture.

Crêpes are traditionally cooked in a small, flat, round pan with short sloped sides, known as a crêpe pan, but small nonstick skillets work just as well. Heat the pan over medium heat and grease with butter or oil to prevent sticking and to add a touch of flavor. With a ladle or small measuring cup, pour a small amount of batter into the pan. Immediately tilt and swirl the pan to spread the batter in a thin, even layer that just covers the bottom of the pan. Cook for a few minutes, then check the doneness of the crêpe by carefully lifting one edge and looking underneath it for a golden color with specks of light brown. With a metal spatula, loosen the edge of the crêpe from the pan, flip, and cook the crêpe on the opposite side until golden. Flip the crêpe out onto a plate lined with parchment paper.

Crêpes can easily be made in advance. Cool them completely on a baking sheet lined with parchment paper, then stack the crêpes. The stack can be wrapped well with plastic wrap and refrigerated for up to 3 days or frozen for later use. To reheat, gently warm the crêpes in a 200°F oven.

Swirl the pan to coat the bottom with the crêpe batter.

Use a thin metal or heatproof rubber spatula to flip the crêpe over when it's cooked on one side.

Apple-Filled Crêpes

SERVES 8

24 Sweet Crêpes (recipe follows)

1½ cups Apple Filling (recipe follows)

2 cups Cinnamon Sauce (recipe follows)

⅔ cup heavy cream

2 tbsp granulated sugar

Finely grated lemon zest, as needed

1. If the crêpes were made in advance, thaw them and let them return to room temperature. Heat the filling and sauce over low heat or in the microwave until heated through.

2. In the bowl or a mixer fitted with the whip attachment, combine the cream and sugar and whip to soft peaks. Fill each crêpe with 2 tablespoons of the apple filling. Top with 3 tablespoons of the sauce and 2 tablespoons of the whipped cream. Serve the crêpes garnished with the lemon zest.

Sweet Crêpes

SERVES 8

2 cups all-purpose flour

¼ cup granulated sugar

½ tsp kosher salt

2 cups whole milk

2 large eggs

1 tbsp unsalted butter, melted

½ tsp pure vanilla extract

Melted butter or vegetable oil to coat pan, as needed

1. In a large bowl, sift together the flour, sugar, and salt. Make a well in the center of the flour mixture.

2. In a medium bowl, whisk together the milk, eggs, melted butter, and vanilla. Add the milk mixture to the flour mixture and stir by hand just until the batter is smooth. Let the batter rest in the refrigerator for at least 1 and up to 12 hours before preparing the crêpes. Strain the batter, if necessary. to remove lumps before preparing the crêpes.

3. Heat a crêpe pan or small skillet over medium-high heat. Brush with the melted butter or oil. Pour about ¼ cup of batter into the crêpe pan, swirling and tilting the pan to coat the bottom with batter. Cook until the first side is set and has a golden color with specks of light brown, about 2 minutes. Adjust the temperature under the pan, if necessary. Using a thin metal or heatproof rubber spatula, lift the crêpe and turn it over. Cook on the opposite side until the crêpe is cooked through, about 1 minute more.

4. Cook the remaining crêpes until all the batter is used up, adding more melted butter or oil to the pan, as needed. Stack the crêpes as you work. The crêpes are ready to fill now, or they can be wrapped well with plastic wrap and refrigerated for up to 3 days or frozen for up to 4 weeks.

Apple Filling

MAKES 2 CUPS FILLING

- ¼ cup applejack or apple-flavored brandy
- ¼ cup apple juice
- 3 tbsp canola oil
- 4 cups peeled, cored, and sliced Granny Smith apples
- 6 tbsp granulated sugar
- 3 tbsp dried currants
- ¾ tsp finely grated orange zest
- 1 tsp pure vanilla extract
- ¼ tsp ground cinnamon
- ⅛ tsp freshly grated nutmeg

1. In a small bowl, combine the applejack or brandy and the apple juice and set aside. In a large bowl, toss the apples with the sugar.

2. Heat a sauté pan over medium-high heat and add 1 tablespoon of the oil. Add about one-third of the sugared apples; they should fit in the pan in a single layer. Sauté the apples until golden on both sides, about 4 minutes. Transfer the apples to a large bowl.

3. Add one-third of the apple juice mixture to the pan, stirring to release the sugar from the pan, and simmer until slightly reduced and thickened, about 30 seconds. Pour the heated apple juice mixture over the sautéed apples in the bowl.

4. Sauté the remaining apples in two more batches as directed above. When you add the final third of the apple juice mixture to the pan, stir in the currants, orange zest, vanilla, cinnamon, and nutmeg. Add this mixture to the bowl with all the sautéed apples and stir the filling gently until the currants are evenly distributed throughout.

5. Place the filling in the bowl set over an ice bath and cool, stirring from time to time. Once the filling has reached room temperature, it is ready to use, or it can be stored in a covered container in the refrigerator for up to 5 days. Warm the filling over low heat or in the microwave, if necessary, to bring it back to room temperature.

Cinnamon Sauce

Try this over French toast or as a topping for ice cream.

MAKES 2 CUPS SAUCE

- 1 tbsp cornstarch
- ¾ cup apple juice
- ½ cup granulated sugar
- ¼ cup fresh orange juice
- ¼ cup light rum
- 2 tbsp fresh lemon juice
- 1 tsp ground cinnamon
- 1 tbsp unsalted butter

1. In a small bowl, combine the cornstarch with ¼ cup of the apple juice and stir until the cornstarch is completely dissolved.

2. In a saucepan, combine the remaining apple juice, ¾ cup water, the sugar, orange juice, rum, lemon juice, and cinnamon. Bring to a boil over high heat and stir until the sugar has dissolved. Add the dissolved cornstarch and return the mixture to a boil, stirring constantly, until thickened and smooth, about 2 minutes.

3. Remove the sauce from the heat and stir in the butter until it melts and is evenly blended. The sauce is ready to serve hot now, or it can be transferred to a bowl set in an ice bath and cooled, stirring it from time to time. Once the sauce has reached room temperature, it can be stored in a covered container in the refrigerator for up to 4 days. Reheat the sauce over low heat or in the microwave.

Crêpes with Zucchini and Mushrooms

This recipe makes a great fall first course, as well as a perfect main dish at brunch.

SERVES 8

1 tbsp olive oil

3 green onions, white and green parts, thinly sliced on the diagonal

2 garlic cloves, minced

1 cup sliced fresh white or wild mushrooms

1 cup shredded zucchini

1 plum tomato, peeled, seeded, and chopped

2 tsp chopped tarragon leaves or ½ tsp dried tarragon

1 cup crumbled feta

1½ tsp fresh lemon juice, or as needed

Kosher salt, as needed

Freshly ground black pepper, as needed

16 Savory Crêpes (recipe follows)

Melted butter, as needed

1. Heat the olive oil in a skillet over high heat. Add the green onions and garlic and sauté, stirring constantly, until softened and aromatic, 2 to 3 minutes. Add the mushrooms and continue to cook, stirring occasionally, until the mushrooms release their moisture and it has cooked away, about 5 minutes more.

2. Add the zucchini, tomato, and tarragon and sauté until the moisture has cooked away, 10 minutes more. Remove from the heat and fold in the cheese. Taste and season with lemon juice, salt, and pepper. The filling is ready to use now, or it can be stored in a covered container in the refrigerator for up to 2 days.

3. If needed, reheat the filling over low heat, stirring occasionally, for about 5 minutes. Place 2 tablespoons of the warm filling in the center of each of the warm crêpes. Fold the right side to the middle and roll up the crêpe.

4. Transfer the crêpes to a buttered baking dish. The filled crêpes can be baked now, or they can be stored in the baking dish well wrapped with plastic wrap in the refrigerator for up to 24 hours or frozen for up to 3 weeks. Thaw before baking.

5. Preheat the oven to 350°F. Brush the crêpes with a little melted butter and bake until very hot, about 10 minutes. Serve at once on warmed plates.

Savory Crêpes

MAKES 16 CRÊPES

2 cups all-purpose flour

¼ tsp kosher salt

2 cups whole milk

2 large eggs

2 tbsp unsalted butter, melted and cooled to room temperature, or canola oil

1. In a large bowl, sift together the flour and salt. Make a well in the center of the flour mixture.

2. In a medium bowl, whisk together the milk, egg, and melted butter. Add the milk mixture to the flour mixture and stir by hand just until the batter is smooth. Let the batter rest in the refrigerator for at least 1 and up to 12 hours before preparing the crêpes. Strain the batter, if necessary, to remove lumps before preparing the crêpes.

3. Heat a crêpe pan or small skillet over medium-high heat. Brush with the melted butter or oil. Pour about ¼ cup of batter into the crêpe pan, swirling and tilting the pan to coat the bottom with batter. Cook until the first side is set and has a golden color with specks of light brown, about 2 minutes. Adjust the temperature under the pan, if necessary. Using a thin metal or heatproof rubber spatula, lift the crêpe and turn it over. Cook on the opposite side until the crêpe is cooked through, about 1 minute more.

4. Cook the remaining crêpes until all the batter is used up, adding more melted butter or oil to the pan, as needed. Stack the crêpes as you work. The crêpes are ready to fill now, or they can be wrapped well with plastic wrap and refrigerated for up to 3 days or frozen for up to 4 weeks.

Crêpes with Goat Cheese and Mushrooms

Use a variety of mushrooms if they are available. Chanterelles, shiitakes, and oyster mushrooms can often be found in your local market.

SERVES 8

2 tbsp olive oil

½ cup minced onion

4 cups sliced fresh white or portobello mushrooms

¾ tsp kosher salt

¼ tsp freshly ground black pepper

16 Savory Crêpes (recipe opposite)

1 cup crumbled fresh goat cheese

Melted butter, as needed

1. Heat 1 tablespoon of the oil in a sauté pan over medium-high heat. Add half of the onions and sauté, stirring frequently, until tender and translucent, about 4 minutes.

2. Increase the heat to high. Add half of the mushrooms. Sauté ,without stirring, until they are browned on one side, 3 to 4 minutes. Stir the mixture and continue to cook over medium heat until the liquid cooks away, about 5 minutes. Transfer to a bowl and keep warm. Repeat the process to cook the remaining mushrooms. Season the mushrooms with salt and pepper and reserve. The mushrooms can be prepared up to this point and then stored in a covered container in the refrigerator for up to 2 days.

3. If needed, reheat the mushroom filling over low heat, stirring occasionally, for about 5 minutes. Place about 3 tablespoons of the filling in the center of each of the warm crêpes and top with 1 tablespoon of the goat cheese. Fold the right side to the middle and roll up the crêpe. Transfer the crêpes to a buttered baking dish; the filled crêpes are ready to bake now, or can be well wrapped and stored in the refrigerator for up to 24 hours or frozen for up to 3 weeks. Thaw before baking.

4. Preheat the oven to 350°F. Brush the crêpes with a little melted butter and bake until very hot, about 10 minutes. Serve at once on warmed plates.

Add a filling to the finished crêpe.

BASIC EGG COOKING

EGGS COOK VERY QUICKLY, so you can easily prepare eggs any style for your guests to enjoy. Choose the freshest eggs you can find for the best flavor. If you have access to locally raised and free-range eggs, so much the better.

Fried Eggs

Fried eggs can be served sunny-side up, over easy, over medium, or over hard. To make sunny-side up eggs, generously coat a pan with oil or butter, heat over medium-high heat, and add the eggs; you can crack them into a cup before pouring them into the pan if you are worried about breaking the yolk. Cook, swirling the pan to keep the egg from sticking, until it is the doneness you want.

EGGS COOKED IN THE SHELL

Fill a deep pot with enough water to hold the eggs comfortably. Bring the water to a simmer. Lower the eggs gently into the pot of simmering water so they don't crack. Calculate the cooking time from the point when the water returns to a full simmer. Lift the eggs from the water, blot off the water, and serve immediately in egg cups with buttered toast. Cooking times are as follows:

3 TO 4 MINUTES FOR SOFT COOKED, WITH WHITES BARELY SET AND YOLK WARM BUT RUNNY

5 TO 6 MINUTES FOR MEDIUM COOKED, WITH WHITES SET AND YOLK HOT AND THICKENED

10 T0 12 MINUTES FOR HARD COOKED, WITH WHITES AND YOLKS COMPLETELY SET

For eggs cooked over, begin as for sunny-side up eggs, and cook long enough for the whites to set completely, about 3 minutes. Use a spatula to turn the egg and continue to cook until it is finished. Cooking times on the second side are as follows:

LESS THAN 1 MINUTE FOR OVER EASY

1 MINUTE FOR OVER MEDIUM

1½ TO 2 MINUTES FOR OVER HARD

Scrambled Eggs

Scrambled eggs make a great brunch buffet dish, because it is as easy to prepare them as a single serving as it is to prepare them for 8 or 10 people, if you have a pan of the right size. This classic breakfast dish is best when served fresh from the pan, but you can keep them warm for up to 15 minutes.

When preparing scrambled eggs for a crowd, plan on using 2 or 3 eggs per person. Crack the eggs into a bowl and blend, using a fork. It's best to do this just before cooking, but if you need to streamline breakfast or brunch, you can make the mixture up to 12 hours in advance. Season the eggs well with salt and pepper. If you'd like, you can also blend in a small amount of milk or cream into the mixture for a more tender texture (we recommend no more than ¼ cup of milk or cream per dozen eggs).

Heat an appropriate-size nonstick skillet over medium-high heat and add oil or butter; don't be afraid to use enough oil or butter to liberally coat the pan. Determining when the pan and fat are properly heated is key. Oil should shimmer but not smoke, while butter should melt and foam but not turn brown or black. Water droplets should skitter over the pan but not cook away instantly. Tilt the pan to coat its entire surface with the fat.

Add the beaten eggs and, using one hand, swirl the pan on the burner and the other to stir the eggs in the opposite direction, using a fork or heat-resistant rubber spatula. Once the eggs set into smooth, small curds and lose their glossy look, roll them onto a warm plate and serve.

Fresh tortillas rolled into trumpets are an appealing way to present scrambled eggs.

Omelets cook quickly enough that they are relatively easy to serve to order, and an omelet station also adds an interactive element for your guests.

Omelets

There are several different styles of omelets. A rolled, or French, omelet starts out like scrambled eggs, but uses one hand to swirl the pan on the burner and the other to stir the eggs in the opposite direction, using a fork or heat-resistant rubber spatula. Once the eggs set into smooth, small curds and lose their glossy look, roll them onto a warm plate and serve.

An American, or folded, omelet is prepared much the same way, but instead of being rolled, an American omelet is folded in half when the eggs start to set. Frittatas, or flat omelets, are baked in the oven; the finished product is dense enough to be sliced into servings. Souffléed omelets are made from eggs that have first been separated into yolks and whites. The beaten whites are folded into the beaten yolks and the dish is prepared by baking the omelet in a hot oven.

Omelets may be filled or garnished with a variety of ingredients. Here are some of our favorites to use alone or in combination:

GRATED CHEESES LIKE CHEDDAR, SWISS, MONTEREY JACK

CRUMBLED SOFT OR FRESH CHEESES LIKE GOAT CHEESE, FETA, OR BLUE CHEESE

SAUTÉED VEGETABLES LIKE MUSHROOMS, SPINACH, OR PEPPERS

SLICED COOKED MEATS OR SAUSAGE

SMOKED FISH

CREAM CHEESE AND FRUIT JELLY OR PRESERVES

DICED SAUTÉED POTATOES

CHOPPED HERBS, ESPECIALLY CHIVES, TARRAGON, BASIL, AND PARSLEY

Be sure to add these types of fillings to the eggs at the appropriate point, so that they are fully cooked and hot at the same time the eggs are finished cooking. Grated or crumbled cheeses will melt sufficiently from the heat of the eggs so they are added just before an omelet is rolled or folded.

To make a French omelet, pour the blended eggs into a hot pan. At the beginning of cooking, stir the eggs with a rubber spatula to encourage even cooking.

At the appropriate stage of cooking, add the desired fillings to the omelet in the pan.

Use a rubber spatula to fold the omelet in thirds.

Carefully roll the omelet directly onto a warm plate.

French Omelet

You can mix the eggs, seasonings, and liquid all at once and keep them in the refrigerator up to 8 hours to simplify your work and keep the kitchen cleaner. In that case, use about ¾ cup of the egg mixture for each omelet.

SERVES 8

24 large eggs

½ cup water or whole milk (optional)

1 tbsp kosher salt

1 tsp ground white pepper

5 tbsp canola or olive oil or unsalted butter

1. For each omelet: In a medium bowl, beat 3 eggs with 1 tablespoon of water or milk, if using, and season well with salt and pepper. Whisk until smooth and evenly blended.

2. Heat a nonstick omelet pan or small skillet over high heat and add the oil or butter, tilting the pan to coat the entire surface.

3. Pour the egg mixture into the pan and scramble it with the back of a fork or wooden spoon. Move the pan and utensil at the same time until the egg mixture has coagulated slightly. Smooth the eggs into an even layer and let the egg mixture finish cooking without stirring.

4. Tilt the pan and slide a fork or spoon around the lip of the pan, under the omelet, to be sure it is not sticking. Slide the omelet to the front of the pan and, using a fork or a wooden spoon, fold it inside to the center. Tilt the pan to roll the omelet onto the plate. The finished omelet should be oval shaped. To give the omelet additional sheen, rub the surface lightly with butter. Serve at once on a warmed plate.

A finished French Omelet

Souffléed Cheddar Omelet

Souffléed Cheddar Omelet

This recipe is easy to double, if you have enough pans to cook the omelets.

SERVES 4

8 large egg yolks

Kosher salt and ground black pepper, as needed

½ cup grated sharp Cheddar

2 tbsp minced chives

Unsalted butter, as needed

8 large egg whites

1. Preheat the oven to 400°F.

2. In a large bowl, beat the egg yolks with a whisk (or use an electric mixer fitted with the whip attachment) until blended. Season with salt and pepper. Stir in the cheese and chives.

3. Grease the entire interior surface of a 10-inch cast-iron skillet with butter. Place it in the oven to preheat for 5 minutes while preparing the remaining ingredients.

4. Meanwhile, in the bowl an electric mixer fitted with the whip attachment, beat the egg whites on low speed until they become foamy and start to thicken, 3 minutes. Increase the speed to medium and beat until the egg whites hold medium peaks when the whip is turned upright, 4 minutes more. Gently fold the beaten whites into the yolk mixture.

5. Pour the egg mixture into the preheated skillet. Set over low heat until the sides and bottom have set, about 1 minute. Return the pan to the oven and bake until the omelet is puffed but fully set and light golden on top, about 15 minutes. Serve at once on a warmed platter or plates.

Frittata

If you would like to double this recipe, bake it in a 9 by 13-inch rectangular baking pan instead of a sauté pan.

SERVES 4

1 cup peeled, small-dice waxy yellow or white potatoes

½ tsp kosher salt, plus more as needed

4 strips bacon, diced

Vegetable oil, as needed

1 yellow onion, diced

8 large eggs

¼ tsp freshly ground black pepper

1. Place the potatoes in a pot with enough cold water to cover by 2 inches. Salt the water. Gradually bring the water to a simmer over medium heat. Cover and simmer until the potatoes are easily pierced with a fork, about 10 minutes.

2. Cook the bacon in an ovenproof nonstick or cast-iron skillet over low heat until crisp, 2 to 3 minutes. Using a slotted spoon, transfer the bacon bits to paper towels to drain, then reserve. Add enough vegetable oil to the bacon fat in the pan, if needed, to make 2 tablespoons, and increase the heat to medium-low. Add the onion. Cook slowly, stirring occasionally, until translucent, 8 to 10 minutes. Add the potatoes and sauté until lightly browned, 8 to 10 minutes more.

3. Meanwhile, in a large bowl, beat the eggs with a whisk just until blended. Season with ½ teaspoon salt and the pepper. Pour the eggs over the onions and potatoes in the skillet, and add the crisp bacon bits to the mixture and stir gently.

4. Preheat the broiler. Reduce the heat under the skillet to low, cover, and cook until the eggs are nearly set, 6 to 8 minutes. Remove the cover and place the skillet under the broiler to brown the eggs lightly, about 3 minutes, watching carefully. Cut the frittata into wedges and serve at once on warmed plates. Frittatas may also be served at room temperature.

Tortillas de Papas

This flat, Spanish-style omelet makes a great brunch or supper dish without the one-at-a-time attention required for French-style rolled omelets.

SERVES 6

3 small red-skinned potatoes (about 1 lb)

½ tsp kosher salt, plus more as needed

½ cup olive oil

Freshly ground black pepper, as needed

2 medium yellow onions, sliced

1 cup quartered artichoke hearts

2 red bell peppers, roasted, peeled, seeded, and cut into strips (see sidebar page 160)

2 tbsp Balsamic Vinaigrette (page 107; see note)

3 tbsp chopped flat-leaf parsley

1 tbsp chopped thyme

12 large eggs

6 tbsp crumbled fresh goat cheese

Fresh herbs (parsley, thyme, or chives), as needed

1. Place the potatoes in a pot with enough cold water to cover by 2 inches. Salt the water. Gradually bring the water to a simmer over medium heat. Cover and simmer until the potatoes are easily pierced with a fork, about 20 minutes. Drain and cool the potatoes. When they are cool enough to handle, cut them into large dice.

2. Heat 3 tablespoons oil in a large sauté pan over medium heat and add the diced potatoes. Season with ¼ teaspoon salt and pepper. Cook until browned, 3 to 4 minutes, and reserve.

3. Preheat the oven to 425°F. Heat the remaining 3 tablespoons oil in another large sauté pan over medium heat and add the onions. Season with ¼ teaspoon salt and pepper. Cook until caramelized, 12 to 15 minutes. Reserve.

4. In a large bowl, combine the artichokes, roasted bell peppers, vinaigrette, parsley, and thyme. Season with black pepper. Add the cooked potatoes and onions and toss gently to combine. The vegetable mixture can be used now, or cooled and stored in a covered container in the refrigerator for up to 2 days.

5. Heat the remaining 2 tablespoons oil in a large skillet with cooking spray, and place over medium heat. Add the vegetable mixture and heat until it is quite hot. Pour in the egg mixture and cook over medium heat until the bottom is set, about 2 minutes.

6. Sprinkle the goat cheese over the top and finish the frittata in the oven until puffed and golden, about 10 minutes. Garnish with the fresh herbs and serve at once.

NOTE *For a great flavor combination, use sherry vinegar in the Balsamic Vinaigrette on page 107.*

With the water at a simmer, gently add the eggs one at a time.

Use a slotted spoon to lift the egg from the water.

Poached Eggs

Poaching eggs creates a tender, delicate texture that works well for a variety of dishes, like Eggs Benedict (page 230). Eggs should be poached in about 3 inches of water. Adding salt and small amount of vinegar to the water can prevent the egg whites from spreading too much and helps the egg proteins to set faster.

Work in small batches to avoid overcrowding the pot. Too many eggs will cause the temperature of the water to drop, extend the cooking time, and just be generally more difficult to handle. The whites should look set and opaque, while the yolks can be cooked to your liking, from soft and runny to very firm.

It might surprise you to learn that poached eggs hold very well for later service. If you're planning to poach the eggs ahead, cook them to slightly less than the final doneness you desire, since they will cook a little further when they're reheated. Using a slotted spoon, lift the cooked eggs from the pot and submerge them in ice water until they're completely chilled. Remove the eggs from the ice water, and place them on clean paper towels to absorb all excess moisture. Hold the eggs on a dry sheet pan in refrigerator until you're ready to reheat them.

If the poached eggs are going to be held for later service, slightly undercook the eggs and submerge them in ice water as they come out of the poaching water.

Eggs Benedict

This is the classic Sunday brunch egg dish. To make Eggs Florentine, replace the Canadian bacon with sautéed spinach.

SERVES 8

2 tsp distilled white vinegar

1 tsp kosher salt

16 large eggs

8 whole English muffins, split into halves, toasted and buttered

16 thick slices Canadian bacon

Hollandaise Sauce (page 155), kept warm

1. Preheat the broiler. In a deep saucepan, combine 6 cups water with the vinegar and salt and bring barely to a simmer.

2. Break each egg into a cup and then slide the egg carefully into the water. Poach until the egg whites are set and opaque, about 3 minutes. Poach the eggs in batches to avoid overcrowding the pan. Remove the eggs from the water with a slotted spoon. Blot on paper towels and trim the edges neatly, if desired.

3. Top each English muffin half with a slice of Canadian bacon and place these on a baking pan. Broil briefly to heat the bacon, 1 to 2 minutes.

4. Top each muffin half with a poached egg and coat with warm hollandaise sauce. Serve at once on warmed plates.

Huevos Rancheros

Huevos Rancheros is a hearty breakfast of fried eggs over refried beans on a corn tortilla topped with cheese, avocado, and salsa. If you prefer, you can make this dish with poached eggs instead of frying them. Make your salsa mild or spicy, or give your guests a choice.

SERVES 8

Eight 6-inch corn tortillas

2 cups Vegetarian Refried Beans (recipe follows, or use purchased)

¼ cup (½ stick) unsalted butter or vegetable oil

16 large eggs

Kosher salt, as needed

Freshly ground black pepper, as needed

1 cup grated Monterey Jack

2 avocados

4 tsp fresh lime juice

1 cup Salsa Fresca (page 57, or use purchased salsa)

½ cup sour cream, as needed

8 cilantro sprigs

1. Preheat the broiler. Heat the tortillas one at a time, in a dry cast-iron skillet over medium-high heat. Place on baking sheets, spread with ¼ cup refried beans, and keep warm.

2. Add enough butter or oil to the skillet to coat it generously. Place the skillet over medium-high heat until it is very hot but not smoking. Crack the eggs directly into the hot butter or oil and reduce the heat to medium-low. Fry the eggs to the desired doneness (page 222), shaking the pan occasionally to keep the eggs from sticking. Season the eggs with salt and pepper.

3. Top each prepared tortilla with 2 fried eggs and 2 tablespoons of the grated cheese. Slide the tortillas under the broiler to melt the cheese, 2 or 3 minutes.

4. Meanwhile, dice the avocados and toss with the lime juice. Divide the avocados among the tortillas. Top each serving with 2 tablespoons salsa and 2 tablespoons sour cream. Garnish with a sprig of cilantro and serve at once.

Vegetarian Refried Beans

The brown-and-pink pinto bean is the standard bean used in frijoles refritos, or refried beans. Refried beans are typically made with lard; this vegetarian version uses corn oil and spices for flavor.

SERVES 8

1 tbsp corn oil

2 cups diced onion

2 tbsp minced garlic

1 cup diced canned tomatoes

½ tsp kosher salt, or as needed

4½ cups cooked pinto beans, or canned pinto beans, rinsed and drained (see sidebar page 232)

1 tsp cumin seeds, toasted, cracked

1 tsp chili powder

Tabasco sauce, as needed

1. Heat the oil in a large sauté pan. Add the onions and garlic and cook, stirring frequently, until the onions are translucent, about 5 minutes.

2. Add the tomatoes, salt, and beans. Mash the beans using a potato masher until a thick heavy paste forms; you can leave about one-third of the beans whole or mash them completely until quite smooth. Cook over low heat, stirring constantly, until the flavor is well developed, about 10 minutes. Season the beans with the cumin, chili powder, and Tabasco. The recipe is ready to use now, or the beans can be cooled and stored in a covered container in the refrigerator for up to 3 days.

REFRIED PINTO BEANS

You can use canned pinto beans or cook them yourself. To prepare dried pinto beans: Rinse and sort dry beans, removing any that are dry or shriveled. Soak for at least 6 and up to 12 hours in cold water in the refrigerator. Drain the beans, pour them in a deep pot, and add enough cold water to cover by 2 inches. Simmer over medium heat until the beans are tender. Add a halved onion, and a bay leaf or epazote leaf to the beans as they simmer, but do not add any salt until they are fully cooked. At that point, you can season them as needed.

Quiche

Quiche is a beautiful, elegant dish that is deceptively simple to make, and it may be served hot or at room temperature. Quiche is most often baked in a tart pan although it can also be baked in a pie pan, tartlet shells, timbale molds, or custard cups for different presentations.

All manner of fillings can be used, so try creating your own quiche with varying blends of cheeses, meats, and vegetables. Veggies to be used as a filling should be blanched or cooked through before adding them to the quiche, and the crust for a quiche is also prebaked.

Prepare the dough according to the recipe, roll it out, and press into the pan. Use a fork to poke holes in the bottom and sides of the dough, then line with a circle of parchment paper, fill with dry beans or uncooked rice, and bake until just golden. This process is known as blind baking. Add the quiche filling and bake until the custard is set and a knife inserted into the center of the quiche comes out clean.

Quiche may also be baked without a pastry crust. Butter a shallow casserole or baking dish. Sprinkle it with grated Parmesan cheese, if desired, and spread the filling ingredients over the casserole bottom. Pour the custard mixture on top. Place the casserole dish in a water bath and bake until a knife inserted near the center of the quiche comes out clean, about 1 hour.

Quiche Lorraine

The traditional version of this recipe includes no cheese, but if you like, you can add some grated Gruyère.

MAKES ONE 9-INCH QUICHE; SERVES 6 TO 8

1 tbsp unsalted butter or vegetable oil

4 slices thick-cut bacon

1½ cups heavy cream or crème fraîche

3 large eggs

Kosher salt, as needed

Freshly ground black pepper, as needed

One 9-inch Quiche Shell (recipe follows), prebaked

1. Preheat the oven to 350°F

2. Heat the butter or oil in a sauté pan over medium heat. Add the bacon and sauté until browned, 2 to 3 minutes. Remove the bacon with a slotted spoon and drain on paper towels.

3. In a medium bowl, whisk together the cream and eggs until blended. Season with salt and pepper.

4. Roll out the dough and line a 9-inch quiche or pie pan. Crumble the bacon evenly over the dough. Pour in the egg mixture gradually, stirring it with a fork to distribute the bacon evenly.

5. Set the quiche pan on a baking sheet and return the quiche to the oven. Bake until a knife blade inserted in the center comes out clean, 40 to 45 minutes. Serve the quiche hot or at room temperature. The quiche can be cooled, wrapped well with plastic wrap, and stored in the refrigerator for up to 2 days. Reheat in a 325°F until hot, about 15 minutes.

Quiche Shell

2 SINGLE SHELLS (USING 9-INCH PANS)

2¾ cups all-purpose flour, plus extra as needed

1 tsp kosher salt

1 cup (2 sticks) cold, diced, unsalted butter or ½ cup (½ stick) diced, cold unsalted butter and ½ cup diced, cold vegetable shortening

½ cup ice cold water

1. In a large bowl, combine the flour and salt and stir with a fork to blend evenly. Cut the butter into the flour using a food processor, pastry blender, or 2 knives until the mixture looks like coarse meal. Add the cold water all at once and mix until a shaggy but evenly moistened dough forms. If necessary, add additional cold water, a few teaspoons at a time. The dough should just hold together when you press a handful of it into a ball.

2. Turn out the dough onto a lightly floured work surface. Gather and press the dough into a ball. Divide the dough into 2 equal pieces for 2 quiche shells, pat them into even disks, wrap well in plastic wrap, and let chill in the refrigerator for 20 minutes. The dough can be stored in the refrigerator for up to 2 days or frozen for up to 4 weeks. Thaw before rolling as directed in the next step.

3. Working on a floured work surface with a floured rolling pin, roll the dough out into a circle, about 12 inches in diameter. Transfer the dough to a quiche or pie pan. Prick the dough evenly over the bottom and sides with the tines of a fork. You can wrap the pans lined with dough at this point and freeze for up to 2 weeks.

4. To prebake the crust: Preheat the oven to 400°F. Line the dough with a piece of parchment or waxed paper and fill about halfway with pie weights, dry beans, or rice. Blind bake until the shell is set and dry, 12 to 15 minutes.

5. Remove the pan from the oven and remove the paper and pie weights. Return the shell to the oven and bake until it is completely dry and a light golden brown, 5 to 6 minutes more. Cool the shell to room temperature before filling.

SEASONAL FRUIT

FRESH FRUIT PLATTERS have long been a brunch staple. Even though, with today's transportation and technology, a huge variety of produce is available at most grocery stores, it is still favorable to buy locally grown produce whenever possible. In most cases, the flavor and condition of local fruits is superior, because the produce has not been shipped. (The exception is citrus fruits, because they actually ship particularly well.)

When making an effort to buy locally grown produce, you must also carefully consider seasonality. Below is a chart of common fruits by growing season; it is helpful as a general guideline, but keep in mind that weather conditions, like early frost and excessive rainfall, can greatly affect growing season and availability.

Seasonal Fruits for Breakfasts and Brunches

SPRING	SUMMER	FALL	WINTER
	Apricots	Apples	Cherimoyas
Apricots	Blackberries	Asian pears	Cranberries
Blackberries	Blueberries	Bananas	Dates
Cantaloupe	Cherries	Gooseberries	Grapefruit
Figs	Guavas	Grapes	Kiwi
Grapefruit	Mangoes	Kumquats	Mandarin oranges and tangerines
Mangoes	Melons	Passion fruit	Oranges
Navel oranges	Nectarines	Pears	Pineapple
Papaya	Peaches	Persimmons	Pomegranates
Pineapples	Plums	Plums	Star fruit
Strawberries	Raspberries	Pomegranates	Ugli fruit

S IDE DISHES AND ACCOMPANIMENTS DO MORE THAN JUST FILL UP EMPTY SPACE ON THE PLATE; THEY ENHANCE THE ENTRÉE BY ADDING COMPLEMENTARY FLAVORS, TEXTURES, COLORS, AND SHAPES. YOU CAN USE SIDE DISHES TO ADD AN EXCITING ELEMENT AND NUTRITIONAL CONTENT TO THE MEAL. YOU CAN PRESENT AN OLD FAVORITE IN A NEW AND EXCITING WAY OR TRY SOMETHING ALTOGETHER NEW. A SIDE DISH CAN BE ANY NUMBER OF SMALL DISHES MADE FROM GRAINS, PASTA, OR VEGETABLES, AND THE WIDE VARIETY OF POSSIBLE SIDE DISHES MAKES THEM THE PERFECT PLACE TO BRANCH OUT WHEN SELECTING RECIPES, ESPECIALLY IF YOU'RE A TIMID COOK OR HAVE THE TENDENCY TO GET STUCK IN A RUT.

SEASONAL VEGETABLES

As discussed in chapter 6 concerning fruits (page 234), seasonality refers to the vegetables that are growing best at a particular time of year. On the next page is a chart of common vegetables and their season. This chart is a good general reference, but be aware that some vegetables will overlap between the seasons and that weather may shorten or lengthen a growing season.

Well-executed vegetable side dishes will complement the flavors of the main course while adding color, texture, and nutritional value to the meal. Trying new seasonings and flavorings in traditional recipes can also add interest to the meal.

Seasonal Vegetables

SPRING	SUMMER	FALL	WINTER
Asparagus	Bell Peppers and Hot Peppers	Arugula	Celery Root (Celeriac)
Artichokes	Carrots	Broccoli	Cardoons
Beets	Chard	Broccoli Rabe (Rapini)	Frisée
Fava Beans	Corn	Brussels Sprouts	Escarole
Fiddleheads	Cucumbers	Cabbage	Sunchokes (Jerusalem Artichokes)
Garlic Scapes and Green Garlic	Tomatoes	Cauliflower	Leeks
Lettuces and Greens	Eggplant	Celery	Rutabagas and Turnips
Peas	Garlic	Chicory	Parsnips
Fennel	Green Beans	Horseradish	Radicchio
Radishes	Green Onions	Sweet Potatoes and Yams	Winter Squashes

MAKING A GREEN SALAD

Salads made from crisp, colorful greens that have been carefully rinsed, spun dry, and dressed with a balanced vinaigrette can be a refreshing counterpoint to the richer dishes of a multicourse meal.

These simple dishes are not difficult or time-consuming to prepare, and they don't even require a recipe. In its most basic form, a green salad—sometimes called a tossed salad, mixed salad, or garden salad—is composed of one or more greens tossed with a dressing.

To make green salads simpler to pull together on the day of the party, clean the greens and spin them dry, and then store in covered containers or ziplock bags. Cut the vegetables and store them separately. Most salad dressings will hold for at least 3 days in the refrigerator, although you might prefer to whisk in fresh herbs, chopped garlic, or shallots at the last minute. When you are ready to serve the salad, combine the greens and vegetables in a salad bowl and toss together with your dressing.

The flavors you choose to add to a salad are dependent on the greens that you select. Greens are usually grouped according to their flavors: they can be mild, spicy, or bitter; sturdy or delicate. You can also look for prepared salad blends that are derived from such traditional combinations as mesclun, which includes different greens according to the season.

The greens are the foundation of the salad, but garnishes add crucial color, texture, and flavor. You may add other vegetables, herbs, nuts, fruits, meats, croutons, cheeses, or even edible flowers to your salad. Most important, the dressing ties all of the salad's components together, contributing a distinct flavor without overpowering the greens.

Panzanella

Panzanella

Panzanella is an Italian bread and tomato salad made with garlic, basil, parsley, olive oil, and vinegar. While this recipe calls for toasting the bread, other variations include soaking the bread in water before tossing it with the remaining ingredients.

SERVES 8

1 baguette, 24 inches long, preferably 2 days old

1 tbsp unsalted butter

½ cup plus 3 tbsp extra-virgin olive oil

¼ cup chopped garlic

2 lb tomatoes, sliced (red, yellow, heirloom, or a combination)

½ cup balsamic vinegar

2 tsp kosher salt, or as needed

1 tsp freshly ground black pepper, or as needed

½ cup loosely packed basil leaves, cut into thin shreds

½ cup flat-leaf parsley, roughly chopped

1. Preheat the oven to 350°F. Cut the baguette into 1-inch cubes. Toast in the oven until crisp and dry, 1 to 2 minutes, stirring occasionally, if necessary.

2. Place the butter and 2 tablespoons of the olive oil into a 10-inch sauté pan over medium low heat. Allow the butter to melt and then add the garlic. Sauté the garlic for 2 to 3 minutes until it is translucent, but not brown. In a large bowl, toss the cooked garlic with the diced bread.

3. In another large bowl, combine the tomatoes, vinegar, the remaining olive oil, salt, and pepper.

4. Just before serving, add the bread, basil, and parsley to the bowl with the tomatoes. Adjust the seasoning with additional salt and pepper, if necessary. Serve at once.

Mediterranean Salad

Choose a variety of olives for this salad. Many markets have an "olive bar" so you can buy a little bit of a number of different types. Remove the pits to make it a little easier for your guests to eat.

SERVES 8

3 tbsp minced canned anchovy fillets

1½ cups Balsamic Vinaigrette (page 107)

1 lb mixed lettuce greens, washed and dried

2 cups quartered brine-packed artichoke hearts, rinsed and drained

2 cups peas, fresh or thawed frozen

2 medium carrot, thinly sliced

½ cup Picholine olives, pitted

½ cup Niçoise olives, pitted

1 cup grated Asiago

½ cup minced flat-leaf parsley

1. In a large bowl, combine the anchovies with the vinaigrette. Add the greens and toss to combine.

2. To make individual servings: Place a bed of 2 cups of the greens in the center of individual salad plates. Top with ¼ cup of the artichoke hearts, ¼ cup of the peas, about 2 tablespoons of the carrots, and about 1 tablespoon each of the Picholine and Niçoise olives. Garnish with 2 tablespoons of the cheese and a sprinkling of parsley. Serve at room temperature.

Asian Vegetable Slaw

Sweet and tangy, this recipe combines the delicious texture of thinly sliced vegetables with a quick and easy vinaigrette, and is sure to be the perfect accompaniment to your favorite Asian entrée.

SERVES 8

- **4 cups shredded Savoy cabbage**
- **4 cups shredded red cabbage**
- **5 carrots, thinly sliced**
- **½ cup chopped cilantro**
- **5 green onions, white and green portions, thinly sliced on the diagonal**

Dressing

- **1 cup peanut oil**
- **½ cup rice wine vinegar**
- **2 tbsp soy sauce**
- **Cayenne pepper, as needed**
- **¼ cup toasted sesame seeds**
- **½ cup chopped toasted peanuts**

1. In a large bowl, toss together the cabbages, carrots, cilantro, and green onions.

2. To make the dressing: In a small bowl, mix together the oil, vinegar, and soy sauce. Pour the dressing over the cabbage mixture and toss to combine. Adjust the seasoning, if necessary with the cayenne.

3. Toss in 3 tablespoons of the sesame seeds and the peanuts. Sprinkle the remaining sesame seeds on the top to garnish. Serve in a bowl or on a platter. The salad can be covered with plastic wrap and stored in the refrigerator for up to 24 hours.

Orange and Fennel Salad

Try seasoning this salad with a specialty salt for an unusual flavor.

SERVES 8

- **1 fennel bulb, trimmed**
- **2 lb navel oranges**
- **¼ cup extra-virgin olive oil**
- **¾ tsp sea salt, or as needed**
- **½ tsp freshly ground black pepper, or as needed**
- **½ cup Niçoise olives, pitted**

1. Slice the fennel thinly across the width of the bulb. Peel the oranges and break them into segments, removing the seeds, if possible.

2. Place the fennel, oranges, and olive oil in a large bowl and toss to combine. Season with salt and pepper. To serve: Divide the salad among 8 plates and garnish with the olives.

Roasted Beet Salad

Take advantage of the amazing variety of beets when they start to appear in your local market. Use red, golden, candy-stripe, or a combination of beets for this colorful salad. For a special presentation, alternate the sliced beets with orange slices.

SERVES 8

- 8 beets, green tops trimmed
- 5 navel oranges, peeled and split into segments (approximately 40 segments)
- ⅓ cup extra-virgin olive oil
- 2 tbsp red wine vinegar
- 2 tbsp lemon juice
- 1 tsp kosher salt, or as needed
- Pinch of cayenne pepper
- 1 cup crumbled fresh goat cheese

1. Preheat the oven to 375°F. Place the beets in a baking dish, add about ¼ inch of water, and cover tightly with aluminum foil. Roast the beets until tender, about 20 minutes. Allow to cool slightly. When cool enough to handle, slip off their skins, or use a paring knife to cut the skin away. Quarter the beets.

2. Place the oranges on a work surface and cut away both ends of the orange segments. Using a sharp paring knife, follow the curve of the orange and cut away the skin, pith, and membrane, leaving the flesh completely exposed. Working to release each segment, or suprême, and keep it intact, slice the connective membrane on both sides of each orange segment.

3. In a large bowl, blend together the oil, vinegar, lemon juice, salt, and cayenne. Add the beets while they are still warm and toss with the dressing. To serve: Divide the beets among 8 plates. Top each salad with 5 orange suprêmes and 2 tablespoons of crumbled goat cheese.

Corn, Pepper, and Jícama Salad

This colorful, crunchy salad is best served at room temperature. Jícama (hee-kah-mah), also known as the Mexican potato, is a root vegetable with a sweet flavor and a texture like an apple. Use a sharp paring knife to trim its thin skin just before using.

SERVES 8

- 2½ cups corn kernels, fresh or frozen
- 1 jícama, peeled and cut into thin strips
- 1 red onion, thinly sliced
- 1 red bell pepper, seeded and cut into thin strips
- 1 green bell pepper, seeded and cut into thin strips
- 1 jalapeño, seeded and minced
- ¼ cup red wine vinegar
- ¼ cup olive oil
- 2 tbsp water
- 1 tsp dry mustard
- 1 tsp kosher salt, or as needed
- 1 tbsp minced garlic
- Freshly ground black pepper, as needed

1. Bring about 2 inches of salted water to a boil over high heat. Add the corn and simmer, covered, until tender, 2 to 3 minutes. Drain well. In a large bowl, combine the corn, jícama, onion, bell peppers, and the jalapeño.

2. In a small bowl, whisk together the vinegar, oil, water, mustard, salt, garlic, and pepper. Add the dressing to the vegetables and toss to coat. Serve immediately.

French Lentil Salad

French green lentils, *lentilles du Puy*, are rounder than classic brown lentils, but if you cannot find them, regular lentils make a fine substitution.

SERVES 8

2 cups French green lentils

¾ cup small-dice carrots

½ cup small-dice celery

1 cup small-dice red onion

¼ lb fresh white mushrooms, thinly sliced

2 tsp Dijon mustard

2 tsp kosher salt, or as needed

¼ cup apple cider vinegar

½ cup olive oil

1. Place the lentils in a medium pot, cover with 4 cups of water, and simmer until the lentils are tender, about 25 minutes. Rinse the lentils in cold water until they are slightly chilled. Drain well.

2. In a large bowl, combine the lentils, carrots, celery, onions, and mushrooms. In a small bowl, mix together the mustard, salt, and vinegar. Stream in the olive oil while whisking to fully combine. Add the dressing to the lentils and toss to combine. Serve at room temperature.

Rice Salad

This colorful salad is substantial enough to feature as main dish for warm weather entertaining.

SERVES 8

1 cup long-grain white rice

8 brined packed artichoke hearts, rinsed, quartered, sliced into eighths

½ cup diced Gruyère

½ cup diced ham

¼ cup Niçoise olives, pitted

¼ cup small green olives, pitted

3 tbsp extra-virgin olive oil

Juice of ½ lemon

2 tsp kosher salt, or as needed

½ tsp freshly ground black pepper, or as needed

2 green onions, white and green portions, sliced thinly on the diagonal

1. Bring 4 cups of salted water to a rolling boil. Add the rice and stir once or twice to separate the grains. Cover the pot, reduce the heat to medium-low, and cook until the rice is tender. Drain any excess water from the rice and transfer to a baking sheet. Spread in an even layer and let the rice cool to room temperature.

2. Place the rice in a large mixing bowl and add the artichokes, cheese, ham, and olives. Season with olive oil, lemon juice, salt, and pepper. Toss well to coat. Just before serving, add the green onions and mix to combine. Serve the salad at room temperature or wrap well and store in the refrigerator for up to 24 hours and serve chilled or at room temperature.

Tabbouleh Salad

This recipe offers a faithful rendition of a salad that, according to many authorities, is more a parsley salad with some bulgur than a bulgur salad with a little parsley.

SERVES 8

3 cups bulgur

2 cups chopped flat-leaf parsley

6 cups diced tomatoes

1 cup finely sliced green onions, white and green portions

¼ cup chopped mint

Dressing

1 cup extra-virgin olive oil

½ cup lemon juice

2 tsp kosher salt, or as needed

2 tsp freshly ground black pepper, or as needed

1. Bring 6 cups of water to a boil. Place the bulgur in a large bowl, add the boiling water, cover, and allow it to soak until the bulgur is tender, about 30 minutes. Drain any excess water, if necessary.

2. Return the drained bulgur to the bowl and add the parsley, tomatoes, scallions, and mint.

3. To make the dressing: In a small bowl, whisk together the oil, lemon juice, salt, and pepper. Pour the dressing over the vegetables, and toss to coat evenly. The salad is ready to serve now, or it can be stored in a covered container in the refrigerator for up to 24 hours.

Black Bean Salad with Lime-Cilantro Vinaigrette

Black beans are commonly found in Southwest-style, Mexican, and Caribbean cuisines. Also known as turtle beans, they are available dried or precooked and canned in the Mexican specialty food section of your supermarket.

SERVES 8

3 tbsp peanut or olive oil

2 tbsp lime juice

2 tbsp chopped cilantro

¼ tsp minced garlic

Kosher salt and freshly ground pepper, as needed

3 cups cooked black beans, drained

3 cups diced bell peppers (assorted colors)

⅓ cup diced red onion

3 tbsp minced jalapeño

1. Combine the oil, lime juice, cilantro, and garlic. Season with salt and pepper.

2. In a large bowl, combine all of the beans, bell peppers, onion, and jalapeño. Add the vinaigrette and toss to combine. Serve at once.

Mixed Bean and Grain Salad

Mixed Bean and Grain Salad

This healthy salad is chock-full of grains and legumes that not only offer a delicious complement to a variety of entrées, but also make nutrition-conscious food both fun and exciting.

SERVES 8

½ lb bulgur

½ lb green or brown lentils

3 oz Israeli couscous

¾ tsp kosher salt, or as needed

2 tbsp red wine vinegar

¼ tsp freshly ground black pepper, or as needed

¼ cup olive oil

½ cup minced flat-leaf parsley

1 cup cooked or canned chickpeas, drained and rinsed

4 sun-dried tomatoes, minced

8 flat-leaf parsley leaves

1. Bring 3 cups of water to a boil. Place the bulgur in a large bowl, add the boiling water, cover, and allow it to soak until the bulgur is tender, about 30 minutes. Drain well.

2. In a medium pot, cover the lentils with water and bring to simmer. Cook the lentils until tender, about 20 minutes. Drain and reserve.

3. Meanwhile, bring 3 additional cups of water to a boil, add ¼ teaspoon of the salt and the couscous. Cook the couscous, covered, until it is tender, 10 to 12 minutes. Drain and rinse with cold water until cool.

4. In a large bowl, mix together the vinegar, the remaining ½ teaspoon salt, and the pepper, then whisk in the oil and add the parsley. Add the bulgur, couscous, lentils, chickpeas, and sun-dried tomatoes. Toss until the salad is evenly dressed. The salad is ready to serve now, or it can be chilled before serving for 15 to 20 minutes. This salad can be held in a covered container in the refrigerator for up to 24 hours.

Greek-Style Orzo Salad with Fennel, Bell Peppers, and Feta

In Italian, *orzo* literally means "barley" but most commonly refers to a small pasta that has a rice or diamond-like shape, which is readily found in the pasta section of grocery stores and cooks very quickly.

SERVES 8

½ lb orzo

¼ cup olive oil

1 red onion, diced

1 red bell pepper, seeded and diced

1 green bell pepper, seeded and diced

1 fennel bulb, finely diced

1 tsp chopped garlic

1 tbsp chopped thyme

½ cup tomato juice

¼ cup chopped flat-leaf parsley

1 cup feta, crumbled

1 tsp freshly ground black pepper, or as needed

1 tsp kosher salt, or as needed

1. Bring a medium pot of salted water to a boil. Add the orzo and cook until tender to the bite. Rinse with cold water and drain. Place in a medium bowl, add 3 tablespoons of the olive oil, and toss to combine.

2. In a large saucepan, sauté the onions, bell peppers, and fennel in the remaining 1 tablespoon olive oil until just tender, about 4 minutes. Add the garlic and thyme and cook an additional 2 minutes.

3. In a large bowl, toss the sautéed vegetables with the orzo. Add the tomato juice. Toss in the parsley, pepper, and feta. Season with salt. Serve immediately or chill in a covered container in the refrigerator for up to 2 days. The salad may be served warm, at room temperature, or chilled.

Curried Rice Salad

Basmati rice, raisins, pumpkin seeds, and curry come together in this unique rice salad. Served at room temperature or lightly chilled, this dish is an excellent alternative to typical rice or potato salads.

SERVES 8

- 2½ cups chicken or vegetable broth
- 1½ cups basmati rice
- 1 tbsp curry powder
- ¼ cup peanut oil
- ¼ cup pumpkin seeds
- 2 tbsp rice wine vinegar
- 3 tbsp golden raisins
- ½ cup chopped onions
- 1 cup diced Granny Smith apple
- ¼ tsp kosher salt, as needed
- ¼ tsp freshly ground black pepper, or as needed
- ½ cup frozen peas, thawed

1. In a medium pot, bring the broth to a boil. Add the rice, lower the heat to medium-low, cover, and cook until tender to the bite, about 30 minutes.

2. Meanwhile, in a small sauté pan, lightly toast the curry powder over low heat, about 30 seconds. Add the oil and pumpkin seeds and toast over medium heat until golden brown, about 3 minutes. Remove the pan from the heat and add the vinegar, raisins, onions, apples, salt, and pepper.

3. Sauté this mixture over low heat for 1 minute. Now, add the peas and cook for an additional minute.

4. Place the curry mixture in a large bowl and allow it to cool to room temperature.

5. When the rice is ready, remove the pot from the heat, add to the curry mixture, and gently stir together. Allow the salad to cool to room temperature and then serve or wrap well and chill in the refrigerator. The salad can be made up to 24 hours ahead of time and may be served at room temperature or chilled.

Soba Noodle Salad

Soba noodles, of Japanese origin, are made from buckwheat and wheat flours, giving them a dark brownish color and nutty flavor. They are widely available in Asian markets, and come in both dried and fresh forms.

SERVES 8

- ½ lb soba noodles
- 2 tbsp rice vinegar
- ¼ cup tamari soy sauce
- 2 tsp light miso
- 6 tbsp sesame oil
- 2 tbsp sesame seeds, plus more as needed
- ½ tsp red pepper flakes
- 3 carrots, cut into thin strips
- 1 bunch green onions, white and green portions, thinly sliced on the diagonal
- 2 cups snow peas, cut in ⅛-inch strips on the diagonal
- ½ tsp kosher salt, or as needed
- 1 tsp freshly ground black pepper, or as needed

1. Bring a large pot of salted water to a boil, add the noodles, and cook until tender to the bite. Rinse with cold water, and drain well.

2. In a small bowl, stir together the vinegar, soy sauce, and miso to combine. Whisk in the oil. Add the sesame seeds and pepper flakes.

3. In a large bowl, add the carrots, green onions, and snow peas. Add the dressing and toss to coat. Add the noodles and adjust the seasoning with salt and pepper. The salad is ready to serve now, or it can be stored in a covered container in the refrigerator for up to 24 hours. The salad may be served chilled or at room temperature. Garnish with additional sesame seeds before serving, if desired.

Soba Noodle Salad

Warm Potato Salad

Warm Potato Salad

Put a new spin on potato salad. The pungent flavors of anchovy, capers, and garlic come together with two delicious vinegars for a refreshing new version of an old favorite.

SERVES 8

2¾ lb waxy potatoes (such as Yukon Gold), quartered

1 cup extra-virgin olive oil

6 tbsp red wine vinegar

2 tbsp balsamic vinegar

½ cup chopped flat-leaf parsley

¼ cup chopped capers

1 tbsp chopped anchovies

1 tsp minced garlic

1 tsp kosher salt, or as needed

¼ tsp ground white pepper

1. Place the potatoes in a large pot with enough cold salted water to cover by about 2 inches. Bring the potatoes to a simmer and cook until they are easily pierced with the tip of a paring knife, 20 to 25 minutes.

2. Meanwhile, in a small bowl, whisk together the oil, vinegar, parsley, capers, anchovies, garlic, salt, and pepper.

3. Drain the potatoes and return them to the pot over low heat for 2 or 3 minutes, shaking the pot, to dry them out and evaporate any excess moisture. Peel and dice the potatoes while still quite hot and place them in a large bowl. Mix the dressing to recombine, and pour it over the potatoes and toss gently to combine. Serve the salad warm or at room temperature. The salad can be made ahead and refrigerated in a covered container for up to 2 days. Bring back to room temperature for service.

German Potato Salad

This is a potato salad made from sliced, cooked potatoes, bacon, onions, and celery. Bacon fat is used in part to flavor the vinaigrette that seasons this dish. This salad is most often served warm or at room temperature for the very best flavor.

SERVES 8

2¼ lb waxy potatoes (such as Yukon Gold)

4 slices bacon

2½ cups chicken broth

¼ cup white wine vinegar

1 cup diced onions

1 tsp kosher salt, or as needed

1 tsp granulated sugar, or as needed

¼ tsp ground white pepper

¼ cup canola oil

2 tbsp mild brown mustard

3 tbsp snipped chives

1. Place the potatoes in a large pot with enough cold salted water to cover by about 2 inches. Bring the potatoes to a simmer and cook until they are easily pierced with the tip of a paring knife, 20 to 25 minutes.

2. Meanwhile, in a skillet, cook the bacon over medium heat until crisp, turning it as needed to cook evenly, about 5 minutes. Remove the bacon slices with a slotted spoon and keep it warm. When cool enough to handle, crumble the bacon into small pieces. Reserve the bacon fat.

3. Drain the potatoes in a colander, return them to the pot over low heat for 2 or 3 minutes, shaking the pot, to dry them out. While the potatoes are still quite hot, remove the peels and slice the potatoes ½ inch thick.

4. In a medium saucepan, bring the broth, vinegar, onions, salt, sugar, and pepper to a boil. Add the oil, rendered bacon fat, and mustard and return to a simmer. Pour the boiling broth-vinegar mixture over the potato mixture. Toss in the crumbled bacon and chives. Toss gently to combine. The salad can be served warm or at room temperature.

VEGETABLES

SELECT YOUR VEGETABLE SIDE DISHES with your main dish in mind. Consider the colors and flavors that will be the best partners. Most of the dishes we've included here are easy to put together and cook. You can keep most of them warm in a covered serving bowl or platter for up to 30 minutes without losing much in the way of flavor or color.

Moroccan-Style Roasted Vegetables

Because these vegetables have different cooking times, they should be roasted separately and combined after cooking for the best result.

SERVES 6

¾ cup sliced red onions

1 cup sliced red bell peppers

⅔ cup zucchini, quartered lengthwise

4 medium leeks, white and light green portions, quartered lengthwise

1 tbsp extra-virgin olive oil

¼ tsp kosher salt

¼ tsp freshly ground black pepper

1⅓ cups sweet potatoes, quartered lengthwise

1 tsp purchased harissa sauce

1. Preheat the oven to 400°F. Place the onions, bell peppers, zucchini, and leeks in a roasting pan. Drizzle the vegetables with the oil and season with salt and pepper. Brush the sweet potato wedges with a thin coat of harissa sauce and place in a separate pan. The vegetables and sweet potatoes can be held in the pan and ready to roast, covered, in the refrigerator, for up to 24 hours.

2. Roast the vegetables and sweet potatoes until cooked and caramelized, 12 to 15 minutes for each. In a large bowl, toss the finished vegetables together to combine. Serve hot or warm.

Roasted Carrots and Parsnips with Fresh Rosemary and Sage

Roasted, sweet root vegetables such as carrots and parsnips become even sweeter when allowed to cook slowly in the oven. By keeping the cuts relatively similar in size, the pieces will all cook in the same amount of time. This side dish is delicious with roasted meats and poultry, particularly in the fall and winter when root vegetables are in season.

SERVES 6

4 parsnips

5 carrots, peeled, cut on the diagonal into ¾-inch-thick slices

3 tbsp olive oil

1 tsp kosher salt, or as needed

1 tsp freshly ground black pepper, or as needed

2 tsp chopped rosemary

2 tsp chopped sage

1. Preheat the oven to 350°F. Peel the parsnips and halve each crosswise where it becomes narrow. Then cut the narrow portions on the diagonal into ¾-inch-thick slices. Quarter the wider portions and also cut them on the diagonal into ¾-inch-thick slices.

2. In a large bowl, toss together the parsnips, carrots, oil, salt, pepper, rosemary, and sage. The vegetables can be prepared to this point and stored in a ziplock bag or a covered container for up to 12 hours.

3. Spread the vegetable mixture out into an even layer in a large shallow baking pan and pour in 2 tablespoons of water. Roast the vegetables in the lower third of the oven until tender, 30 to 35 minutes. Serve hot.

Roasted Carrots and Parsnips
with Fresh Rosemary and Sage

Asian-Style Sweet-and-Sour Green Beans with Water Chestnuts

These beans are both easy to prepare and feature a refreshing Asian flavor profile that is a quick and easy complement to your favorite Asian-inspired entrée. The water chestnuts add a crisp texture and a refreshing flavor to the dish.

SERVES 8

1 lb green beans, trimmed, cut into 2-inch lengths

2 tbsp soy sauce

2 tbsp hoisin sauce

2 tbsp rice wine vinegar

1 tsp hot pepper sauce, or as needed

2 tsp peanut oil

1 garlic clove, minced

One 8-oz can water chestnuts, drained and sliced

1 tsp dark sesame oil

1. Place the green beans in a steamer basket and set in a saucepan over 1 inch of boiling water; the water should not touch the bottom of the steamer basket. Cover and steam until the green beans are just tender, about 5 minutes. Drain.

2. In a small bowl, combine the soy sauce, hoisin sauce, vinegar, and the hot pepper sauce. Put the peanut oil in a wok or large skillet and set over high heat. Add the prepared green beans and garlic. Stir-fry the beans for 2 minutes. Add the soy sauce mixture and cook, stirring, 2 minutes more. Stir in the chestnuts and drizzle with the sesame oil. Serve at once.

Buttered Green Beans with Tarragon and Shallots

The light and delicate aniselike flavor of tarragon offers a delicious complement to this simple combination of green beans, shallots, and butter.

SERVES 8

2 lb green beans, trimmed

1 tbsp minced shallots

1 tbsp unsalted butter

1 tbsp chopped tarragon

Kosher salt, as needed

Freshly ground black pepper, as needed

1. Bring a pot of salted water to a rolling boil. Add the green beans and cook, uncovered, until the beans are bright green and just barely tender, about 3 minutes. Drain the beans in a colander and rinse with cool water. The beans can be prepared to this point and stored in a ziplock bag or a covered container in the refrigerator for up to 24 hours.

2. In a large skillet or sauté pan, heat the butter over medium-high heat. Add the shallots and cook, stirring frequently, until tender, about 2 minutes. Add the beans and sauté until warm, 2 to 3 minutes more. Stir in the tarragon, season with salt and pepper, and serve immediately.

Sautéed Brussels Sprouts with Crisp Pancetta

The majority of the preparation work when making this recipe comes in removing the core and pulling the Brussels sprout layers apart. This is well worth the effort, as the tender leaves cook quickly and evenly to beautiful bright green color.

SERVES 8

- 6 cups Brussels sprouts, trimmed
- 2½ oz pancetta, roughly chopped
- ¼ cup extra-virgin olive oil
- ½ cup chopped white onion
- 1 tbsp unsalted butter
- 1 tsp kosher salt, or as needed
- ½ tsp freshly ground black pepper, or as needed

1. Slice each Brussels sprout in half lengthwise and cut out the core with the tip of a paring knife. Gently pull the layers of leaves apart.

2. Heat a large sauté pan over medium heat and add the oil and pancetta. Render the fat from the pancetta until the pancetta gets lightly crispy, 3 minutes. Remove the pancetta and reserve.

3. Add the onions to the pan with the rendered pancetta fat and cook over medium-high heat, stirring frequently, until translucent, about 5 minutes. Add the butter and swirl to melt.

4. Add the Brussels sprouts and 1 to 2 ounces water. Sauté over medium heat, tossing to coat. Cook until the leaves are tender and bright green. Season with salt and pepper. Top with the crispy pancetta and serve immediately.

Sautéed Swiss Chard

Swiss chard can be found in the produce aisle near other leafy greens. Although white and red chard are typically found in most grocery stores, rainbow chard makes this dish truly beautiful.

SERVES 6

- ½ cup pine nuts
- 3 tbsp olive oil
- 6 tbsp minced shallots
- 2 tbsp minced garlic
- 2 bunches Swiss chard, torn into pieces
- 1 tsp kosher salt, or as needed
- ½ tsp freshly ground black pepper, or as needed
- ¼ cup dry white wine

1. Heat a small sauté pan over medium heat. Add the pine nuts to the dry pan and toast, agitating the pan every 30 seconds, to prevent burning. Toast until the nuts are light golden color on all sides, about 4 minutes total.

2. Heat the olive oil in a large skillet over medium-high heat. Add the shallots to each pan and cook, stirring frequently, until translucent, about 5 minutes. Add the garlic and cook until aromatic, about 2 minutes.

3. Add the chard to each pan, and season with salt and pepper. Sauté the chard until it is just barely wilted, about 5 minutes.

4. Add the wine, cover the skillet, and steam the chard until the spines are tender and the liquid has almost evaporated, 5 minutes. Serve hot.

Grilled Belgian Endive

Grilling adds a smoky flavor to the endive. Try this with small heads of radicchio if you'd like a bolder color on the plate.

SERVES 8

8 heads Belgian endive

Kosher salt, as needed

Juice of 1 lemon

Olive oil, as needed

Lemon Vinaigrette (recipe follows)

1. Peel down the endive to form smaller, uniform heads. Bring a medium pot of salted water to a simmer over medium-high heat and add the lemon juice. Add the trimmed endive and simmer until the core of the endive is tender enough to pierce easily with the tip of a paring knife, about 10 minutes. Remove the endive from the pot, drain well, and reserve. The endive can be prepared to this point and stored in a covered container in the refrigerator for up to 24 hours.

2. Preheat a gas grill to medium-low; turn one burner off. If you are using a charcoal grill, build a fire and let it burn down until the coals are glowing red with a heavy coating of white ash. Spread the coals in an even bed on one side of the grill. Clean the cooking grate and rub lightly with a little vegetable oil.

3. Brush the endive lightly with olive oil and grill over direct heat until the first side is colored and shows dark grilling marks, about 3 minutes. Turn once and grill on the second side over indirect heat until very hot, 2 minutes more.

4. Arrange the endive on a platter and coat lightly with the vinaigrette. The endive can be served hot, warm, at room temperature, or cold.

Lemon Vinaigrette

MAKES 1 CUP

⅓ cup fresh lemon juice, plus as needed

2 shallots, minced

½ tsp granulated sugar

¾ cup extra-virgin olive oil

Kosher salt and freshly ground black pepper, as needed

In a small bowl, whisk together the lemon juice, shallots, and sugar. Slowly whisk in the oil. Season with salt, pepper, and additional lemon juice, if needed. The dressing can be made in advance and held for up to 2 days.

Sautéed Snow Peas with Sesame Seeds

This versatile recipe adds a refreshing element to almost any main dish, and using seasonal vegetables eliminates the need for heavy garnishes.

SERVES 8

1 tsp kosher salt, or as needed

1 lb snow peas, trimmed, strings removed

2 tbsp peanut or canola oil

2 tbsp toasted sesame seeds

Freshly ground black pepper, as needed

1. Bring a large pot of salted water to a rolling boil over high heat. Add the snow peas to the boiling water and cook until they are bright green, but still crisp, about 1 minute. Drain at once in a colander and place in a bowl filled with ice water. When the snow peas are chilled, drain them and reserve until you are ready to finish them by sautéing. They can be stored in a ziplock bag in the refrigerator for up to 12 hours.

2. Heat the oil in a large skillet over medium-high heat. Add the snow peas and toss until they are evenly coated and very hot, about 2 minutes. Add the sesame seeds and season with additional salt and the pepper, if needed. Serve hot.

Pan-Steamed Lemon Asparagus

If you have a choice, opt for thicker asparagus. They have a richer flavor. This dish cooks quickly, so you can have it ready to serve in about 5 minutes, as long as you've done all the trimming, peeling, chopping, and measuring ahead of time.

SERVES 8

2 bunches asparagus

2 tbsp olive oil

¼ cup minced shallots

4 tsp minced garlic

¼ cup lemon juice

¼ cup dry white wine

1. Trim off the bottoms the asparagus spears so that the asparagus are equal in length.

2. Heat the oil in a large sauté pan over medium heat. Cook the shallots and garlic, stirring frequently, until translucent, about 2 minutes. Add the asparagus and stir until bright green and coated with the oil, shallots, and garlic.

3. Add the lemon juice and white wine to the pan, cover, and steam the asparagus until cooked through, about 3 minutes. Serve immediately on warmed plates or platter.

Haricots Verts with Toasted Walnuts

Haricots verts is the French term for extra-thin, delicate green beans. Tossed with walnuts, shallots, and garlic, they make an elegant side dish for cuts of beef and various chicken dishes. Regular green beans may be substituted if haricots verts are unavailable.

SERVES 8

2 lb haricots verts, trimmed

1 tsp olive oil

2 tbsp minced shallots

2 garlic cloves, minced

¼ cup chopped toasted walnuts

¼ tsp kosher salt, or as needed

Freshly ground black pepper, as needed

2 tbsp unsalted butter

1. Bring a pot of salted water to a rolling boil. Add the haricots verts and cook, uncovered, until the beans are bright green and tender, about 4 minutes. Drain the beans in a colander and rinse with cool water. The beans can be prepared to this point and stored in a ziplock bag or covered container in the refrigerator for up to 24 hours

2. In a small sauté pan, heat the oil over medium heat. Add the shallots and garlic and cook, stirring frequently, until the shallots are translucent, 3 to 4 minutes.

3. Add the haricots verts, walnuts, and butter to the pan and toss until the haricots verts are hot and evenly coated with the butter, shallots, and garlic. Season with salt and pepper and serve hot.

Broccoli with Orange-Sesame Sauce

Complement one of your favorite Asian dishes with a side of this lightly steamed broccoli, seasoned with orange, honey and ginger and topped with crunchy sesame seeds.

SERVES 8

2 lb broccoli florets

1 cup fresh orange juice

2 tbsp honey

1 tbsp peeled, grated ginger

1 tbsp fresh lemon juice

2 tsp dark sesame oil

2 tbsp sesame seeds, toasted

1. Place the broccoli in a steamer basket and set the basket in a saucepan over 1 inch of boiling water; the water should not touch the bottom of the steamer. Cover and steam until the broccoli is just tender, 8 to 10 minutes. Drain.

2. In a small saucepan, combine the orange juice, honey, and ginger and bring to a boil. Cook over medium-high heat until the sauce thickens, about 3 minutes. Stir in the lemon juice and sesame oil, and cook for 2 minutes more.

3. Arrange the broccoli in a serving bowl, top with the sauce, sprinkle with the sesame seeds for garnish. Serve immediately.

Sweet and Spicy Sautéed Apples

These sautéed apples provide the perfect balance to a savory dish. For a sweet version to be served on top of your favorite ice cream, just eliminate the cayenne pepper.

SERVES 8

4 Granny Smith apples, peeled, cored, and cut into wedges

½ cup packed brown sugar

¼ tsp ground cloves

¼ tsp ground cinnamon

½ tsp kosher salt, or as needed

Pinch of cayenne pepper (optional)

¼ cup (½ stick) unsalted butter

6 tbsp Calvados

1. In a medium bowl, toss the apples with the brown sugar, cloves, cinnamon, salt, and cayenne, if using.

2. In a large sauté pan, heat the butter over high heat. Add the apples and sauté, stirring only occasionally, until the sugar has caramelized and the apples are golden brown, about 10 minutes. Deglaze the pan with the Calvados, scraping up any browned bits from the bottom, and cook until the liquid has reduced by half.

3. The apples are ready to serve now, or they can be cooled and stored in a covered container in the refrigerator for up to 3 days. Reheat over low heat or in the microwave until very hot. Serve hot.

Braised Greens

Use any cooking green you like in this recipe, including escarole, dandelion or mustard greens, or spinach.

SERVES 8

3 lb collard greens or kale

2 slices pancetta or bacon, minced

1 cup minced onions

3 garlic cloves, minced

½ cup dry white wine

1 ham hock

1¼ cups chicken broth

Kosher salt, as needed

Freshly ground black pepper, as needed

1. Preheat the oven to 350°F. Bring a pot of salted water to a rolling boil over high heat.

2. Meanwhile, prepare an ice bath in a large bowl. Strip the leaves from the collards or kale, discard the stems, and cut the leaves into bite-size pieces. Add the leaves to the boiling water and cook until they are tender and wilted, about 3 minutes. Drain at once in a colander and place in the ice bath until cool. Drain again and squeeze out excess moisture.

3. In a Dutch oven or other flameproof casserole, render the pancetta or bacon over medium heat. When the pancetta or bacon is a light golden color, add the onions and garlic and cook, stirring frequently, until aromatic, about 1 minute. Add the blanched greens and wine and stir to release any browned bits from the bottom. Cook until the liquid is reduced by half.

4. Add the ham hock and broth. Season with salt and pepper. Transfer to the oven and braise until tender, 30 to 45 minutes. Remove the ham hock, if using, and cut any lean meat from the hock. Dice the ham and stir it into the greens.

5. Remove the greens from the pan and place them in a serving bowl. Place the Dutch oven with the cooking liquid back on the stovetop and cook over medium-high heat until it is reduced by half. Add the liquid back to the greens and adjust the seasoning with salt and pepper. The greens can be served now, or stored in a covered container in the refrigerator for up to 3 days. Reheat, if necessary, over medium heat and serve very hot.

Brussels Sprouts with Mustard Glaze

Make sure to sort out any exceptionally large or small sprouts, as they will not cook evenly or in the same amount of time.

SERVES 6

6 cups Brussels sprouts, trimmed

½ cup chicken broth

2 tsp whole-grain mustard

½ tsp whole mustard seeds (optional)

1. Bring a large pot of salted water to a rolling boil. Add the Brussels sprouts and cook until until tender, 5 to 6 minutes. If the Brussels sprouts are quite small, reduce the cooking time; increase the cooking time for larger sprouts.

2. In a saucepan, heat the broth, mustard, and mustard seeds over medium heat. Add the Brussels sprouts and toss to coat with the mustard mixture. Serve hot.

Brussels Sprouts with Mustard Glaze

Ratatouille with Couscous (page 265)

Ratatouille

This is another terrific dish that improves if it is allowed to sit overnight. Pair it with couscous or polenta to make a meatless main dish.

SERVES 8

1 tsp olive oil

⅔ cup diced red onion

1½ tbsp minced garlic

1 tbsp minced shallots

1 tbsp tomato paste

5 plum tomatoes, seeded, sliced ¼ inch thick

1 cup medium-dice zucchini

1 cup medium-dice red bell pepper

1½ cups medium-dice eggplant

1 cup medium-dice yellow squash

1 cup vegetable broth

1 tbsp minced basil

¼ tsp dried oregano, as needed

½ tsp kosher salt, or as needed

¼ tsp freshly ground black pepper, or as needed

1. Heat the oil in a medium saucepot over medium-high heat. Add the onions, garlic, and shallots. Sauté until the onions are translucent, 6 to 7 minutes. Add the tomato paste and sauté until brown, 3 to 4 minutes.

2. Add the tomatoes, zucchini, bell peppers, eggplant, squash, and broth. Bring to a gentle simmer and stew, stirring occasionally, until the vegetables are tender, about 15 minutes. The ratatouille can be cooled and stored in a covered container in the refrigerator for up to 3 days or in the freezer for up to 4 weeks.

3. Reheat in a saucepan or the microwave until very hot, if necessary, and season with the basil, oregano, salt, and pepper. Serve hot.

Vegetable Gratin

SERVES 6

¼ cup olive oil, plus as needed

1 medium red onion, thinly sliced

2 red bell peppers, seeded and cut into strips

1 green bell pepper, seeded and cut into strips

¼ cup julienned sun-dried tomatoes

3 garlic cloves, peeled and crushed

½ cup pitted, chopped kalamata or Niçoise olives

¼ cup chopped basil

2 tsp chopped oregano

Kosher salt and freshly ground black pepper, as needed

1 medium zucchini, thinly sliced

1 medium yellow squash, thinly sliced

2 cups crumbled feta

3 large eggs, beaten

2 cups heavy cream

1. Heat the oil in a large sauté pan over medium-high heat. Add the onions and sauté, stirring frequently, until tender and translucent, 6 minutes. Add the bell peppers, sun-dried tomatoes, and garlic, and cook, stirring frequently, until the peppers are tender, about 3 minutes. Stir in the olives, basil, and oregano. Season with salt and pepper.

2. Spread this mixture evenly in the bottom of a shallow baking dish or casserole. Layer the zucchini and yellow squash over the onion mixture. Sprinkle with the cheese.

3. Preheat the oven to 350°F. In a large bowl, whisk together the eggs and cream. Season with salt and pepper and pour over the vegetables. The dish can be assembled to this point and stored, covered, in the refrigerator for up to 4 hours. Cover with aluminum foil and bake until the squashes are tender and the custard has thickened, about 20 minutes. Remove the cover and bake long enough to give the top a golden color, 3 to 4 minutes more. Let the gratin rest for 5 minutes before serving.

Creamed Swiss Chard with Prosciutto

As this dish proves, creamed vegetable dishes don't have to be bland. The assertive taste of chard paired with prosciutto is enhanced, not masked, by the addition of heavy cream.

SERVES 8

3 tbsp olive oil

½ cup diced prosciutto

½ cup minced yellow onion

1 tbsp minced garlic

12 cups chopped Swiss chard

⅔ cup heavy cream

Kosher salt, as needed

Freshly ground black pepper, as needed

⅓ cup grated Parmesan

¼ tsp freshly grated nutmeg

1. Heat the oil in a large sauté pan over medium heat. Add the prosciutto and sauté until aromatic, about 1 minute. Increase the heat to high, and add the onions and garlic. Sauté, stirring constantly, until the garlic is aromatic, about 1 minute more.

2. Add the Swiss chard and sauté just until the leaves wilt, about 5 minutes. Add the heavy cream and bring to a simmer. Cook the Swiss chard until it is tender, about 5 minutes.

3. Season generously with salt and pepper, remove from the heat, and stir in the cheese and nutmeg. The chard can be prepared to this point, cooled, and stored in a covered container in the refrigerator for up to 8 hours. Reheat over low heat or in the microwave, if necessary. Serve immediately in a warmed bowl or on warmed plates.

Stewed Chickpeas with Tomatoes, Zucchini, and Cilantro

Native to the Mediterranean region, chickpeas are commonly found in the cuisines surrounding the Mediterranean Sea and those of the Middle East. Here chickpeas are combined with tomatoes and zucchini for a hearty and delicious side dish that can be made in a snap and only improves with time.

SERVES 8

3 tbsp olive oil

3 tbsp minced garlic

3 cups small-dice zucchini

1 cup peeled, seeded, and diced tomatoes, juices reserved

3 cups cooked chickpeas, rinsed and drained

2 tbsp chicken or vegetable broth

¼ cup chopped cilantro

1 tsp kosher salt, or as needed

½ tsp freshly ground black pepper, or as needed

¼ cup fresh lime juice

1. Heat the oil in a large sauté pan over medium heat. Add the garlic and cook, stirring frequently until aromatic, 2 minutes. Add the zucchini and tomatoes and sauté until the zucchini is tender, about 8 minutes.

2. Add the chickpeas and enough broth to keep them moist. Stew until heated through, 6 to 7 minutes. The stew can be prepared to this point, cooled, and stored in a covered container in the refrigerator for up to 2 days. Reheat, if necessary, over low heat or in the microwave. Add the cilantro and season with salt, pepper, and lime juice. Serve warm.

GRAINS

STEAMED GRAINS AND PILAFS are a good match for a wide range of foods. These simple techniques are easy to update with some additional aromatics or garnish ingredients. You may add ingredients like herbs or spices to the grain as it steams, or you may add them after the grain has cooked, as a garnish. Steamed grains can be reheated successfully, but if at all possible, try to time your cooking so that the grain won't need to sit more than 20 or 30 minutes.

Pilafs are another great option for grains. A pilaf means that some aromatics, typically onions, shallots, leeks, or garlic, are gently cooked in oil or butter before the grain is added. Finishing the pilaf in your oven means virtually hands-off, worry-free cooking with no need to stir.

Basic Rice Pilaf

Pilaf is a method of cooking commonly used for grains. The grain, such as rice, is sautéed in butter or another fat along with aromatics such as onion, shallot, or garlic before hot liquid, such as broth is added. Started on the stovetop, pilaf is typically finished in the oven, which is a convenient way to have your hands free to finish other accompaniments in the meantime.

SERVES 8

2 tbsp olive oil

⅓ cup diced onion

1 garlic clove, bruised

1½ cups long-grain white rice

2½ cups chicken or vegetable broth

1 tsp kosher salt, or as needed

Freshly ground black pepper, as needed

1 dried bay leaf

1 sprig thyme

1. Preheat the oven to 350°F. Heat the oil in a medium ovenproof saucepan over medium heat. Add the onions and garlic and cook, stirring frequently, until the onions become translucent, about 3 minutes.

2. Add the rice, water, salt, pepper, bay leaf, and thyme. Bring the mixture to a boil.

3. Cover the pot tightly and transfer to the oven. Bake until the rice is tender and has absorbed all of the liquid, about 18 minutes. Remove and discard the bay leaf and thyme. Fluff the rice with a fork to separate the grains and release steam. Serve hot.

Spicy Dill Rice

Dill, cardamom, and chile peppers come together and lend an interesting twist to basmati rice. Packed with flavor, this rice is terrific with poultry or seafood entrees.

SERVES 8

2 tbsp peanut oil

1 cup chopped onions

1 jalapeño, chopped

1 tsp ground cardamom

1½ cups basmati rice

½ cup chopped dill

1 tsp kosher salt, or as needed

2¼ cups chicken or vegetable broth

1. Preheat the oven to 350°F.

2. Heat the oil in an ovenproof saucepan over medium heat. Add the onions, jalapeño, cardamom, and cook, stirring frequently, until the onions are tender, about 3 minutes. Add the rice and stir constantly until the grains are coated with fat. Add the dill and salt and sauté, stirring frequently, over low heat for 2 minutes.

3. Add the broth, cover, and cook in the oven until the liquid is absorbed, about 16 minutes. Gently fluff with a fork to separate grains. Serve hot.

Coconut Rice with Ginger

You can create your own variations here by adding additional flavorings to the rice before fluffing it with a fork: Add one or more of the following: raisins, slivered almonds, cashew bits, green chiles, or toasted shredded coconut.

SERVES 8

¼ cup (½ stick) unsalted butter

4 garlic cloves, minced

2½ tbsp minced ginger

1½ cups long-grain white rice

2 cups coconut milk

1 cup water

1 tbsp kosher salt, or as needed

1 tsp freshly ground black pepper

1. Preheat the oven to 350°F.

2. In an ovenproof saucepan, heat the butter over medium heat. Add the garlic and ginger and sauté until aromatic, about 2 minutes. Add the rice and sauté until the grains are coated with butter, 2 minutes more.

3. Add the coconut milk, water, salt, and pepper. Bring the mixture to a boil and cover with a lid or aluminum foil. Cook the rice in the oven until tender, about 16 minutes. Fluff the rice with a fork. Serve hot.

Wild Rice Pilaf

Any combination of garnishes can be added to the cooked pilaf, including sliced toasted almonds, sliced green onions, or a favorite dried fruit that has been diced and rehydrated slightly in a touch of apple juice, white wine, or warm water.

SERVES 6

3 tbsp olive oil

6 tbsp minced shallots

2 tbsp minced garlic

1½ cups wild rice blend

4½ cups chicken or vegetable broth

1 tsp kosher salt, or as needed

½ tsp freshly ground black pepper, or as needed

1. Preheat the oven to 350°F.

2. Heat the oil in a medium ovenproof saucepan over medium heat. Add the shallots and garlic and cook, stirring frequently, until translucent, 3 to 4 minutes.

3. Add the rice and toast, stirring constantly, until aromatic, 2 to 3 minutes. Add the broth and bring the mixture to a boil. Cover, transfer to the oven, and bake until the rice is tender to the bite, about 35 minutes. Season with salt and pepper, if necessary. Fluff with a fork. Serve hot.

Barley and Wheat Berry Pilaf

This pilaf has a rich, almost nutty flavor that pairs well with roasted or grilled meats, or make it the centerpiece of a meatless menu.

SERVES 6

1 cup wheat berries

3 tbsp unsalted butter

½ cup minced yellow onion

½ cup minced carrot

¼ cup minced celery

1½ cups pearled barley

4 cups chicken broth

1 sprig thyme

1½ cups chopped kale or collard greens

Kosher salt and freshly ground black pepper, as needed

1. Preheat the oven to 350°F.

2. Place the wheat berries in a bowl and add enough cold water to cover them by about 2 inches. Soak for at least 8 and up to 12 hours.

3. Heat the butter in a pot over medium-high heat. Add the onion, carrot, and celery and sauté, stirring frequently, until the onions are translucent, 5 to 6 minutes. Add the barley and sauté until it is coated with butter and has a "toasted" aroma, 2 or 3 minutes.

4. Add the broth and bring to a simmer. Add the wheat berries and the thyme sprigs. Stir once or twice, cover the pot, and place in the oven to cook until the barley and wheat berries are tender and have absorbed all the broth, 50 to 60 minutes. After the pilaf has cooked for 45 minutes, add the kale or collards greens. Remove and discard the thyme. Season with salt and pepper. Serve hot.

Couscous

Couscous originated in the cuisines of North Africa and is a form of pasta, not a grain, as many people think. This quick couscous recipe can be tailored with a number of variations; some are listed below. Different sizes of couscous take different amounts of time to cook, so read the directions on the package.

SERVES 8

2 tbsp unsalted butter

2 tbsp kosher salt, or as needed

2 cups couscous

1. In a medium saucepan, bring 3 cups of water to a boil. Add the butter and salt. Stir in the couscous, making sure that all of it is wet.

2. Cover, set the saucepan aside, and let the couscous rest until it is tender and has absorbed the water, 15 to 20 minutes. If you wish to make the couscous in advance, it can be stored in a covered container in the refrigerator and reheated in a microwave until very hot. Fluff the couscous with a fork to break up any clumps.

PINE NUT AND RAISIN COUSCOUS *After the couscous and water are combined, stir in ½ cup each golden raisins and toasted pine nuts.*

CURRY COUSCOUS *Add 2 tablespoons of curry powder with the butter.*

POLENTA

POLENTA IS A THICK PORRIDGE made from coarsely ground cornmeal that is cooked by simmering in water, broth, or milk. (Other cereals and meals, like oatmeal, grits, and farina are prepared in the same way.) Use one hand to slowly pour the measured polenta into the simmering liquid. Whisk or stir constantly with the other hand as you add the polenta to keep it from clumping up. Once you have added all the polenta, continue to cook over medium to low heat, stirring often. The more you stir, the creamier the finished product will be.

Basic Creamy Polenta

Instead of serving this as a creamy polenta, pour it into a baking dish to cool and firm. Then, you can cut it into pieces to grill, broil, or sauté until crisp, golden, and very hot.

SERVES 8

- **4 cups water**
- **1 tsp kosher salt, as needed**
- **¾ cup coarse yellow cornmeal**
- **¼ cup (½ stick) unsalted butter**
- **½ cup grated Parmesan (optional)**

1. Bring the water for the polenta to a simmer in a deep pot. Add salt and slowly add the cornmeal, making sure you whisk continuously. Let simmer gently, stirring from time to time, until the polenta is done, about 45 minutes.

2. Remove the polenta from the heat, adjust the seasoning, and add the butter and cheese, if using, mixing vigorously until combined. Serve at once.

   JALAPEÑO JACK POLENTA *Reduce the Parmesan to ¼ cup and add 1 cup grated Jalapeño Jack along with the butter.*

POTATOES

POTATOES ARE ONE OF THE MOST POPULAR of all side dishes. We've include some basics for boiled potatoes with herbs, whipped potatoes, and a potato gratin. To boil potatoes, put them into a deep pot and cover with cold water. Put the pot over the heat and let the water come slowly to a simmer; this tactic cooks potatoes evenly so that you end up with a rich, creamy texture.

Potato Purée

You can make this classic comfort food as rustic or as elegant as you like. For a home-style touch, use an old-fashioned potato masher to smash the potatoes, leaving some texture to the dish. To give the dish a refined, lighter-than-air texture, use a food mill or potato ricer to purée the potatoes and then whip with an electric mixer.

SERVES 6

- **2¼ lb russet potatoes, peeled and quartered**
- **¾ cup (1½ sticks) unsalted butter**
- **1 cup whole milk**
- **1 cup heavy cream**
- **1½ tsp kosher salt, or as needed**
- **¾ tsp freshly ground black pepper, or as needed**

1. Place the potatoes in a large pot with enough cold salted water to cover by about 2 inches. Bring the potatoes to a simmer and cook until they are easily pierced with the tip of a paring knife, 20 to 25 minutes.

2. Meanwhile, in a small saucepan, melt the butter. Add the milk and cream and stir to combine. Keep warm.

3. Drain the potatoes and return them to medium heat. Add the cream mixture, and mash the cream into the potatoes using a potato masher or a handheld blender. Season with salt and pepper and transfer to a serving bowl. Serve immediately or dot the surface with butter,

or drizzle with some cream, and keep warm in a 200°F oven for up to 30 minutes.

FRIED GARLIC AND ASIAGO MASHED POTATOES *While the potatoes are boiling, melt the butter over medium-high heat. Add 6 tablespoons roughly chopped garlic and fry until light golden brown, about 5 minutes. Add the cream and milk and simmer long enough for the flavors to blend together, about 2 minutes. Add the garlic mixture to the potatoes and mush. Stir in ½ cup grated Asiago and season with salt and pepper.*

ROSEMARY AND SAGE MASHED POTATOES *Add 2 tablespoons each of chopped rosemary and chopped sage to the cream-butter mixture and allow to steep while the potatoes are boiling. Add the herb mixture to the potatoes and mash with a potato masher or hand blender. Season with salt and pepper.*

Pouring a layer of cream onto mashed potatoes will prevent a skin from forming while they're being kept warm for service.

Oven-Roasted Potatoes

Never underestimate a simple, sure favorite. Potato wedges tossed with a bit of oil and herbs provide an excellent accompaniment for classic favorites, such as pork loin or beef tenderloin.

SERVES 6

2 lb russet potatoes, peeled and cut into wedges

1½ tbsp olive oil

2 tsp chopped rosemary

4 garlic cloves, minced

1 tsp kosher salt, or as needed

½ tsp black peppercorns, crushed

1. Preheat the oven to 400°F.

2. Toss the potatoes with the oil, rosemary, garlic, salt, and pepper. Spread the potatoes in a single layer on a baking sheet.

3. Roast the potatoes in the oven until browned on one side, about 15 minutes. Flip the potatoes and continue roasting until they are golden brown on the second side and tender, about 15 minutes. Serve hot.

Parslied Potatoes

Parslied Potatoes

These tender, creamy potatoes, flecked with fresh green herbs, are a flavorful and beautiful complement to poached, roasted, or grilled meats and fish. Try fingerlings or other small potatoes, including baby Yukon Gold or banana potatoes.

SERVES 6

1½ lb small red-skinned potatoes, peeled if desired

Kosher salt, as needed

3 tbsp unsalted butter

3 tbsp chopped flat-leaf parsley

Freshly ground black pepper, as needed

1. Place the potatoes in a pot with enough cold salted water to cover by about 2 inches. Bring the potatoes to a simmer and cook until they are easily pierced with the tip of a paring knife, 20 to 25 minutes. Drain in a colander.

2. Return the potatoes to the pot and place over very low heat to dry them out, shaking the pot occasionally to keep them from sticking.

3. Add the butter and toss the potatoes in the butter until it melts and the potatoes are very hot and evenly coated. Add the parsley and season with salt and pepper, as needed. The potatoes can be kept warm in a 200°F oven for up to 30 minutes. Serve very hot.

Sweet Potato Cakes

Russet potatoes, chives, and sage balance the flavor of sweet potatoes in these creamy cakes.

SERVES 8

3 russet potatoes, peeled, quartered

2 sweet potatoes, peeled, quartered

⅔ cup fresh bread crumbs

⅓ cup whole milk

2 tbsp mayonnaise

2 tbsp chopped chives

1 tbsp chopped sage

½ tsp kosher salt, or as needed

¼ tsp freshly ground black pepper, or as needed

1. Preheat the oven to 250°F.

2. Place all the potatoes in two separate pots and add enough salted water to cover by about 2 inches. Bring the potatoes to a simmer and cook until the potatoes are tender enough to pierce easily with the tip of a paring knife, about 15 minutes for the sweet potatoes and about 25 minutes for the russet potatoes.

3. Drain the potatoes and place on the baking sheet. Place the potatoes in the oven to steam-dry, about 5 minutes. Remove from the oven and increase the oven temperature to 475°F.

4. Pass the hot potatoes through a food mill or potato ricer set over a large bowl. Allow to cool slightly. Stir in the bread crumbs, milk, mayonnaise, chives, sage, salt, and pepper.

5. Form the potato mixture into 16 small cakes, about ½ inch thick. Spray a baking sheet with cooking spray and arrange the cakes on the baking sheet. The cakes can be shaped and then stored, well wrapped, in the refrigerator for up to 24 hours.

6. Bake until the cakes are golden on both sides, turning, if necessary, as they bake, using a gentle touch so they don't fall apart, about 12 minutes total. Serve hot.

Potato Gratin

Add some grated Gruyère to the gratin by scattering a handful on each layer of potatoes. For a crisp texture, you may also want to add a thin topping of equal parts fresh bread crumbs mixed with grated Parmesan before you bake the gratin.

SERVES 6

1½ lb red or Yukon gold potatoes

1 garlic clove, minced

Kosher salt, as needed

Ground white pepper, as needed

1½ cups heavy cream

1. Preheat the oven to 325°F. Grease an 8 by 8-inch baking pan with butter.

2. Peel the potatoes and use a slicer or mandoline to cut them into slices ¹⁄₁₆ inch thick.

3. Scatter the garlic in the prepared pan, then layer the potatoes in the pan, seasoning each layer with salt and pepper and drizzling with cream. Pour the last of the cream over the top and press to completely submerge the potatoes in the cream. You can prepare the gratin ahead to this point, cover well, and store in the refrigerator for up to 24 hours.

4. Cover with aluminum foil and bake for 45 minutes. Remove the foil. With the back of a large spoon, press on the potatoes to bring any juices and cream to the top. Return to the oven and bake, uncovered, until the potatoes are lightly browned on top and tender when pierced with a fork, 20 to 25 minutes more. Let the gratin rest for 10 minutes before cutting into portions and serving.

HE LAST COURSE ENCOMPASSES ELABORATE SWEETS LIKE CAKES, TORTES, PIES, AND PASTRIES, AS WELL AS CUSTARDS, PUDDINGS, CRÊPES, SOUFFLÉS, CHEESE PLATES, AND SIMPLE FRUIT DESSERTS. YOU DON'T HAVE TO SPEND HOURS TO MAKE GREAT DESSERTS. THE KEY IS TO TRY APPROACHING BAKING IN A SYSTEMATIC, METHODICAL WAY. BEFORE YOU BEGIN, GATHER ALL THE EQUIPMENT AND MEASURE OUT THE INGREDIENTS CALLED FOR IN A RECIPE.

Chefs call this *mise en place*, or "putting in place." Read and re-read your recipes carefully; you may need to sift dry ingredients together, melt and cool some ingredients, or permit others to warm slightly at room temperature. Be sure to plan ahead, so that your frozen desserts are perfectly chilled and set when you want to serve them, pastry doughs are ready to roll out when your filling is complete, and cakes are adequately cooled before you start to frost and decorate them.

Desserts must be served at the proper temperature. Refrigerate plates for cold or frozen desserts for at least 20 minutes. Likewise, warm or hot desserts stay at their proper temperature longer if you warm the plates in a low (200°F) oven for 10 minutes before plating the food.

A large part of a last course's appeal is the artful arrangement of colors, shapes, textures, and temperatures on the plate. Sauces are an easy way to make a dessert more memorable. Something as simple as pudding can be taken to a new level of presentation and flavor when accompanied by a brandied cherry coulis or classic caramel sauce. Don't be afraid to experiment with new flavors, color combinations, and placement on the plates, but you should always take time before the party to figure out these details—the moment you're plating a frozen dessert for a twelve-guest dinner party is not the time to ponder over where to drizzle the sauce.

A special garnish can also be an attractive addition to a plate. A scattering or dusting of finely chopped nuts, confectioners' sugar, cocoa powder, or chocolate shavings is a lovely and easy, finishing touch. You can use a stencil to create a pattern on the plate or simply sift or sprinkle the garnish over the dessert or entire plate. A sprig of a fresh herb or an edible flower is another exciting option, as long as the flavor complements the dish.

THE CHEESE PLATE

AS A LAST COURSE, A COMPOSED PLATE OF ONE CHEESE with one or more accompaniments can be a nice alternative to a sweet dessert. A variety of approaches can be taken when creating a cheese plate, but the key is finding a balance of flavors that, when combined, enhance the overall taste experience. Think about your chosen cheese's acidity or bitterness, sweetness or saltiness, body, richness, and texture, and then pair it with other foods with complementary attributes. Three types of foods have a natural affinity for cheese and make excellent accompaniments: wine and beer, bread and crackers, and fruit. A few other traditional pairings are: balsamic vinegar, honey, olives, and nuts.

A cheese plate composed of one cheese with accompaniments makes a great last course. Here, blue cheese is paired with pears, walnuts, and local honey.

When the cheese plate is one course in a larger meal, a guest should be served no more than 3 ounces of cheese. Remember that cheese is a rich protein, and you don't want to overwhelm your guests.

Neatness and visual appeal are essential to a composed cheese plate. Keep cheeses whole as long as possible, and when you do cut them, the individual portions should refer back to the shape of the whole cheese; for instance, wheels should be cut into pie-shaped wedges, pyramids into triangles, and logs into rounds. There are a couple exceptions to this rule: very hard cheeses, especially those of the grana style, will need to be served as irregular chunks chiseled off whole, and the softest of cheeses are impossible to cut with a knife, so you'll need to use a spoon or spreader.

Because cheese is a living food, it is critical to store it at the proper temperature. Cheese should never be allowed to sit out at room temperature for extended periods of time. Always keep cheeses covered or wrapped in the refrigerator. Waxed paper or aluminum foil work well, because they allow the cheese to breathe but not to dry out. In general, blue cheeses should be kept separate from other cheeses, especially bloomy rinds, and at a colder temperature to keep the interior mold from spreading too much. Never freeze cheese—it will destroy the texture. Before serving, every cheese should be aromatized, or allowed to come to room temperature, to bring out the fullest flavor.

COOKIES

THE PERFECT ACCOMPANIMENT TO COFFEE AND TEA, cookies also make a fittingly sweet conclusion to almost any meal. Biscotti are meant for dipping, whether your preference is a glass of sweet dessert wine or a pot of Earl Grey tea. These cookies are baked twice and have great lasting power. You can make biscotti well ahead of time and keep them at room temperature for 3 days.

An eye-catching assortment of thoughtfully selected sweets is a nice finish to any gathering, from a sit-down dinner to a cocktail party..

ENTERTAINING

Almond Anise Biscotti

These classic biscotti never lose their appeal. Serve them with coffee, espresso, tea, or a fine bottle of Vin Santo.

MAKES 32 BISCOTTI

2 cups bread flour

1 tsp baking powder

3 large eggs

¾ cup granulated sugar

1 tsp anise extract

½ tsp kosher salt

1⅓ cups whole almonds

2 tbsp anise seeds

1. Preheat the oven to 325°F. Line 2 baking sheets with parchment paper. Sift the flour and baking powder into a large bowl.

2. In the bowl of an electric mixer fitted with the whip attachment, whip the eggs, sugar, anise extract, and salt on high speed until thick and pale yellow, about 5 minutes. Reduce the speed to low and mix in the flour mixture just until incorporated. Using a rubber spatula, fold in the almonds and anise seeds.

3. Mound half of the dough on each of the prepared baking sheets and shape into a log about 3 inches wide and the length of your baking sheet. Bake until light golden brown, about 30 minutes. Remove from the oven and cool the logs on the baking sheets set on wire racks for 10 minutes. Lower the oven temperature to 275°F.

4. Remove the logs from the pans and place on a work surface. Using a serrated knife, cut each log crosswise into ½-inch-thick slices. Place the slices back on the lined baking sheets, cut side down, and bake, turning the biscotti once halfway through the baking time, until they are golden brown, about 20 minutes. Transfer the biscotti to wire racks to cool completely. The biscotti can be stored in airtight containers at room temperature for up to 3 days.

Chocolate Biscotti

Biscotti are perfect to serve with coffee or hot chocolate. For a change, try adding macadamia nuts, almonds, or hazelnuts to the batter.

MAKES 4 DOZEN BISCOTTI

3½ cups cake flour

½ cup unsweetened cocoa powder

2 tsp baking powder

5 large eggs

1¼ cup granulated sugar

2 tbsp instant coffee powder

2 tsp vanilla extract

⅓ tsp almond extract

⅓ tsp kosher salt

1¾ cup bittersweet chocolate chunks

1. Preheat the oven to 325°F. Line 2 baking sheets with parchment paper. Sift the flour, cocoa powder, and baking powder into a large bowl.

2. In the bowl of an electric mixer fitted with the whip attachment, whip the eggs, sugar, coffee powder, vanilla and almond extracts, and salt on high speed until thick and pale yellow, about 5 minutes. Reduce the speed to low and mix in the flour mixture just until incorporated. Using a rubber spatula, fold in the chocolate chunks.

3. Mound half of the dough on each of the prepared baking sheets and shape into a log about 3 inches wide and the length of your baking sheet. Bake until a skewer inserted in the center of the logs, about 30 minutes. Remove from the oven and cool the logs on the baking sheets set on wire racks for 10 minutes. Lower the oven temperature to 275°F.

4. Remove the logs from the pans and place on a work surface. Using a serrated knife, cut each log crosswise into ½-inch-thick slices. Return the slices to the lined baking sheets, cut side down, and bake, turning the biscotti once halfway through the baking time, until they are golden brown, about 20 minutes. Transfer the biscotti to wire racks to cool completely. The biscotti can be stored in airtight containers at room temperature for up to 3 days.

Rugelach

Fill these as indicated in the recipe, or use your favorite jam and nuts, and throw in a few chocolate morsels if you like.

MAKES 36 COOKIES

2 cups bread flour

½ cup all-purpose flour

½ tsp salt

1½ cups (3 sticks) unsalted butter

10 oz cream cheese

1 cup raspberry jam

2 cups pecans, chopped

½ cup whole milk

Cinnamon-Sugar: ½ tsp sugar mixed with ½ cup sugar

1. Preheat the oven to 375°F. Line 3 baking sheets with parchment paper. Sift the flours and salt into a large bowl.

2. In the bowl of an electric mixer fitted with the paddle attachment, mix the butter and cream cheese together on medium speed until smooth, about 5 minutes. Reduce the speed to low and mix in the flour mixture until just combined, scraping down the bowl as necessary to blend evenly.

3. Turn out the dough onto a work surface. Roll the dough into a rectangle approximately 10 inches wide by 14 inches long and ½ inch thick. Fold the dough in thirds, like a letter. Divide the dough into four equal portions, wrap tightly in plastic wrap, and refrigerate for 2 hours or up to overnight.

4. Roll out the first piece of the dough into a rectangle 12 inches wide by 18 inches long and ⅛ inch thick. Spread ¼ cup of the jam evenly over the surface and sprinkle with 1 cup of the chopped pecans.

5. Beginning with the 18-inch side, roll the dough into a log. As you roll, the log will stretch to approximately 24 inches long. Brush the log with the milk and sprinkle with 2 tablespoons of the cinnamon-sugar. Cut the log into sections ¾ inch long. Repeat the process with the remaining three pieces of dough.

6. Place the cookies on the prepared baking sheets, spacing them 2 inches apart, and bake until golden brown, about 20 minutes. Transfer to wire racks and cool completely. The cookies can be stored in an airtight container at room temperature for up to 2 days.

Chocolate Chunk Cookies

Make these cookies super-size to take on picnics or serve at kids' parties, or miniaturize them to include as part of a cookie plate to serve at a tea or reception.

MAKES 45 COOKIES

3½ cups all-purpose flour

2 tsp baking soda

1 tsp kosher salt

1½ cups (3 sticks) unsalted butter

1 cup granulated sugar

⅔ cup packed light brown sugar

3 large eggs

2 tsp pure vanilla extract

2¾ cups semisweet chocolate pieces

1. Preheat the oven to 375°F. Line 4 baking sheets with parchment paper. Sift the flour, baking soda, and salt into a large bowl.

2. In the bowl of an electric mixer fitted with the paddle attachment, cream the butter and both sugars on medium speed, scraping down the bowl occasionally, until the mixture is smooth and light in color, about 5 minutes.

3. In a medium bowl, combine the eggs and vanilla and add to the sugar mixture in three additions, mixing until fully incorporated after each addition and scraping down the bowl as needed.

4. Add the flour mixture on low speed, mixing just until incorporated. Blend in the chocolate pieces by hand with a wooden spoon.

5. Drop tablespoons of the dough onto the prepared baking sheets, spacing them about 1½ inches apart. Bake until golden brown, about 10 minutes. Transfer to wire racks and cool completely. The cookies can be stored in an airtight container at room temperature for up to 2 days.

CUSTARDS

CUSTARDS AND PUDDINGS ARE A STUDY IN THEME and variation. They are prepared from a limited range of basic ingredients that marry well with both familiar and exotic flavors. They might be served hot or cold. They might be baked, stirred, molded, or chilled. However they are prepared and served, they are characterized by a creamy, rich texture.

Some desserts in this section, such as crème brûlée and pots de crème, are served in the same container in which they are baked. Crème caramel, however, is traditionally unmolded to let the sauce flow out over the custard.

When unmolding a custard, first loosen the edges by carefully running a paring knife around the inside of the mold. Press the knife flush to the side of the mold to avoid cutting into the custard.

Crème Caramel

A perfectly smooth, silken custard is a fitting end to almost any dinner party. Remember to make this dessert the day before your event so that the caramel has time to liquefy into a sauce.

SERVES 6

1 cup granulated sugar

⅛ tsp fresh lemon juice

3 tbsp warm water

2 cups whole milk

⅛ tsp salt

3 large eggs

2 large egg yolks

2 tsp pure vanilla extract

1. Preheat the oven to 325°F. Bring some water to a boil to make a water bath. Coat six 6-ounce ramekins or custard cups lightly with cooking spray and set them on a kitchen towel in a deep baking pan.

2. In a heavy saucepan, combine ½ cup of the sugar with the lemon juice and bring to a boil over high heat, stirring constantly. Once all the sugar has dissolved, stop stirring and start swirling the pan, continuing to cook until the sugar is a rich golden brown, 3 to 4 minutes.

3. When the caramel is a deep golden brown, add the warm water and stir over low heat until any hard bits are dissolved. Pour a ⅛-inch layer of caramel into the bottom of each prepared ramekin or cup.

4. In a medium saucepan, combine the milk, ¼ cup of the sugar, and the salt over medium heat and bring to a simmer. Remove from the heat and keep warm.

5. Meanwhile, in a large bowl, whisk the eggs and egg yolks with the remaining ¼ cup sugar. Temper the eggs by gradually adding about one-third of the hot milk mixture, whisking constantly. Add the remaining hot milk, whisking constantly. Add the vanilla and stir to combine. Strain the custard through a fine-mesh sieve into a bowl and then pour or ladle into the prepared ramekins or cups, filling each three-fourths full.

6. Place the baking pan on a pulled-out oven rack. Add enough boiling water to come halfway up the sides of the ramekins or cups. Carefully slide the rack back into the oven and bake until the custard edges have set and a nickel-size spot in the center jiggles slightly when a custard is gently shaken, 20 to 25 minutes.

7. Remove the custards from the water bath. Let the custards cool on a wire rack, wrap individually, and refrigerate for at least 24 hours or up to 3 days before unmolding and serving.

8. To serve: Warm a sharp paring knife in warm water and run it around the edges of each ramekin. Turn the custards out onto chilled plates.

Ricotta Cheesecake

MAKES ONE 8-INCH CAKE; SERVES 8

Graham Cracker Crust

1½ cups graham cracker crumbs (about 12 crackers)

2 tbsp granulated sugar

¼ cup (½ stick) unsalted butter, melted

Ricotta Filling

⅔ cup whole-milk ricotta

½ cup granulated sugar

1 lb cream cheese

2 large eggs, lightly beaten

1 tsp pure vanilla extract

1 tsp fresh lemon juice

1 tbsp cornstarch

3 tbsp bread flour

3 tbsp unsalted butter, melted and kept warm

1. Preheat the oven to 350°F. Lightly spray an 8-inch round cake pan with cooking spray and wrap the outside carefully with aluminum foil.

2. To make the crust: In a small bowl, stir together the crumbs, sugar, and butter. Press the crumbs down into a compact layer in the prepared pan, covering the bottom and sides of the pan. Bake the crust for 5 minutes. Remove from the oven and allow the crust to cool while preparing the filling.

3. Purée the ricotta and sugar in a food processor until smooth, 3 to 5 minutes. In the bowl of an electric mixer fitted with the paddle attachment, mix the cream cheese with the ricotta mixture on medium speed until smooth, about 10 minutes, scraping down the bowl with a rubber spatula as needed.

4. Add the eggs and mix on low speed until very smooth, scraping down the bowl thoroughly. Add the vanilla, lemon juice, cornstarch, and flour to the batter and blend on medium speed until smooth. Gradually add the melted butter, scraping down the bowl as needed, until evenly blended.

5. Spread the batter in an even layer over the crust. Drop the pan onto the counter from the height of 1 inch to release any air bubbles. Place the pan in a shallow baking dish and place the dish on a pulled-out oven rack. Add about 1 inch of boiling water. Carefully slide the rack into the oven and bake until the cheesecake edges are set but the center is still soft and the cake is starting to pull away from the sides and the top is just starting to brown, 50 to 60 minutes.

6. Remove the pan from the water bath and cool the cheesecake in the pan on a wire rack, then refrigerate for at least 3 hours or up to 24 hours before unmolding. To unmold: Run a spatula or thin-bladed knife around the inside edge to loosen the cake. Unlatch the clamp to open the pan sides and lift the form away from the cake. Cut the cheesecake into slices and serve.

MOUSSE AND CREAMS

THE TERM *MOUSSE* **COMES FROM A FRENCH WORD** meaning "frothy, foamy, or light." Creams are similar to puddings and generally include eggs, sugar, and milk, cooked until thick. Both mousses and creams can be served on their own as a dessert, but they are also frequently used to fill pastries including tarts, cream puffs, or éclairs, as well as fillings for layer cakes.

A well-made mousse should have an intense flavor with added smoothness and richness from the cream. The color should be even throughout every portion.

Mango Mousse

A small quantity of rum intensifies the tropical flavors of this mousse. Since the rum is not boiled in this dish and won't lose any flavor, be sure to choose a rum with a flavor you enjoy. Rums that are golden or dark have more pronounced flavors because they are typically aged longer.

SERVES 6

1 large mango

¼ cup dark rum or water

1 package (2¼ tsp) powdered unflavored gelatin

2 cups heavy cream

½ cup granulated sugar

2 large egg whites

Finely grated lime zest, as needed

1. Peel the mango and cut the flesh away from the pit. Purée the mango in a food processor or blender until very smooth. You should have about 1½ cups. Set aside.

2. Place the rum or water in a shallow bowl and sprinkle the gelatin over the liquid in an even layer. Stir to break up any clumps and allow the gelatin to soften, undisturbed, for about 3 minutes.

3. Heat the softened gelatin in a double-boiler over barely simmering water or in a microwave for about 20 seconds on low power, until the granules melt and the mixture is clear.

4. In a chilled large bowl, whip the cream by hand or with the whip attachment of an electric mixer until it starts to thicken, and then gradually add half the sugar while continuing to whip to medium peaks. Transfer the cream to a separate bowl if you used your electric mixer, and thoroughly wash and dry the mixer bowl and whip attachment to whip the egg whites.

5. In the cleaned bowl of an electric mixer fitted with the whip attachment, whip the egg whites on low speed until they are foamy. Increase the speed to high and gradually add the remaining sugar while continuing to whip until the meringue holds medium peaks.

6. Place the mango purée in a large bowl. Stir the melted gelatin into the purée. Working by hand with a rubber spatula, fold the whipped cream into the mango purée just until evenly blended. Add the meringue in 2 additions, folding the mixture just until blended.

7. Pipe or spoon the mousse into six 6-ounce molds, pudding dishes, wineglasses, or soufflé cups. Refrigerate the mousse for at least 3 hours or up to 24 hours. Garnish with lime zest just before serving in the molds.

Chocolate Mousse

Choose a good bittersweet chocolate for this luscious dessert. This recipe calls for the egg yolks to be cooked over simmering water. Instead of a double boiler, we recommend that you do this step by setting a mixing bowl on top of a saucepan that has about 1 inch of simmering water in it. You'll find it much easier to whip the yolks as they cook.

SERVES 8

4 large egg yolks

1 tbsp brandy

¼ cup granulated sugar

1½ cups coarsely chopped bittersweet chocolate, melted

1 cup heavy cream

2 large egg whites

Chocolate shavings or curls (see sidebar next page)

1. Combine the egg yolks with the brandy and 2 tablespoons of the sugar in a stainless steel bowl set over a saucepan with 1 inch of simmering water. Whisk until the mixture is thick, light, and very warm (about 110°F), 6 to 8 minutes.

2. Add the melted chocolate. Remove the bowl from the saucepan and whip by hand or with a handheld mixer on high speed until cool.

3. In a chilled large bowl, whip the cream by hand or with the whip attachment of an electric mixer to medium peaks. Transfer the cream to a separate bowl if you used your electric mixer and carefully clean the mixer bowl and whip attachment before whipping the egg whites.

4. In the cleaned bowl of an electric mixer fitted with the whip attachment, whip the egg whites on low speed until they are foamy. Increase the speed to high and gradually add the remaining 2 tablespoons sugar while continuing to whip until the meringue holds medium peaks.

5. Add one-third of the egg white to the chocolate mixture and gently fold until incorporated. Fold in the remaining egg white, then fold in the whipped cream until just blended.

6. Pipe or spoon into serving dishes, cover, and chill for at least 3 hours or up to 24 hours before serving. Scatter chocolate shavings or curls over the mousse just before serving.

MAKING CHOCOLATE SHAVINGS AND CURLS

Chocolate shavings and curls are simple to create and add an impressive element to any finished cake. The chocolate should be in a large piece and it is best to have it at room temperature. Set a 1-inch-thick piece of chocolate on a piece of parchment or waxed paper on a baking sheet. Stabilize the baking sheet by placing a very lightly moistened towel under it and brace the sheet against a wall or another sturdy backing.

Hold a chef's knife or a vegetable peeler so the blade is at a 45-degree angle to the surface of the chocolate, then scrape the blade across the surface without digging into the block or gouging it. To make short shavings, use a short stroke. Longer strokes will produce longer shavings, which may curl slightly.

Chocolate shavings are quite thin and should not be touched with bare hands. The heat of your hands could easily melt them. Instead, use a spatula, preferably offset, to lift the shavings and scatter or pile them on top of a dessert. If you make shavings in advance, use the spatula to transfer them to a parchment paper–lined container and store at room temperature.

For an easy chocolate decoration, microwave a block of chocolate for a few seconds to soften it slightly, and then use a vegetable peeler to cut curls.

Pastry Cream

Pastry cream is a perfect filling for éclairs and cream puffs. You can add a variety of flavorings in addition to the chocolate variation we offer below. Try adding up to ¼ cup of a cordial or liqueur such as Kahlúa, Grand Marnier, or Amaretto, a few tablespoons of honey or maple syrup, or a teaspoon of finely grated citrus zest.

MAKES 3 CUPS

¼ cup cornstarch

½ cup sugar

2 cups milk

8 large egg yolks

2 tsp pure vanilla extract

1. Stir together the cornstarch with the ¼ cup of the sugar in a small bowl to remove any lumps in the cornstarch. Add ½ cup of the milk. Add the egg yolks and vanilla extract to the cornstarch mixture and whisk together until the mixture is completely smooth. Set aside.

2. In a medium saucepan, stir together the remaining 1½ cups milk with the remaining ¼ cup sugar until the sugar has dissolved. Place over medium heat and bring to a bare simmer. Remove the pan from the heat.

3. Add about one-third of the hot milk into the egg mixture, whisking constantly. Return the tempered egg mixture to the remaining hot milk in the saucepan. Return the pan to the heat and continue cooking, vigorously stirring with a wire whisk until the mixture comes to a boil and the whisk leaves a trail in the cream.

4. Pour the pastry cream into a shallow container and cool over an ice bath or in the refrigerator. Stir the pastry cream from time to time as it cools. Once it is cool, cover the surface directly with plastic wrap and store in the refrigerator until you are ready to use it. It will last for up to 3 days.

CHOCOLATE PASTRY CREAM *Add 1 tablespoon unsweetened cocoa powder to the cornstarch and sugar in step 1. Add 3 ounces melted dark or semi-sweet chocolate to the milk when it comes to a boil in step 2, whisking until it is evenly incorporated.*

Diplomat Cream

This cream can be used as a filling for a number of pastries, such as éclairs and cream puffs. Or use it to fill tartlet shells, and then simply top with fresh berries or clementine segments.

MAKES 3 CUPS CREAM

1 cup heavy cream

2 tbsp water

¾ tsp powdered unflavored gelatin

1 cup Pastry Cream (opposite)

1. In the bowl of an electric mixer fitted with the whip attachment, or by hand in a large bowl with a wire whisk, whip the heavy cream to soft peaks . Cover and refrigerate.

2. Place the water in a shallow bowl. Sprinkle the gelatin in an even layer over the water and allow the gelatin to soften, undisturbed, for about 3 minutes. Melt over barely simmering water while stirring constantly.

3. Blend the melted gelatin into the freshly prepared and still-warm pastry cream. Strain, then cool over an ice water bath to 75°F.

4. Gently blend approximately one-third of the reserved whipped cream into the pastry cream mixture. Fold in the remaining whipped cream, thoroughly incorporating it.

5. Immediately pipe the cream into the prepared pastries. Cover and refrigerate until the cream is completely set.

DOUGHS FOR TARTS AND PASTRIES

IF YOU HAVE PASTRY DOUGHS READY TO WORK WITH, or if you have a source for good pastry doughs, you can prepare an almost limitless number of different pastries. Most pastries can be assembled up to 8 hours before you serve them.

The notion of making pastry doughs from scratch can induce instant panic in some, but it doesn't have to be that way.

Rich Short Dough for Tarts

Chilling short dough makes it easier to roll out and prevents sticking. If the dough is very cold, however, let it rest at room temperature for 5 to 10 minutes to make rolling easier. Dust the work surface, rolling pin, and the top of the dough very lightly with flour. Roll in all directions with even, steady pressure to make a large circle.

When transferring rolled-out dough to a pie or tart pan, avoid stretching or tearing it. One way to do this is to fold the dough round loosely in half. Lift the folded dough with both hands, position it over one side of the pan, then carefully unfold the dough. If you are using a fluted tart pan, press the dough against the sides to fill in the fluting for the best appearance after unmolding.

Pâte à Choux

Pâte à choux, or cream puff paste, is a cooked dough. It expands dramatically as it bakes in the oven and puffs up to make a hollow shell.

To prepare the dough: Bring the butter and water, or a combination of water and milk, to a rolling boil. Add the flour to this mixture all at once and stir vigorously with a wooden spoon until it forms a ball in the pan.

Add the eggs to this hot mixture carefully, blending each addition in well. At this point, you must work quickly so that you do not overcook the eggs.

Once the eggs are blended into the dough, it can be dropped from a spoon to make cream puffs. To make éclairs, transfer the dough to a pastry bag with a plain tip and pipe out little logs. Leave about 2 inches between pâte à choux pastries to allow them to expand as they bake.

Bake these pastries until the dough forms a crisp shell. You'll know it is properly baked when it has a deep golden yellow color and you can't see any beads of moisture on the outside. After you take the shells from the oven, cut a small slit on the bottom to let the steam escape. You may want to pull any moist crumbs from the interior before you fill them with a cream, mousse, or ice cream.

Blitz Puff Dough

Puff pastry, known to professionals as "roll-in" or "laminated" dough, consists of many layers of dough separated by layers of butter.

Traditional laminated dough can take up to 2 days to prepare and eats up a lot of space in the refrigerator, but blitz puff dough is a practical alternative that is easy to prepare and keeps well in the freezer.

Folding blitz puff pastry creates layers within the dough that trap moisture and add volume to the finished product. More folds will yield finer and more even layers with less height. Fewer folds yield a lighter product with irregular layers and more height. To give the dough a "four-fold," imagine that the rectangle is divided into quarters, and fold the outer quarters in to the middle so that their edges meet. Then fold the dough in half, as if closing a book. This type of fold quadruples the number of layers in the dough. Tightly wrap the folded dough in plastic wrap and allow it to rest in the refrigerator for 30 minutes.

Repeat the "four-fold" process two more times, refrigerating and turning the dough 90 degrees each time before rolling the dough back into a rectangle. After completing the final four-fold, wrap the dough in plastic wrap and allow it to chill in the refrigerator for at least 1 hour before using and up to 8 hours. Wrapped tightly in plastic wrap, the dough can also be frozen for up to 4 weeks for later use.

Rich Short Dough

This is the classic dough for dessert tarts. It is made in a processor similar to that used in making sugar cookies. Once the dough is baked, you can fill the shell with mousse, fresh fruits, or pastry cream.

MAKES 24 OUNCES DOUGH; ENOUGH FOR 48 TARTLETS

1 cup (2 sticks) unsalted butter, softened

1 cup plus 2 tbsp confectioners' sugar, sifted

½ tsp pure vanilla extract

7 large egg yolks

3 cups cake flour, sifted

1. In the bowl of an electric mixer fitted with the paddle attachment, cream together the butter, confectioners' sugar, and vanilla on medium speed, scraping down the bowl periodically, until smooth and light in color, 3 to 4 minutes.

2. Add the egg yolks gradually, scraping down the bowl and blending until smooth after each addition. Add the flour all at once and mix on low speed until just blended.

3. Turn out the dough onto a lightly floured work surface, divide the dough in half, and gather each half into a smooth ball. Wrap tightly with plastic wrap and refrigerate for at least 1 hour before rolling. The dough can be refrigerated for up to 1 week or frozen for up to 4 weeks.

4. Working with one disk at a time, remove the dough from the refrigerator, unwrap, place on a lightly floured work surface, and scatter a little flour over the top. Alternatively, place the dough between sheets of parchment or waxed paper. Roll out the dough into a circle about 2 inches wider than the diameter of your tart pan and about ⅛ inch thick. For tartlets, roll out the dough and cut it into circles with a cookie cutter, about 1 inch wider than the diameter of your tartlet pan.

5. Fold the dough in half or roll it loosely around the rolling pin, and gently lift and position it over the pan. Unfold or unroll and ease the dough into the pan without stretching, making sure that the pan's sides and rim are evenly covered. Press the dough gently against the sides and bottom. Trim the overhang to 1 inch (or ½ inch for tartlets). Tuck the dough overhang under itself and flute the edges.

6. To bake unfilled tart and tartlet shells: Preheat the oven to 350°F. Prick the dough with the tines of a fork and chill in the refrigerator until the dough is firm, at least 10 minutes and up to 2 hours. Bake until very light golden brown, 10 to 12 minutes. Cool completely in the pans set on a wire rack before filling. Reserve in airtight containers at room temperature still in the pans for up to 3 days before filling, if desired.

Pâte à Choux

MAKES 24 CREAM PUFFS OR MINI ÉCLAIRS

1 cup whole or low-fat milk

½ cup (1 stick) unsalted butter, diced

2 tbsp granulated sugar

½ tsp salt

1 cup bread flour, sifted

4 large eggs

Egg wash: 1 large egg whisked with 2 tbsp cold milk or water (optional)

½ cup sliced blanched almonds (optional)

1. Preheat the oven to 375°F. Line 2 baking sheets with parchment paper.

2. To make the pâte à choux: Combine the milk, butter, granulated sugar, and salt in a saucepan over high heat and bring to a boil. Reduce the heat to medium, add the sifted flour all at once, and stir well. Cook, stirring constantly with a wooden spoon, until the dough begins to come away from the sides of the pan, about 5 minutes.

3. Transfer to the bowl of an electric mixer fitted with the paddle attachment and beat on medium speed until cooled to body temperature. Add the eggs one at a time, beating well and scraping down the bowl with a rubber

spatula after each addition. Transfer the pâte à choux dough to a pastry bag with a plain round tip, shape as desired, and bake (see variations below). Once baked, the shells can be frozen for up to 3 weeks. Thaw before filling

CREAM PUFF SHELLS *For cream puffs, pipe or spoon the dough into 24 equal-size balls (about the size of a golf ball) onto the prepared baking sheets, spacing them about 2 inches apart. To coat the shells with sliced almonds, brush the unbaked puffs very lightly with egg wash. Scatter the puffs with the sliced almonds.*

Bake until the pastries are puffy and lightly browned, about 10 minutes. Lower the oven temperature to 325°F and continue to bake until the puffs appear dry and a rich golden brown, another 10 to 12 minutes. Remove from the oven and cool completely on wire racks before splitting and filling.

MINI ECLAIR SHELLS *Use a pastry bag to pipe the pâte à choux into small logs, about 1½ inches long and ½ inch in diameter. Bake until the pastries are puffy and lightly browned, about 15 minutes. Lower the oven temperature to 325°F and continue to bake until the puffs appear dry and a rich golden brown, another 10 to 15 minutes. Remove from the oven and cool completely on wire racks before splitting and filling.*

Blitz Puff Pastry

Use this dough to make savory or sweet pastries to serve as appetizers or desserts.

MAKES 3 POUNDS DOUGH

4½ cups all-purpose or cake flour

1 cup plus 6 tbsp ice water

1 tbsp salt

2 cups (4 sticks) unsalted butter, cut into large dice

1. Combine the flour, salt, butter, and water in a food processor and pulse until barely mixed. Alternatively, mix by hand, in a large bowl. Combine the flour and butter. Toss until all the butter is coated with flour. Add the water and salt and mix until a shaggy mass is formed.

2. Turn out the dough onto a lightly floured marble slab or another cool surface. Shape into a square. Roll the dough into a rectangular piece, ½ inch thick. Fold the right and left edges of the dough into the center of the rectangle so they meet and do not overlap. Fold the dough in half where the two edges meet to create 4 layers. Tightly cover the 4-layer rectangle in plastic wrap and refrigerate for at least 2 and up to 24 hours.

3. Unwrap the dough and place it on a lightly floured work surface with the long edge parallel to the edge of your work surface. Roll it out and fold it as described above and refrigerate it, in between each roll and fold, until you have completed a total of 4 folds.

4. The dough is now ready to roll, cut, and shape as desired, or it can be stored, tightly wrapped in plastic wrap, in the refrigerator for up to 3 days or in the freezer for up to 4 weeks.

Lemon Meringue Tartlets

We love this dessert as part of a buffet. You can prepare the tartlet shells and the lemon curd a few days ahead of time so that you only need to prepare the meringue and assemble the tartlets on the day of your party.

MAKES 24 TARTLETS

Lemon Curd

½ cup (1 stick) unsalted butter, cubed

⅔ cup granulated sugar

½ cup fresh lemon juice

1 tbsp finely grated lemon zest

7 large egg yolks

24 prebaked tartlet shells made from Rich Short Dough, page 284

Meringue

2 large egg whites

⅔ cup granulated sugar

1. To make the lemon curd: In a medium saucepan, combine half of the butter, half of the sugar, and all of the lemon juice and zest and bring to a boil over medium heat, stirring gently to dissolve the sugar, about 3 minutes.

2. In a medium bowl, blend the egg yolks with the remaining sugar. Temper by gradually adding about one-third of the lemon mixture, stirring constantly with a whisk. Return the tempered egg mixture to the saucepan. Continue cooking, stirring constantly with the whisk, until the mixture thickens and comes to a simmer, 2 to 3 minutes. Stir in the remaining butter.

3. Strain the lemon curd into a large shallow bowl. Cool over an ice bath, stirring constantly, until the curd reaches room temperature. The curd can be prepared up to 2 days in advance and stored in a covered container in the refrigerator.

4. To make the meringue: Place the egg whites in the bowl of an electric mixer fitted with the whip attachment. Beat on high speed until they become frothy, then add the sugar. Beat the meringue on high speed until it holds medium peaks, about 8 minutes.

5. To assemble and finish the tartlets: Preheat the broiler to high. Spoon or pipe about 2 teaspoons of the lemon curd into each tartlet shell. The curd should just come to the top of the shell without overflowing. Pipe or spoon the meringue on top of the tartlets and transfer to a baking sheet. Broil the tartlets just until the meringue is lightly browned, about 2 minutes. Serve immediately or refrigerate the tartlets for up to 8 hours before serving.

Cranberry Pecan Tartlets

Make the tartlet shells ahead of time so that you can fill them as soon as the filling mixture is cooked.

MAKES 24 TARTLETS

Filling

¼ cup (½ stick) unsalted butter

½ cup light corn syrup

⅓ cup packed light brown sugar

1 large egg

¾ tsp pure vanilla extract

24 prebaked tartlet shells made from Rich Short Dough (page 284)

½ cup chopped pecans

½ cup pecan halves

12 fresh cranberries, halved

1. Preheat the oven to 350°F. Set the prebaked tartlet shells, still in the pans, on a baking sheet.

2. To make the filling: In a medium saucepan, combine the butter, corn syrup, and brown sugar. Bring to a simmer over medium heat, stirring, until the sugar has dissolved, about 3 minutes.

3. Whisk the egg by hand until it is pale in color and light in texture, about 5 minutes. Blend in the hot sugar mixture and the vanilla.

4. Place 1 teaspoon of the chopped pecans in each tartlet shell. Pour 1½ teaspoons of the filling over the chopped pecans The filling should just come to the top of the shell without overflowing. Arrange the pecan halves and halved cranberries on top of the filling.

5. Bake the tartlets until the filling is set, 5 to 7 minutes. Allow to cool completely in the pans on wire racks before unmolding . Serve at room temperature or chilled. The cooled tartlets can also be stored, in a covered container, in the refrigerator for up to 3 days.

Bittersweet Chocolate–Orange Tartlets

Instead of making individual tartlets, you can line a tart pan with dough and prebake it as described on page 284. This recipe will fill two 8-inch pans.

MAKES 24 TARTLETS

Filling

¾ cup heavy cream

3 tbsp granulated sugar

1 tbsp finely grated orange zest

6 large egg yolks

¾ cup good-quality bittersweet chocolate, melted

2 tbsp orange-flavored liqueur

24 prebaked tartlet shells made from Rich Short Dough (page 284)

1. Preheat the oven to 325°F. Set the prebaked tartlet shells, still in the pans, on a baking sheet.

2. To make the filling: In a medium saucepan, combine the cream, 2 tablespoons of the sugar, and the zest and bring to a boil. Remove from the heat, cover, and steep for 5 minutes.

3. In a large bowl, blend the egg yolks with the remaining tablespoon sugar. While whisking constantly, gradually add about one-third of the hot cream mixture into the yolks. Then blend in the remaining cream mixture. Add the chocolate and liqueur and blend well. Strain.

4. Divide the filling evenly among the tartlet shells, filling them just to within ⅛ inch of the top. Bake the tartlets just until the custard sets, about 10 minutes. Allow to cool completely in the pans on wire racks before unmolding. Serve at room temperature or chilled. The cooled tartlets can also be stored, in a covered container, in the refrigerator for up to 3 days.

Cream Puffs

Although not essential, we like to coat the cream puffs with a sprinkling of sliced almonds.

MAKES 24 PUFFS

½ cup heavy cream

2 tbsp confectioners' sugar, plus more as needed

½ tsp pure vanilla extract

1 cup Pastry Cream (page 282)

24 Cream Puff Shells, baked (page 284)

1. In a large bowl, whip the heavy cream by hand or with a handheld electric mixer to medium peaks. Add the sugar and vanilla and continue to whip just long enough to blend.

2. Fold the whipped cream into the pastry cream with a rubber spatula until it is evenly blended. This step can be completed up to 8 hours before you assemble the cream puffs. Store in a covered container in the refrigerator.

3. Slice the tops off each of the baked pastries and reserve the tops. Spoon about 2 teaspoons of the filling into the base of each cream puff, letting it mound slightly.

4. Place the reserved tops of the puffs on the filling. The assembled pastries can be stored in a covered container in the refrigerator for up to 8 hours. Just before serving, dust lightly with confectioners' sugar.

VARIATION *Place a slice of strawberry or a few blue-berries on top of the pastry cream if you wish.*

Mini Chocolate Éclairs

MAKES 24 ÉCLAIRS

½ cup heavy cream

2 tbsp confectioners' sugar, plus more as needed

½ tsp pure vanilla extract

1 cup Pastry Cream (page 282)

24 Mini Éclair Shells, baked (page 284)

1½ cups Chocolate Glaze (page 302), warm

1. In a large bowl, whip the heavy cream by hand or with a handheld electric mixer to medium peaks. Add the sugar and vanilla and continue to whip just long enough to blend.

2. Fold the whipped cream into the pastry cream with a rubber spatula until it is evenly blended. This step can be completed up to 8 hours before you assemble the éclairs. Store in a covered container in the refrigerator.

3. Slice the tops off each of the baked pastries and reserve the tops. Spoon about 2 teaspoons of the filling into the base of each éclair shell, letting it mound slightly.

4. Dip the tops of each éclair shell into the chocolate glaze. Set them on a cooling rack set in a baking sheet until the chocolate has set a little.

5. Place the glazed tops on the éclairs. The assembled pastries can be stored in a covered container in the refrigerator for up to 8 hours.

Berry Napoleon

The filling for this fresh berry napoleon is made by lightening a basic pastry cream with whipped cream known as *crème légère* and flavoring it with rum and vanilla.

SERVES 8

12 oz Blitz Puff Pastry (page 285)

Confectioners' sugar, as needed

Crème Légère

1 cup whole milk

⅓ cup plus 2 tbsp granulated sugar

2 tbsp cornstarch

2 tbsp all-purpose flour

3 large egg yolks

1 tsp pure vanilla extract

1 tbsp dark rum

2 cups heavy cream

2 pints fresh raspberries, or as needed

8 lemon balm sprigs or mint leaves

1. Preheat the oven to 375°F. Line a baking sheet with parchment paper. On a lightly floured surface, roll out the puff pastry into a rectangle 12 inches wide by 16 inches long and about ⅛ inch thick. Using the tines of a fork, prick the pastry all over. Place the pastry on the prepared pan. Cover with a second piece of parchment paper and top with another baking sheet to keep the pastry flat as it bakes. Bake the pastry for 15 minutes.

2. Remove the top baking sheet and parchment paper and generously dust the pastry with the confectioners' sugar. Increase the oven temperature to 425°F. Bake the pastry until the sugar turns a dark golden brown, 5 minutes longer. Remove the pastry from the oven and let cool completely in the pan set on a wire rack.

3. To make the crème légère: In a small saucepan, bring the milk just to a boil. Set aside. In a medium saucepan, blend ⅓ cup of the granulated sugar, the cornstarch, and flour. Add the egg yolks and stir. Add the hot milk in a stream, whisking constantly.

4. Cook the mixture over medium heat, whisking constantly, until it comes to a boil. Simmer for 3 minutes over low heat, whisking constantly. Strain through a fine-mesh strainer into a large bowl. Stir in the vanilla and rum. Set aside and let cool.

5. Using an electric mixer fitted with the whip attachment or a handheld wire whisk, in a large, chilled bowl, whip the cream and the remaining 2 tablespoons granulated sugar until medium-stiff peaks form. Gently fold the whipped cream into the cooled mixture. Place the crème légère in a pastry bag fitted with a plain tip and set aside.

6. Cut the pastry into twenty-four 2-by-4-inch rectangles. Reserve 8 of the best-looking rectangles for the napoleon tops. Lay out 8 rectangles. Cover each rectangle with the berries and pipe the crème légère over the berries. Add a second layer of pastry and make another layer of berries and crème légère. Top each napoleon with one of the rectangles reserved for the tops. Dust with confectioners' sugar and garnish with raspberries and lemon balm or mint leaves. Serve the napoleons at once, or they can be stored in a covered container in the refrigerator for up to 8 hours.

CAKES

AMERICAN CAKES TYPICALLY CONSIST OF TWO LAYERS of buttery cake, filled and frosted. You may slice a sponge or butter cake and fill it with an icing, Bavarian cream, jam, whipped soft ganache, or another filling. The cake may be covered with an icing or glaze. The icings, glazes, fillings, sauces, and decorating techniques that you choose can turn an ordinary cake into a unique, elegant dessert.

Cutting the Cake Into Layers

To cut a baked cake into thinner layers, set the cake on a flat, stable surface. Use a ruler to divide the cake into

Before splitting a cake into layers, trim any uneven areas from the side and top.

Lightly score the cake all the way around. When you start slicing, be sure to keep the knife perfectly level as you work your way through the cake using the score line as a guide.

equal layers. Working from one side to the other, cut horizontally through the cake with a serrated knife, using a gentle back-and-forth sawing motion. Brush away loose crumbs from each layer using a pastry brush. Whether you are assembling the cake directly on a serving plate or have a turntable or cake stand, "cement" the bottom layer to the plate or stand with a dollop of icing. This keeps the cake from shifting around as you work.

Filling the Cake

Different fillings have different consistencies, requiring various approaches. For a jam filling, spread an even but rather thin coating over the cake layer. Creamy and foamy fillings, like whipped soft ganache and buttercream icing are spread in a slightly thicker layer. If the filling layer is too thick, the cake layers may start to slide apart and some of the filling may ooze out of the cake.

Leave a rim around the edge of the cake unfilled to allow for the filling to spread after the next layer is placed on it. Let the filled cake rest for an hour to let the layers settle into position before icing the cake. If the filling contains eggs or cream, be sure to store it in the refrigerator.

Spreading the Crumb Coat

Set the cake on a decorating turntable, cake stand, or plate. If you are using a cake plate, put strips of waxed or parchment paper under the edges of the cake to catch drips that would otherwise fall on the plate. Remove the strips from under the cake once the cake is fully iced.

The crumb coat is an initial coat of icing or jam spread on the cake to keep cake crumbs from showing in the finished icing. Spread the icing or jam evenly but thinly over the tops and sides of the cake. Let this coating set up for about 1 hour in the refrigerator.

Icing the Cake

Once the crumb coat is set, spoon a generous amount of icing onto the cake's top. Using a back-and-forth stroke with a level palette knife, spread the icing in an even layer that extends over the top edge of the cake. Scoop up the icing with your palette knife and hold the knife vertically to spread icing on the sides. Again, use a generous amount so that you create a layer thick enough to completely coat the cake.

If you wish, at this point you may use a cake comb or the teeth of a serrated knife to make a design on the sides of the cake, or create scallops and swirls with the tip of your palette knife or the back of a spoon. Any remaining icing can be piped on the top.

Cutting and Serving the Cake

Cakes that are frosted and filled can be challenging to slice neatly, unless you are properly prepared for the task. Use a large, sharp knife with a thin blade to cut through the cake. Have ready the knife, a tall container (such as a pitcher) filled with hot water, and a clean kitchen towel. After you make each cut, dip the knife in the water and wipe away the cake and icing that cling to the blade. Dry the blade before making each cut. Insert the blade under the slice to lift it and steady the slice by holding the back of a table fork against the wide end of the slice. Set the cake slice down on the plate, standing upright, and hold the back of the fork at the wide end of the slice to hold the cake in place as you slide out the knife blade. If the slice of cake is too tall or too thin to stand up, lay it on the plate with one of the cut sides facing down.

Gently scoring the top of a cake with a sharp knife will make it easier to cut the cake into neat, even slices at the table.

If freezing a cake layer, such as the top of a wedding cake, be sure to package it carefully and label it clearly with the date.

Vanilla Sponge Cake

Frost and fill this cake with lightly sweetened whipped cream and add a layer of fresh fruit to the filling for a simple and delicious dessert. These cakes keep well in the freezer; if you have them on hand, you can make an almost instant dessert that your guests might think came from a bakeshop.

MAKES TWO 8-INCH CAKE LAYERS

- **6 tbsp (¾ stick) unsalted butter, plus more as needed**
- **1 tbsp pure vanilla extract**
- **1¼ cups granulated sugar**
- **5 large eggs**
- **5 large egg yolks**
- **2 cups cake flour, sifted twice**

1. Preheat the oven to 375°F. Lightly butter two 8-inch cake pans and line with parchment paper.

2. In a small saucepan, melt the butter over low heat. Remove from the heat, add the vanilla, and stir to combine. Set aside to cool.

3. In the bowl of an electric mixer, combine the sugar, eggs, and egg yolks and set the bowl over a pan of barely simmering water. Whisking constantly with a wire whisk, heat until the mixture is warm to the touch or reaches 110°F on a candy thermometer.

4. Remove the bowl from the heat and attach it to the mixer fitted with the whip attachment. Whip the eggs on medium speed until the foam is 3 times the original volume and no longer increasing in volume, 5 minutes.

5. Fold the flour into the egg mixture using a rubber spatula. Blend a small amount of the batter into the melted butter and then fold the tempered butter back into the remaining batter.

6. Fill the prepared cake pans about two-thirds full. Bake until the top of each layer is firm to the touch, about 30 minutes. Let the layers cool in the pans for a few minutes before turning them out onto wire racks. Let cool completely before finishing the cake with filling and frosting. The cake layers can also be wrapped well and frozen for up to 4 weeks.

Yellow Butter Cake

This cake is buttery and rich with a fine texture, almost like a pound cake. Ice and fill the cake with Simple Buttercream (page 295) for a classic American-style layer cake.

MAKES TWO 8-INCH CAKE LAYERS

- **3½ cups cake flour**
- **2 cups granulated sugar**
- **1 tbsp baking powder**
- **½ tsp salt**
- **1 cup (2 sticks) unsalted butter, diced, softened**
- **1 cup whole milk**
- **4 large eggs**
- **2 large egg whites**
- **2 tsp pure vanilla extract**

1. Preheat the oven to 350°F. Coat two 8-inch round cake pans lightly with cooking spray.

2. Sift the flour, sugar, baking powder, and salt into the bowl of an electric mixer fitted with the whip attachment. Add the butter and ½ cup of the milk. Mix on medium speed until smooth, about 4 minutes, scraping down the bowl with a rubber spatula as needed.

3. In a medium bowl, blend the eggs, egg whites, the remaining ½ cup milk, and the vanilla. Add the egg mixture to the batter in 3 additions, mixing for 2 minutes on medium speed after each addition. Scrape down the bowl between additions.

4. Divide the batter evenly between the prepared pans. Bake until the layers spring back when touched lightly in the center, 35 to 40 minutes.

5. Remove the layers from the oven and cool completely in their pans on wire racks. Release the sides and bottom of the layers from the pans with a narrow metal spatula or a table knife before unmolding and finishing the cake with filling and frosting. The cake layers can also be wrapped well and frozen for up to 4 weeks.

Angel Food Cake

In order to reach a lofty height, angel food cake needs to cling to the sides of the pan, both as it bakes and while it cools. This is why the pan is ungreased and the cake is cooled upside down. Some angel food cake pans have little "feet" on the rim to hold the cake above the tabletop or counter. If your pan has no feet, place the inverted pan on a bottle with a long, relatively thin neck

MAKES ONE 9-INCH TUBE CAKE

- **1 cup cake flour**
- **1¼ cups granulated sugar**
- **½ tsp salt**
- **12 large egg whites**
- **2 tbsp water**
- **1 tsp cream of tartar**
- **1 tsp pure vanilla extract**

1. Preheat the oven to 350°F. Sift the flour, ¼ cup of the sugar, and salt twice onto parchment or waxed paper and set aside.

2. In the bowl of an electric mixer fitted with the whip attachment, whip the egg whites and water on low speed until foamy, 2 minutes. Add the cream of tartar and continue to whip until the egg whites form soft peaks, 2 minutes. Add the vanilla, then gradually add the remaining 1 cup sugar while whipping. Continue to whip until the egg whites are glossy and form medium peaks, 3 to 4 minutes.

3. With a rubber spatula or wide spoon, gently fold the sifted flour mixture into the egg white mixture. Spoon the batter into an ungreased 9-inch angel food cake pan, run a butter knife through the batter once to ensure that there are no air pockets, and smooth the top. Bake until golden brown on top, 40 to 45 minutes.

4. Turn the cake pan upside down and let it cool completely. Then, use a spatula or thin knife to release the cake from the sides of the pan and turn it out carefully onto a plate. The cake can also be wrapped well and frozen for up to 4 weeks.

NOTE *Because angel food cake is so light and bouncy, it is actually easiest to pull it apart into pieces than to cut it. Special cutters that look like oversized combs do the job without crushing the cake. If you do not have a cutter for angel food cake, use a serrated knife and a light touch as you cut.*

Flourless Chocolate Soufflé Cake

This dense, rich cake really needs no accompaniment, but a puff of lightly sweetened whipped cream and a spoonful of fresh berries are always a nice addition.

MAKES ONE 8-INCH CAKE

- **5 oz bittersweet chocolate, chopped**
- **¾ cup (1½ sticks) unsalted butter, plus more as needed**
- **10 large eggs**
- **⅔ cup granulated sugar**
- **¼ cup Grand Marnier or another orange-flavored liqueur**

1. Preheat the oven to 375°F. Grease the bottom of an 8-inch round cake pan and line it with parchment paper. Use another piece of parchment paper to form a collar around the inside edge of the pan, allowing the paper to extend 3 inches above the top of the pan. Secure the collar in place with tape. Butter the paper generously.

2. Stir the chocolate and butter together in the top of a double boiler until melted and smooth, or melt them in the microwave on low power in 15- to 20-second increments. There may be a few lumps left, but they will melt as the chocolate cools to room temperature.

3. Separate 9 of the eggs. Set aside. In the bowl of an electric mixer fitted with the whip attachment, beat the 9 egg whites on medium speed until frothy. Gradually add ⅓ cup of the sugar. Whip the egg whites on high speed until medium peaks form, about 4 minutes. Transfer the meringue to a separate, large bowl.

4. Rinse out the mixing bowl and the attachment and return it to the mixer. With the whip attachment, beat the 9 egg yolks, the remaining whole egg, and the remaining ⅓ cup sugar on medium speed until a dense foam that falls in ribbons from the whip forms, scraping down the bowl with a rubber spatula as needed, about 5 minutes. Add the liqueur and the cooled chocolate mixture. Continue whipping until the batter is evenly blended, 1 minute.

5. Remove the bowl from the mixer and fold half of the meringue into the egg-yolk mixture until the batter is evenly blended, lighter in texture, and smooth. Fold in the remaining meringue, folding only until blended evenly.

6. Pour the batter into the prepared pan and bake until the cake just starts to pull away from the sides and the center no longer jiggles when the pan is gently shaken, 45 to 50 minutes.

7. Let the cake cool completely in the pan on a wire rack. Then, turn it out by placing a serving plate over the pan and inverting. Turn the cake upright before slicing and serving. This cake can be well wrapped and stored in the refrigerator for up to 3 days.

Simple Buttercream

MAKES 4 CUPS FROSTING; ENOUGH TO FILL AND ICE AN 8- OR 9-INCH CAKE

1 cup (2 sticks) unsalted butter, softened

4 cups confectioners' sugar, sifted, plus more as needed

1 tsp pure vanilla extract

⅛ tsp salt

¼ cup heavy cream or whole milk, plus more as needed

1. In the bowl of an electric mixer fitted with the paddle attachment, cream the butter on medium speed until it is very light in texture, about 2 minutes. Add the confectioners' sugar, vanilla, and salt and mix on low speed until the sugar and butter are blended, 3 to 4 minutes, scraping down the bowl with a rubber spatula as needed.

2. Increase the speed to medium and, with the mixer running, add the cream or milk in a thin stream. Increase the speed to high and whip the buttercream until very smooth, light, and a good spreading consistency, about 3 minutes. Adjust the consistency, if necessary, by adding a bit more confectioners' sugar or cream.

3. Use the buttercream to fill, ice, and decorate a cake. Once blended, the buttercream can be stored in a covered container in the refrigerator for up to 2 weeks. To use after refrigeration, let the buttercream soften at room temperature for about 15 minutes. Transfer it to the bowl of an electric mixer fitted with the paddle attachment, and beat until it is a smooth, light spreading consistency, 3 to 4 minutes.

CHOCOLATE BUTTERCREAM *Replace ½ cup of the confectioners' sugar with unsweetened cocoa powder and/or melt up to 2 ounces bittersweet chocolate and add along with the cream or milk.*

PIPING WITH A PASTRY BAG AND TIPS

Pastry bags and tips are great tools to have in the kitchen. They make it easy to add fillings to pastries and cakes as well as to shape doughs like pâte à choux uniformly. Cloth and vinyl bags can be washed and reused. Disposable pastry bags are inexpensive and work equally well.

Pastry tips are available in a wide array of shapes and sizes. The number of the tip can tell you what size and shape it is. Plain round tips are numbered 2 through 6. Open star tips are numbered 14 through 84 and closed star tips are numbered 23 to 233. The smaller the number, the smaller the opening and the finer the design.

To fill a pastry bag: Position the tip securely in the bag's opening or in a coupler or tip holder. Fold down the bag's top to create a wide cuff, then transfer the ingredient to the bag with a large spoon. Support the bag under the cuff with your free hand while filling it with the other. Use a tall container to support the bag if you need to use both hands, folding down the cuff around the edge of the container. Fill the pastry bag only two-thirds full. Twist the bag to close it, compressing the mixture and releasing any air pockets.

To pipe: Hold the filled bag at a 45-degree angle to the surface you're piping onto, and use your dominant hand to slowly and steadily squeeze the bag. Use your other hand to guide and steady the tip. Release the pressure on the bag as you lift it away to make clean lines without tails.

To make a shell border: Use a pastry bag with your choice of plain or star-shaped tip. The larger the opening of the tip, the larger the shells will be. Fill the piping bag and press out any air bubbles before you begin to avoid blowouts of icing as you work. Hold the tip of the pastry bag at a 45-degree angle close to the surface. Use even pressure to squeeze the icing out with one hand. Use your other hand to guide the tip of the bag. As you squeeze, lift the tip very slightly to allow the icing to fan forward in a rounded shape. When the shell is the size you want, ease the pressure on the bag and pull the tip toward you and down toward the cake, cutting it off. Continue making shells all the way around the cake, starting each new shell at the end of the previous one.

Whether you are piping decorations or making a border, it is always a good idea to practice on parchment or waxed paper before working on a cake surface. Wash the tips and reusable pastry bags thoroughly after each use in warm, soapy water and dry them completely inside out.

Here are a few borders that can be piped using a star tip.

Borders piped using a straight tip.

ICE CREAM AND OTHER FROZEN DESSERTS

CHURNED FROZEN DESSERTS LIKE ICE CREAM, SORBET, and sherbet get their soft spoonable texture from being stirred with a dasher while they are cooled to below the freezing point in an ice cream maker. But ice cream does not represent the entire universe of frozen desserts. Frozen soufflés, granitas, semifreddos, and parfaits are just a few of the frozen desserts that can be made even without an ice cream maker.

To scoop a frozen dessert, make sure that your scoop is clean and dry. If the scoop is wet, it can introduce ice crystals that will give your frozen dessert an unpleasant gritty texture. You can also use a large, sturdy spoon to scrape curls of ice cream from the top of a large block.

If your frozen yogurt, ice cream, or sorbet is too firm to scoop or scrape easily, let it rest in the refrigerator for about 30 minutes before serving. Warming frozen desserts in the microwave for 15 or 20 seconds on low power also softens them just enough to scoop. Fresh or poached fruit, cookies, pies, cakes, and dessert sauces such as chocolate, caramel, and raspberry are all great accompaniments to many frozen desserts.

To take the stress out of serving ice cream to a big crowd, pre-scoop the ice cream into paper cupcake cups and keep them in the freezer until you're ready to serve.

French-Style Ice Cream

This classic custard-style ice cream has a rich golden color from egg yolks.

MAKES ABOUT 1¼ QUARTS ICE CREAM; SERVES 8

6 large egg yolks

2 cups granulated sugar

3 cups heavy cream

1 vanilla bean, split lengthwise

1. Make an ice water bath by filling a large bowl with about 2 inches of ice water. Set aside.

2. In a medium bowl, whisk together the egg yolks with ½ cup of the sugar until thickened.

3. In a heavy saucepan, combine the cream, the remaining 1½ cups sugar, and the vanilla bean and cook over medium heat. Bring to a simmer, stirring constantly.

4. While stirring constantly, slowly pour about 1½ cups of the hot cream mixture into the egg yolk mixture to temper the eggs. Stir the tempered egg mixture back into the remaining cream mixture and continue to cook over low heat, stirring constantly, until the custard is thick enough to coat the back of a spoon, about 5 minutes. Immediately pour the custard through a fine-mesh sieve into another medium bowl. Put the bowl with the custard in the ice bath and stir every few minutes until it is quite cool.

5. Retrieve the vanilla bean and, with the tip of a paring knife, scrape the seeds from the vanilla pod into the custard, then discard the pod.

6. Transfer to a storage container, cover, and refrigerate the custard for at least 4 hours or up to overnight. Freeze in an ice cream maker according to the manufacturer's instructions. Pack the ice cream in storage containers and place in the freezer for at least 2 hours and up to 5 days before serving.

Chianti Granita with Summer Berries

The brilliant colors and lush fruity flavors of this dessert make it the perfect ending to a summer celebration.

SERVES 8

¾ cup warm water

1 cup granulated sugar

1½ cups Chianti

⅓ cup fresh lemon juice

⅓ cup fresh orange juice

2 cups fresh raspberries, blueberries, blackberries, red currants, or sliced strawberries

12 mint leaves, thinly sliced, for garnish

1. Chill 8 serving bowls or wineglasses in the freezer.

2. Combine the warm water and sugar in a large bowl. Add the wine, lemon juice, and orange juice. Pour the mixture into a 9-by-13-inch nonreactive metal pan and place the granita in the freezer. Stir the mixture every 30 minutes until it is completely frozen, 3 hours. The granita can be stored, covered, in the freezer for up to 3 days.

3. To serve: Using a sturdy spoon or an ice cream scoop, scrape out the granita into the chilled serving bowls or wineglasses. Top with the fresh berries and garnish with the sliced mint leaves.

PALATE CLEANSERS

Sorbets are not just desserts; they are also traditional French palate cleansers, served to guests between the courses of a meal to cleanse their mouths of lingering flavors before the next dish is served. A palate cleanser is not a full course, so it should be a relatively simple preparation (think bright, fresh flavors like lemon, lime, and mint) and served in a very small amount—no more than a few bites.

A palate cleanser, such as the Lemon-Champagne Sorbet pictured here, is served to prepare guests to receive the next course.

Lemon-Champagne Sorbet

Serve this with biscotti or other cookies for a sweet and simple conclusion to a brunch or lunch.

SERVES 8

1½ cups water

¼ cup granulated sugar

½ cup fresh lemon juice

2½ cups champagne, prosecco, or another sparkling wine

1 large egg white

1. In a medium bowl, combine the water and sugar and stir until the sugar is fully dissolved. Add the lemon juice and champagne.

2. In another medium bowl, whip the egg white until foamy. Add to the sugar syrup, mixing well. Chill in the refrigerator for at least 1 hour and up to 8 hours.

3. Freeze in an ice cream machine according to the manufacturer's instructions. Place it in the freezer for at least 2 hours before serving. The sorbet will last up to 3 days in the freezer, but if it has been stored longer than 2 hours, let the sorbet "temper" for 30 minutes in the refrigerator before serving.

NOTE *If too much sugar is added to the sorbet, it will be too dense to freeze properly, so follow the recipe carefully.*

FRUIT DESSERTS

THE CLASSIC END TO A MEAL IN MANY CULTURES is perfectly ripe piece of fresh fruit, often as an accompaniment to carefully selected cheeses. You may present fruits already sliced if they are large or unwieldy, for instance pineapple or melons. Another approach for smaller fruits is to simply wash them well and let your guests slice them. This tactic works best for fruits like apples, pears, peaches, plums, apricots, and grapes.

Desserts made with fruit are another popular option. Here, we've assembled a few classics. Crisps are simple to prepare and you can make them with a wide variety of seasonal fruits, alone or in combination: plums, pears, apples, peaches, nectarines, apricots, or berries. They can be made ahead of time and reheated to serve warm from the oven. Shortcakes are another easy option. Fresh fruits are sliced and combined with a little sugar, then left to sit long enough for the natural juices in the fruit to dissolve the sugar and make a light, delicious syrup that soaks into the shortbread.

Strawberry Shortcakes with Clabbered Cream

SERVES 10

3 pints strawberries, hulled and quartered

3 tbsp granulated sugar

½ cup fresh orange juice

1 tsp minced orange zest (see Notes)

Shortcakes

3 cups all-purpose flour

⅓ cup granulated sugar

1 tbsp baking powder

1 tsp salt

½ cup (1 stick) unsalted butter, cold, cut into pieces

¾ cup whole milk, cold

1 large egg, beaten

6 oz (¾ cup) clabbered cream (see Notes)

1. In a large bowl, combine the strawberries, sugar, orange juice, and zest. Stir to coat the berries evenly and let them sit at room temperature while making the shortcakes. The berry mixture can be made in advance and stored in a covered container in the refrigerator for up to 8 hours.

2. To make the shortcakes: Preheat the oven to 375°F. Sift the flour, sugar, baking powder, and salt together into a large bowl. With your fingertips, or using a pastry blender, work in the butter pieces until the mixture is the texture of coarse cornmeal. Make a well in the center and pour in the milk. Mix with a wooden spoon until the mixture pulls away from the side of the bowl.

3. On a lightly floured work surface, roll out or pat the dough to a thickness of ½ to ¾ inch; it will appear very rough and flaky. Using a 3-inch round cutter, cut out 10 shortcakes (see Notes).

4. Place the shortcakes on an ungreased baking sheet. Brush the tops with the beaten egg. Bake until the shortcakes just begin to turn golden, 15 to 20 minutes. Remove from the oven and use immediately, or let the shortcakes cool on a wire rack and store in an airtight container at room temperature for up to 2 days. Re-warm in a 250°F oven for 5 minutes just before serving.

5. To serve: Split each shortcake horizontally in half and place the bottom piece on a dessert plate. Layer the strawberries with some of their juice and a generous dollop of clabbered cream over the shortcake and finish with the shortcake top over the cream.

NOTES *To make minced orange zest: Using a vegetable peeler, remove just the colored portion of the peel, then mince the peel with a sharp knife.*

When cutting out the biscuits, be careful not to twist the cutter or the shortcakes will not rise around the edge.

Clabbered cream is a cultured pasteurized cream available in some specialty foods stores. Lightly whipped, unsweetened, heavy cream, sour cream, or crème fraîche may be substituted.

Rhubarb Crisp

Add sliced fresh strawberries to this crisp in the spring, or replace with apples, pears, or a combination of the two for a fall or winter dessert. Top the crisp with some ice cream or lightly sweetened whipped cream, if you wish.

SERVES 8

2 lb rhubarb, cut into ½-inch lengths (about 6 cups)

1 cup granulated sugar

3 tbsp all-purpose flour

Topping

1 cup all-purpose flour

⅓ cup lightly packed brown sugar

1 tbsp granulated sugar

¼ tsp ground cinnamon

⅓ cup (¼ stick plus 1 tablespoon) unsalted butter, softened

½ cup walnuts, toasted and chopped (see page 45)

1. Preheat the oven to 375°F. In a large bowl, combine the rhubarb, granulated sugar, and flour. Spread the mixture into an even layer in an unbuttered 2-quart baking dish.

2. To make the topping: In a large bowl, combine the flour, brown and granulated sugars, and the cinnamon. With your fingers, or using a pastry blender, work the butter into the flour mixture until the whole mixture is crumbly. Add the walnuts and stir to combine. Distribute the topping evenly over the rhubarb.

3. Bake until the topping is golden brown and the rhubarb is tender when pierced with a paring knife, 30 to 45 minutes. If the topping is brown but the rhubarb is not yet tender, cover the baking dish with aluminum foil and continue to bake 5 to 10 minutes more.

4. Remove the crisp from the oven and let sit for 10 to 15 minutes before serving. Serve warm. The crisp can be prepared in advance and stored, covered, in the refrigerator, for up to 2 days. Reheat in a 300°F until warm and the topping is crisp, about 15 minutes.

DESSERT SAUCES

ADD A DESSERT SAUCE LIKE CHOCOLATE OR CARAMEL sauce or brandied cherry coulis to a dish of ice cream—your own or a high-quality purchased ice cream—or set them out to let your guests make their own sundaes. Dress up a simple slice of angel food or sponge cake with a drizzle of sauce.

Use dessert sauces to decorate your plates. Spoon and spread a "swoosh" of sauce or drip the sauce onto the plate to make drops or transfer the sauce to a squeeze bottle or a cup with a spout and use to swirl it onto the plates.

Brandied Cherry Coulis

Mixed with additional warmed, whole pitted cherries, the coulis can be used as a filling for dessert crêpes (see page 218 for a crêpes recipe).

MAKES ABOUT 1½ CUPS COULIS

¾ cup pitted fresh or frozen cherries

½ cup water

½ cup dry red wine

6 tbsp granulated sugar

¼ cup brandy

Small pinch of ground cinnamon

In a small saucepan, combine the cherries, water, wine, sugar, brandy, and cinnamon over low heat. Simmer until the cherries are tender, 8 to 10 minutes. Purée in a blender or food processor until smooth. Strain through a fine-mesh sieve and let cool. The coulis is ready to use now, or it can be stored in an airtight container in the refrigerator for up to 5 days.

Caramel Sauce

Serve this sauce over ice cream or use it as a topping or glaze for profiteroles and éclairs. You can also add this to the basic ice cream recipe (page 297) for a caramel swirl.

MAKES 1¼ CUPS SAUCE

1 cup granulated sugar

3 tbsp water

A few drops fresh lemon juice

Pinch of salt

½ cup heavy cream, warmed

2 tbsp unsalted butter

1. In a heavy saucepan, combine the sugar, water, lemon juice, and salt. Cook over medium heat, stirring gently with a wooden spoon, until the sugar melts, about 1 minute. Continue to cook, without stirring, until the sugar turns a deep golden brown, about 2 minutes more.

2. Remove from the heat and carefully add the cream. Stir until smooth and evenly blended. Add the butter and stir gently to blend. The caramel sauce is ready to serve now, or it can be stored in a covered container in the refrigerator for up to 7 days. To rewarm, heat gently in a heavy saucepan over low heat, or briefly in the microwave on medium power.

NOTE *Since sugar burns easily, be sure to use a heavy pot to prevent scorching when making this caramel. A few drops of lemon juice help prevent the caramel from forming sugar crystals and becoming grainy. Carefully add the warmed cream off the heat, as the hot caramel will foam up and may spatter when the liquid is added.*

Chocolate Sauce

Use this sauce to make a chocolate fondue. Select ripe but firm fruit to cut into pieces: pineapple, bananas, strawberries, cherries, plums, or pears. Or use it as a glaze to coat éclairs or cakes.

MAKES ABOUT 2 CUPS SAUCE; SERVES 8

1 cup heavy cream

2 tbsp granulated sugar

2 tbsp unsalted butter

5 oz bittersweet, semisweet, milk, or white chocolate, coarsely chopped

2 tbsp dark rum, brandy, Grand Marnier, framboise, Kahlúa, Tia Maria, Amaretto, or Frangelico (optional)

In a heavy saucepan, combine the cream, sugar, and butter and bring to a boil over medium-high heat. Remove the pan from the heat, add the chocolate, and let the mixture rest for 2 to 3 minutes. Stir until the chocolate is completely melted and the sauce is very smooth. When the sauce is cool, stir in the liquor, if desired. Transfer the sauce to a clean bowl or jar and cover tightly. Store, refrigerated, for up to 1 week. Rewarm the sauce over low heat or in the microwave before serving.

CHOCOLATE GLAZE *Reduce the quantity of heavy cream to ⅔ cup.*

ART OF PLANNING A MENU FOR A GET-TOGETHER IS DECIDING WHAT BEVERAGES YOU WANT TO OFFER. THE FINAL DECISIONS REST UPON A NUMBER OF FACTORS: TIME OF DAY, YOUR PERSONAL PREFERENCE, YOUR GUESTS, AND THE NATURE OF THE EVENT.

MATCHING BEVERAGE CHOICES TO THE OCCASION

I wanted to start everyone off with my sister's favorite brunch drink, a Mimosa made with prosecco and garnished with fresh berries. I've borrowed plenty of champagne flutes and commissioned the kids to add a spoonful of raspberries to each one. I'll have the orange juice in my most elegant pitcher and pop open the champagne when everyone arrives. I'll also have a selection of fresh juices to top off with a splash sparkling water for a virgin mimosa so that everyone can join in the toast.

No matter what the occasion, you'll want to have a few beverage options for your guest. Children's parties are a perfect time to make fresh lemonade or iced tea. Family gatherings almost always demand great, freshly brewed coffee and tea. Beer and wine work at outdoor affairs or elegant dinner parties. Depending upon the type of celebration, you may want to include some champagne or champagne cocktails. Brunch almost requires Mimosas and Bloody Marys. Punches and nogs are perfect for holiday open houses and receptions.

NONALCOHOLIC ALTERNATIVES

I object to having a house full of children hopped up on soda and sugary drinks, so I've decided to make some simple standbys: lemonade and fruit-flavored iced tea. This way I can control how much sugar goes into the drinks, and how much waste this party generates. A simple garnish, like a slice of fruit, makes the drinks special, and no one has expired yet from lack of a carbonated drink.

Always make sure to have nonalcoholic libations on hand and immediately accessible to your guests. Standard choices include individual bottles of water, seltzer or club soda, sparkling water, tonic, or an array of sodas, but also consider beverages like sparkling cider. If smaller children will be attending, include juice boxes on your shopping list, though many times parents will bring their own.

If you're of the mind and have the energy and time, you can also prepare something special for your non-tipplers, like fresh lemonade (page 305) for a summertime party or a simmering pot of mulled cider (page 331) when the weather gets cold.

Classic Lemonade

When you buy lemons for lemonade, select fruit that is heavy for its size with relatively thin skins for the most juice. Let the lemons warm to room temperature and roll them under your palm before juicing them.

SERVES 8

6⅔ cups cold water

½ cup granulated sugar

1 cup fresh lemon juice

8 lemon slices

1. In a small saucepan, combine ⅔ cup cold water with the sugar and bring to a boil. Stir to dissolve the sugar.

2. Combine the syrup with the lemon juice in a pitcher and add 6 cups cold water. Stir to combine. Pour into glasses filled with ice. Garnish each serving with a lemon slice. The lemonade can also be stored in the refrigerator for up to 24 hours.

RASPBERRY LEMONADE *Purée 1 cup of fresh or thawed frozen raspberries through a wire-mesh sieve into a small bowl to remove the seeds. You should have about ⅓ cup of purée. Add the purée to the syrup and lemon mixture in step 2.*

GINGER LEMONADE *Peel a piece of fresh ginger, about ¾ inch long, and cut it into thin slices. Add the ginger slices to the sugar and water in step 1. Strain the ginger out of the syrup before cooling and using to prepare the lemonade in step 2.*

Agua de Jamaica

Agua de Jamaica is a delicious cold herbal tea from Mexico with a refreshing taste and a beautiful ruby red color that comes from hibiscus flowers. These flowers are known as *jamaica* in Spanish (pronounced *ha-MIKE-ah*). The flowers can leave stains, so use stainless steel or glass containers instead of plastic, aluminum, or ceramic.

SERVES 8

2 cups dried jamaica flowers (hibiscus)

1¼ cups granulated sugar, plus more as needed

3 medium oranges, cut in half

1. In a medium saucepan, bring 2 quarts of water to a boil. Add the hibiscus and sugar and stir while the mixture boils for 1 minute.

2. Squeeze the juice from the oranges into a noncorrosive medium bowl and place the orange halves in the bowl as well. Pour the hibiscus mixture into the bowl and steep for 1 hour.

3. Strain through a sieve, pressing on the hibiscus and oranges to extract as much liquid as possible. Taste the liquid for strength and sweetness. If it is too pungent, add water. If it is too tart, add sugar. Pour into a pitcher, cover, and chill in the refrigerator for at least 2 hours and up to 2 days.

Raspberry-Lime Cooler (front) and Mediterranean Cooler

Raspberry-Lime Cooler

This is a great nonalcoholic drink. If you added some vodka, gin, or rum, it would be known as a "rickey."

SERVES 8

⅔ cup raspberry purée (see page 305)

⅔ cup fresh lime juice, about 5 limes

Two 1-liter bottles club soda or sparkling water

8 lime wedges

Combine the raspberry purée and lime juice in a pitcher. Add the carbonated water and stir gently to combine. Pour into tall glasses filled with ice and garnish each serving with a lime wedge.

Mediterranean Cooler

Look for bottled pomegranate juice in the produce section of well-stocked supermarkets or health food stores. You can also substitute other juices for those we recommend here. Grapefruit and cranberry juice makes a Seabreeze. Orange and cranberry makes a Madras. A modest amount of club soda gives the drink a little spritz without getting too bubbly. You can also add some vodka, gin, or rum to give the drink a kick.

SERVES 8

4 cups fresh tangerine juice

2 cups pomegranate juice

2 cups club soda or sparkling water

1. Juice the tangerines and strain the juice to remove any seeds or unwanted pulp. Combine the tangerine juice with the pomegranate juice in a pitcher and chill.

2. When ready to serve, add the carbonated water and stir to combine. Pour into highball glasses straight up or over ice, if desired.

COFFEE AND TEA

BE SURE TO PLAN FOR COFFEE AND TEA SERVICE if you're having an evening get-together, and most certainly for brunch. If it's a large gathering and buffet style, your best bet is to buy, borrow, or rent a large coffee urn and plan to let guests serve themselves. If possible, offer both caffeinated and decaffeinated coffee. For sit-down service, your regular coffeemaker will likely do the trick, or you can have thermal carafes on hand to allow you to make two pots (or make a pot of caffeinated and a pot of decaf) before serving everyone at the same time.

For tea at the end of a buffet, you can plan to either make it on a cup-by-cup basis or offer individual pots of tea if there aren't large numbers of tea drinkers, in the crowd. Use a larger teapot for bigger gatherings or for tea parties. Tea water should be at a full boil when you add it to the tea. It is a nice touch to have several different teas on hand for guests to choose from, including at least one that is decaffeinated.

For coffee or tea service, be sure you have sufficient creamers and sugar bowls to put out on the table, as well as lemon wedges and honey for tea drinkers and an artificial sweetener for those can't have sugar.

Another end-of-meal option for buffets is to offer a coffee bar that includes carafes of coffee and all sorts of add-ins like fresh whipped cream, peppermint stick stirrers, flavored syrups, and liqueurs like Kahlúa, Amaretto, or Nocello. You could also offer specialty coffee drinks like Irish coffee as a grand ending to a grand evening.

Brewing Coffee

The characteristics of a cup of coffee depend on three factors: the coffee itself, the water, and your coffeemaker. Brewed coffee should be served while it is still very hot. It can also be chilled in the refrigerator to use for ice coffee or frozen coffee drinks.

Coffee service is an excellent end to a formal meal.

THE COFFEE

Whole beans maintain their quality longer than pre-ground coffee, so grind the coffee yourself using a coffee grinder or a coffee mill. For the best flavor, do this just before brewing the coffee. Each type of coffeemaker calls for a specific degree of grind. Drip-style coffeemakers normally use a fine grind, while press or plunger-style pots use a slightly coarser grind. Always be sure to look at the instructions that come with your specific coffee pot.

The standard ratio for brewed coffee calls for one "measure" of coffee, equal to 1½ to 2 tablespoons of ground coffee, to every 6 ounces of water. If you would like stronger coffee, simply use a higher ratio of coffee to water.

You can store whole coffee beans in a dark, covered container at room temperature for several days. For longer storage, keep the beans in the freezer.

Freezing brewed coffee in ice cube trays is a great trick for keeping iced coffee from becoming diluted by melting ice cubes.

Formal tea service is the ideal time to bring out your delicate china and opulent serving pieces.

THE WATER

Always start with fresh, cold water. If your tap water has an unpleasant odor or has a water softener or other chemicals added, use filtered or bottled water to brew your coffee. For the best extraction, a coffeemaker should bring the water to around 190°F. If the water is not hot enough the coffee may taste weak; if it is too hot, the volatile oils that give coffee its rich aroma may be lost.

THE COFFEEMAKER

Drip-style coffeemakers hold ground coffee in a basket lined with a disposable paper filter or a reusable gold mesh or nylon filter. The brewed coffee then drips automatically into a glass pot. Espresso machines brew coffee with pressure. Finely ground, dark-roasted coffee is packed into a basket and water is forced through the grounds. The result is a thick, intensely flavored coffee. A press pot brews coffee by letting the grounds steep in hot water for a few minutes. Pushing down the plunger separates the grounds from the coffee. No matter what type of coffeemaker you choose, be sure it is very clean before using.

Brewing Tea

No matter what type of tea you choose to use, there are some basic brewing guidelines that always hold true:

- Fill your kettle with fresh, cold water. If your tap water has an unpleasant odor or has a water softener or other chemicals added, use filtered or bottled water. Bring the water to a full boil and then pour some into your pot to preheat it. Once the pot is hot, pour out the hot water and add your tea. You may use premade tea bags or loose tea that is either added directly to the pot or put inside a tea ball.

- Most teas require at least two or three minutes for a proper infusion; herbal teas make take four or five minutes to infuse properly. Remove the tea bags or tea ball once the tea reaches your desired strength. If you've added loose tea to the pot, then the leaves will stay in the pot and the tea will get stronger as it sits. In that case, you should always have a second pot filled with hot water so that guests can adjust the intensity of their own cups.

Frozen Coffee

If you don't have an espresso maker, use triple the amount of coffee you normally use to brew coffee.

SERVES 2

6 oz brewed espresso, cold (4 shots)

½ cup coffee ice cream

⅓ cup whole milk

¼ cup heavy cream, whipped

¼ tsp ground cinnamon, or as needed

Blend the espresso, ice cream, milk, and ¼ cup crushed or cracked ice in a blender until smooth. Pour into chilled tall glasses and garnish each serving with a dollop of whipped cream and a sprinkle of cinnamon.

Café au Lait

The French have given us this wonderful steamy coffee drink, perfect to enjoy with a buttery brioche or a pastry for breakfast. Serve café au lait in large heated cups or in French café-au-lait bowls, essentially large cups without a handle.

SERVES 1

3 oz brewed espresso, hot (2 shots)

¼ cup whole milk

Ground cinnamon, as needed (optional)

1. Steam the milk using a milk steamer. Alternatively, in a small pan, bring the milk to a simmer over low heat and use a whisk to whip the hot milk until frothy.

2. Combine equal parts of espresso and hot milk in a heated cup. Garnish with a little cinnamon, if desired.

Chai Tea

Chai is a popular Indian beverage made from black tea, milk, a sweetener, and spices. A spice mixture known as chai masala may include cardamom, cinnamon, ginger, and peppercorns to give the drink its heady aroma. Some sugar or honey is essential to bring out all the flavors.

SERVES 8

12 bags Darjeeling tea

3 cinnamon sticks, 1½ inches each

4 tsp sliced ginger

1 tbsp cardamom pods

1½ tsp fennel seed

2 to 3 cloves

⅛ tsp black peppercorns

1 vanilla bean, split in half lengthwise

¼ cup honey, or as needed

3 cups whole milk

1. In a medium saucepan, bring 1½ quarts water to a boil. Add the tea bags, cinnamon, ginger, cardamom, fennel, cloves, peppercorns, and vanilla bean. Reduce the heat and simmer the mixture for 10 minutes, stirring occasionally, until it becomes aromatic and a medium brown color.

2. Add the honey and milk and stir to dissolve the honey. Bring to a boil and remove from the heat.

3. Strain the liquid through a sieve, pressing on the tea bags and spices to extract as much liquid and flavor as possible. Taste the liquid for sweetness and add more honey, if desired. The chai can be served immediately in tea cups as a hot drink, or chilled to serve in tall glasses over ice. The chai can be refrigerated for up to 2 days.

Cappuccino or Café Latte

Cappuccino is a shot of espresso mixed with an equal amount of milk, topped with a froth of milk, served in a cup. Lattes have double or even triple the amount of milk, along with a frothed milk topping. Lattes are usually served in glasses rather than cups.

SERVES 1

3 oz brewed espresso, hot (2 shots)

½ cup whole milk, as needed

Ground cinnamon, as needed (optional)

1. Steam the milk using a milk steamer. Alternatively, in a small pan, bring the milk to a simmer over low heat and use a blender to whip the hot milk until frothy.

2. For each cappuccino, combine a shot of espresso and ¼ cup of hot milk in a heated cup. For each latte, combine a shot of espresso with ½ cup milk. Top with a bit of frothed milk and garnish cinnamon, if desired.

If frothing the milk using a machine, keep the tip of the frothing wand submerged in the milk until it reaches the proper temperature.

The ideal foam consistency for lattes and cappuccinos.

Immediately pour the steamed milk into the coffee drink and use a spoon to top with the foam.

SERVING WINE AND BEER

Serving Wine

IF YOU'LL BE SERVING BEER, make sure you have a selection of beer types. This is an opportunity to try out a range of beers. And make sure that your selection runs the gamut from lighter tasting to heavier, "hoppier" beers. You want to make sure that your guests can find a beer that they like, even if it might not be to your taste.

Technically speaking, different beers should be served in different types of beer glasses. If you are hosting an event with beer aficionados, it might be a nice touch to offer your beer selection in the proper glass. In general, either a pilsner or a pint glass will suffice to serve most styles of beer. You can even serve beer in a Collins glass.

With the recent upsurge of microbreweries in America has come a newfound respect for the "working man's drink." Artisan beer is a complex beverage that, much like wine, may be evaluated in terms of color, aroma, mouthfeel, and finish.

Choosing the right wine for your celebration is easiest if you have an idea of the foods you plan to serve. If you are having a reception, you could offer a medium-body white and red wine and one sparkling option, such as prosecco or cava. You may want to choose specific wines to accompany different courses for a dinner party. The general advice here is to match the wine to the food. If you are serving foods with a specific flavor profile, such as Spanish, Italian, or California, then choose a wine from the appropriate part of the world. If you are choosing foods to accompany a special wine, take into account where the wine came from and match your dishes to the wine. If you feel overwhelmed about choosing wines, ask a friend or relative to help, or go directly to your wine shop and ask them for suggestions.

Serve red wines at room temperature and serve white wines chilled. You can keep white or blush wines, and even beer, in ice buckets if you have them available. Or, use small galvanized metal buckets, or any other appropriate improvised container. If your refrigerator is already bursting at the seams, back-up bottles can be kept on ice in coolers under or behind your bar area, in the refrigerator, or even—if you're serving a crowd and space is at a premium—in your washing machine or your bathtub, which you have very sensibly filled with ice.

If you can't refrigerate all your beverages ahead of time, keep in mind that it takes only about 30 minutes to chill a bottle of wine when it's in ice, as opposed to chilling it in the refrigerator, which can take up to 4 hours. The same holds for beer, though the chilling times are faster.

To make it easier for guests to pour themselves a glass of wine, you can open the bottles ahead of time and close them up with a stopper. There are many different styles of wine openers. No matter what type of opener you like to use, try to get the corkscrew in the center of the cork. You'll be less likely to split or break the cork.

If you want to decant a wine, you can complete the process up to 1 hour before your guests arrive. Open the wine and then carefully pour the wine from the bottle into the decanter. If you are decanting a wine that has sediment, light a candle and position it so that it shines through the neck of the bottle as you pour. As soon as you see the sediment start to flow into the neck, stop pouring.

WINEGLASSES

There is a plethora of different styles of wineglasses. For your event, keeping it simple can be the best way to go. Have an all-purpose wineglass that you can use to serve both red and white wine by the glass for your cocktail reception. For a sit-down dinner, having different glasses for white wine and red wine is a nice touch.

Champagne or sparkling wine should always be served in a tall slender, footed glass. The champagne flute is an iconic glass. The flute can also be used for sparkling wine cocktails such as a mimosa. Champagne saucers should be avoided as they allow the bubbles from the wine to escape too quickly.

The Fun of Champagne (and Other Sparklers)

Champagne is never a bad choice to kick off a party or to conclude it. You can fill flutes to hand your grateful guests as they come through the door, or indulge them in any number of delicious champagne-based cocktails (page 315). If you're serving champagne, another idea is to have filled glasses set out on a table for guests to take as soon as they come through the door, which is a lovely way to welcome people into your home.

Shopping for sparkling wines does not have to mean breaking the bank. Look for American selections from California, the Willamette Valley, the Finger Lakes, even New Mexico. If you're on a budget, think cava, sparklers made outside of Barcelona, Spain, as well as Italy's delightful prosecco.

Champagne is sold in a number of different-size bottles from the diminutive quarter-bottle or "split" (6.3 fluid ounces) to half-bottles (12.7 fluid ounces) to 750-milliliter bottles (the standard size, which supplies 25.4 fluid ounces) to the magnum (50.8 fluid ounces and equal to 2 standard bottles). Even bigger bottles are sold, though they are difficult to find and unwieldy to pour from: the Jeroboam (equal to 4 bottles) Rehoboam (equal to 6 bottles), Methuselah (equal to 8 bottles), Salmanazar (equal to 12 bottles), the Balthazar (equal to 16 bottles), and the Nebuchadnezzar (equal to 20 bottles). When you buy champagne, get the right size bottle for your party. Unpoured champagne doesn't hold all that well, though you can carefully stopper it and keep it refrigerated for up to 12 hours. There will be some loss of carbonation, however.

A standard 750-milliliter bottle yields five, 5-ounce glasses, assuming you are using a standard champagne flute. Of course, your glass may be larger or smaller. See some tricks for pouring champagne on page 314, whether you plan to serve it on its own or in a cocktail such as a Mimosa or Kir Royale.

OPENING AND POURING CHAMPAGNE

If you're going to be serving sparkling wine, be sure to open the bottles safely. As much as you may think an exploding bottle of champagne says fun, it can also mean a trip to the emergency room if one of your guests happens to find himself or herself in the trajectory of that errant cork, which is, essentially, a speeding projectile.

To open, loosen and remove the foil wrapper around the cork. Then, untwist the wire cage that holds the cork in place. Keep your finger on top of the cork so that it doesn't fly out when you aren't ready. Wrap a clean napkin around the bottle and the cork to get a secure grip. Be sure you aren't aiming the bottle in anyone's direction and keep the bottle at a 45-degree angle as you open it. Then, twist the cork in one direction and the bottle in the other and gently ease the cork out. If you've done this properly, there may be a small pop, but there shouldn't be a big bang or an eruption of champagne. The point is to keep the bubbles in the champagne and to get the champagne into the glass.

To pour, use the so-called two-stage approach to prevent champagne and other sparkling beverages from running over the top of your glass. The first pour, sometimes referred to as "priming" the glass, doesn't fill the glass. Carefully pour in enough champagne to fill the glass only one-third to one-quarter full. The bubbles may rise almost to the top of the glass. When they settle down, you can finish filling the glass without overflows. If you are filling a lot of glasses, prime them all first, then make a second pass to fill them all.

Remove the foil and loosen the cage with six half-turns.

Hold the bottle at a 45-degree angle, and, using a napkin to hold the cork steady with your thumb, twist the bottle in one direction with your other hand and the cork in the other.

Catch the cork in the napkin. You will hear a soft hiss as carbon dioxide escapes with the cork, but you should try to avoid a loud pop.

Since foam forms when it is poured, sparkling wine should always be poured in stages. Pour a base, then, when the foam has settled, pour again to finish filling the glass.

Bellini

To make peach purée, put about 1½ cups of fresh peaches in a blender and purée until smooth. You should have about ¾ cup. It's best to make the purée just before serving the drink, but if you add a few drops of lemon juice and keep it well-covered and in the refrigerator, it will last up to 2 hours.

SERVES 4

¾ cup peach purée

16 oz champagne or sparkling wine

Pour 3 tablespoons of the peach purée into each champagne flute and top with the champagne or sparkling wine.

NOTE *If you prefer, you may add peach schnapps to the recipe to replace all or some of the peach purée.*

Mimosa

Mimosas are enduringly popular champagne cocktails that have become a brunch classic. Use fresh squeezed orange juice and good-quality champagne. If blood oranges are in season and available, try them for a dramatic twist on the standard mimosa.

SERVES 7

One 750-ml bottle champagne or sparkling wine

2¼ cups fresh orange juice

Fill 7 champagne flutes one-quarter of the way with champagne or sparkling wine, allow the bubbles to settle, then fill glasses half-full. After the bubbles have settled again, add 2½ oz of orange juice to each glass, or until glasses are three-quarters full.

Mimosas

COCKTAILS AT HOME

I wanted to show off my recently acquired bartending skills and my home bar, so I decided to serve a variety of cocktails at my New Year's Eve open house. This involved a good bit of advance planning and setup, but it was a lot of fun. I made the decision early on that I would not run the blender every 5 minutes to make frozen drinks—too noisy! (I confess, though, that it is something I love to do at more intimate get-togethers where making a big pitcher of frozen margaritas is part of the whole gestalt). Instead, I planned a festive eggnog to honor the season (as well as to show off the beautiful silver punch bowl and cups that I inherited from my great-grandmother).

If you are more comfortable offering just wine and beer, no one is going to complain. However, it can be a fun to offer, a house drink that reflects the theme or type of party and celebrates the time of year. For an outdoor get-together, a refreshing pitcher drink, such as a fruit-filled sangria (page 328) or a fresh lime and mint-fueled mojito (page 321), would be just the ticket. Frozen drinks are classics for such occasions, but once you have more than ten people, that becomes a lot of ice-grinding time, so you might want to limit those to smaller soirees.

If you are planning a cocktail party, you'll want to have the basics for traditional cocktails. Knowing your crowd and what you guests like to drink is helpful; some groups prefer gin over vodka, others like dark rum instead of light.

If you are purchasing alcohol for your event, remember that, while the quality of your cocktail depends upon the quality of the ingredients you use to make them, it is not necessary to purchase the best-quality alcohol if you are going to be mixing it. When you are at your local liquor store, ask the salespeople what they recommend you purchase for your event.

Here's a list of basics that will have you ready to make classic and contemporary cocktails for your guests:

VODKA	CAMPARI
GIN	BITTERS
SCOTCH	MIXERS: CLUB SODA, TONIC WATER, COLA, GINGER ALE, SPARKLING WATER OR SELTZER, BLOODY MARY MIX
WHISKEY/BOURBON	
RUM	
SWEET AND DRY VERMOUTHS	GARNISHES: TWISTS AND WEDGES OF LEMON AND LIME, OLIVES, COCKTAIL ONIONS, MARASCHINO CHERRIES, CELERY STICKS
TRIPLE SEC	
TEQUILA	

The right glassware makes an impression, so you may want to have:

HIGHBALL AND LOWBALL GLASSES	MARGARITA GLASSES
OLD-FASHIONED GLASSES	WINEGLASSES
ROCKS GLASSES	SNIFTERS
MARTINI GLASSES	CORDIAL GLASSES

There are some basic tools you should have on hand to mix and serve drinks:

JIGGERS OR SHOT GLASSES FOR MEASURING	SWIZZLE STICKS, BAR SPOONS, OR SOME OTHER UTENSIL AVAILABLE FOR STIRRING
ICE BUCKET AND TONGS	
COCKTAIL SHAKER AND STRAINER	KNIFE AND CUTTING BOARD; CHANNEL KNIFE FOR CUTTING TWISTS
BLENDER	
MUDDLER	CONTAINERS FOR GARNISHES
BOTTLE OPENER AND CORKSCREW	SEVERAL CLEAN, FOLDED-UP DISH TOWELS SET ASIDE DISCREETLY, IMMEDIATELY AVAILABLE FOR EMERGENCY WIPE-UP
CITRUS JUICER OR REAMER	
COCKTAIL PITCHER	
ICE BUCKET AND TONGS OR SCOOP	COCKTAIL NAPKINS

Common bar equipment, clockwise from top right: blender, hand juicer, Hawthorn strainer, julep strainer, jiggers, paring knife, muddler, hand reamers, glass cocktail shaker, bar spoon (inside glass shaker), and traditional cocktail shakers.

And no matter what kind of bar setup you have, it's a good idea to keep a garbage can set close by, otherwise you'll have a buildup of spent cans and bottles.

Setting up the Beverage Area

Whether you have one bar area or several, you'll want each fully equipped—unless you're planning on serving one specialty drink that you will be making fresh throughout the party, like martinis or frozen margaritas. For wine or beer, make sure you have several openers and corkscrews available at each station. A single opener is guaranteed to disappear.

If you're serving water or soda, you might offer pitchers, large 2- or 3-liter bottles, or individual servings in bottles or cans. If you're serving from pitchers or large bottles, you should probably offer guests ice for their drinks. Ice buckets are a good idea, as they have lids and are insulated, meaning your ice will stay ice that much longer. But in a pinch, again, any attractive container will do. In either case, make sure you provide tongs for guests to grab their cubes.

IDEAS FOR KEEPING PUNCH COLD

You want your punch to stay as cold possible, but you don't want to add ice cubes to it, because they will dilute the punch; the same goes for sangria. Here are some ideas for keeping it cool:

- Pre-chill punch bowls and pitchers. Add ice cubes to your punch bowl or pitcher about 30 minutes before adding a punch or beverage. Pour out the ice before you add the punch.

- Use frozen fruit instead of ice. Add a bag of individually quick-frozen berries just before serving, or chunks or slices of appropriate fruit that you froze the night before. To freeze your own fresh fruit, cut it into chunks or spears if necessary, spread the fruit in a single layer on a baking sheet, transfer to the freezer and freeze until solid. You can transfer the fruit to containers or ziplock bags for longer storage.

- Make a frozen ring of the beverage. This works best for fruit juices. Pour a portion of any nonalcoholic drink into a ring mold or Bundt pan and let it freeze solid. Do this the day before. To unmold the ring, turn the mold upside down and let warm water run over the mold until the frozen drink starts to fall out. Note, however that drinks that contain alcohol won't freeze solid.

Whatever you choose to do, get the setup ready as much as you can the night before: set out the glasses in an attractive arrangement, the red wine, openers and corkscrews, and small cocktail napkins to wipe away any drips, as well as any ice buckets, tubs, or coolers you might be using. If you're going to have a specialty drink station, again, set it up as much as you can ahead of time. Place a bottle of each of the liquors or mixers needed (if they don't need to chilled) on the table, with extras behind or underneath the bar. If you need a blender or other special equipment and ingredients (muddler, reamer, pitcher, cocktail shaker, margarita salt), set that all out as well, in addition to the glasses you will be serving the drinks in.

MAKING AND SERVING COCKTAILS

Cocktails are a balance of flavors and too much or too little of an ingredient can have a negative impact on your beverage. For a novice bartender, measuring your ingredients will ensure that you serve a properly made drink. Jiggers and shot glasses let you measure out the components of a drink easily.

There are two different styles of cocktail shakers: cobbler and Boston shaker. The cobbler cocktail shaker consists of a mixing tin, strainer, and cap. The pieces neatly fit together and can be made out of metal or glass. The ingredients are measured into the mixing tin. The strainer fits into the top of the mixing tin, and the cap covers the openings in the strainer. You hold the mixing tin with one hand, and use the other hand to hold the cap in place. After shaking the drink to combine the ingredients, you remove the cap and pour the drink through the strainer into the glass. If the drink is to be served "on the rocks," you add ice to the glass before pouring in the drink.

Garnishing Drinks

A slice of citrus fruit or a maraschino cherry is the classic garnish for some cocktails, but you may want to try something new. Mint, cranberries, chocolate, or even candy canes can add flavor and pizzazz to your beverages. If you like to use maraschino cherries, try using brandied cherries instead.

Cut or prepare the garnishes for your drinks on the day of the event, as close to party time as possible. After you prepare all of your vegetable or citrus garnishes, place them in a glass and cover them with a damp towel until you are ready to start serving the drinks to keep them fresh.

Martinis may be garnished with a twist of lemon peel, but some people prefer pitted green olives. Try replacing plain olives with olives stuffed with blue cheese or even truffled cheese. Or replace the olives with almonds or cocktail onions.

Have celery on hand for Bloody Marys, cut into long sticks; use the heart and keep the leaves intact.

Gin- or vodka-and-tonic calls for lemon or lime wedges or slices, as do Cuba Libres. If you make a small incision in the slice or the wedge, you can hang the fruit on the rim of the glass more easily.

For some drinks, the garnish is sugar or salt to coat the rim of the glass A classic known as a Sidecar, for instance, is served in a glass with a sugared rim, while margaritas get a salted rim. To rim a glass, have some sugar or salt in a plate or shallow bowl. Use a wedge of the appropriate citrus to moisten the rim of the glass; just rub it around the rim. Then take the glass and dip it in either salt or sugar so that you create a thin coating all the way around the glass. Move the glass around in the salt or sugar until it is properly coated. Shake off the excess and then pour in the drink. If you plan on serving a lot of drinks that require a sugar or salt rimmed glass, you can prepare the glasses before the event.

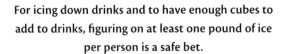

HOW MUCH ICE?

For icing down drinks and to have enough cubes to add to drinks, figuring on at least one pound of ice per person is a safe bet.

Make sure that the ice is fresh and has no noticeable odors or aromas (unless you meant to make flavored cubes as described below). Old ice can add an unpleasant flavor to your drink. Keep your ice in covered container, so that it won't be "contaminated" by falling food or other foreign objects. Never use a glass to scoop out the ice; if the glass breaks, the ice becomes unusable. Instead, set out an ice scoop or tongs.

For specialty cocktails or nonalcoholic drinks, consider making flavored ice cubes. Cubes made from lemonade, fruit juices, coffee, or tea mean that drinks stay cold and don't end up watered down. Pour the drink of your choice into ice cube trays and put them in the freezer. You can also create custom ice cubes, specially flavored to suit your beverages, by added flowers, lemon zest, or different fruit juices to water and freezing them a day or two ahead of time.

Preparing Glasses for Beverages

When you are preparing for the event, make sure your glassware does not have any unsightly soap residue or water spots. You might have to take a damp towel to "polish" the glass to ensure the glass is spotfree. You want to make sure the cloth that you are using to polish the glass is not too wet, or it will leave lint residue on the glasses. A lint-free cloth is ideal for polishing glassware. When you are polishing the glasses, check the cleanliness of the glass and look for lipstick residue. It can be very embarrassing if you serve a drink in a glass that is not clean.

Some people like to place their martini glasses in the freezer before the event. It is a nice touch, but it is not necessary. You can always chill the martini glass with ice before you make the drinks. All of your other glasses should be at room temperature including the glassware that you plan on serving beer in.

STRAIGHT/NEAT

SERVING A DRINK EITHER STRAIGHT OR NEAT is exactly as it sounds, you are serving alcohol without any other liquids or ice. Scotch and bourbon are often served this way. Cognac or brandy is almost always served this way. It is simply pouring an alcohol spirit into a glass.

ROCKS

WHEN YOU SERVE ALCOHOL WITH ONLY ICE, you have made a drink on the rocks. A common style of this drink is Scotch on the rocks. A drink that you serve on the rocks might use a lemon twist as a garnish.

MUDDLED

THE MOST COMMON MUDDLED DRINKS are an old-fashioned and a mojito. You gentle smash the ingredients and allow the flavors of the ingredients to be released and combined. To muddle, you place the ingredients in the bottom of a mixing glass and, with the muddling stick, smash together the ingredients, and then add your alcohol and other ingredients.

Old-Fashioned

SERVES 1

1 orange slice

1 maraschino or brandied cherry

Splash simple syrup (recipe follows)

Dash of angostura bitters

2 oz bourbon or rye whiskey

Splash of club soda (optional)

Combine the orange slice, cherry, simple syrup, and bitters in a mixing glass and muddle the contents together. Add the whiskey and ice, stir until cold, and pour into a cocktail glass. If you choose, top with club soda.

Simple Syrup for Cocktails and Cold Beverages

2 CUPS SYRUP

2 cups sugar

1 cup cold water

Stir the sugar and the water together in a saucepan over low heat until the sugar has completely dissolved. Pour the syrup into a bottle or jar and let it cool. The syrup can be stored in a covered container at room temperature for up to 7 days.

NOTE *This syrup can be used with iced tea and coffee, as well as to make cocktails. If you want to flavor your syrup, you can add strips of citrus zest, slices of ginger, or a cinnamon stick to the syrup while the sugar is dissolving. Strain these flavorings out before storing the syrup.*

Mojito

Mojitos are a delicious blend of rum, lime, and mint for an interesting change from mimosas and Bloody Marys at brunch. They get their fizz from a splash of club soda.

SERVES 8

6½ limes

⅔ cup superfine or granulated sugar, or as needed

½ cup coarsely chopped peppermint

2 cups white rum

4 cups club soda

8 sugar cane swizzle sticks (optional)

1. Cut the limes into quarters and add them to a pitcher along with the sugar. Mash the limes and sugar together using the back of a wooden spoon until the juices from the limes have been released and the sugar has mostly dissolved into the lime juice.

2. Add the mint to the pitcher and mash it together with the lime-sugar mixture. Pour the rum and the club soda into the pitcher and stir together.

3. Put two pieces of the mashed quartered limes in each tall glass and add ice cubes. Pour the mojito over the ice and garnish with a sugar cane swizzle stick, if desired.

BERRY MOJITO *Add 1 cup raspberries, blackberries, blueberries, or strawberries to the recipe and muddle them with the mint and lime.*

MANGO OR PINEAPPLE MOJITO *Add 1 cup mango or pineapple chunks with the mint and lime and muddle them together.*

SHAKEN OR STIRRED DRINKS

DO YOU SHAKE OR STIR A MARTINI? The general rule of thumb is: if it is straight alcohol, as in a martini, it is stirred. If you have fruit juice, cream, or multiple ingredients, you shake it in a cocktail shaker. To stir a drink, place the alcohol in a mixing glass, add ice and with a bar spoon stir the drink until the contents are chilled. Strain the beverage with a julep strainer into a cocktail glass.

For drinks that you shake, place the contents in a cocktail or Boston shaker, add ice, and shake the contents until they are chilled and well incorporated. The length of time you shake depends of the contents. Drinks with cream or raw egg will need to be shaken longer than drinks that are made with fruit juices.

With some drinks, such as a Bloody Mary, you do not want to incorporate too much air in a drink. Instead of shaking or stirring, you might roll the drink. This is the process of pouring the contents of the drink from one part of the mixing tin to the next. You do this until the ingredients are well incorporated. When your drink is well incorporated, strain the contents into a cocktail glass.

Martini

Dry martinis may have only a few drops of vermouth, while a regular martini has the full ½-ounce measure noted here. Be sure to ask your guests how dry they like their martinis before adding the vermouth!

SERVES 1

3 oz vodka or gin

½ oz dry vermouth, as needed

Combine the vodka or gin and vermouth in a mixing glass filled with ice (the less vermouth you add, the drier the martini will be). Stir with a bar spoon until cold. Strain into a chilled cocktail glass. Garnish with olive or lemon twist, or both.

NOTE *Martinis can be made in large batches and mixed in a cocktail pitcher.*

DIRTY MARTINI *Add ½ ounce olive brine and garnish with an olive.*

GIBSON *Garnish with cocktail onions.*

Sidecar

SERVES 1

2 oz brandy

1 oz fresh lemon juice

1 oz Cointreau

1 orange slice

Combine the brandy, lemon juice, and Cointreau in a cocktail shaker with ice and shake until cold. Strain into a sugar-rimmed cocktail glass. Garnish with an orange slice.

Martini

Manhattan

Manhattan

SERVES 1

2 oz bourbon or whiskey

1 oz sweet vermouth

Dash of angostura bitters

1 brandied cherry

Combine the bourbon or whiskey, vermouth, and bitters in a mixing glass with ice and stir with a bar spoon until cold. Strain into a chilled cocktail glass and garnish with the brandied cherry. The drink can also be served on the rocks.

PERFECT MANHATTAN *Replace half of the sweet vermouth with dry vermouth.*

Margarita

SERVES 1

2 oz Blue Agave tequila

1 oz Cointreau or another orange liqueur

1 oz fresh lime juice

Simple Syrup, page 320, as needed (optional)

Combine the tequila, liqueur, and lime juice in a cocktail shaker with ice. Shake until the contents are cold and strain or pour into a cocktail or margarita glass. If you prefer your margarita frozen, pour the contents in a blender and purée until smooth. If you like your margaritas a little on the sweeter side, add some simple syrup.

CADILLAC *Using a bar spoon, gently pour ½ ounce of Grand Marnier over the top of your drink.*

POMEGRANATE MARGARITA *Add ½ oz pomegranate juice and ¼ oz simple syrup to the recipe. Garnish with pomegranate seeds.*

BLOOD ORANGE MARGARITA *Add ½ oz blood-orange juice to the recipe.*

A Cadillac, a variation of a classic margarita, is made by floating a shot of Grand Marnier on top of the drink.

Bloody Mary

SERVES 1

2 oz vodka

4 oz tomato juice

¼ oz fresh lemon juice

1 tsp prepared horseradish

Pinch of kosher salt

Pinch of celery salt

Pinch of freshly ground black pepper

4 dashes Tabasco sauce

4 dashes Worcestershire sauce

1 celery stalk

1 lemon wedge

Combine all of the ingredients except for the celery and lemon wedge in a cocktail shaker with ice. Pour the contents from one mixing tin to the other to incorporate the ingredients, then pour the contents into a Collins or highball glass filled with ice. Garnish with the celery stalk and lemon wedges.

NOTE *For large crowds: Fill a pitcher with Bloody Marys and set out glasses with ice and garnish for guests to pour their own cocktail.*

BLENDED AND FROZEN DRINKS

FROZEN DRINKS ARE A GREAT ADDITION to your summer parties. A typical frozen drink is made by blending a flavorful liquid or soft fruits, liquor, and ice. The key to making them is a blender powerful enough to crush the ice and fully blend the ingredients, otherwise, you may end up with ice chunks in your drinks. Add the ingredients for you drink to the blender jar, place the lid or cover securely in place, and then turn on the machine. It's a good idea to hold the lid in place as the drink is blending. You can hear when you drink is ready to serve by the change of the sound of the blender. If the blender sounds like it is straining, add a little liquid to help the blender break down the ice.

Piña Colada

SERVES 1

2 oz light rum

1 oz pineapple juice

1 oz coconut cream

1 pineapple wedge

1 maraschino cherry

Combine the rum, juice, and coconut cream in a blender with ice. Blend until smooth. Pour out the contents into a cocktail glass. Garnish with the pineapple wedge and maraschino cherry.

CHI CHI *Substitute vodka for the rum.*

Piña Coladas

PUNCHES, MULLED DRINKS, AND NOGS

A PUNCH BOWL BRIMMING WITH A SPECIAL DRINK is a great option for large gatherings. You can choose to make punches virgin or alcoholic, but if you have a few different age ranges, make sure that they look and taste quite different, so you can tell at a glance if someone dipped from the wrong bowl. If you don't have a punch bowl, you can serve these drinks from pitchers instead.

Sangria

SERVES 8

One 750-ml bottle dry Spanish red wine (rioja)

2 orange slices

2 peaches, sliced

1 apple, sliced

½ cup granulated sugar

1 cup fresh orange juice

5 oz Spanish brandy

1. Combine all of the ingredients in a pitcher and stir together. Let infuse in the refrigerator for at least 6 and up to 24 hours.

2. To serve, pour or ladle the chilled sangria and some of the fruit into wine or collins glasses filled with ice.

Tom and Jerry

If you are concerned about serving raw eggs to your guests, you can substitute pasteurized eggs.

SERVES 12

6 large eggs

¾ cup confectioners' sugar

10 fl oz brandy, plus more as needed

12 cups whole milk

Freshly grated nutmeg, as needed

1. Separate the eggs. In a large bowl, beat the egg whites until frothy. Whisk in ½ cup of the confectioners' sugar and beat until stiff peaks form. Set aside.

2. In another large bowl, beat the egg yolks with the remaining ¼ cup confectioners' sugar and 4 tablespoons of the brandy until light and lemon colored,. Fold the egg whites into the egg yolks and refrigerate the mixture for at least 2 and up to 4 hours.

3. Just before serving, in a large pot, heat the milk over medium-low heat until hot; you will see wisps of steam rising from the surface, but do not let it come to a full boil. Reduce the heat to low to keep the milk hot.

4. To finish the Tom and Jerrys: For each serving, pour 2 tablespoons brandy (or more if desired) and 1 large heaping tablespoon of the egg mixture into a heatproof punch cup. Stir to combine and then fill the cup with the hot milk. Place another tablespoon of the egg mixture on top and grate a little nutmeg on top.

Red Sangria

Eggnogg

Eggnog

Add a shot of brandy, bourbon, or rum to each portion of eggnog before serving it to the adults, if you wish.

SERVES 8

2 cups whole milk

2 cups heavy cream

¾ cup granulated sugar

2 large eggs

½ tsp pure vanilla extract

⅛ tsp kosher salt

Ground cinnamon or freshly grated nutmeg, as needed

1. In a heavy saucepan, combine the milk, 1 cup of the heavy cream, and ½ cup of the sugar and bring the mixture to a simmer.

2. Meanwhile, in a medium bowl, blend the eggs with the remaining ¼ cup sugar, the vanilla, and salt. Gradually add about half of the hot cream mixture to the eggs to temper them, then return the egg mixture to the saucepan.

3. Simmer over very low heat until the mixture is heated to 165°F. Continue to simmer, stirring constantly, for 3 minutes more.

4. Strain the eggnog through a wire-mesh sieve into a large bowl and cool down rapidly in an ice bath. Transfer to a pitcher or jar, cover well, and chill for at least 2 hours and up to 24 hours before serving.

5. To serve: Whip the remaining cup of heavy cream and fold it into the eggnog. Pour into teacups and garnish with a dusting of ground cinnamon or nutmeg.

Mulled Cider

You may be able to find pear cider to use instead of the more widely available apple cider. If possible, buy cider that has not been pasteurized for the freshest, fullest apple or pear flavor.

SERVES 8

2 quarts unfiltered apple or pear cider

1 cinnamon stick

3 or 4 whole cloves

3 or 4 allspice berries

Freshly grated zest of 1 orange

8 thin orange slices

1. In a medium saucepan, combine all of the cider, the cinnamon stick, cloves, allspice, and zest. Simmer until the flavor of the spices and orange zest are infused into the cider, about 20 minutes.

2. Strain the cider and pour into heated mugs. Garnish each portion with an orange slice.

AFTER-DINNER DRINKS

After-dinner drinks (also known as postprandial drinks) can run a fairly wide gamut, from cordials and liqueurs like Grand Marnier, Sambuca, Amaretto, or Tia Maria to dessert wines meant to be accompanied by crisp, dry cookies. You might prefer to offer a wonderful cognac or brandy. Or you might like to serve composed coffee drinks (Irish coffee is a strong cup of coffee made stronger by the addition of a good Irish whiskey and a bit of sugar, then topped with whipped cream, for instance.) Fortified wines such as Port, Madeira, or Marsala make a good companion for some cheeses. The Italian tradition of serving herbed and spiced drinks, known collectively as *digestivos,* is a delightful end to an Italian-inspired meal.

Digestivo is the Italian term for an alcohol, believed to aid digestion, served after a meal. Some of the most popular are Averna, Cynar, and Fernet Branca.